AFGHAN CRAFTSMEN

AFGHAN CRAFTSMEN

First published in Great Britain in 1994
by Thames and Hudson Ltd, London

First published in the United States of America in 1994
by Thames and Hudson Inc., 500 Fifth Avenue, New York, New York 10110

This edition first published in Scandinavia in 1994
by Rhodos International Science and Art Publishers A/S, Copenhagen

EDITORIAL COMMITTEE: Ida Nicolaisen and Poul Christian Matthiessen
COPY EDITOR: Niels Peder Jørgensen

British Library Cataloguing-in-Publication Data
A catalogue record for this book is available from the British Library

ISBN 0-500-01612-7

Library of Congress Catalog Card Number: 94-60295

Lay out : Sunna & Ruben Blædel
Production Rhodos
Printed and bound in Denmark

Asta Olesen

AFGHAN CRAFTSMEN

The Cultures of Three Itinerant Communities

Ida Nicolaisen
Editor-in-Chief

THE CARLSBERG FOUNDATION'S NOMAD RESEARCH PROJECT

THAMES AND HUDSON

RHODOS INTERNATIONAL SCIENCE AND ART PUBLISHERS

EDITOR'S PREFACE 7

ACKNOWLEDGMENTS 15

I. FIELDWORK AMONG ITINERANT PEOPLES 17
Reassessment of the Fieldwork 32

II. EAST AFGHAN ECONOMY AND SOCIETY 36
Main Features of the Rural Economy 36
Ethnic Identity and Occupation 44
Crafts, Trades, and Religious Patronage 51

III. THE MUSALLI THRESHERS 57
Introduction 57
Land and People in Laghman 58
Mythical Origin 67
Historical Origin 73
The Occupation of Grain-cleaning 76
Pay and Working Conditions in Laghman 87
Migrant Threshers in Kabul 93
Threshing: a Threatened Profession 98
Additional Incomes 101
Poverty and Dependency 106
Organizing the Community 108
Musallis in Helmand 112
Social Organization 119
Summary 126

IV. THE SHAYKH MOHAMMADI PEDLARS 131
Introduction 131
Mythical and Historical Origins 132
The Trade of the Past 144
Shaykh Mohammadi Trade Today 153
Apprenticeship 160
Activities of the women 161
The Saray Khwaja Summer Camp 163
Barter and Profits 167
Economic Conditions 179
Social Organization 182
Conflicts and Solidarity 192
Political Structures 198
Summary 201

V. THE GHORBAT SIEVEMAKERS 206
Introduction 206
Mythical Origin 207
Historical Origin 213
The Production of Sieves 221
Apprenticeship 230
The Marketing of Sieves 231
Summer Migrations 235
Wintering in Jalalabad 241
Women's Peddling 248
Men's Additional Activities 254
Economic Stratification 260
Household and Marriage Patterns 264
Political Structures 270
Group Identity and Cohesion 276
Summary 378

VI. CONCLUSIONS 284

APPENDIX: The *Kesb Nāma* 291

BIBLIOGRAPHY 310

GLOSSARY

INDEX

EDITOR'S PREFACE

DANISH NOMAD RESEARCH - AN OVERVIEW

Pastoral nomads have always fascinated the more earthbound peoples among whom they live. Forever on the move with tents and belongings, and with their flocks of goats, sheep, cattle, yaks, camels, horses, or reindeer, these elusive folk have captured our imagination. They call into question the very way of life that we peasant or urban people live by defying our idea of a stable and secure homestead. They stir our emotions by questioning values that we take for granted, and by offering a vision of an alternative and, as we tend to believe, carefree existence.

Awe and respect for the Scythians, Huns, Old-Turks, Mongols, and the Arab Bedouins, all of whom carved out for themselves a prominent place in the history of the Old World, lie deep in the Western mind. Images of Tibetan nomads and their yaks, existing at altitudes where agriculture is impossible because there are too few frost-free days, of Tuareg mounted on the camels with which they held sway over the Sahara desert for centuries, controlling trade between the Atlas and the West African states, or of the Masai wandering with their cattle through the tall grasses of the East African savannah are part of our perception of the world. Some of these images are out of date, but still they persist for these are people who arouse our curiosity. Although far away in space and time they yet manage to enrich our lives.

Pastoral nomadism is a way of life confined to the Old World. Until the first decades of the 20th century, pastoral nomads pursued their way of life over a broad belt in the arid and semi-arid zone which stretches from North Africa through the Middle East, and into the heart of Central Asia. Other pastoralists wandered with their cattle on the East African plains and in South Africa, while a range of nomadic groups whose lives were based on reindeer herding lived in Northern Scandinavia and out across the tundras and forests of European and Asian Russia. The living conditions of all these peoples have now changed, but some still keep livestock and continue their migratory way of life.

Each of these pastoral societies represents or represented a unique adaptation to the environment, understood in the widest sense of the word, i.e. as the natural, social, and cultural surroundings which influence their way of life. Pastoral nomadism and the cultures of pastoral peoples are fascinating fields of research in themselves. Scholars have long been intrigued by the environmental understanding and detailed botanical knowledge of nomads, by their sophisticated techniques for handling domesticated animals, and the subtle strategies which they utilize to survive under conditions which are unforseeable and often very harsh. Pastoral nomadism is a highly specialized occupation but, through economic exchanges with agriculturalists and urban communities, the nomads are or have been an important part of the wider society.

In Denmark serious scholarly interest in the cultures and societies of pastoral nomads, including the nature, history, and transformation of nomadism, dates back almost a century. During this period explorers, photographers, and scientists - geographers, archaeologists, linguists, botanists, zoologists, and not least anthropologists - have made a substantial contribution to the documentation and understanding of a range of pastoral societies and of pastoral nomadism in general.

Geographically, Danish research efforts have centered on three areas: Central Asia, South West Asia, and North Africa. From these regions scholars and explorers have brought back rich collections of artefacts to Danish museums which, together with field notes, photographs, films, and music recordings, have formed part of the documentation of a range of nomadic cultures and their ingenious technical, esthetical, and symbolic expressions. Others turned their energies to lengthy in-depth studies of the ecology, culture, and social organization of pastoral groups.

A substantial part of these studies and unique collections have not been published to date. To remedy this the Carlsberg Foundation's Nomad Research Project was formed to arrange a series of publications of which this is the fourth. The project deals with the cultures of nomads as different as the Mongols, Tibetans, Kirghiz and Turkmen of Central Asia, Pashtun nomads of Afghanistan, the Lurs of Iran, the Bedouin of Qatar, the Tuareg of the Sahara, and the Kreda and Haddad of Chad.

Just as the lives of nomadic peoples have changed over time, so the theoretical interests of the Danish anthropologists who endeavoured to record, understand, and describe such peoples have also changed. The problems which interested these investigators and the questions they asked were long influenced by the kind of culture-historical ethnology which dominated Danish anthropology until the early 1950's and the emphasis on subsistence systems and material culture studies which was an essential part of this academic tradition.

Anthropology was established as a university discipline in Denmark only in 1945. Prior to that time it was pursued by scholars who had been trained as geographers. These were either attached to the Department of Geography at the University of Copenhagen or were curators in the Department of Ethnography at the National Museum of Denmark. Among the former were Professor H. P. Steensby (1875-1920) and Professor Gudmund Hatt (1884-1960), while most notably among the latter were Dr Carl Gunnar Feilberg (1894-1972), who later became Professor of Human Geography, and Dr Kaj Birket-Smith (1893-1977), who became Copenhagen University's first Lecturer in Ethnography.

The historical roots and development of anthropology in Denmark had a marked influence on the theoretical perspectives which scholars brought to the study of pastoral societies. It characterized their concept of nomadism and defined the scientific problems which occupied them. Their focus was on the typology, origin, and historical transformation of pastoral nomadism.

Arising from his expedition to North Africa in 1908 H. P. Steensby argued, as had the French scholars A. Bernard and N. Lacroix, that the various forms of pastoral nomadism in that region had developed from subsistence systems based on both agriculture and animal husbandry in adaptation to increasingly scarce resources. Gudmund Hatt, in his studies of reindeer nomadism, suggested that this had its roots in a hunting culture in which tame reindeer had been used as decoys. In later works though he discussed the origin of nomadism in more general terms, he ultimately returned to links with elements of hunting cultures. Feilberg, who carried out fieldwork among Lur pastoralists in Persia in 1935 (cf. *Les Papis*, Copenhagen, 1952), dealt with the history of nomadism through an intricate analysis of the structure and distribution of the black tent (*La Tente Noire*, Copenhagen, 1944).

Parallel with this theoretically oriented research on pastoral nomadism, impressive collections of ethnographic specimens from a wide range of pastoral peoples were finding their way into the National Museum of Denmark. The most important of these were those made by Ole Olufsen (1865-1929) in the Pamirs, West Turkestan, and North Africa, by Henning Haslund-Christensen (1896-1948) in Mongolia, and by C. G. Feilberg from his fieldwork among the Lur. After the Second World War the National Museum in Copenhagen and the Prehistoric Museum, Moesgaard near Aarhus received new collections. A major Tibetan one was donated by His Royal Highness Prince Peter of Greece and Denmark (1908-1980). The collections were further enriched by Lennart Edelberg (1915-1981) and Klaus Ferdinand (b.1926) who carried out research among Afghan nomads. Edelberg also made substantial field collections among the Lur, while Ferdinand did the same among the Bedouins of Qatar. Finally, Johannes Nicolaisen (1921-1980) and Ida Nicolaisen (b.1940) brought back collections from the Tuareg of the Sahara and the Sahel, and the Kreda and Haddad of Chad.

The earliest of the major Danish collections of nomad artefacts are those from Ole Olufsen's expeditions to the Pamirs and West Turkestan almost a century ago. Olufsen was a military man with a keen interest in geography and the exploration of little known regions of the earth. He was appointed Honorary Professor of Geography at Copenhagen University. In 1896-97 and 1898-99 he organized and led two expeditions to the Pamirs and West Turkestan under the auspices of the Royal Danish Geographical Society. In the course of these he gathered topographical, meteorological, hydrographical, zoological, and botanical data. Olufsen travelled widely within the Emirate of Bokhara and Russian Turkestan. He was interested in the cultures of the various ethnic groups and collected some 700 artefacts among the pastoral Kirghiz and Turkmen, the Uzbeks, and various urban ethnic groups. Later expeditions in 1908 and 1922-23 took Olufsen to North Africa where he collected botanical, mineralogical, and ethnografic specimens, including a tent and numerous other objects from among the Tuareg. Although Olufsen published accounts of his travels, his most enduring contributions lie in the opening up of new research areas for others and in the ethnographic collections which he brought back.

A unique Mongol collection of some 3,000 artefacts was put together by the Danish explorer and ethnographer Haslund-Christensen, assisted by Georg Söderbom, his Swedish colleague on the Sven Hedin expedition. Unlike most other collectors of museum specimens of the time, Haslund-Christensen understood the necessity of providing detailed information on the use, the place of origin, and the circumstances under which the artefacts were obtained. The collection includes objects of everyday life such as tools, costumes, jewellery, and household utensils from most of the twenty or so Mongol groups, but mainly from the Chahar Mongols. The exquisite garments of this magnificent collection, a total of more than 400 pieces, are analyzed and described by Henny Harald Hansen in Mongol Costumes, published in this series.

Haslund-Christensen had come to Mongolia in 1923 with five other adventurous young Danes on the initiative of the physician Carl I. Krebs (1889-1971) to establish a farm South-West of Lake Baikal in Uriankhai. During the three years he spent there, Haslund-Christensen came to know and like the Mongols. He learned the language and much about their culture. In 1926 he left the farm, went to Ulan Bator and later to Peking, where he was engaged between 1927 and 1930 by the Swedish geographer and explorer Sven Hedin as a caravaneer for the Sino-Swedish Expedition. In the years 1927-1935 this expedition went from Kalgan through the Gobi Desert to Xinjiang and to the Torgut Mongols in the Tien Shan Mountains. Haslund-Christensen made a unique collection of 60 folk songs, which he recorded on wax cylinders, and a fine ethnographic collection for the Riksmuseet in Stockholm.

While Sven Hedin was mainly occupied with the mapping and exploration of Central Asia, Haslund-Christensen had developed a genuine and deep interest in the cultures of the peoples he met on his travels and he felt obliged to collect as much information on Mongol traditions as possible before the impact of the outside world penetrated any further and changed them forever.

In 1936-37 Haslund-Christensen was back in Mongolia, this time on his own, to collect artefacts for the National Museum of Denmark, which was planning to open in a new building with greatly enlarged exhibition space in 1938. Despite the difficulties caused by the Japanese occupation of Manchuria and Inner Mongolia, Haslund-Christensen succeeded in spending several months with the Eastern Mongols. In 1938-39 he was occupied with a second expedition to Central Asia, this time under the auspices of the Royal Danish Geographical Society, together with the linguist Kaare Grønbech (1901-1957) and the archaeologist Werner Jacobsen (1914-1979). In the course of this expedition the Southern part of Inner Mongolia was surveyed and this resulted in additional ethnographic collections for the National Museum. Thanks to Georg Söderbom a large collection of artefacts representing materials and objects used in everyday life was obtained from Mongol nomads.

In the years 1947-56 the Third Danish Expedition to Central Asia, organized and led by Haslund-Christensen, carried out ethnographical, botanical, zoological, geographical, physical-anthropological, and linguistic research in Afghanistan, Chitral, Kashmir, Ladakh, Sikkim, and Assam. It was in the course of this expedition, in 1948, that Haslund-Christensen died in Kabul. Of the dozen scholars who over the years participated in the expedition, only two carried out ethnographic research on nomadic peoples. They were H.R.H. Prince Peter, and the botanist Lennart Edelberg. Prince Peter, who had studied social anthropology with Bronislaw Malinowski in London, worked mainly among Tibetans from his base in Kalimpong (see *A Study of Polyandry*, The Hague, 1963). Among other things he made an outstanding collection of clothing, tools, implements, and household belongings among Tibetan nomads. In Afghanistan Lennart Edelberg carried out botanical research in the course of which he developed a keen interest in the cultures of the transhumant peoples of Nuristan and Afghan nomads. As a result of these experiences Lennart Edelberg came to argue the need for long-term studies of these peoples and it was for the purpose of satisfying these needs that the next Danish Expedition to Afghanistan devoted itself. His work from 1947 to 1949 resulted in important ethnographic collections being sent back to the museum in Denmark.

Lennart Edelberg was later, in 1964, a member of the Danish Archaeological Expedition to Luristan. Again he took the opportunity to make ethnographic collections, this time among the Lur nomads whom Feilberg had studied thirty years earlier. It is the studies and collections of these very scholars which provide the ethnographic data on which *Nomads of Luristan*, the second volume in this series, is based

In the early 1950's Danish research among pastoral peoples changed its theoretical and methodological scope. A new generation of trained anthropologists was emerging, spearheaded by Johannes Nicolaisen who was to become the first Professor of Anthropology at Copenhagen University, and Klaus Ferdinand who established the discipline at Aarhus University and directed the Ethnographic Department at the Prehistoric Museum at Moesgaard. With them began the kind of prolonged field research and empirical in-depth studies of pastoral peoples considered indispensable today if an understanding of another culture is to be achieved. Although both Nicolaisen and Ferdinand maintained an interest in historical analysis and the study of material culture, their emphasis was different and problems of social organization, economy and the cultural understandings of the nomads came into the foreground, as did the changes that these nomadic societies were undergoing.

Johannes Nicolaisen began his studies of North African nomads in 1947 as a student of anthropology with fieldwork among Berber and Arabic speaking pastoral groups in and just South of the Atlas mountains in Algeria, an area he revisited in 1950. It was the Tuareg, however, who captured his fascination and whose society and culture became the main subject of his research when he had earned his university degree. Nicolaisen spent more than three years among these people between 1951 and 1964, living and travelling with them on camelback. All in all he visited the Tuareg nine times, studying the changes which in particular the Ahaggar and Ayr groups were experiencing.

Nicolaisen had familiarized himself with British social anthropology at University College, London between 1952 and 1954, and the theoretical issues discussed there had a profound impact on his analysis of Tuareg society. Although maintaining a culture-historical perspective, the social organization of the Tuareg became a key area of his data collecting. His works examine in detail the intricate kinship systems, socio-political organization, slavery, and the religion of these nomads, as well as the ecological adaptations and socio-economic transformations of various Tuareg groups. Despite his substantial contributions to nomad studies Nicolaisen left a considerable part of his works unpublished. It is intended to remedy this in the present series. In 1963 he and Ida Nicolaisen, his wife and fellow anthropologist, took up the study in Chad of a hunting and gathering people, the Haddad, who lived among the pastoral Kreda on terms similar to slavery. This work is also to be published in the present series.

For Klaus Ferdinand Afghan nomadism, in particular the form practised by Pashtun and Aimaq groups, became the main focus of his research interests. In 1953-55 he was in Afghanistan as a member of the Henning Haslund-Christensen Memorial Mission. This was led by H.R.H. Prince Peter and had as its other members Lennart Edelberg and the photographer Peter Rasmussen (1918-1992). On this expedition Ferdinand worked with culture-historical studies of various forms of pastoral nomadism: semi-nomadism, trading nomadism, and 'true' pastoral nomadism. A particular interest in the course of this research concerned an investigation of tent types. Prince Peter and Ferdinand were the first to document the existence of special summer trading bazaars set up and managed by the nomads in Central Afghanistan.

Klaus Ferdinand continued his ethnographic studies and museum collecting activities in 1960, 1965-66, and 1974, partly together with his wife Marianne, among nomads in East and Central Afghanistan. Little was known at that time of the social organization, economic life, and culture of these people despite the fact that pastoral nomads had played an integrative economic role in the history of modern Afghanistan. Over time Ferdinand's investigations turned increasingly to trade and trading systems of the nomads and the socio-cultural conditions within which these unfold.

In 1975 Klaus Ferdinand returned to Afghanistan to pursue the study of nomadic traders and the now rapidly changing economies and cultures of the nomads. This time he was accompanied by three of his students: Birthe Frederiksen (b.1949), Asta Olesen (b.1952), and Gorm Pedersen (b.1949), each of whom was to conduct separate fieldwork among the Afghan nomads. Birthe Frederiksen carried out her work among the Hazarbuz of the Mohmand tribe, Gorm Pedersen among the Zala Khan Khel of the Ahmadzai tribe, both groups which relied on or had been heavily involved in trading in the past. Asta Olesen took up the study of non-pastoral nomads, the highly specialized itinerant craftsmen and peddlers who practice so-called peripatetic nomadism. The present volume contains her analysis. Ferdinand devoted his own time to the collecting of information on the history of nomad bazaars and traditional caravan activities and trade routes. All of these studies will be published in this series.

In 1959 Ferdinand took part in the Danish Archaeological Expedition to Qatar, which was part of a programme of extensive Danish archaeological investigations in the Gulf States, initiated by Professor P. V. Glob. Together with the photographer Jette Bang (1914-1964) he studied both Northern and Southern groups of Bedouin and collected ethnographic specimens. His study of these little known and nowadays sedentarized nomads appeared as the first volume of the series, under the title Bedouins of Qatar.

Taken as a whole, these Danish studies of nomadic cultures and societies are widely different in kind, reflecting the educational background, interests, and theoretical orientation of the explorer or scholar who carried them out, the length of time spent in the field, and the period in which the expedition or fieldwork took place. As ethnographic data they must be appreciated and analysed against this background. Museum collections cannot be fully understood by viewing them simply and uncritically as adequate and objective representations of the cultures which produced them. Invariably, each collection is a result of selection by the fieldworker who has made choices on the basis of implicit or explicit criteria of representation, and as such what is brought back represents to some degree Western cultural principles, scientific ideas, and esthetic values over time. Removed from their original context the objects are then rearranged in exhibitions where they may give the impression of replicating such abstract wholes as, for example, Mongol culture. The interpretations and evaluations of the ethnographic collections and other ethnographic data which are to be presented in this series of publications take such issues into consideration.

After 1979 it became apparent that Danish research among pastoral peoples had reached a new phase. Afghanistan, a country where no less than eight Danish anthropologists had been working during the 1970s was closed to further fieldwork for the forseeable future. Afghan refugees, including pastoral nomads, poured by the millions into neighbouring Pakistan and Iran following the communist takeover in 1979, the Soviet invasion, and the ensuing war. Luristan, another core area of Danish research interest, was likewise barred to foreign researchers due to the political changes which followed the coming to power of Ayatollah Khomeni and his government. At the same time, the situation of pastoral nomads all over the world had been radically transformed due to changed ecological, demographic, economic, social, and not least political conditions. In the Sahel region severe droughts brought starvation to man and beast both in the 1970s and the 1980s and several pastoral groups were at the brink of extinction. Demographic pressure and the ensuing competition over land and pastures between nomads and peasants put severe strain on many a pastoral economy. Trade and transport, a significant economic aspect of pastoral economies in many regions, had run into difficulties. Camels and horses lost out in competition with lorries, trade routes were closed by political intervention, and traditional items of local manufacture and trade were replaced by new industrially produced goods. In the Gulf the oil adventure put an end to the traditional way of life of the Bedouins. The Bedouins of Qatar among whom Klaus Ferdinand had carried out research in 1959, gave up their nomadic migrations in the 1960s when the men obtained employment at the refineries and in other petroleum related fields. A main obstacle to the continuous existence of pastoral nomads in most cases was and is nevertheless the development of modern bureaucratic administrations in areas where pastoral nomads have had virtual autonomy, and the interests of governments in getting the nomads settled and under control.

Against this background it is evident that anthropological research is today faced with an entirely new situation and must address itself accordingly. New problems of inquiry and analysis force themselves upon the researcher, not only in the wake of insights already gained and of issues on the current theoretical agenda, but first and foremost because of the socio-economic changes and political obstacles that pastoral nomads are facing all over the world, and the radical transformations that their cultures have already undergone within living memory. It is also clear that ethnographic collections and the unpublished data on the lives and traditions of these various pastoral peoples, which in some cases are already of the past, attain a new significance in this situation. Each of these cultures represents a singular social and cultural experiment in the history of mankind. As such each of them carries evidence that is significant to the overall effort to explore the common denominators of cultural and social formation and the factors which limit the variability of these, which is the ultimate goal of anthropology.

The greatest value of the collections and studies, however, lies perhaps in the fact that they serve to document unique cultural histories which are not only of significance to the descendants of these intriguing nomadic peoples, but are important as both symbols and records of ethnic identity.

In 1985 the Carlsberg Foundation received an application for funds for the preparation and publication of this fine and varied Danish research on nom'ad cultures. The initiative for this came from Klaus Ferdinand. In the past, the Carlsberg Foundation had funded a considerable part of the field research among pastoral nomads. In 1986 the Board of Directors of the Carlsberg Foundation decided to grant funds to support the study and writing up of unpublished materials from the Danish ethnographic collections and the cultural and social data from anthropological field research among pastoral nomads of Central and South West Asia, Qatar, and North Africa. Accordingly, a substantial grant was given to THE CARLSBERG FOUNDATION'S NOMAD RESEARCH PROJECT for a five year period.

The work was supervised by a committee chaired initially by Professor Henrik Glahn, and later by Professor Poul Christian Matthiessen, both of the Carlsberg Foundation. The other members were the late Professor Tove Birkelund of the Carlsberg Foundation, Associate Professor Klaus Ferdinand, Curator of the Ethnographic Department of the Prehistoric Museum, Moesgaard, Curator Rolf Gilberg of the Danish National Museum, and Associate Professor Ida Nicolaisen of Copenhagen University. Niels Petri of the Carlsberg Foundation carried the secretarial burden, assisted by Sven Dindler.

In 1990 an editorial committee was formed with Poul Christian Matthiessen and Ida Nicolaisen as members. Ida Nicolaisen was appointed Editor-in-Chief of the series. In 1993 Per Øhrgaard took over from Matthiessen and Gunver Kyhn from Petri.

I would like to take this opportunity to thank the National Museum of Denmark, the Prehistoric Museum at Moesgaard, the Institute of Anthropology, Copenhagen University, the University of Aarhus, and Danish and foreign colleagues for help and interest in the work presented here. I wish moreover to express my gratitude to the Carlsberg Foundation for the generous support it has given to the Danish Nomad Research Project and the series of publications which will fulfill the aims of that project. Over the past century the Carlsberg Foundation has enabled the National Museum of Denmark and the Prehistoric Museum, Moesgaard to acquire the collections which are now the jewels in their ethnographic crowns. It has offered Danish scientists unique opportunities to record the way of life of a range of pastoral peoples in the Pamirs, in Mongolia, Afghanistan, Iran, Qatar, and North Africa. Last but not least, it has provided scholars with the opportunity to analyse their field data and/or the associated museum collections for publication in this series.

Ida Nicolaisen
Editor-in-Chief
Copenhagen, April 1994

ACKNOWLEDGMENTS

Many persons and institutions have offered their generous assistance and cooperation during my research on itinerant groups in Afghanistan. The original field research, conducted within the framework of the "Danish Scientific Mission to Afghanistan 1975-76" was financially supported by The Danish Council for Development Research for which I am very appreciative.

I will be forever grateful to the many Musalli, Shaykh Mohammadi and Ghorbat families who allowed me into their homes and for a while shared their troubles, tales, and teas with me. While their present fate is uncertain, I hope that my account has done justice to their past. In my research, I enjoyed the competent and inspiring assistance of Mohammad Azim Safi who was not only an enthusiastic interpreter-cum-assistant but has remained a close friend ever since. My interest in Afghanistan was initially inspired and maintained by Klaus Ferdinand, Head of the Department of Ethnography and Social Anthropology, Aarhus University. Klaus has also been most generous in sharing his own profound knowledge and experience on Afghanistan with hopeful students. He has always been a constructive and encouraging critique and adviser. I will remain grateful to Klaus and Marianne, who practice truely Afghan hospitality in a Danish setting. I wish to thank my fellow travellers on the Afghan scene, Birthe Frederiksen and Gorm Pedersen, for all our shared experiences and fruitful discussions over the years.

My special thanks are due to Ida Nicolaisen, chief editor of The Carlsberg Foundation's Nomad Research Project, who has offered many critical comments and valuable advice during the writing of this book. Steven Sampson made editorial revisions of my English manuscript and I have benefitted from his reading of the manuscript with fresh eyes. I also wish to thank Sven Dindler for his practical assistance in the initial phase, Bente Wolff, whose meticulous work at the computer rendered the manuscript readable, the artists Jørgen Mühlmann-Lund (drawings), Elsebeth Morville (maps), and Ahmet Yurtaslan (kinship diagrams), for their excellent drawings, and Klaus Pedersen at the Carsten Niebuhr Institute, who has corrected my transliteration of local terms. Where no photo credits are given the pictures are taken by the author during 1975-6.

Finally, I wish to thank the Carlsberg Foundation for financial support during the preparation of this volume.

Copenhagen, April 1994
A.O.

CHAPTER I

FIELDWORK AMONG ITINERANT PEOPLES

On 13 October 1975, the police station register for the Kote Sangi quarter of Kabul listed some 186 families belonging to 17 different communities camping within its area of jurisdiction. According to the police, most of these people owned some land in the eastern parts of the country, but heat and poverty during the slack season of agricultural work had forced them to Kabul and surrounding areas to find wagework for the summer.

Their white canvas tents were pitched in the many open spaces of Kote Sangi or within its equally many four-walled enclosures, a sign that Kote Sangi, at the western outskirts of Kabul city, was not yet a fully built-up area. Throughout the fringe areas of Kabul, and especially in Kote Sangi and the northern area of Yakatut, similar clusters of white tents could be found. Their numbers grew significantly during the following weeks, up to the beginning of December, whereupon they would gradually disappear before the real onset of winter. In the spring, from mid-April to mid-May, the tents would again mushroom all over the area, remain in a reduced number through the summer, until the next autumn rush. Such tent camps were thus not an Afghan version of shanty-towns but part of a cycle of widespread seasonal migrations, which for generations has been a regular feature for a significant part of the Afghan population.

Most of the time, the authorities tolerated the camping of the migrants, as long as they remained inconspicuous. Still, the local police stations kept a keen eye on them, registering every household and demanding that each group appointed a responsible "headman" as well as a settled person to guarantee their good behaviour. Among the local population in Kote Sangi, three local representatives (*maliks*) acted as "guarantee persons" for the migrants vis-a-vis the authorities. If anyone committed any violation of law, the *maliks* were responsible for summoning them.

The police were correct in their assessment that the inhabitants of these white tents were all poor migrating peoples, although in terms of basic economic activities they belonged to at least four different categories: (1) One major category consisted of small peasants, tenants, and agricultural labourers from eastern Afghanistan who for at least two generations had migrated to Kabul for the summer. They came mainly for harvest work in the rural areas around the city, but when the harvest was over, sought employment in construction, transport, or small-scale trade. Returning to their home areas in the autumn, for the second harvest there, they might

1.0 Modern part of Kabul (Photo: Gorm Pedersen, Spring 1976).

try to supplement their earnings with similar kinds of work. Although such seasonal migrations had taken place for decades, the number of people who undertook them was increasing due to centralization of land ownership and the gradual impoverishment of Afghanistan's peasantry, particularly since the 1930s. (2) Another large category were poor pastoral nomads, who increasingly sought employment in wage labour along their traditional migration route, which began at their winter areas in the east. The nomads engaged in both harvest work in the rural areas and in construction and transport work in urban neighbourhoods. For a growing number of poor nomads, these forms of employment were in the mid-1970s as economically important as their traditional pastoralism.[1] (3) Yet another category consisted of specialized craftsmen – mainly rural artisans living in Laghman and Nangarhar during winter. This category included a number of endogamous descent groups with occupations such as threshing, sievemaking, potterymaking, knifemaking, barber, and petty trade. These groups also practiced their traditional occupations in their summer dwelling areas, and they had apparently been migrating for generations. They explained that they migrated because the summer area offered them a better market for their products. In case their traditional profession did not provide sufficient income, these groups might also take on additional wage labour of the same kind as the peasants and pastoral nomads. (4) The last category included a number of mainly itinerant groups without any permanent residence. They consisted of endogamous descent groups, frequently of non-Afghan origin, engaged in various trades such as bangle-selling, animal training (monkeys or snakes), prostitution, and the like (Rao 1981, 1982).

It was the latter two categories of migrating, occupationally specialized descent groups, who interested me during my field research in Afghanistan in 1975-76. The fieldwork took place within the framework of the Danish Scientific Mission to Afghanistan, 1975-76, headed by Associate Professor Klaus Ferdinand of Aarhus University. Two fellow students of mine, Gorm Pedersen and Birthe Frederiksen also took part in the Mission, and like Klaus Ferdinand studied patterns of socio-economic change taking place among Pashtun pastoral nomads. While migratory lifestyle was thus a common theme of the Mission, my focus on the itinerant craftsmen and

1.1 Sievemaker camp in one of the many open spaces of Kabul's Kote Sangi quarter (May 1975).

1,2 Most tent-dwellers prefer to camp in a walled-in enclosure in order to ensure a measure of privacy. A low mud-wall is often built in front of the tent to provide shelter for the outdoor cooking (Outskirts of Kabul , spring 1975).

traders deviated from the traditional connotation of "nomadism" as *pastoral* nomadism. Even among Pashtun nomads pastoral nomadism could no longer be taken for absolutely granted. As migrating communities, itinerant craftsmen and traders differed in a number of significant ways from their fellow migrants, and hence, in their resource extraction, adaptation to the physical and social environment, and in their social and cultural interaction with the settled society. These were the general features I sought to elucidate. My particular interest centred on itinerant groups as migratory variants of the overall East Afghan occupational specialization along ethnic lines and the socio-economic maintenance of these communities.

The fieldwork, from mid-April 1975, lasted 12 months and was carried out among Shaykh Mohammadi pedlars, Musalli threshers and Ghorbat sievemakers. Both the Shaykh Mohammadi pedlars and the Musalli threshers considered themselves as belonging to the Laghman Province, where they spent the winter in houses, while undertaking summer-migrations to, respectively, the Koh-i Daman area north of Kabul, and the agricultural zones surrounding Kabul. The picture was less uniform for Ghorbat sievemakers: Some were fully nomadic, migrating between Kabul and adjoining provinces during summer and Laghman/ Jalalabad during winter. Others were semi-nomadic and stayed in houses during winter, either in Jalalabad or in their traditional summer-areas such as Charikar, Kabul, or Ghazni. Still others were settled in other parts of the country: the north, areas around Kandahar, or Herat.

This study, based on fieldwork conducted seventeen years ago, poses special problems. All the primary data and most of the background material pre-date the so-called Saur Revolution of 1978 and the subsequent Soviet occupation during 1979-89. The general political unrest, resistance struggle, and civil war in the country since then have had disastrous consequences for the population, having led to the breakdown of the economy and affected all aspects of life. Thousands of Afghans have died during the war and millions have been forced into exile, prima-

1.3: Potter families from Laghman may also migrate to Kabul and adjoining areas for the summer. These families from Charbagh had set up their workshop along the Jalalabad road just outside Kabul (Spring 1975).

1,4-6 Like other craftsmen in Afghanistan, the potter works on the ground with the wheel lowered into a hole.

rily in neighbouring Pakistan and Iran. Regrettably, I have no information regarding the fate of the Musallis, Shaykh Mohammadis, and Ghorbats during all this turmoil. In war even more than in peace, poor and marginal people are easily ignored, and inquiries regarding their whereabouts have yielded no results. Thus I have no choice but to restrict my account timewise to the mid-1970s, where reliable information is available on the relevant topics. While I have remained with the original focus of the research and its theoretical foundation, new perspectives have appeared in light of more recent studies and theoretical interests. These perspectives will be discussed later in this chapter, following a brief presentation of the actual circumstances and problems involved in studying marginalized, itinerant communities.

In spite of these limitations, the relevance of this study is that it fills a gap in our all too scanty knowledge of the pre-war Afghan society, adds a new perspective to the little researched subject

1,7 -8 The craft of smithery is very specialized. Here a couple of knife-smiths from Haiderkhani in Laghman have set up their workshop on the sidewalk in the town of Paghman, north of Kabul (Summer 1975).

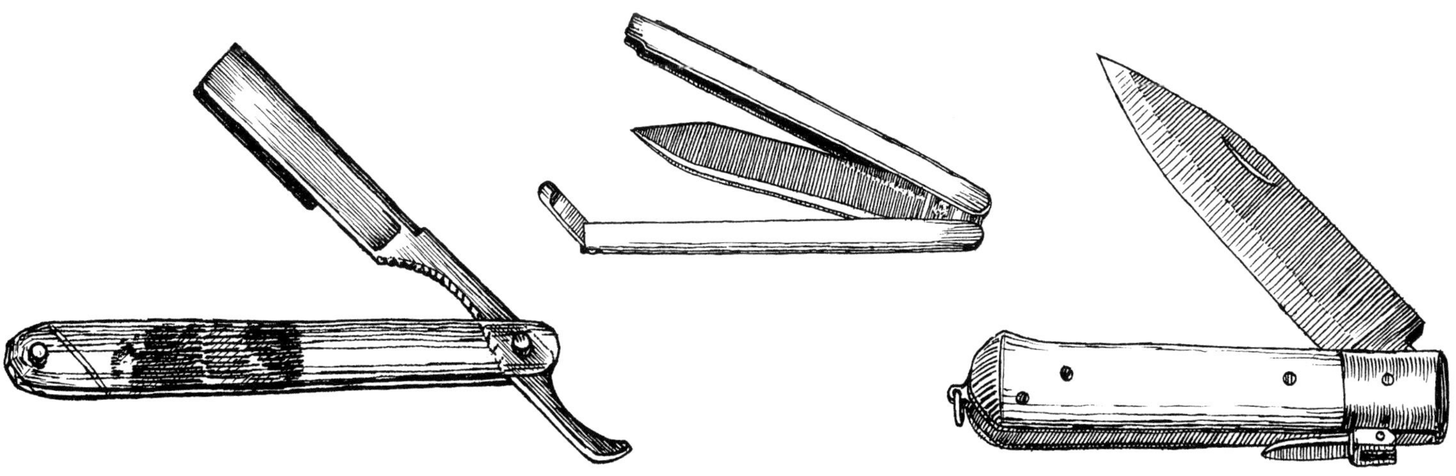

1,9-11 Knives of high quality are produced in many localities in Afghanistan. The blades are normally made from second-hand steel, typically the leaf springs of jeeps, and hardened by being heated and hammered out.

of Sufism in Afghanistan, and last but not least, contributes to general anthropological debate on the social construction of identity.

My fieldwork began in the end of April, 1975. I was to spend a couple of months in Kabul, learning some basic Farsi while awaiting the arrival of the other members of the Danish Scientific Mission, Klaus Ferdinand, Birthe Frederiksen, and Gorm Pedersen.[2] During this period, I met the Indian anthropologist Aparna Rao, who was also about to start field research among itinerant and supposedly "gypsy-like" groups in Afghanistan.[3] We joined forces for a couple of months, and greatly assisted by my subsequent interpreter Mohammad Azim Safi,[4] we screened Kabul and adjoining areas for tent-dwellers – or more specifically, for those who lived in white tents, as the black goat-hair tents are occupied exclusively by pastoral nomads. As the Danish Scientific Mission began its activity, and I had chosen the groups among whom I wanted to conduct my fieldwork, our ways split.

In Rao's and my own search for the occupants of the white tents, it became obvious that being itinerant, as well as ethnically and occupationally despised, makes people less than inviting towards strangers, not to mention female, foreign researchers. The initial suspicion and rejecting attitude of the itinerant people was paralleled by the local authorities' anxiety about our interest in such "outcaste" groups. As a consequence, we were called to local police stations on the periphery of Kabul, where we had to provide lengthy explanations regarding our research, permissions, etc.[5] Later on, I learned to avoid this harassment by duly advising the local authorities before contacting any itinerant groups, but only to end up with the problem of having to reject an offer of an armed police guard to protect me during my field visits!

The concern of local authorities was real. They considered the itinerant groups socially inferior, often criminal, and certainly immoral, and the local police officers were not very keen to take on the responsibility of allowing a foreign, single woman to visit such people, not to mention live among them. Eventually, my resourceful interpreter M. Azim Safi had to go to

1,12-13 A wood-turner at work at the roadside.

1,14 Among the fully itinerant groups are the monkey-trainers, Shādibāz, here in the Kote Sangi area of Kabul (May 1975).

the Ministry of Interior and personally guarantee my safety – a mission for which his elder brother, a university professor, equipped him with a pistol so that he could live up to his Pashtun word of honour! Similarly, while residing in the summer camp of the Shaykh Mohammadi pedlars in Saray Khwaja, my host there, the snake-charmer Mirza Gul, also had to guarantee my physical safety to the local authorities. Consequently, throughout my stay, he slept in front of the door to the family's little hut, with his hunting gun at his side. The little blue tent I had brought along, was considered unsafe for me to stay in, as robbers and highwaymen, supposedly plentiful in Koh-i Daman, immediately would spot it as a suitable target. Hence the Shaykh Mohammadis found it more suitable to let the interpreter sleep in the tent!

Afghan state authorities have no positive image among the population. Central authority has traditionally been associated with "forced settlement, forced labour, military service, taxation and bureaucratic arbitrariness" (Fröhlich 1970). Even though the settled population's conception

1,15 A Shādibāz with his monkey, Kabul (Photo: Klaus Ferdinand, Sept. 1954).

has taken a more positive turn during this century, the itinerant peoples have had less reason to revise their opinion. They may have been less subject to taxation, but were continually at the mercy of the local police in obtaining permission to camp, having to register in each new locality and provide names of settled "guarantee persons". While possession of an identification card was mandatory for men, it required registration of a permanent address, which automatically meant being drafted for two years' national service. While their *duties* towards the State were well-defined, the itinerants' *rights* were less obvious, and in all official encounters they were *a priori* considered less respectable and reliable than settled people. Consequently, vis-a-vis the authorities, itinerant people followed the strategy of attracting as little attention as possible, so as to be least affected.

Bias against itinerant peoples was not applied indiscriminately to all migrating tent-dwellers, however. The largest community of migrating peoples were the Pashtun pastoral nomads, and neither among the authorities nor among the settled population were they regarded with such a negative image as were the itinerants. While the authorities may well have regarded the pastoral nomads as potentially uncontrollable and thus sought to have them settled, in the eyes of the other Afghans, the Pashtuns represented a free and dignified life. Like itinerant women, Pashtun nomad women were not veiled, but this was not taken as a sign of lack of chastity. On the contrary, in Afghan poetry and oral tradition nomad women have been celebrated for chastity, loyalty, beauty, and bravery. The difference in perceptions of itinerants and pastoral nomads is probably due to the fact that the latter were part of the dominant Pashtun community, for whom they represented a cherished, uncomplicated past. Moreover, the Pashtun nomads have played a significant political and military role in Afghan history. Their positive image as compared to the itinerants thus derived from the political force and military power they represented in contrast to the almost complete political and military impotency of itinerant minority groups.

Becoming the involuntary objects of anthropological field research obviously did not conform to the itinerants' strategy of attracting minimal attention, and I was initially looked upon with suspicion, if not for my own intentions then for the troubles I would no doubt bring and the extra surveillance by the authorities. The itiner-

I,16-17 Camp of itinerant prostitutes, north of Pul-i Khumri (Photo: Gorm Pedersen, April 1975).

ants' fears turned out to be well-founded. During our initial survey, Aparna Rao and I paid a visit to a camp of Ghorbat sievemakers in Yakatut, near Kabul. Reluctantly, they lived up to Afghan norms of hospitality by inviting us to sit down and have tea. As soon as the tea appeared, however, so did a police officer. He had come to oust the Ghorbat from their camp site, but seeing foreigners among them, he ordered us as well as our reluctant host to come along to the police station. During the resulting commotion, our host's tent was left unguarded and the family's identification papers were stolen together with a document stating the paternity of a child, custody over whom the divorced parents were contesting. Not only was the father's possibility to claim his child, whom the mother had taken, seriously damaged, but even worse, when applying for new identity cards, it was discovered that one of the Ghorbat men had not performed his national service although he was 30 years old. Consequently, he was immediately drafted, and as penalty for his late appearance had to serve additional time. Needless to say, after these events it took some time before anthropologists were welcome guests in the sievemaker camps!

Ultimately, good relations were established with all three groups, who generously received me and my interpreter and spoke about themselves and their lives while sharing their tea, anxieties, and fairy tales with us. Initial attitudes towards me varied significantly among the three groups. The Ghorbat sievemakers were on their guard, suspicious and in some cases directly resentful, and it took considerable time to establish a relaxed, confidential relationship with them. A directly hostile, rejecting attitude existed among other groups, such as the monkey-training Shādibāz, the Vangāwālā banglesellers and J̌ogis of the north, with whom I came in sporadic contact during the initial survey. The Musalli threshers, on the other hand, readily accepted the idea of somebody wanting to write a book about their occupation, no doubt nourishing the hope that information regarding their poor conditions might make them eligible for land allocation. The difference in expectations between the Ghorbat sievemakers and the Musalli threshers is significant in this respect. The Ghorbats had repeatedly had the experience of having their property taken over by the authorities, while the Musallis had seen several hundred relatives allocated land in the Helmand Valley Project. The Shaykh Mohammadi pedlars appeared neither to expect much trouble nor any benefits arising from my work. However, this was also the only group to whom somebody had introduced me and my work, and I did not have to worry about my credibility. Everything was taken care of by my host and his relatives. Hence, circumstantial factors certainly played a role in forming the initial attitudes of the three groups. However, their different social situations also had an effect. The Ghorbat were certainly the most marginalized, the Musalli felt the most disadvantaged and exploited, while the Shaykh Mohammadis were the most self-assertive, considering themselves the economic and social equals of all other groups, a view which was not corroborated by the settled community.

1,18 Mirza Gul, my host in the Shaykh Mohammadi camp in Saray Khwaja. At the time he earned his living by catching snakes in the mountains and curing snake and scorpion bites. Mirza Gul did his utmost to make my stay comfortable and to facilitate my data collection.

1,19 Interview session in the Shaykh Mohammadi camp in Saray Khwaja (Photo: Gorm Pedersen, Dec. 1975).

Reassessment of the Fieldwork

The initial focus of my fieldwork among itinerant groups in Afghanistan was to regard them as a variant of the general East Afghan occupational specialization along ethnic lines. My objective was thus to determine how these groups related to the dominant agricultural production system, how their occupational specialization was maintained socio-economically and culturally, and how their economic activities were affected by development in Afghan society generally.

At the time of research, no studies of similar kind had taken place in Afghanistan, and there existed no systematic record of these small specialized groups. Subsequently, Aparna Rao, who carried out the related study of "gypsy-like" groups (*Jat*) at the same time, has published on the subject (notably Rao 1982), including an anthology on such itinerant or "peripatetic" groups in cross-cultural perspective (1987). Re-

1,20 Mohammad Azim Safi, my untiring interpreter, is checking up on sieves in Dahan-i Ghori. Besides all his other commendable qualities, Azim's good sense of humour was an irreplaceable asset in the fieldwork situation (Photo: Gorm Pedersen, Feb. 1976).

garding the Ghorbat sievemakers, aside from the work of Rao and myself (see Ch. V), no other studies have dealt with this group.

I began my fieldwork with an initial survey of specialized communities ranging from threshers, potterymakers, knifemakers, tinkers, riveters of chinaware, sievemakers, snake-charmers, monkey-trainers, bangle-sellers, pedlars, etc.. I finally chose Musalli threshers, Shaykh Mohammadi pedlars, and Ghorbat sievemakers for detailed study. These three groups vary in their pattern of itinerancy as well as in the nature of their occupation and its relationship to the dominant agricultural economy. Hence, the three groups were selected according to their assumed ability to elucidate the scope and variety of ethnic occupational specialization in Afghanistan, its historical background, and its maintenance today:[6]

The Musallis, supplying a labour service, i.e. threshing and winnowing, to their home-villages in Laghman were economically dependent upon local landowners and socially and politically integrated in their local communities. Their relations to the landowning community in their summer areas around Kabul were mainly of economic nature and although long-lasting, less stable. On the other hand, the Shaykh Mohammadi pedlars, by virtue of their petty trading, were not tied to any specific settled community, instead serving a wide, ever-changing range of customers. In their attempt to maximize benefits from their peddling activities, they displayed a higher spatial and economical flexibility. This lack of attachment to a specific settled community, in addition to their spatial concentration, enabled the Shaykh Mohammadis to maintain a comparatively strong social and political position vis-à-vis the settled community in their home-area. Finally, the sievemakers, as small independent craftsmen, were as economically autonomous as the pedlars, but their higher degree of nomadism, the low status of their occupation as being ritually "unclean", and their religious minority position as Shi'as, maintained them as a marginal community in political and social matters. They had only feeble contact with the settled society. Here their autonomy constituted a form of isolation rather than independence.

My general anthropological interests at the time were influenced by the Marxism dominant at Danish universities during the 1970s. This theoretical orientation was reflected in the primarily economic formulations of the research design. The selection of groups for study was thus based mainly on economic criteria, and my data collection centred on a detailed account of their past and present economic activities, both in their technological aspects and social organization. Information on kinship and marriages was collected in order to analyze the socio-economic maintenance of these mainly endogamous, occupationally specialized descent groups.

No anthropologist is ever in full command of his or her fieldwork and data collection. I was no exception. Invariably, it happened that I was supplied with information on matters which I had not asked about, had not planned to investigate, or was unable to understand. This applied particularly to the many legends, tales, and stories which elderly people in all three communities found considerably more exciting or less dangerous to relate than they did satisfying my tedious questions on economics. I should add that even at that time I was tempted to agree with them.

In substance, the present description of the three groups' economic relations differs little from my original analysis hereof carried out 16 years ago.[7] However, the material on the groups' historical background and their various legendary accounts associated with it, has been reworked in light of a growing recognition of the importance of Sufism in Afghanistan. Both the discovery of a close connection between these legends and those of the urban guild-associated craftsmen and the central role played by legends in the construction of identity in all three communities opened new dimensions for the analysis of my original field data.

Together with the often overlooked cultural homogeneity which connects the many ethnic groups in Afghanistan, the analysis confirmed my original conception of the three itinerant communities as exemplifying the general occupational specialization in East Afghanistan. In spite of their migratory lifestyles, they shared many socio-economic and cultural features with other, settled, communities of specialized craftsmen. In their relations to the surrounding society, the itinerants vary in degree rather than kind. On the other hand, I had chosen "itinerancy" as a selection criteria, which was still justified by the fact that this way of life related to a specific set conditions for socio-economic existence and reproduction of these communities. This study will demonstrate how migrations were related to the respective group's occupation of specific socio-economic niches, representing a continual process of adaptation to the surrounding society both historically and at an individual level. The economic relations and the nature and degree of itinerancy also defined the groups' negotiating power, and hence, their socio-political relations, with the surrounding, settled communities. Finally, I will argue that the "complex" of itinerancy, descent, and occupation were significant factors in defining the inferior social position and status of these communities, but that this complex simultaneously explained the central role played by legendary tales of origin in their self-identification.

Identity is not a constant, of course, and its different meaning for the three groups will be demonstrated along with examples of reinterpretation and change of identity. Finally, I have also attempted to relate the material on kinship and marriage to group maintenance and social status.

The problem remains however, that the Musalli, Shaykh Mohammadi, and Ghorbat communities differed in a number of ways, and so did my conditions for carrying out fieldwork among them. Hence, my data about the three groups are not completely parallel, a fact which complicates a truly comparative analysis. In addition, reevaluating field data collected well over a decade ago brings with it the limitation, that any new perspectives which may appear, cannot be followed up by additional questions. Hence, while lacuna and open questions remain in this presentation, it is my hope that they will arouse the curiosity rather than the annoyance of the reader, and thus become an inspiration for colleagues dealing with the anthropology of itinerant groups. Continous warfare since 1978 has torn apart the fabric of Afghan society, leaving no segment of the population unaffected. In focusing on three itinerant groups, this study not only seeks to understand an often neglected aspect of Afghan society, but also to elucidate a past, which, although recent, is forever gone.

NOTES:

1 Ferdinand, personal communication, May 1976. For a more detailed account of this development among pastoral nomads, see also Ferdinand (1968).

2 During these two months, I was fortunate to have the family of the famous classical singer, *Ustād* Yaqub Qassemi, open their home to me and 'adopt' me as a daughter of the family. The Qassemis were and still are among the most broad-minded and warm-hearted of families, embodying the highest principles of the famed Afghan hospitality. I will always be grateful to them for having allowed me into the closed circle of Afghan family life.

3 Rao ultimately chose to conduct her fieldwork primarily among the sievemaking Ghorbat, whom I also selected as one of three groups for further study. She has published widely on Afghan itinerant groups in general and on Ghorbat in particular (Rao 1981, 1982, 1982a, 1983, 1986, 1987, 1988).

4 Mohammad Azim Safi assisted me throughout my fieldwork, and its relative success was due mainly to him. He was not only a skilled interpreter, but soon developed into a skilled anthropological fieldworker as well, having a remarkable ability to relate to people of all communities irrespective of their social background. Azim Safi also provided me with a solid introduction to Afghan social, political, and cultural life, from which I still benefit – not to mention our lasting, close friendship. While in Kabul, Laghman, and Helmand, I benefitted from the warm hospitality of his extended family. They have my thanks.

5 On one occasion, it was only the timely intervention of the Indian Embassy, which helped not only Aparna Rao but also me out of difficulties, for which I still owe them my appreciation.

6 According to these selection criteria, it could be argued that a community of entertainers should also have been selected for study. They were left out for mainly practical reasons: lack of time, since three groups already might prove too large a task, and because the entertainer communities would have proven considerably more unapproachable than the other groups, in view of their more pronounced social marginality.

7 The results of the fieldwork were presented in a field report to Aarhus University (Olesen 1977) and in a couple of shorter articles (Olesen 1982, 1985).

CHAPTER II

EAST AFGHAN ECONOMY AND SOCIETY

The livelihoods of all three itinerant communities, Shaykh Mohammadi, Musalli and Ghorbat are primarily dependent upon the rural production system and market conditions in their areas of migration. The threshing services of the Musallis are aimed exclusively at grain-producing households, the main market for the Ghorbats' sieves are rural households generally, just as the Shaykh Mohammadis traditionally ply their trade only in rural areas. In the following section, the relevant features of the East Afghan rural economy will be outlined so as to set the framework for a more detailed description of the activities of each community.

Ethnic occupational specialization in East Afghanistan is not simply an economic, but a socio-cultural phenomenon as well. Ethnic affiliation and occupation are intricately interwoven and subject to a social ranking reminiscent of the caste system of the Indian Subcontinent. The linkage between ethnic affiliation and occupation will be described as will the low social ranking of certain occupations, so as to provide the background for later discussion of the social integration of the three groups in the settled society.

Itinerant communities are in many respects socially and economically marginalized. They live on the fringes of society, displaying a number of distinct features. While they may thus appear as communities apart, I will argue that they nevertheless comprise the overall West and Central Asian cultural tradition in which crafts and craft guilds are linked to a quasi-religious origin and setting, creating respectability and an esprit de corps even among the most stigmatized occupations. This phenomenon has tended to escape the focus of research on Afghanistan. However, a proper understanding of the many myths and legends recorded among the three groups is essential for understanding how they construct their identity.

Main Features of the Rural Economy

Eastern Afghanistan is the most fertile and densely populated part of the country. Like in the rest of Afghanistan, around 80% of the population lives on agriculture. Because of very limited rainfall during summertime, up to 80% of the cultivated area must be irrigated, mainly from canals drawing water from rivers. Arable land, which forms only a minor portion of the total area, is located in the four major valley systems of the region: (1) the Kabul valley, an area of high level basins surrounded by mountains, (2) Kohistan-Panjshir, including the wide basin of

Koh-i Daman and Charikar, leading to the steep valleys of Nijrab and Tagab, (3) Ghorband, lying in an east-west direction from Charikar to Shibar Pass, and (4) Nuristan, a region of wild, narrow mountain valleys (Dupree 1973: 10-12).

The general population density in Afghanistan was not very high in 1975, around 25 persons per km^2, as the main part of the country consists of either non-arable mountain (mostly in the east) and desert land (mostly in the west).[1] The cultivated areas, however, were densely populated, which is illustrated by the fact that a population density of 981 persons per km^2 cultivated land was calculated for the rural areas around Kabul (Hahn 1965, II: 18), a figure which would be hardly less for other parts of East Afghanistan.

Differences in altitude create great climatic variation in East Afghanistan. While Kabul lies approximately 1,800 metres above sea level, Laghman and Nangarhar are located at 8-900 metres, a difference reflected in the subtropical temperatures in the latter areas as compared to the agreeable summers and freezing cold winters of Kabul.

The main crops at the higher altitudes have been wheat, corn and barley. Around Kabul, the cultivation of vegetables as a cash crop at the expense of grain cultivation had taken place since the 1950s-60s. In Paghman and Koh-i Daman, north of Kabul, fruit is abundant, particularly grapes; raisins thus constitute a major export commodity. Two annual grain crops can be grown in these areas, provided there is sufficient water, if the first crop is wheat, then the second crop (e.g. maize) should have a short growing-season, since winter begins in November and ends in March.

In the provinces of Laghman and Nangarhar, wheat would be the first crop followed by paddy, as these are among the main rice-cultivating areas of the country. In addition, many citrus fruits are grown, particularly in Nangarhar.

Compared to neighbouring Iran and Pakistan, the economic stratification in Afghan society has been comparatively limited. Poverty was much more equally distributed in Afghanistan and never reached the appalling stages seen in the Indian Subcontinent. The vast majority of cultivators were small peasants, but with a numerically limited group of big landholders owning very large tracts of land.[2] Huge regional differences did exist, however. The most fertile and densely populated areas of East Afghanistan were almost completely dominated by the small peasantry, and large estates were virtually non-existent.[3] In the northern provinces, which to a large extent had come under cultivation only during this century, there existed large landholdings, and the same was true for south-western Afghanistan.[4]

Differences in ownership patterns in the various regions was complemented by differences in technological development and in the overall agricultural economy. While mechanization and cash-cropping (notably cotton) was widespread both in the northern and south-western provinces, agricultural production in the eastern (and central) provinces was carried out using simple implements, and oxen were used as draught animals. In 1975, in the high valley of Karenj in Laghman, I even observed a man who was ploughing his field, using his two wives as draught animals. Ploughs, harrows, and other implements were simple wooden tools fitted with iron shares, manufactured by local artisans. The cultivation of land in these areas, was thus very labour intensive, and during peak periods the cultivator had to contract additional labour for example in order to transplant the paddy and for harvest work. Normally, the additional labour

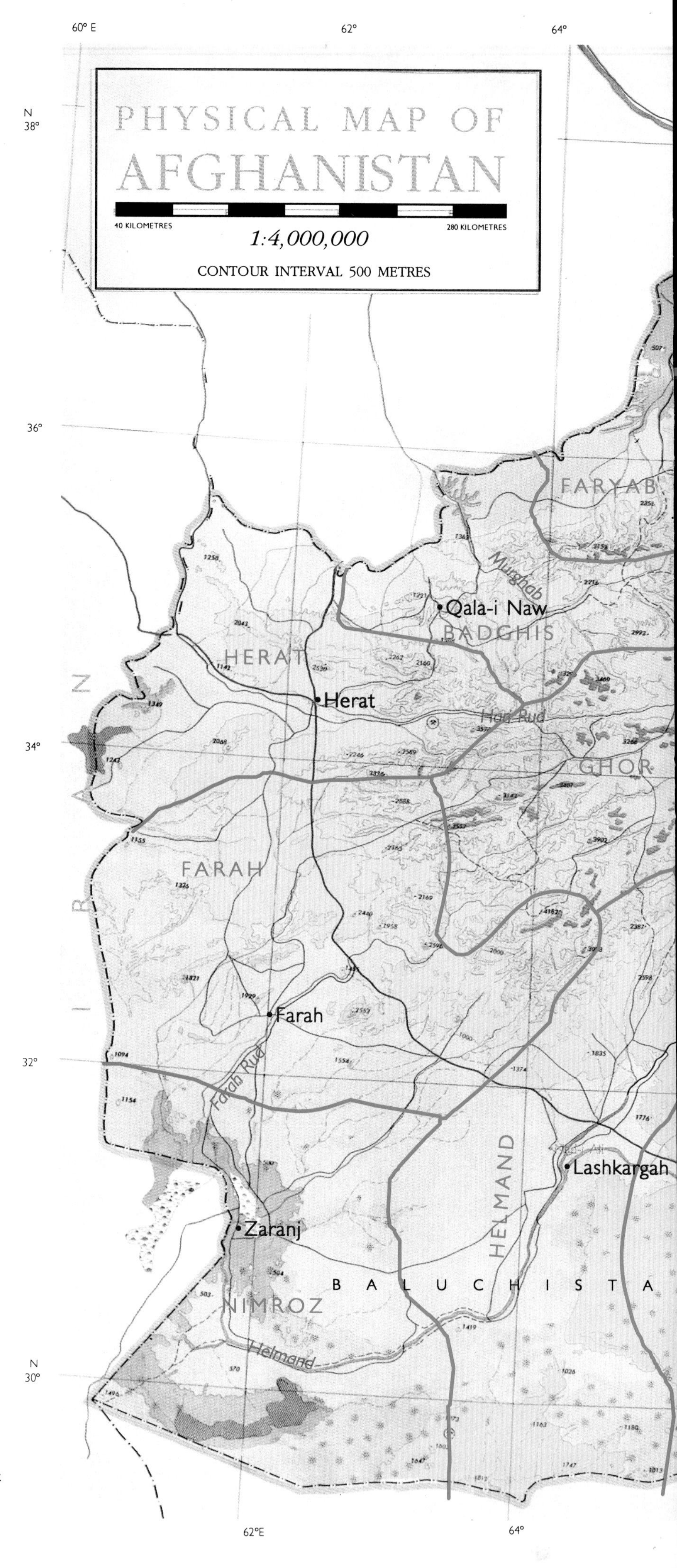

21 Physical Map of Afghanistan (Source Cartographic & Cadastral Survey Institute, Kabul, 1975-6)

U S S R
CHINA
Shibarghan
Balkh
Mazar-i Sharif
Tashqurghan
Kunduz
Khanbad
Taluqan
Faizabad
Aibak
Baghlan
Pul-i Khumri
SALANG PASS
PANJSHIR
NURISTAN
GHORBAND
Charikar
Mahmud -i Raqi
Bamiyan
BAMIYAN
HAZARAJAT
KABUL
Kabul
Mehtar-lam
Asadabad
BAJAUR
SWAT
Jalalabad
Maidan Shahr
NANGARHAR
Peshawar
Baraki Barak
WARDAK
LOGAR
Ghazni
Gardez
KATAWAZ
GHAZNI
KHOST
PAKTIA
Urgun
Uruzgan
Arghandab
Gomal
Indus
Kalat-i Ghilzai
ZABUL
Kandahar
Quetta
P A K I S T A N
SAMANGAN
BALKH
BAGHLAN
KUNDUZ
TAKHAR
BADAKHSHAN
MINE
INTERNATIONAL BOUNDARY
RIVER
HIGHWAY
CONTOURS AND SAND
PROVINCES
ALTITUDE SCALE
7485
5000
4000
3000
2000
1000
500
HEIGHTS IN METRES
66°
68°
70°
72°
74°
38°
36°
34°
32°
30°

2,2 Relief of Afghanistan, with elevations in metres (Source: Dupree, 1973)

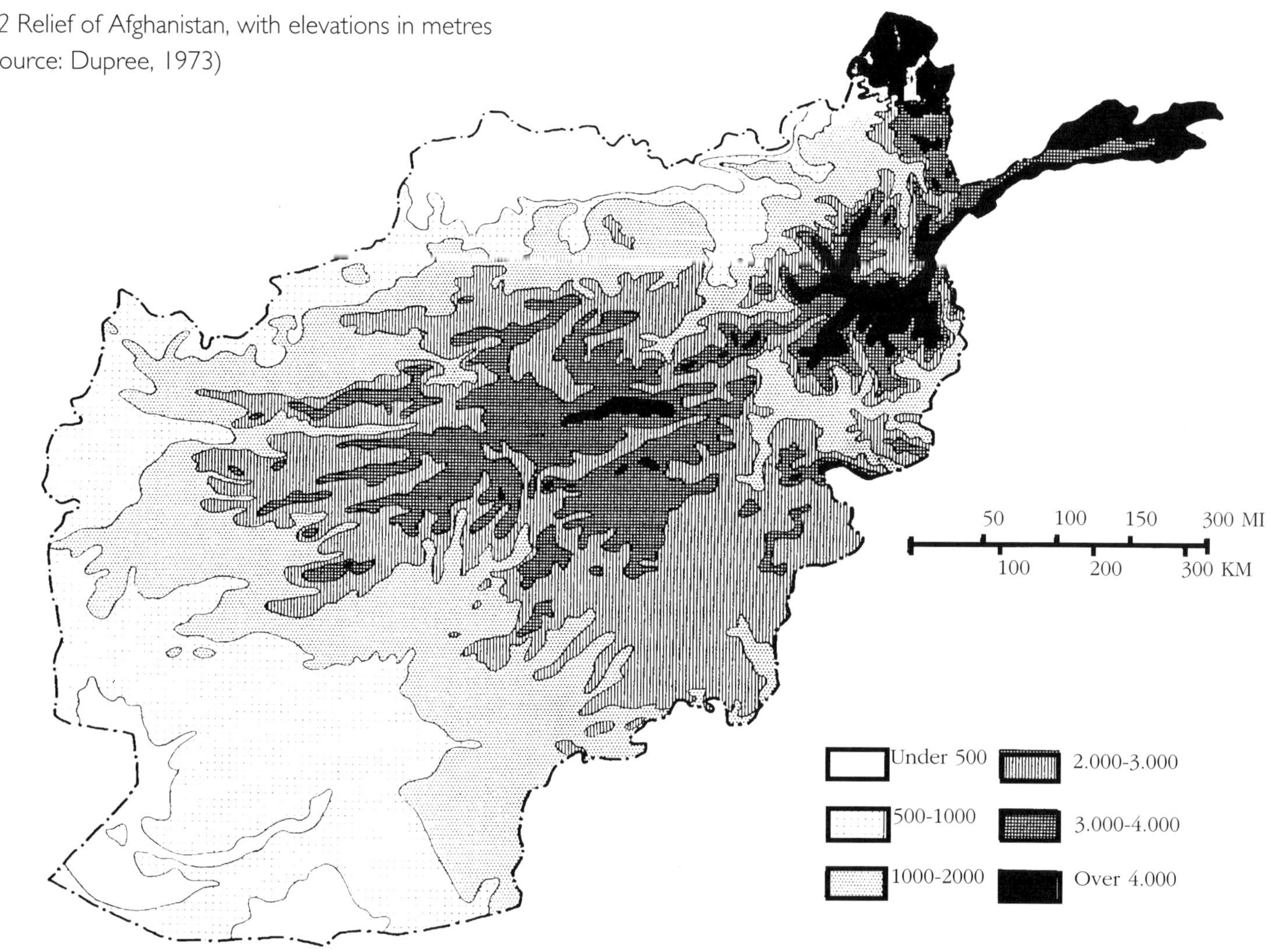

force of poor landless people, both from within and outside the village, were hired on a daily basis.[5]

In East Afghanistan, a large proportion of the population was therefore fully or partly employed within the agricultural sector, and the lack of alternative employment possibilities in, for example, the urban sector left no other choice. On the basis of research in the Kunduz, Badakhshan, and Parwan provinces, Barin Zuri points out that the Afghan rural economy, while not characterized by permanent underemployment, could certainly be described as having considerable seasonal underemployment. In fact, both the domestic workforce of the agricultural households as well as hired labourers displayed an excess of work-hours during the months of September-October (i.e. the period of harvest in the researched provinces), while they were underemployed for the remaining 10 months of the year (Barin Zuri 1981). While a permanent rural-urban migration (up to the mid-1970s) had only taken place on a limited scale as compared to other developing countries, seasonal migration had become a common response for the rural workforce.

In East Afghanistan the picture was the same. An increasing number of poor, rural people thus undertook summer migrations, particularly to Kabul and surrounding areas, where employment chances were best. They did so mainly in the four months between the spring and autumn harvests of the eastern river valleys, i.e. a period of relative underemployment here. Hence, the labour migrants exploited the staggered harvest seasons of the high Kabul basin and the low-lying eastern river valleys.

In the rural areas, the labour migrants might take up harvest work and when that ended, turn to other kinds of temporary employment or petty trading within the urban sector. Petty trading and various kinds of occasional labour in construction (*gilkārī*, lit. mudwork), transport as porter, or using a donkey (*kharkārī*, lit. donkey-work) or *karachī* (a two-wheeled cart), were in popular parlance referred to as *gharībī* (lit. poor man's work). The term *gharībī* is very apt, as only poor people with no other possibilities engaged in these kinds of work, and earnings were so limited that the people were bound to remain poor.

Afghan villages have been described as largely self-sufficient units, except for items like tea, sugar, salt, iron implements, cloth, mirrors, trinkets, kerosene, lamps and lamp chimneys, matches, etc. which people obtained from either a town bazaar or itinerant pedlars. "Until recently, the Afghan village had two interesting peculiarities when compared to other Asian villages: no bazaars and no wheels. Therefore, few full-time specialists live in the village" (Dupree 1973: 132). However, the eastern-most areas like Laghman and Nangarhar, where cultivation was particularly intensive, differed from this overall picture as a certain division of labour existed within agriculture itself: apart from the actual cultivators (be they owner-cultivators, share-croppers, or tenants) and the ordinary blacksmith, there existed a number of specialists in charge of specific kinds of work such as threshing and rice-shelling.

The general artisan sector in Afghanistan during this century had suffered considerable setbacks due to competition from both domestic and imported industrial products. Other factors contributing to the decline of rural crafts were the gradual turn towards a money economy and the increasing market orientation of part of the population (Grötzbach 1972: 251). However, due to the overall stagnation within the agricultural sector and its low technological level, many traditional crafts associated with agricultural production still survived and had remained little affected by competition from industrial products.

The rural craftsmen of East Afghanistan exhibited a wide variety of settlement forms, ranging from the completely settled way of life to semi-nomadic and nomadic forms. Settled craftsmen such as the rural blacksmiths, and some semi-nomadic groups like the Musalli threshers, to be described in a later chapter, were found in most villages; one or two such households would provide full time craft services to the landholding community in return for a certain share of the crop. In the terminology of Rao (1987: 12), such craftsmen were attached to their customers, in the sense of working primarily for a given village community. Other craftsmen occasionally formed separate village communities and engaged in seasonal migrations. This might be the case when their products or services depended either on the availability of specific raw materials or on a low, seasonal or irregular demand. Such specialized communities could be found among potterymakers, gold- and knife-smiths,

2,3 The Alishang valley, next to Maskurah, April 1975 (Photo: Gorm Pedersen). pp. 42-3

leatherworkers, specialized groups of carpenters, weavers, small traders, etc. These groups were unattached to agricultural production, living independently and visiting their customers at more or less regular intervals. Examples are the knifesmiths of Haiderkhani, who numbered more than fifty families, the famous potterymakers of Charbagh, with more than eighty families, or the 150 families in the Shaykh Mohammadi pedlar community of Maskurah. These communities were composed of patrilineal descent groups who maintained the same occupations for generations. They sold their products in or outside the region and were economically independent of the landowning groups. Many of these occupational specialists undertook seasonal migrations to other provinces in order to sell their produce: many potterymakers, both from Laghman and Nangarhar, went to Kabul and the Koh-i Daman area north of Kabul during summer time, setting up a workshop with kilns and selling their pots to the surrounding villages. Their choice of location was very much determined by the local availability of good clay, such as that found around Qala-i Murad Beg in Koh-i Daman. Equally so, the Shaykh Mohammadi pedlars of Maskurah went to four different localities in Koh-i Daman for the summer, while the knifesmiths of Haiderkhani migrated to Paghman, where they set up their forge under a shade on the sidewalk.

By the mid-1970s some of these crafts were disappearing due to competition from industrial products, as had occurred with the weavers, or they were undergoing changes due to the overall technological and economic development as was the case of the Shaykh Mohammadi pedlars. Their trade routes, overall migration patterns, and supply of merchandise had changed during the last couple of generations, but there was little indication that they were to disappear as a specialized community of pedlars.

Finally, some craftsmen were entirely nomadic. They lived in tents all year round or rented rooms on a short-term basis in different locations and visited their customers in different areas on a seasonal basis. When they rented rooms for longer periods of time (for example during the winter months), it would normally be in towns rather than in villages. This was the case for the Shaykh Mohammadi chinaware riveters, the cotton codders, and the Ghorbat sievemakers.

This latter category of nomadic, non-pastoral people also included a number of non-Afghan groups who pursued various professions, including juggling, animal performance (mainly monkeys and snakes), peddling bangles, and other petty trinkets, fortune-telling, cupping, prostitution, etc.[6] These groups were all highly stigmatized, and were commonly referred to as "*Jat*", a generic term which implies both low descent and low occupation.

Ethnic Identity and Occupation

A striking feature of Afghanistan is its ethnic multiplicity, with its many languages and local dialects which the visitor encounters all over the country. Many authors have attempted to capture this heterogeneity of the Afghan population in the form of ethnic indexing and mapping. Most recently, Orywal has identified no less than 57 ethnic groups (Orywal, 1986).[7] Parallel with ethnic diversity is the diversification of languages. Along with the two principal (and official) languages of Afghanistan, Persian and Pashto (each with several regional dialects), there exist a host of minor languages and dialects, including Dardic and Turkic languages.

2,4 The irrigated flat lands stand in stark contrast to the dry hills in the southern Laghman province. In the background is Diwa village, Alishang valley (Photo: Gorm Pedersen, Dec. 1975).

The religious situation of Afghanistan is more uniform, as the majority (approximately 80%) adhere to the Hanafi Sunni doctrine. A sizeable minority are Imami Shi'as, some small groups are Ismaili Shi'as and there exist smaller, though economically well-off units of Indian Sikhs and Hindus. Afghanistan also has a Jewish community, although many have migrated to Israel over the past generation.

It is important to note, however, that these features of ethnic heterogeneity also contain a considerable degree of cultural homogeneity. This applies not only in terms of Afghanistan's dominant Islamic heritage, but also in the patrilineal family structure and range of settlement forms, which often cut across ethnic divisions. An additional factor may be that although Afghanistan's many peoples have not co-existed peacefully and the boundaries of present-day Afghanistan were not consolidated until the end of the last century, Nuristan being the major exception, these peoples have nevertheless been in continual contact with each other, whether it be relations of peace, warfare, or commerce.

In Afghan society, a man[8] defines his identity primarily according to his *qawm*, which may refer to his ethnic/tribal unit, and for non-tribals, to their ethnic and locality characteristics.[9] This means that an individual primarily conceives himself as a member of a collectivity, an ethnic, tribal, local, or religious community, and he relates to members of the same or other communities and is perceived by these as part of a collectivity. Below *qawm*-membership, a man is identified by his specific kinship relations, as the son of so-and-so.[10] Subordinate to all these relational aspects of identity come individual characteristics, such as economic position (landowning/non-landowning), occupation, etc.

Qawm affiliation is neither an absolute nor an unchanging category. Particularly in a heterogenous society like the Afghan, *qawm* names and *qawm* affiliation, both for individuals and groups, may change over time, quite apart from the fact that *qawm* identity is not only relational but to a large extent also a situational concept.[11] Since reference to *qawm* affiliation is used to define a person's identity in the social world, it may be invoked in a segmentary fashion, either to stress the shared identity of two parties or, depending on circumstances, to stress their lack of common bonds.

Hence, in Afghan society, a person's identity has primarily been constituted by membership and socialization within a specific social segment such as the family, tribe, local community, or ethnic group. Until the middle of this century, the relationship between the Afghan state and the population has also been based on the same concept of segmented communities. The central authorities were not concerned with the integration of these various groups. Rulers have often maintained power through a skillful strategy of divide-and-rule vis-à-vis the various tribes, religious, and ethnic groups, in order to maintain communal segregation. The rulers related to communities – be they tribal, religious, or localized – rather than to individuals in matters of conscription, taxation, legal matters, and political alliances. The first Afghan ruler to introduce the concept of citizen as opposed to the traditional concept of a collectively defined subject was King Amanullah (1919-29). His efforts in this respect, as well as his general reform policy, met with considerable opposition, however, and were largely abolished following the civil war in 1929 (Poullada 1973). Not until the introduction of parliamentary democracy in the 1960s, was the concept of a free, equal and independent citizen fully recognized by the Afghan state. Among the population at large, however, primordial loyalties and in-group solidarity remain important factors in defining their social universe (Olesen 1992).

In relation to primarily artisans and craftsmen, the concept of profession (*kesb*) equals *qawm* as a marker of identity, and the two terms frequently tend to be used synonymously. The reason is that, traditionally, a person was by and large born not only into a *qawm* but also into an occupation; in the 1970s sons were to a large extent still are, trained to take over their father's occupation. From this it followed, that those in small *qawm*s were directly associated with specific professions, and hence, the meaning of *qawm* and *kesb* became practically indistinguishable in daily usage.

In Afghanistan, as in any other society, men are not born equal. Economic and political differences are related to and duplicated by status distinctions along ethnic, occupational, and religious lines. A well-defined, generally agreed upon ranking of *qawm*s cannot be established. *Qawm*-affiliation has neither a constant meaning in time or space nor is it unchanging at the individual level. A person may strive to increase his social respectability by claiming membership of another *qawm*. The term Tajik is particularly ambiguous and is at times used as a sort of "residual category". If one does not belong to one of the major, more well-defined groups, one may call oneself Tajik, or claim to be Tajik in order to hide one's real background. Yet one can only make a successful claim to Tajik identity provided one is a *Fārsīwān*, a Persian-speaker. In his survey of ethnic classifications in Tashqurghan, North Afghanistan, Centlivres often received the following response: "I am a Tajik, but my father or grand-father was Uzbek". The change of *qawm* identity was partly associated with language, since the process was described as "Uzbek becoming *Fārsīwān*", i.e. Persianophone, which in the popular conception meant Tajik. Centlivres concludes that the term Tajik implies a certain integration into the Persian-speaking urban communities (Centlivres 1972: 158).

Wealth is an important status criterion, but far from the only one. In the rural setting, ownership of land is highly valued, as it renders a man economically independent. Within the tribal ethos of Pashtun society, land ownership has traditionally been the precondition enabling a man to act in the local political arena. Trade activities are respectable, too, at a certain level, since the income generated guarantees economic independence and enables a man to act with honour. Hence, among the bazaar trades, Centlivres refers the following popular saying from Tashqurghan about the ranking of people: first shopkeeper, then artisan and then worker ("*awal dokāndār, bāz kesp wa kār, bāz mazdūrkār*") (1972). "To be in somebody's bread", i.e. to be earning a salary, has irrespective of the factual economic conditions the connotations of being a *nawkar* (servant), which is seen as socially degrading because it limits one's freedom to act with honour.

The situation of the different crafts is more ambivalent, especially because regional variations play a role. In their respective studies of the Tashqurghan bazaar, both Centlivres (1972) and Charpentier (1972) discuss the social status associated with various trades and crafts. Both state that income and capital are generally recognized means of acquiring high social status. Charpentier points out that a formerly respectable craft like silver-smithery has suffered a decline in status in concordance with its economic decline. The ranking of professions may thus change over time, and from place to place. Blacksmithing for example, is generally considered inferior (Kieffer in Centlivres 1972), but this was not the case in Tashqurghan, where blacksmiths' earnings were comparatively good and the craft rather developed. While disagreement may exist as to the individual ranking of the majority of crafts, certain crafts are generally deemed inferior because they are considered "unclean", "servant-like", religiously disapproved, or associated with low morality. This applies to tanners, ropemakers, cloth-dyers, sievemakers, professional threshers, and musicians; the disapproval of the latter is embodied in the Afghan saying, "Song and dance are Satan's daughters" (Shah 1982: 118).

Much discussion has occurred regarding the extent to which the social ranking of various professions and *qawms* among the Muslims on the Indian Subcontinent can be compared to the caste system of Hinduism.[12] This discussion is also relevant for eastern Afghanistan. Nevertheless, the relative poverty of Afghanistan combined with tribal and Islamic notions of equality have rendered the social stratification less pronounced and rigid here as compared to neighbouring countries. In the Afghan context, there is no generally accepted nor religiously supported ranking of either *qawms* or occupations. Only at the lowest strata of occupations do caste-like features become more pronounced, in

2,5 The village blacksmith makes and repairs most of the agricultural tools (Laghman, April 1975).

the sense that endogamous groups carrying out inherited crafts are associated with notions of "uncleanliness", which may find some religious support. It must be emphasized, however, that "inferiority" and "uncleanliness" are associated with the profession rather than with the person. For Muslim Afghans, everybody is born equal before God, and this is not true of the Hindu caste system.

At the bottom of the Afghan social hierarchy, then, the various ranking systems tend to overlap with inferior *qawm*s pursuing what are considered inferior occupations. When these facts are combined with yet another socially unacceptable feature, that of an itinerant life-style, the foundation is laid for a stigmatized and socially marginal existence associated with superstition and prejudice, nourished by lack of information about or personal acquaintance with the itinerant population. For the general public, low status craft groups are lumped together under the common term *Jat*.[13] During my fieldwork I found this term used contemptuously about all three groups among whom I did research, the Musalli threshers, the Shaykh Mohammadi pedlars and the Ghorbat sievemakers.

It is to the credit of Rao that the widespread perception of *Jat* as referring to a specific socio-

2,6The blacksmith in Diwa (Photo: Klaus Ferdinand, 1955).

economic group in Afghanistan has been corrected (Rao 1981, 1982). Rao's analysis of the popular usage of *J̌at*, a term known from the Indian Subcontinent,[14] indicates that, in Afghanistan it is applied indiscriminately to several ethnic and socio-economic groups. *J̌at* clearly has derogatory connotations, and no group accepts to be classified as such, but instead refers to themselves by other names. This is despite the fact that each of these groups may classify others as *J̌at*. More specifically, Rao finds that *J̌at* was applied to at least six groups, partly of Iranian and partly of Indian origin: Baluch, Ghorbat, Jalāli, Pikrāǰ, Shādibāz, and Vangāwālā. Apart from their different ethno-linguistic origins, the groups also differ according to occupation and degree of nomadism (Rao 1982: 26-33).

In view of this, and according to these groups' own usage of the term, it seems most plausible to treat the concept of *J̌at* not as a generic term for these six groups or possibly more, but, rather, as a symbol or verbal indicator of the extreme marginalization and inferior status associated with certain *qawms*, professions, and lifestyles. In this respect the six groups above occupy the bottom rung of the Afghan social ladder.

Crafts, Trades, and Religious Patronage

The three communities researched, the Musalli threshers, the Shaykh Mohammadi pedlars, and the Ghorbat sievemakers, all experience their itinerant lifestyle, occupation and descent, as being considered inferior by the settled society. The groups share the norms and values of the surrounding society and thus acknowledge their own "shortcomings". They find compensation or partial rehabilitation in myths and legends which tell of their holy descent or claim religious initiation and patronage of their profession. They may be considered social outcasts, but in fact see themselves as a "chosen people". This phenomenon is not peculiar to these three groups nor to itinerant groups as such, but is part of the overall cultural tradition among professional groups in Muslim West Asia.

From his study of the Tashqurghan bazaar, Centlivres informs us that the crafts, like elsewhere in the Muslim world, are organized in guilds (*aṣnāf/ṣunuf*, pl.). The guilds function as corporate groups. They have a patron of religious origin, who in the remote past is supposed to have initiated the craft, perhaps following a revelation. From the patron the craft has been transmitted until the present day through a series of initiated master craftsmen. This original mythical master is referred to as the *pīr* of the craft, and respect is paid him as a kind of guardian of the profession. Artisans of the same profession refer to each other as *hampīr*, i.e. as people devoted to the same *pīr*. Associated with each craft and *pīr* is a specific religious writing, *risālat*, which constitutes a sort of professional code concerning the craft, sacralizing it as *ḥalāl*, or religiously commendable (Centlivres 1972: 163-72).[15]

While the impact of modernization has led to the breakdown of the guild system in most West Asian countries, Centlivres stresses that Tashqurghan's guilds are very much alive and integrated into the daily life of the artisans and, to a lesser degree, the traders. The continued existence of guilds in Afghanistan in the 1970s should probably be seen as an effect of the economic "backwardness" of the country.

Guild systems have primarily been an urban phenomenon, but Centlivres points out that the tendency of each occupation to have its own *pīr* is equally widespread among the rural artisans. This was certainly confirmed during my own research. I was continuously told legends of the founding *pīrs* or protectors of various occupations. A Musalli informant directly referred me to seek further information in the publication entitled *Kesb Nāma* ("Book of Occupations"), a *risālat* covering potters, blacksmiths, carpenters, barbers, laundrymen, and dyers.[16]

In his treatise on *jihād*, Schleifer elaborates on the spiritual dimensions of "pious chivalry", *futuwwa*, as the key to the historical integration of craft guilds into the emerging Sufi orders (*ṭarīqāt/ṭuruq, pl.*). As "economic units", the craft guilds were sacralized by the concept of *futuwwa*, which characterizes the *jihād* as a vocation, implicit in a frequently quoted *ḥadīth* which appears in one of the most popular collections of medieval (13th century) Islam (Schleifer 1983: 194):

> "Verily Allah has prescribed proficiency in all things. Thus, if you kill, kill well; if you slaughter, slaughter well. Let each one of you sharpen his blade and let him spare suffering to the animal he slaughters."

2,7 The blacksmith in Diwa (Photo: Klaus Ferdinand, 1955)

2,8 The itinerant weavers had virtually disappeared from the countryside by the mid-1970s, losing out in competition with industrial products (Photo: Klaus Ferdinand, 1955).

Schleifer goes on to point out that the term *iḥsān* here translated as "proficiency", is used by the Prophet in the sense of "sincerity", i.e. to do things for the sake of God alone and not for outer appearance or convention. He argues that:

> "The concept of *futuwwa* of the craft guilds synthesized these two meanings, whereby the perfection of their work for which the craftsmen *strived* under the tutelage of a master was not for his own sake (a livelihood can be made with shabby goods) but for the sake of God and thus a Way for perfection of his *soul*" (1983: 195).

The concept of *futuwwa* not only contained a chivalrous challenge to be truly noble and brave but held the (Sufic) promise of *ma'rifa* (the intuitive knowledge of God) in the perfection of one's craft. In this context Schleifer sees the Sufi orders as a source of doctrine and guidance for the guild system that provided a profound measure of vocational dignity and social security in ordinary economic life (1983: 199). The relation-

2.9 The potter at his wheel. In the southern Laghman, there are a number of villages dominated by certain craftsmen, such as potters and knife-makers (Photo: Klaus Ferdinand, 1955).

2,10 In spite of his low social position, the village barber has several important tasks, including the circumcising of boys and cooking at village celebrations. The photo shows a barber at work in Mehtarlam, the administrative centre of the Laghman province (Photo: Gorm Pedersen, April 1975).

ship between the religious orders and the guilds could also take on direct forms. As Trimingham (1971: 25) points out, a particular guild and its members tended to be linked with a particular order and saint. While the hierarchial structure of the guilds was reflected in the organizational structure of the orders, the guilds on their side adopted the concept of spiritual heritage, in the sense that each group claimed attachment to ancestors, whether true or mythical, whose parentage was morally significant. This is easily discernible in Afghanistan, and extends far beyond the regular network of urban guilds. Rural and even itinerant craftsmen and traders who are not part of proper guild organizations also refer their occupation to an original founder/initiator *(pīr)*.

Besides the regular status hierarchy of the various occupations, Centlivres observed an alternative religio-mythical stratification among the craftsmen of Tashqurghan which literally reversed the established order. There was a hierarchy of *pīr*s in which professions usually considered the most inferior found themselves at the top on account of the virtue of their *pīr*, e.g., the barbers' Salman, the tanners' Axī, the dyers' Isā and the ropemakers' *Imām* Jafar.[17] In this way, poor or despised professions obtained religio-mythical status by force of their *pīr*. According to Centlivres, the various Afghan hierarchies preclude a simple comparison with the caste system or any absolute and rigid status system (1971: 171).

The sacralization of professions through an alleged religio-mythological origin and, in many cases, a continued attachment to a proper religious order or *pīr* is thus a common feature of Afghan social life. Equally widespread among Afghan urban, rural, and peripatetic craftsmen is the effort to compensate a socially low or despised position in ordinary life by elevating the position of their *pīr* within the spiritual domain. However, the precise relationship between the Afghan craft guilds and the Sufi orders is unclear, since no specific study on the guilds or on the religious orders in Afghanistan has been carried out. It nevertheless seems clear that the overall cultural environment has established a pattern which is also discernible among rural and itinerant craftsmen, even though they exist outside the proper guild structure of the urban centres. This will be apparent in the subsequent studies of the Shaykh Mohammadi, Musalli and Ghorbat.

NOTES:

[1] Reclamation of land for agricultural purposes has taken place, but has not been able to offset population growth. Since the turn of the century, huge areas in Turkestan have come under the plough, and after the Second World War, several thousand landless families were settled by the ambitious US-financed Helmand Valley Project. In the 1970s, another irrigation scheme, this time Soviet-financed, was carried out in the Nangarhar province where landless people also were being settled.

[2] According to Davydov, 42% of the landowners owned less than 2 *ǰarīb* (1 *ǰarīb* = 0.195 ha), 94% owned less than 50 *ǰarīb* of land, which however amounted to less than 27% of the cultivated area, while 0.2% of landowners possessed 50% of the cultivated area (Davydov's informations, published 1962, are quoted from Grötzbach 1972: 205).

[3] In 1975-76, I approached the local authorities in Laghman in order to obtain information about the actual land distribution, but to no avail. It was not clear whether the authorities simply did not want to supply the information or whether it did not exist, but the latter is not unlikely. During the land reform which followed the Saur Revolution in 1978, the insufficiency or nonexistence of cadastral surveys became clear, this was one reason for the failure of the land reform. Moreover, while most of the landless population dwelled in East Afghanistan, hardly any land was available for redistribution there. The landless people had to go mainly to southwestern Afghanistan if they would have any hope of receiving land through the reform (see also Olesen 1983 for a discussion of the Saur Revolution, the subsequent land reform and the popular response to it).

[4] This is reflected in Toepfer's survey of villages in seven provinces, where he found that while average farm size in Nangarhar was 4.9 *ǰarīb*, it was 71.0 *ǰarīb* in Helmand (Toepfer 1972).

[5] The overall technological and economic stagnation of Afghan agriculture has been discussed by many authors. It can be summed up by increasing indebtedness of the peasantry, centralization of land ownership, and drainage of the economic surplus from agriculture into either trade or additional land ownership, without the subsequent productive investments (see, for example, Hahn 1964-65, Grötzbach 1972, Toepfer 1972, Kanne 1974).

[6] See Rao (1982) for a brief list of these groups, their habitats, economic activities, religions, mother tongues, etc.

[7] The methodological and theoretical problems involved in reaching a meaningful definition of ethnic group and ethnicity are amply reflected in the highly varying results of successive ethnic maps of Afghanistan. For a very relevant discussion of the problems involved, see Digard (1988).

[8] The term "man" is used deliberately here rather than the gender-neutral term "person", since Afghan society is not only patrilineal and patrilocal, but patriarchy is also the established norm. However, while the "patri"-dominance is formally recognized in all domains of social life, the endogamous marriage pattern prevalent in all social groups brings about a close correlation between matrilateral and patrilateral relatives, which blurs the distinction and strengthens the matrilateral ties. In addition, the normative description of the (lack of) influence of women and of matrilateral relatives also tends to undercommunicate the considerable *actual* influence they often exercise.

[9] The term "ethnic group" is used here according to F. Barth's definition (1969: 10-11). In accordance with Narrol, Barth presents the following criteria: an ethnic group is (1) largely self-perpetuating, (2) shares fundamental cultural values, realized in overt unity in cultural forms, (3) makes up a field of communication and interaction, (4) has a membership which identifies itself, and is identified by others, as constituting a category distinguishable from other categories of the same order.

[10] Incidentally, for a woman, the most important aspect of her (adult) identity is the number of (male) children born, which is reflected in the fact that she hardly ever would be referred to by her name, but as "the mother of so-and-so" (name of the eldest son).

[11] For further discussion, see Tapper (1988) and Centlivres and Centlivres-Demont (1988).

[12] For example Leach (1962), Barth (1962), S. Ahmad (1977), Berland (1977), Hayden (1987).

[13] See Rao (1982: 23-33) for a discussion of the term *J̌at*, its distribution, origin, and general usage in Afghanistan today.

[14] See, for example, Westphal-Hellbush and Westphal, 1964.

[15] Centlivres collected a number of *risālat*s in Tashqurghan and describes their content as follows: The *risālat* begins with an invocation of God, then presents the [illegible] chain from creator to *pīr*, perhaps comprising a prosopopoeia of the *pīr* himself, thanking God for the power entrusted to him. Then follows a series of questions and answers regarding the actual exercise of the profession as well as the prayers prescribed for carrying out each of its technical operations. Centlivres suggests with reference to Kassim et al. (1927: 250) that these prayers, said in Arabic, play the role of magic formulas rendering the technique effective. Finally, the *risālat* states the obligation of the craftsman to recopy the text, keep it, read it, or have it read once a week or once a month (Centlivres 1972: 167).

[16] See abridged translation of *Kesb Nāma* in Appendix I. In their study of potterymaking in Pakistan, Rye and Ewans came across a potter in Dir who slavishly followed all the instructions of the *Kesb Nāma*. He had bought the book some 30 years earlier and considered it holy, a view which had also been emphasized to him by a mullah. Professor Matson has also seen a copy of the book in the possession of a potter in Charikar, Afghanistan (Rye and Ewans 1976: Appendix 5).

[17] Salmān-i Fārsi is a popular figure in Muslim legend and a national hero of Iran. He is supposed to have left his father's house near Isfahan when still a boy, seeking the Prophet, who, he was told, would revive the religion of Abraham. On the way to Arabia, Salmān was sold as a slave. In Medina, he met the Prophet, with whose aid he purchased his freedom. Little is known of Salmān-i Fārsi as a historical figure; his fame is due largely to his nationality; he has become a prototype of the Persians who were converted to Islam and who played a central role in the spread of Muslim Islam (*Encyclopaedia Britannica*, 1985, X: 359). Salmān's position as *pīr* of the barbers is founded on the legend that he carried out the first ritual shaving of the Prophet's head (Centlivres 1971: 166).

Axī, or Akhī, probably refers to *Akhī* Evren, a 14th-century saint of the *futuwwa* orders of Kirshehir (Central Anatolia) (Centlivres 1971: 166). In their Anatolian form these orders were called *Akhilik*. *Akhī* Evren is said to have been a tanner and was the *pīr* of the tanners and all trades concerned with the treatment of leather. Over time, the *Akhi Bābā*s, the descendants of *Akhī* Evren, guardians of his shrine as well as heads of all tanners in the Ottoman Empire, gained a position of considerable power among craftsmen in general, and *Akhī* Evren became the *pīr* not only of the tanners but of all Turkish guilds. The influence of his cult has stretched as far as Turkestan (*The Encyclopaedia of Islam* ,1983, II: 966-9).

Isā is identical with Jesus, who in Islam is counted among the major prophets.

Imām Jafar is the 6th *imām* in the Shi'a tradition.

CHAPTER III

THE MUSALLI THRESHERS

Introduction

In the densely populated lower Alishang and Alingar river valleys of Laghman, threshing, winnowing, and sifting of grain constitute a specialized occupation, carried out by a distinct and internally related group of people, commonly referred to as "Musallis" (i.e. from the prayer carpet). In fact, "Musalli" is neither a *qawm*-name nor does it mean "thresher", although *muṣallī-tūb* is used to designate the profession. In the following, this occupation will simply be referred to as "threshing" even though it includes other work processes as well. The Musallis, who are originally of Indian descent, have for generations had the hard, dusty work of threshing as their exclusive prerogative. Along with other specialized occupations in the villages, threshing has been inscribed in a traditional system of mutual rights and obligations, reminiscent of the jajmani-system of the Indian Subcontinent, in which the specialists' relations to the landowning community are regulated.[1] The Musallis are among the poorest of the rural population, and this in addition to their *qawm* and the economic dependency implied by their occupation, leave them as one of the lowest-ranking social groups in the villages; in fact, only the barbers are considered socially inferior to the Musallis.

It is only in the fertile central and southern parts of Laghman that threshing constitutes an occupation in itself and that Musallis are found. They live dispersed, with one to three families per village, mostly as tenants in rented houses.[2] In the upper parts of Laghman, cultivators thresh and clean their grain themselves as is the case in other parts of Afghanistan. Threshing being a seasonal occupation, the Musallis, after cleaning the grain from the spring harvest during the month of June, will migrate to the higher-lying Kabul area, where the harvest season is one month later[3]. Here they dwell in tents in larger groups, cleaning the grain of the local landowners, whereupon they return to Laghman in time for the autumn harvest towards the end of October. While the Musallis thus are involved in the production system of two regions, socially and economically they basically belong to Laghman, where their relations are of a permanent nature as compared to their ad hoc character in the Kabul area during the summer migrations.

This chapter begins with a brief outline of the Laghman province and its agricultural production system, which forms the economic and social background for the Musallis and their occupational niche. There exist no written sources as to the origin and history of the Laghman Musallis and recourse had to be sought in their own oral

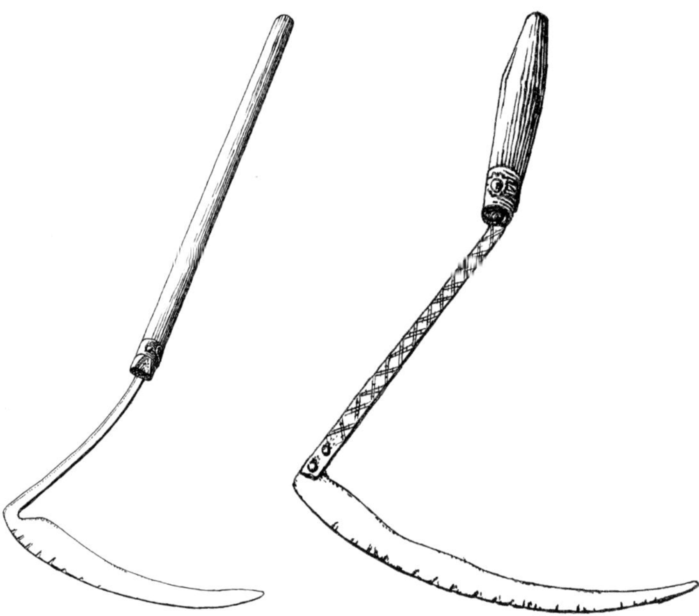

3,1-2 In the small agricultural plots in Laghman, all harvest work is carried out by use of a sickle, either short- or long-handled.

accounts, which, however, centre far more on legendary tales of origin in a distant, mythological past than on more recent historical events. Rather than constituting historical evidence, the legendary accounts are important to the Musallis' conception of themselves, of their *qawm,* and occupation. Hence, these legends also seem to be subject to the Musallis' interpretation and adaptation in response to changing external conditions. The actual historical origin of the Musallis is unclear, but on the basis of 19th century British sources from the Indian Subcontinent, it seems plausible to assume that the Laghman Musallis originate from menial castes of the Punjab in former British India.

The next section of this chapter describes the occupation of threshing along with the work organization of the Musallis in Laghman and Kabul, and their socio-economic relations to the settled population, in view of the changing conditions in the agricultural sector. A gradual breakdown in the traditional occupational specialization in Laghman had been underway, resulting in competition among poor people for all unskilled wage work, but also, in 1975, in attempts to form an interest organization among a section of Musallis. Yet another development has affected the lives of the Musallis, the gradual settlement of several hundred Musalli families by the government in the Helmand Valley Project area since the 1950s.

The final section of this chapter discusses the internal social organization of the Musalli community, including household composition, marriage patterns, and the conception of *qawm,* its delimitation and meaning as a social category in relation to their integration and social position in the settled community. The question ultimately arises as to which extent the Musallis' seasonal migration has left a distinct imprint on their lifestyle as compared to that of the settled population, including their incorporation of cultural features normally associated with urban artisans' groups.

Land and People in Laghman

The Laghman Province of East Afghanistan is one of the most fertile agricultural areas of the country owing to its subtropical climate and abundant water supply. The region is traversed by the Kabul, Alingar, and Alishang rivers.[4] Entering Laghman from the south, turning off the Kabul-Jalalabad highway, the road follows the joined Alishang-Alingar river upstream through the wide valley until it bifurcates at the village of Tirgarhi, and enters the narrower but still densely populated Alishang and Alingar river valleys. Further north lies the mountainous, thinly populated Nuristan area, from where the

3,3 A Pashto-speaking Musalli family in Mohammad Khel.

rivers spring, and which even today is still relatively inaccessible.

As all agricultural production in Laghman depends on irrigation water from canals derived from the rivers, the separation between desert and arable land is razor-sharp. The cultivated areas of the valley bottoms stand out as sprouting green against the greyish-brown, barren hills and mountain slopes, which cannot be reached by irrigation water.[5] The scarcity of arable land means that not an inch is wasted for human settlement; hence, the villages are either located at the edge of the cultivable areas or at high-lying or otherwise useless land.

The building style is uniform throughout the area, and differences in wealth can mainly be deciphered from the size of dwellings. All private houses are made from built-up mud walls (*pakhsa*) or occasionally of sun-dried brick finished with a coat of a waterproofing mixture of mud and straw. The roofs of all buildings are flat and form an integral part of the living space: fruit

and vegetables are spread out for drying here, in the sunny days of winter it is a pleasant place for relaxation as compared to the cold and damp rooms, and in the oppressive heat of summer, the whole family sleeps in the fresh air on the roof. The building style is primarily geared to ensure the protection of the inhabitants and their possessions; hence, even the most humble house is surrounded by a 2 m high wall with only one entry door or gate, and there are no windows facing the street. The more wealthy families live in virtual fortresses (*qal'a*) with 3-4 m high boundary walls and regular watch-towers in each corner. Inside, a courtyard is found and perhaps a small plot with a few fruit-trees or vegetables. Along the sides of the perimeter are built rooms one or more stories high, all with windows facing towards the courtyard. Here, a nuclear or extended family may live. And the complex normally also contains small rooms, in which a poor, landless family may live for free in exchange for certain services. Such rooms, however, may have a separate entry. Walking through the villages of Laghman, or anywhere else in East Afghanistan, faceless walls meet the eye, giving no clue as to what is within. This uninviting appearance, brought about by the need for a man physically to protect his home and family, is fully justified both by past and present Afghan experiences of the central power and of private feuds. Like the contrasts in the landscape, the intimidating appearance of the houses is counteracted by the overwhelming hospitality of their inhabitants.

The population of the Laghman Province is ethnically very mixed. While local legends tell of *kāfirs* (i.e. infidels) who were the original inhabitants, historically at least, it can be established that Tajiks occupied the area prior to the incursion by Pashtuns.[6] Gradually, Ghilzai Pashtuns aided by the (Pashtun) rulers in Kabul and their local governors, spread into the province, taking over large parts of the land.[7] British reports from 1914 explain, that while Pashtuns were occupying both sides of the Kabul river and the Alingar valley, Tajiks dominated the Alishang valley, while the lower parts of Laghman from Tirgarhi to Darunta were ethnically mixed (Adamec 1985: 485). For revenue purposes, Laghman was thus sub-divided into what became known as *Laghman-i-Afghania* and *Laghman-i-Tajikia* (ibid.). While Tajiks and Pashtuns tended to dominate in the respective areas, this division was by no means exclusive, and many villages have from ancient times had a mixed population, where at least the various specialist groups have belonged to ethnic minority communities. With the ethnically mixed population follows a diversity of languages in Laghman: the main languages are Pashto and the Laghmani dialect of Persian, but Kohistani, Pashai, and Nuristani dialects are also spoken.

Although arable land is scarce in Laghman, agriculture is still the dominant occupation, complemented only by crafts and trading; there are no cities in the area, but several hundred villages and a few minor towns. There are few landowners with large holdings, but most of the land is owned by smallholders, frequently with plots of less than 1 ha.[8] Due to the hot climate and low altitude, two grain crops per year can be harvested

3,4 A young Musalli woman with her child.

3.5 In the mountainous, northern parts of the Laghman province with little agricultural land and a dispersed population, there are no Musallis and few other specialists in the villages. Photo from the Karenj valley in upper Alishang.

3,6 Mehtarlam, the provincial centre of Laghman, has a small bazar. The other settlements in the province are villages of varying size.

in Laghman, and grains, occupying 80-85% of the land, are by far the most important crop.[9] Wheat is normally grown in spring followed by a second crop of paddy or maize, which in many places are grown on rotation basis.

The Laghman province has traditionally had a comparatively developed division of labour in the form of occupational specialization along ethnic lines. This is also the case for the other fertile eastern regions of Kunar (Christensen 1980) and Nangarhar, while it is nonexistent in other more thinly populated and less fertile areas. This occupational specialization has many characteristics in common with that of the Indian Subcontinent, in the sense that it is inscribed in a system of political and economic clientship and involves a certain informal hierarchy of occupations.[10]

The basic structure of the village communities centres on the patron-client relations tying non-landowning groups such as sharecroppers, agricultural labourers, and various specialists to the landowners.[11] A sharecropper is not only economically dependent upon the landowner but is also expected to support his landlord in local disputes. In return, the latter extends to his clients loans, political support, and protection (Kakar 1979: 120). At the bottom of the social ladder are the agricultural labourers and other occupational groups, consisting mainly of endogamous descent groups. While the sharecropper is dependent upon a single landowner, the specialists are attached to the community, or rather to the local landowners, as a group. The village specialists can be divided into two basic categories[12] : (1) Artisans directly related to agricultural production, such as blacksmiths and carpenters. These are obliged to repair and maintain the agricultural tools and implements, and as payment they receive from the local landowners a portion of the crop at harvest, irrespective of the actual amount of work carried out during the year. Only when doing work unrelated to agriculture will the artisans be paid cash. (2) Persons carrying out specific kinds of agricultural labour, such as threshers and rice mill workers, or special personal services such as barbers who have an important social function in the community. These are also paid with a certain amount of produce from the landowners at harvest time.

An old Laghmani explains how the system still works:

> "Carpenters, blacksmiths, and barbers are paid in kind at harvest time. First, they are paid at the reaping time, when they get some sheaves , and at the time when the stack is ready, they get a share – these three groups get an equal share. If the carpenter serves the blacksmith, he does it for free, as they need each other. But if he works for other landless people, he gets payment in money. If he makes, for example, a door for a landowner, he is paid in money. His payment in kind is just for his work on the agricultural tools ... If the blacksmith wants to take his grain to the mill, he will do it for free. The carpenter will get the Friday share of the mill as payment for his maintenance of the mill ... The blacksmiths are one *qawm*, and so are the carpenters. They don't give their daughters to non-professionals."

As is the case with the sharecroppers, the relationship between the artisan groups and the landowners is based on a complex net of economic, political, and social relations in which the specialists are the clients of the landowning community and expect to be protected by their patrons. Christensen (1980) has given an account of a similar system from the neighbouring province of Kunar, where exchange relations between the artisans and the landowning group are referred to by the term *kalin* (yearly)[13]. Among the Musallis of Laghman, I did not hear the relationship coined in a specific term.

While landownership generates the highest status in the local community, the occupations of thresher and barber are singled out as particularly inferior or unclean, as well as being associated with a range of services for the local community. In spite of its low status, a few people of other professions have during the last generation taken up grain cleaning as an occupation. They have done so out of dire need, be they landless peasants or other traditional specialists like rice mill workers (*pāykūbt*). The latter have traditionally been of the *qawm*s of Hussein Khēl, Hazarmeshi, and Ibrahim Khēl. For the far ma-

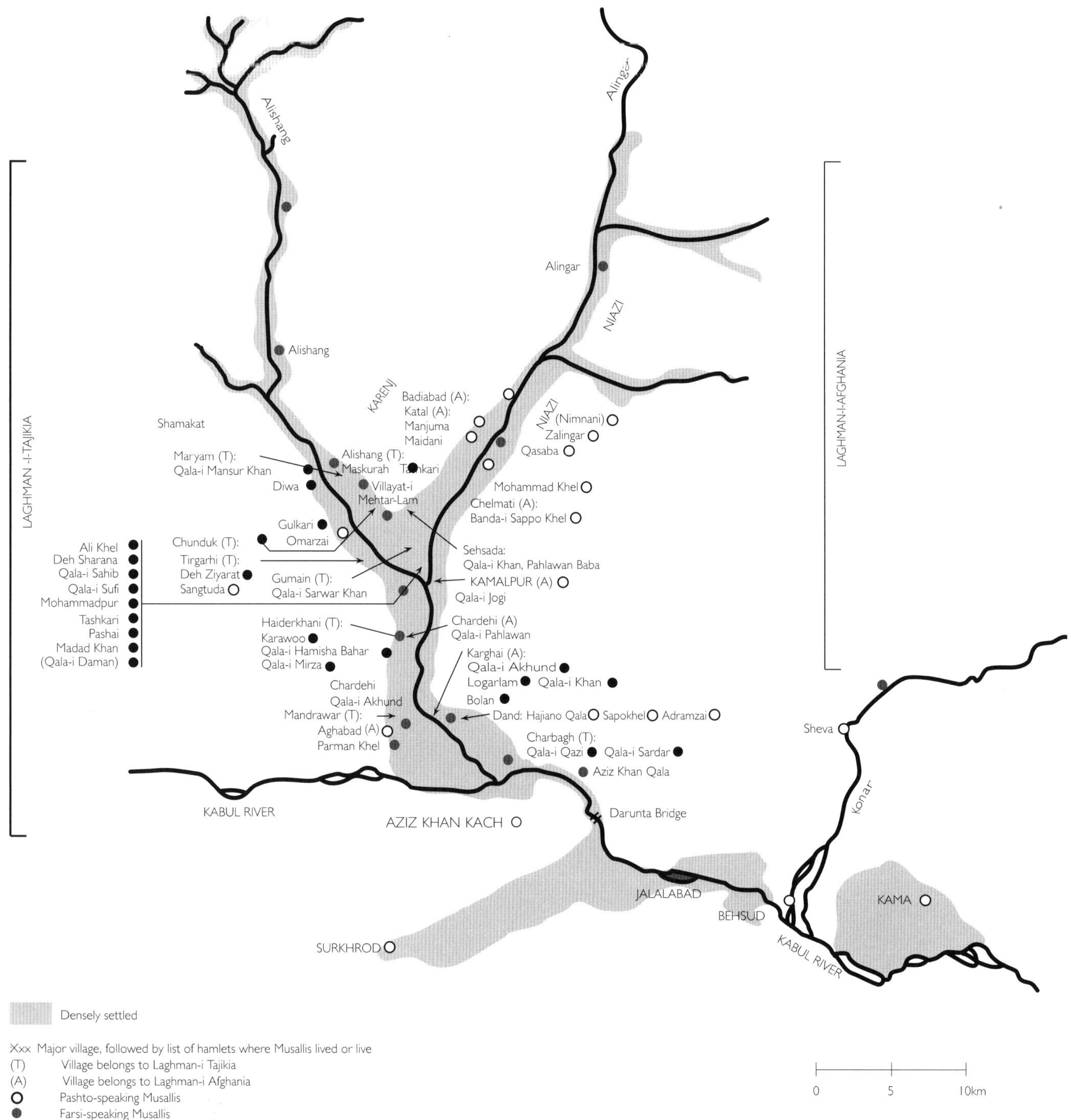
Location of Musallis in Laghman
Alishang
Alingar
Alingar
NIAZI
Alishang
KARENJ
Shamakat
Badiabad (A):
Katal (A):
Manjuma
Maidani
NIAZI
(Nimnani)
Zalingar
Qasaba
Maryam (T):
Qala-i Mansur Khan
Alishang (T):
Maskurah
Tankari
Diwa
Villayat-i
Mehtar-Lam
Mohammad Khel
Chelmati (A):
Banda-i Sappo Khel
Gulkari
Omarzai
Ali Khel
Deh Sharana
Qala-i Sahib
Qala-i Sufi
Mohammadpur
Tashkari
Pashai
Madad Khan
(Qala-i Daman)
Chunduk (T):
Tirgarhi (T):
Deh Ziyarat
Sangtuda
Gumain (T):
Qala-i Sarwar Khan
Sehsada:
Qala-i Khan, Pahlawan Baba
KAMALPUR (A)
Qala-i Jogi
Haiderkhani (T):
Karawoo
Qala-i Hamisha Bahar
Qala-i Mirza
Chardehi (A)
Qala-i Pahlawan
Karghai (A):
Qala-i Akhund
Logarlam
Qala-i Khan
Bolan
Chardehi
Qala-i Akhund
Mandrawar (T):
Aghabad (A)
Parman Khel
Dand: Hajiano Qala
Sapokhel
Adramzai
Charbagh (T):
Qala-i Qazi
Qala-i Sardar
Aziz Khan Qala
LAGHMAN -I-TAJIKIA
LAGHMAN-I-AFGHANIA
Sheva
Konar
KABUL RIVER
AZIZ KHAN KACH
Darunta Bridge
JALALABAD
BEHSUD
KAMA
SURKHROD
KABUL RIVER
Densely settled
Xxx Major village, followed by list of hamlets where Musallis lived or live
(T) Village belongs to Laghman-i Tajikia
(A) Village belongs to Laghman-i Afghania
Pashto-speaking Musallis
Farsi-speaking Musallis
No dot: Affiliation uncertain or not known
0
5
10km

3,7

jority of professional threshers, however, the occupation has been inherited over generations.

Mythical Origin

'Musalli' is the term commonly used in Laghman about all professional threshers irrespective of their origin. The threshers relate that the first Musalli was given this name by serving the Prophet as his prayer rug (*muṣallā*) carrier (see account below). In the Laghman province, threshers can be divided into two groups:

(1) Pashto-speaking Musallis:

A group of at least 30 interrelated families found almost exclusively within the Pashtun-dominated areas. They call their *qawm* Shāhi Khēl, i.e. King Khēl, and some of them claim Pashtun descent. The group had formerly been much bigger, but more than 200-300 families have received land from the government and settled in the Helmand province.[14]

(2) Persian-speaking Musallis

A group of at least 150 related families located mainly within the Tajik-dominated areas. They also call their *qawm* Shāhi Khēl, but both groups deny being interrelated and challenge the others' right to use the name. They explain that they arrived from India a few generations ago, and a couple of elderly people still know a few words of the 'Inku' language, presumably Hindko. A smaller number of their relatives have been settled by the government in Helmand.[15]

Both groups, like most Laghmanis, are bilingual in Persian and Pashto, but their first language tends to be that which dominates the village where they live.[16]

All the original grain-cleaners of Laghman prefer to be known as Shāhi Khēl, but this *qawm*-name is known hardly by anybody outside their own ranks. Instead, they are generally referred to as "Musallis" or by, what they consider as the derogatory term, "Chungars"/"Changars". The actual origin of the grain-cleaners is of little concern to other Laghmanis, who suppose them to be of low descent. A poor Pashtun reflects: "The Musallis are those *Ḥabashī*[17] or Chungars, about whom we hear in the stories: 'There was a king and his wife was in love with a Chungar ... '. By *qawm* they are *Ḥabashī*."

Even if others do not bother about their origin, it is of great concern to the Musallis themselves, who reject both the term "Chungar"/ "Changar", and to some extent that of "Musalli" too, claiming that these names have been imposed upon them, out of contempt, by the local Laghmanis. Whenever Musallis outlined their ancestry to me, as they invariably did even though I was inquiring about their economic situation, they would insist that they were superior to Musallis in other parts of Laghman. In fact, they were so concerned about their origin, that a virtual "mythical battle" went on between the two groups of original grain-cleaners. The Musallis' use of derogatory names about each other is similar to other itinerant groups referring to each others as *Jat*. The strategy is to elevate one's own group socially by distancing it from, real or imaginary social inferiors, such as "Chungars" or *Jat*. In this way, they find themselves supporting the dominant cultural discourse on itinerant groups in general, which confines all of them to a very low social status.

The Musallis themselves consider grain cleaning to be a low, unclean occupation. Hence, the Pashto-speaking Musallis who claim Pashtun descent, can be viewed as attempting upward mobility within the existing norm system, just like their *qawm* name of Shāhi (King) Khēl does. Although both groups call themselves Shāhi Khēl, they hold different stories of origin. The Pashto-speaking group claims to be descendants of the "original" Musalli:

> "When Adam and Eve left Paradise they had not yet copulated ... [but wanted to have a baby] ... Adam prayed two *rak'at* of *nafl* and then he put a big piece of glass (*shīsha*) in front of himself and prayed to God.[18] And there appeared Shish (*alai-hi 's-salam*) whose descendants are those *jūlahā* [weavers].[19] Then Adam asked Eve to do the same. She also prayed two *rak'at* of *nafl* and brought a prayer carpet (*muṣallā*) and prayed to God. From the carpet the Musalli appeared. They called him *Musalli* because he was created from the *muṣallā*."

Both the Pashto and Persian-speaking groups agree that the first Musalli was the prayer rug carrier of the Prophet, from which derives, the Musallis' position as *sīyāl*s (respectable equals), at least for the Pashto-speaking group, who claims to be his descendants[20]. As one informant states:

> "And in the Qor'an it is written that nobody could order a Musalli to do something – to bring him a cup of tea. The Musalli is more holy [i.e. religiously respectable] than the descendants of the Prophet himself because the Musalli has served the Prophet. The children of the Prophet have not served Him as much as the Musalli."

This legend of having been "original" *Muslim*s rather than later converts, parallels the Pashtuns' claim of being descendants of a companion of the Prophet. In both cases, the implications are the inherent quality of Muslimness embodied in Pashtunness/Musalliness (Anderson 1984: 274). Their respectable descent, however, does not prevent other professionals in Laghman from pointing out, that decent (*sīyāl*) people do not hold a profession as degrading as grain cleaning. The Pashto-speaking Musallis relate, that they have inherited the actual occupation of *muṣallī-tūb* from a more recent ancestor, *Khwāja* Safa *Walī*.[21] He is said to be buried in Asheqan-wa-Arefan in Kabul, and the Musallis tell that on his tomb there grows one winnowing tray (*chaj*), one broom and one pitchfork.[22] In spite of this effort to make *muṣallī-tūb* a respectable and religiously sanctioned profession, there is also a legend telling how the Musallis, from their original position of respectability, have fallen to their present-day low and despised social position. This is explained as a kind of Fall from Grace, which they have brought upon themselves:

> "The first Musalli at the time of the Prophet was brooming Jerusalem with his beard. He was also cleaning and giving barley to the winged horse of the Prophet – Burāq – on which He went to the seventh sky to visit God. Another part of the Musalli's duty was to carry the prayer carpet of the Prophet.
>
> "One day the Prophet asked the Musalli what he got out of his work. The Musalli answered: "Dust and ashes". Then the Prophet said: "Well, then let that be your lot for the rest of your time.'"[23]

In one version of this legend, the Prophet, in addition to condemning them to "dust and ashes", also assumes control over the wind, which had formerly been the prerogative of the Musallis. The wind is very important for the Musallis, as the initial threshing of grain depends on it.

The Persian-speaking Musallis do not claim to be descendants of the first Musalli, and some even claim that the first Musalli left no descendants at all. They explain their own ancestry as follows:

(1) "The Shāhi Khēls had a kingdom in Punjab. The kingdom was razed and so we scattered ... Our grand-parents have told us that we had the Punjabi language. We are not ourselves from Laghman. One of our ancestors became a servant of a Musalli and in this way himself became a Musalli. We have forgotten our former language."

(2) "We are actually Shāhi Khēls – our ancestors have learned *muṣallī-tūb* from the Musallis. Some ancestors of ours came from Hindustan where a king had forced them to take flight [emigrate]. They came here when the world had become dark for them. They started to work with the Musallis until they learned their work and intermarried with them. But our ancestors said that we are Shāhi Khēls."

Hence, while the mythical ancestry of the Pashto-speaking Musallis as descendants of the first Musalli stresses their qualities as *sīyāl* people with inherent religious qualities, the Persian-speaking Musallis compensate for their low position by an alleged royal origin. Another version links the Persian-speaking Musallis' name with a more recent ancestor, Shāhi *Bābā* or Mahmad *Bābā* about whom nothing more is known.[24] There is even disagreement about whether his grave is in Katal, Laghman or in Bajaur, Pakistan. More important than their biological ancestry, however, is the fact that the Persian-speaking Musallis were brought from barbary into civilization by the famous *pīr* Shams Tabrizi, whose disciples (*murīds*) they still are.[25] They also mentioned that the founder of the occupation of *muṣallī-tūb* should be the archangel Jibrail [Gabriel], but no further stories are related in this connection:

"Shāhi Khēl was a *qawm* which was very unruly. They were thieves – they were the kind of thieves whom neither the king nor the people could oppress. The people became very furious and complained to the king telling him, that there were people who robbed their houses at night and that they could not catch them. The king tried his best but was not able to arrest those people. ... But there was Shams *Ṣāḥib*[26] – it was said that only this *walī* could bring people under control. So the people went to Shams *Ṣāḥib* and told him, that 'Unless you find these people, we do not know what to do – neither the king nor the people can do anything about it'. As Shams was a *walī* [saint] and was endowed with knowledge, he went ahead ... and found the people, the Shāhi Khēls, in a big jungle. They had placed a big cooking pot on the fire, there was *pilaw* and kebab and everything, and they were enjoying themselves.[27] During the night, they went robbing, and in the daytime they went back to the jungle. When Shams *Ṣāḥib* entered the jungle, they received him with respect. He told them that 'You have got neither this world nor the next – at nighttime you go and rob people and during the daytime you hide yourselves in this jungle. Why don't you get out of here and see the world?' They told him: 'What would it help to see the world if we have not got any profession through which we can earn our living?' Shams *Ṣāḥib* told them: 'Come out, I will give you a profession'. He brought all of them out of the jungle and when they reached settled areas, he told them to stay there. He split them up. One of them he sent – let us say – to Karawoo, another to Tirgarhi, another to Kalakot and Haiderkhani.[28] In this way he scattered them, and in each village he told them to take the pitchfork and to winnow the stacks belonging to the people there. In this manner our profession was given to us by *Ḥaẓrat-i* Shams *Ṣāḥib.*[29] Neither the Prophet nor anybody else has carried out this profession. Those who clean the wheat stacks are the Shāhi Khēls and they are the *qawm*, I described."

The Persian-speaking Musallis still consider themselves the disciples of Shams Tabrizi and tell many stories of the miracles he performed. Shams Tabrizi is buried in Multan, Pakistan, but one of his descendants, called Shah Agha, who lives in Behar, still turns up every year to collect tribute of money or rice or wheat, *naṣr*, from the Musallis.[30] An elderly woman told me that:

" ... a descendant of Shams *Ṣāḥib* comes to Kabul and also to Laghman. His name is Shah Agha, he does the *faqīrī.*[31] His father also collected tribute. We pay them as much as we can afford, 30-50 Afs, some 1-1.5 *sēr* at a time.[32] He has other disciples, *murīds*, than the Musallis and he comes to our camp in Kabul, too.

"Those people [i.e. the descendants of Shams Tabrizi] are easily recognizable as they wear *chiltar* [i.e. the cirklet around the head cloth of the Arab type]. ... They are very, very dwarf-like. The holy offspring are like that."

A man from the same group disclaimed that the above-mentioned Shah Agha is the Musallis' *pīr* and tried to clarify their relationship to him in the following manner:

"Contrary to what others say, he [Shah Agha] is not our *pīr* but our *khalīfā*, and they say it because of their ignorance, and also because people call us *panǰ-pīra* [people with five *pīrs*]. Others are supposed to have only four because there are four sects."[33]

What is meant by this last distinction between *pīr* and *khalīfā* is not entirely clear. *Pīr* can denote both a spiritual leader of a Sufi order and the initiator of a craft, while *khalīfā* more specifically refers to a Sufi adept who has been designated by his spiritual mentor as successor, with the right to initiate others into the Sufi order (*ṭarīqāt*). Accordingly, the distinction between *pīr* and *khalīfā* may be, that the Musallis do not venerate Shams Tabrizi and his descendants because Shams *Ṣāḥib* was the initiator or *pīr* of *muṣallī-tūb*, but rather, because of his role as spiritual leader (*khalīfā*) of a *ṭarīqāt*. The use of this distinction serves to stress that the Persian-speaking Musallis' performance of *muṣallī-tūb* is not divinely ordained but simply accidental, a twist of fate.

As mentioned, the two groups of Musallis not only have different tales of origin, but also slander each other. The Pashto-speaking Musallis are thus familiar with the Persian-speaking Musallis' alleged origin, but recount it with a negative twist, as the following story told by a middle-aged man illustrates:

"Those in Ali Khel, Gumain, and some other places are Chungars – originally they came from India. In the olden days people said that they lived in jungles. They were brought out of it by a hook, which is called *chugak* and these people are therefore called *Chungars*.[34] They have holes in their ears when they are born, and they also practice making holes in the ears of people, considering it a good omen. ... The Chungars speak Hindko – if they had not come from India, how would they have learned that language. ... *We* are all pure Pashtuns, and the Chungars have taken our occupation after they were brought out of the jungle. Our ancestors all had this occupation."

The Persian-speaking Musallis respond with slander aimed at the original Musalli, the alleged ancestor of the Pashto-speaking Musallis:

"Why is it that [the original] Musalli was a congenital idiot? Because he was wandering around in the deserts at the time of the Prophet. When the Prophet came up to him one day, he began to run away. So the Prophet decided to play a trick on him and to catch him. He threw some raisins on the ground and the Musalli just picked them up like a dog and ate them. ... He was an idiot because instead of kissing the feet of the Prophet and His hands, he went for the raisins. ... So finally the Prophet caught him by that trick. ... As the Prophet knew that he was but an idiot who couldn't do anything, He told him: 'My son, eat with me and carry my prayer carpet'. So he did that until he grew up. ... Actually he is called '*muṣallā wardar*' which means 'the prayer rug carrier', but people shorten it into 'Musalli'. So when he had become a strong young man, the Prophet thought, 'Well, let him go on his *gharībī*'. One night He said to him: 'Tomorrow I will give you your share at morning prayer time.' This was overheard by a Hindu – that is why Hindus now wake up at night. The next day the Musalli, that congenital idiot, was sleeping until noontime. But the Hindu went very early [to the court of the Prophet] and was asked: 'What do you want?'. He answered: 'I want wealth'. He was told. 'All right, take it'. That is why Hindus are rich and that is why Musallis sleep until noontime without having taken their ablution or prayed. Well, when he [the Musalli] came he was told that his share had been taken by the Hindu. He went after the Hindu and started fighting with him. He tried to grab the Hindu by the head ... but instead of fighting, the Hindu tried to keep his turban on his head. ... So the Hindu told the Musalli: 'I will pay you a definite amount of money per year if you let me go'. The Hindu gave him some money and went away. That is why Hindus have been paying tribute to the Muslims. The Musalli was told [by the Prophet] to go away and to do as he pleased. This is why the Musalli plays the drum. He makes winnowing trays, he makes pitchforks, he works as a barber, doing *dumgarī*, he threshes the stacks and also is a messenger, doing *qaṣidī*."

So far we have been referring to two groups of Musallis, both calling themselves Shāhi Khēl, living in different parts of Laghman and claiming to be distinct and unrelated. Nevertheless, the two groups are quite familiar with each other's legends. Some versions even combine elements from both groups. For example, *Khwāja* Safa *Walī*, ancestor of the Pashto-speaking Musallis, was said to have learned *muṣallī-tūb* from Shams *Ṣāḥib* of Tabriz, *pīr* of the Persian-speakers. An analysis of Musalli marriage patterns indicates that marriages have taken place between the two groups, and in case of distant relatives, there exist contradictory claims as to whether a family belongs to one or the other group of Musallis. Hence the two different groups of Musallis in Laghman do not constitute clear-cut and mutually exclusive categories of people.

This observation was further reinforced by a visit to Helmand, where at least 200-300 Musalli families from various localities in Laghman have been settled since the late 1950s. Many of these families trace their relations to both groups of Musallis in Laghman, and I did not find any parallel to the discourse on "fake" vs. "real" Shāhi Khēl. Even their legends of origin (which they were generally hesitant to relate during my short stay), combine elements from the myths of both Laghman groups.

Although both groups of Afghan grain-cleaners claim that they are internally unrelated, some of the Persian-speaking Musallis give more matter-of-fact explanations:

"We are by ancestry Shāhi Khēls – we took wives from the Musallis and mixed. Our ancestors were not Musallis. We are considered *khwāharzāda* [sister's offspring] of the Musallis. ... Before our ancestors intermarried with the Musallis, they were transport-workers using cows. They would transport things for people on the old road to Kabul, the road of Badpakht."

"We are all Shāhi Khēls. All those who can clean stacks are Shāhi Khēls all over the country. But [because of intermarriages] the Shāhi Khēls themselves have split off into many tribes."

"Now the distinction between Shāhi Khēl and Musalli has disappeared. All of us are now called Musallis. Take me for example. My paternal grandfather and grandmother were Musa Khēls. My father married into the Musallis, couldn't do anything else, so he took up *muṣallī-tūb* and we learned it. So we are now called Musallis."

These explanations may well be close to historical fact. The conflict between the two groups of Musallis, a conflict fought on the "battle field" of mythology, may be explained in two ways, (1) Either the two groups actually have separate Indian origins (see next section), whereupon they each gradually assumed threshing as their main occupation and eventually intermarried. (2) Or they may historically have constituted a single group, which over the years evolved into two groups due to dispersal of settlement. The migration to Helmand of more than 200-300 families meant that the connecting links between Musallis in various localities in Laghman disappeared. This may have resulted in the present situation, where other Musallis, unless specific kinship relations are known, are defined not only as non-*qawmi* but also as non-Shāhi Khēl.

One problem remains, however: why this intra-Musalli conflict about "fake" vs. "real" Shāhi Khēl? Why do Musallis slander each other as 'Chungar'? Retrospectively, I can only hint at some tentative answers, since at the time of the field research I had accepted the existence of two distinct *qawms*. As mentioned previously, in the conception of the local population of Laghman (and Kabul), a thresher is a Musalli, and a Musalli is socially inferior. The two groups of Musallis in Laghman, who continue to carry out the occupation of threshing, have followed two strategies in order to counter this image of social-occupational inferiority.

Those Musallis living mainly in the Pashtun-dominated areas of Laghman deny any Punjabi origin, claim Pashtun descent, and speak Pashto as their first language, all of which accords well with the Pashtun classification of the world. To be on the safe side, they also claim to be descendants of the original Musalli, which ultimately proves that they are *sīyāl* people, i.e. equal to anybody, and by implication original, true Muslims. As far as the degrading character of threshing is concerned, this is countered by referring to a holy person, *Khwāja* Safa *Walī* as the initiator of the occupation, which is thus sacralized and rendered *ḥalāl* (see Ch. II).

The Persian-speaking Musallis have opted for other strategies by recognizing their Punjabi descent but negating any original connection to threshing, apparently considering the occupation as more degrading than their descent. One version of their origin myths claims royal descent and downfall, while another tells of a civilizating process brought about by *pīr* Shams Tabrizi, a myth which lends religious credibility to the *qawm*.

While the strategy of the Pashto-speaking Musallis aims at upgrading the occupation of *muṣallī-tūb*, that of Persian-speakers focusses on the *qawm* of Shāhi Khēl. Hence, this might explain why each group must reject the other's versions as bogus in order to maintain the credibility of their own. Whether this is a comparatively new situation brought about by the emigration from Laghman of a substantive proportion of the community is not known. Among the Shāhi Khēl immigrants in Helmand, however, the situation seems quite different:

The Musallis in Helmand have left all this behind and started afresh simply as "Shāhi Khēls", in a social environment, where "Musallis" are not found and generally not known, and where threshing as a profession does not exist. This was clearly reflected in their reluctance to discuss their situation in Laghman in the past, or to relate their legends of origin, which their relatives in Laghman readily offered. Instead, the Helmand Musallis focus their concerns on Shāhi Khēl's inter-relations with other settled groups in the area, particularly the extent to which they were managing better than these. Hence, they sought to build up "Shāhi Khēl" as a socially respected *qawm*. In view of these efforts the internal discourses in Laghman were not only irrelevant but would even be harmful to their new identity of "Shāhi Khēl", where there were no traces left of the "Musalli" or of *muṣallī-tūb*.

Historical Origin

The historical origin of the names of the traditional Afghan grain-cleaners, "Shāhi Khēl", "Musalli", and "Chungar"/"Changar" can all be traced to the Indian Subcontinent, in most cases to Punjab. Ibbetson, in his comprehensive record of Punjabi castes, informs us, that the Chúhras, one of the traditional scavenger castes, are called Musallis (northwest of Lahore) or Kutána (southwest of Lahore), when converted to Islam, provided that they have given up the eating of carrion and removal of night-soil.[35] In the Frontier towns, however, the Musallis still remove night-soil. Here they may sometimes be called 'Sháhi Khel' as well, although this name would seem to be more generally used for Chúhras who have settled on the upper Indus and taken to working in grass and reeds like the Kutánas (Ibbetson 1974(1916): 217-19).

Whatever the historical development, it appears that at least in parts of Punjab, threshing has been the traditional occupation of the Musallis. Ahmad (1974) describes them as sweepers of the village and as threshers of grain. In his study of the village of Sahiwal in West Punjab in 1964-65, Ahmad writes that "traditionally, members of the Mussali caste known as Mehnati Mussali specialize in this work", i.e. the threshing of grain (1977). Westphal-Hellbusch, on the other hand, describes itinerant Musallis near Sargodha in Pakistani Punjab who were selling ropes and mats, while others near Chekkian, who owned camels and goats, were engaged in transporting grass, reeds, and rushes (1980).

In the above works, there is no indication as to the origin of the name "Musalli" apart from Ibbetson's information that the name signifies a change of religion and partly of occupation by local Chúhras – and that a Musalli is considered socially above a Chúhra (Ibbetson 1974(1916)). The Musallis' myth in Afghanistan of the first Musalli being the prayer rug carrier of the Prophet may be connected to those Musalli-groups working in grass and reeds, and who produce mats for domestic purposes, since in this area simple prayer-mats are frequently made of grass.

In accordance with Ibbetson's remark that Musallis on the Frontier are called Shāhi Khēl, Barth says that in the Swat valley thong- and sievemakers and dancers are called Shāh khel/ kashkôl (1959: 17). The term "Chungar", like "Musalli" and "Shāhi Khēl" can also be traced to Punjab. Crooke in fact, writes that "Chungars" are peculiar to the Punjab, that the name "Chungar" seems to mean "sifter of grain". This and reaping are their chief occupation (Crooke 1977(1906): 141).

Ibbetson, however, who lists the "Changar" among the "vagrant and criminal tribes", specifies that among these, the men are reapers while the women are employed in sifting grain for grain-dealers. Incidentally, Ibbetson's imperial classification matches the Afghan Musalli legend, which tells of ancestors who were "robbers and thieves"! (Ibbetson 1974(1916): 205). Leitner agrees with Crooke regarding the meaning of the name "Chungar" or "Changar": "I am inclined to think that 'Changar' is simply 'sifter' from 'chhánna'; for sifting wheat from chaff is their occupation" (Leitner 1880: 1). As far as their occupation is concerned, Leitner continues:

> "The Changars, as I know them, pick up what they can find, carry grass and assist Banias in threshing wheat, taking what falls on the ground from the sieve as their portion. A nasty custom exists among the Changars of washing the undigested entire grain out of the dung of horses and using it for their consumption; and it is said that it was one of their ancestors doing so 'on a journey beyond the hills' that led to his proscription and to his becoming the founder of the tribe of Changars" (Leitner 1880: 3).

According to Leitner, the Changars are to be found in many localities of present-day Pakistan. They themselves maintain that they

"have come from Darap near Siálkot, and that their ancestors have descended from the Kashmir and Pathan hills ... They indicate Lahore, Ludhiana, Amritsar, Ferozepur, Multan, Jullundur, Peshawar and 'stage beyond Peshawar' as their principal 'locales'" (Leitner 1880: 2).

Berland, in his study of peripatetic groups in Pakistan in the 1970s, also makes a passing remark to the Changars, who "are nomadic artisans who specialize in weaving reed baskets used by urban and village laborers. They also manufacture threshing baskets and brooms and weave fishnets" (1982: 58). Occupationally, then, there seems to be an overlap between the Changars and the Chúhras-cum-Musallis.

There is good evidence that at least the Persian-speaking Musallis in Laghman may well be of Changar-descent, despite their vehement denials. In his short comments on the Changars, Ibbetson mentions that they claim to have been converted to Islam by Shams Tabriz of Multan (1974: 205). Equally so, Leitner refers to several caste names within the Changar tribe, one of which is "Magharé". By comparison, a knowledgeable elderly Afghan Musalli woman from the Persian-speaking group mentioned Shāhi Khēl as being one of four sub-groups called "Magra", while the Musallis of Chahrdehi (in Laghman) should be known as "Joni". These names were supposed to be in the "Inku" language, but she did not know the meaning of them.[36] No reference can be found connecting "Shāhi Khēl" to the Changars, but Leitner remarks, that "as usual with tribes of questionable origin, that of Rajput is claimed by some Changars" (1880: 1). In an Afghan context, claiming Rajput descent would serve no purpose; and moreover, unless one was trying to pass as a Pashtun, as is the case with the Pashto-speaking Musallis, the name "Shāhi Khēl" ("King Khēl") may be as good a choice as any.

In 1975-76, Musallis were found in most but not all villages in central and southern Laghman. It seems probable that in the past there were professional grain-cleaners in virtually every village in this region, but by the mid-1970s many had left Laghman. Between 1950 and 1976, more than 350 Musalli families had thus received land and been settled in Helmand and Baghlan. An indication of their past presence can be found for example in the village of Qawal Khel, where at least for a couple of decades no Musallis have lived. Here the peasants received a separate payment called *chungarī* for cleaning the grain stacks. *Chungar*, here was a local, derogatory name for Musalli.

It cannot be established with any certainty, however, whether the Musallis' original immigration to Laghman occurred at one point of time, over several separate immigrations, or as a gradual influx of people. Neither can it be established for how long the Musallis have been in East Afghanistan. Adamec provides a list of different taxes collected in the Laghman district in 1879-80, which includes "*chaudharana* paid to masullis [presumably a printing error for Musallis] for cleaning grain at Khirman, who in return hand a share of R5 to R20 to the State". Subsequently, in lists of revenue sources in *Laghman- i -Tajikia* and *Laghman- i -Afghania* during the year 1879-80, Adamec refers to *chungarana* yielding a revenue of 384 Kabuli rupees and 151 Kabuli rupees from the two areas, respectively (Adamec 1985: 495). The term *chungarana* is not explained, but as *chungar* is a commonly used term for Musallis, one may assume that the *chungarana* is identical with the above-mentioned *chaudharana* (and *chungarana* being correct in view of the many printing errors in this work). On the basis of the above rates, the number of Musallis in the two areas at this time (1879-80) can thus be estimated as 20-80 families in *Laghman-i-Tajikia* and 8-30 in *Laghman-i-Afghania*.

However, as statistical information on Afghanistan, even in the 1970s was very inaccurate, to say the least, the above information can best be taken as an indication that in 1879 the Musallis were so well-established in both the Tajik- and Pashtun-dominated areas of Laghman that they had become subjects of revenue-collection (which they apparently no longer were in the 1970s). Equally so, in January 1892, the British Kabul Agency diarist reported that "twenty Musalis (sweepers) and 40 prisoners have been engaged to clean the grain in the Kabul store".[37] Hence, also at that time, Musallis were found in the Kabul area, but from the context it is not clear whether they were settled there or came from elsewhere. Today, the Musallis do not winter in Kabul.

The Occupation of Grain-cleaning

In rural Laghman, the agricultural year revolves around the two harvest- seasons, which are not only peak labour periods but also offer additional income opportunities. It is during harvest time that agricultural households have the greatest need to hire outside labour, so that poor and landless villagers as well as some pastoral nomads may find employment as reapers, being paid 1/20 of the crop harvested by them. The Musallis may take part in the reaping, but otherwise their main task comes later.

While the grain is being harvested, the peasants prepare the threshing ground: A corner of a field is cleared of vegetation and stones, the earth compacted, and finally the surface smoothed with wet mud like a platform. The sheaves are then laid to form a big round stack, and the peasant carries out the first threshing.[38] This is done by tying eight to ten oxen and donkeys side by side to a pole in the centre of the stack and driving them round it. Through this process, which is called *gundīmal* (Persian)/ *ghubal* (Psh.), the spikes are broken off the straw. In the Kabul area, the peasants achieve the same effect by using a threshing sledge (*supir*) drawn by a couple of oxen.[39] The threshing sledge breaks the whole wheat stalk and turns it into chaff (*bus*) which can be used as animal fodder. In Laghman, this initial threshing breaks off only the spikes from the wheat plant, and the remaining straw, called *sawāra*, is used mainly as fuel.[40]

Hereafter, the Musalli's work begins: He brings along his own implements, which consist of a broom (*ǰarū*), a wooden pitchfork (*chārshākh*), a winnowing tray (*chaǰ*) made by himself, a flail (*gundī-chūba*), weighing anywhere from 500 g – 5 kg), a wooden shovel (*rāshbīl*), and sieves of different mesh-size (*katabīz*, *maydabīz*). Since the peasant's initial threshing breaks down and disperses the stack, the Musalli begins by sweeping it together again. His next task is to separate spikes from the straw by threshing with the pitchfork. A good wind is required to carry away the straw while the heavier spikes fall to the ground. As the threshing goes on, in the periphery of the threshing ground only straw will be found, while closer to the stack an increasing proportion of spikes will be mixed in the straw. To demarcate the limit beyond which no further threshing is required, the Musalli puts sticks with coloured cloth in the ground. This demarcation of the stack is called *chukak*. The threshing of the stack goes on until spikes and straw are completely separated.

After this, the Musalli threshes the spikes (*gundī-takānī*) with a flail to loosen the grain and the chaff, empty spikes (*gundī/shughak*) and grain are then separated by winnowing with the winnowing-tray. This final winnowing does not require any wind. The last cleaning is done with sieves of different fineness.[41]

With each step in the process, the Musalli sweeps the stack together, and after the final gleaning, decorates the cleaned stack of grain. (In Dar al-Aman in Kabul I saw a carefully piled grain stack on which nice patterns had been drawn, and it was decorated with flowers, a wooden shovel, and a pocket-knife. On top of the stack was placed a vessel with incense.) When the stack has been decorated the landowner comes and the cultivator weighs the

3,8 In Laghman, the initial threshing of grain is carried out by using oxen or donkeys to tread upon the grain stack, whereby the spikes break off the plant (Photo: Klaus Ferdinand, 1955).

3,9 From a young age children learn to take part in the daily work (Laghman, 1975)

3,10-11 Musallis winnowing the stack with a pitchfork after the initial threshing by animals. The wind carries the straw away, while the heavier spikes fall to the ground (Oct. 1975).

stack, upon which the Musalli and other specialists receive their traditional share of the crop in return for their services during the year. The remainder of the crop is divided between landowner and sharecropper. When the stack has been divided and carried away, children, poor widows, or other destitute people glean the ground once more and thereby gain some extra kilograms of grain. This gleaning is called *kalpī*. The stubble left on the fields is free for anybody to collect; poor people like the Musallis collect stubble for use as fuel.

When the peasant has transported the wheat home, yet another cleaning is required before it can be taken to the flour mill (*āsīyā*). Musallis may be called upon to do this work for the peasant which includes sifting the grain in a sieve and winnowing (*sang-chaj̆*) it with a winnowing tray (*chaj̆*) to separate small stones (*sang*). Some Musallis claim that this work, called *āsīyāī* (lit. of the mill), is only required in Kabul because wheat from this area has more impurities in it than wheat from Laghman. This is because the threshing floor in Laghman is prepared by the peasant, who renders it smooth with mud, while in Kabul the wheat stacks are thrown on any flat surface where there may be dirt and animal dung. A payment of 4 *sēr* per *kharwār* is mentioned in this connection.[42] In Laghman, where the wheat presumably is less impure when brought to the house, the women of the household do the final cleaning before it is sent to the flour mill.

Paddy is threshed much like wheat, although the paddy stem, which is flexible, does not break by using the threshing-sledge or letting animals tread out the stack, only the paddy spikes break off the straw. Another difference is that the threshing does not remove the husk of the paddy grain, which instead has to be separated in the stamp mill (*pāykūb*). Despite the extra labour costs of milling, however, the yield from a paddy stack is higher than from wheat: a paddy stack only produces 10 *sēr* per *kharwār* waste material while in a wheat stack around half the stack would be waste material. The Musallis' payment for cleaning paddy would be 3/4-1 *sēr* per *kharwār* cleaned paddy; the pay is less than for wheat since the threshing work is less. In many regions corn and paddy are rotation crops and the Musallis also clean the corn, and at times even *māsh*, for which they receive 3 *sēr* per *kharwār*.[43]

The de-husking of the paddy (*pāykūbtī*) used to be the traditional occupation of the *qawms* of Hussain Khēl and Hazarmeshi. After the Musalli has cleaned the paddy, it is par-boiled in large clay containers. Par-boiling makes the grain more elastic so that it does not break so easily during the actual shelling process of the stamp water-mill. The par-boiling supposedly also increases the vitamin content of the grain (see Ferdinand 1959). After parboiling the paddy is dried by being mixed with heated sand. The rice mill worker then sifts away the sand and de-husks the rice in the mill. This work requires the

3,12-12a After being cleaned, the grain is arranged in a pile and nicely decorated with patterns. The stack is now ready to be weighed, and the cultivator and the various specialists will received their traditional share of the harvest. The photo *3,12* from Laghman shows the pole to which the animals were tied while treading upon the stack. 3,12a is from Dar al-Aman in Kabul, and here the peasants used a threshing sledge instead of animals for the initial threshing.

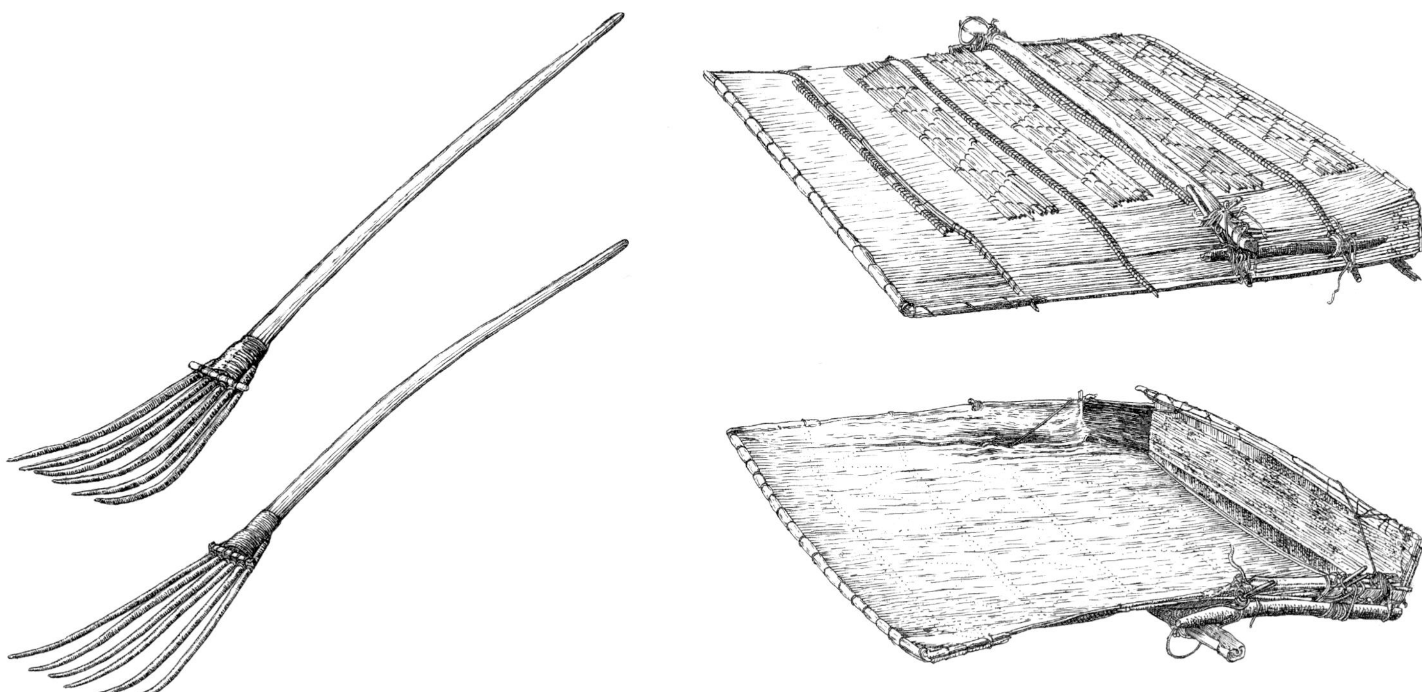

3.13-14 The wooden pitchfork is used for winnowing the stack in order to separate the spikes from the straw.

3,17-18 The *chaj*, a winnowing tray used for the final cleaning of grain, is used both by Musallis on the threshing floor and in the households for removing the last impurities from the grain and other crops prior to consumption.

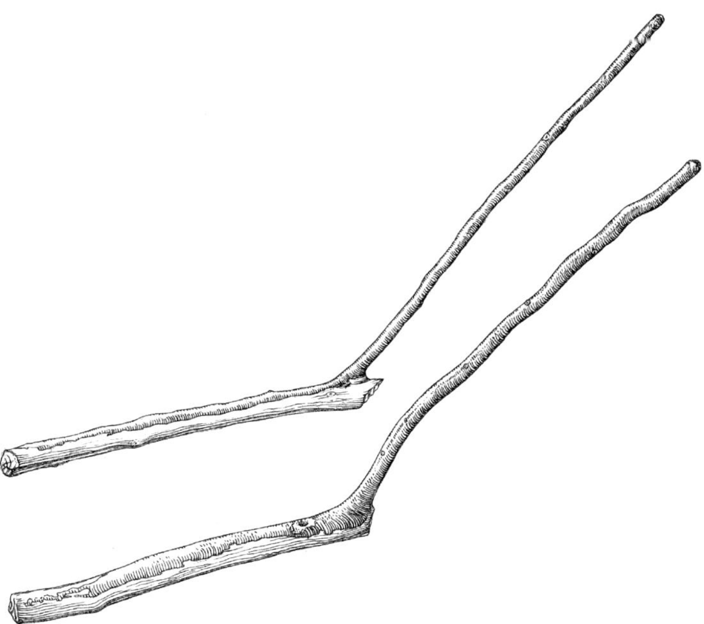

3,15-16 The wooden flails used by the Musallis for threshing the grain may weigh up to 5 kg.

cooperation of three persons: one to feed the paddy into the mill, one to collect the rice and husks, and one to separate the rice and husks with a winnowing tray.

The rice mill worker is paid for his work in kind: From 1 *kharwār* of paddy, he shall deliver 43 *sēr* of rice to the peasant and 2 *sēr* of rice to the mill-owner; i.e. to the landowner on whose land the water mill is erected. The remainder belongs to the rice mill worker as payment for his work and may amount to some 5 *sēr*, depending upon the percentage of water in the paddy. The chaff which is separated from the grain is also part of the rice mill worker's share, and it will be used as fuel in the drying of rice in the oven (*batta'ī*). Some Musallis state that,

3,21-5 The traditional process of par-boiling and dehusking paddy in Laghman was described in detail by Ferdinand (1959: 224): "In the Laghmān villages we saw rows of pottery jars in the various stages of paddy-boiling ... . We were told that it was usual for the paddy just to be brought to the boil, and then allowed to simmer for a whole night. The next morning the jars were inverted to allow the water to run off, and shortly afterwards the damp paddy was ready for drying by being mixed with redhot sand."This took place by a beehive-shaped clay lined oven, about 2.5 metres high ...with openings in the side, a smaller where a young man threw rice hulls on the fire and, in intervals, provided a strong draught with a plaited fan, and a large opening from which hot sand was removed with a little iron spade. The sand was poured upon dark yellow damp paddy in a large flat wooden bowl ... , and the sand and paddy were mixed together for a few moments, before the steaming mass was emptied onto a large sieve, and the sand sieved away with a rolling action. The dry, light yellow paddy is now ready to go to the stampmill" (Photos: Klaus Ferdinand, Alishang valley, Feb. 1955).

3,23

3,22

3,24

3,25

3,26-7 In the 1970s par-boiling of paddy was still being carried out as described by Ferdinand (1959). While par-boiling and dehusking used to be the occupation of the Hazarmeshi and Husayn Khêl *qawms*, by the mid-1970s these *qawms* and the Musallis had begun to encroach upon each other's monopolies.

3,26

3.28-9 In the mid-1970s par-boiling of paddy had been "modernized" by replacing the pottery jars with a large metal container placed directly on the fire.

3,30 The crash-drying of paddy is here carried out by placing it in the pottery bowls built into the fireplace, upon which the paddy is par-boiled. Hence, the heat of the par-boiling is at the same time used to dry the paddy, helping to save fuel.

3,31 Water-driven rice stamp-mill in Diwa.

3,20 In the 1970s, most mills in Laghman were still run by water power. Rivers and many small streams make water power abundant in the Laghman Province. Here is a double-armed stampmill for dehusking paddy (Diwa, April 1975).

when de-husking paddy, they are being paid in broken rice (*du-kat*), since the paddy-owner wants his 43 *sers* of "proper" rice. This broken rice is consumed mainly by the household as it is of very poor quality for cooking.

One Musalli, who had turned to rice mill work from *muṣallī-tūb* explained that he might process 15-20 *kharwār* paddy per season, i.e. 8-11 t of paddy. Since he did not own any land, the paddy owners demanded that he supply a guarantee person before they would give him their paddy for processing. Although Laghman in 1975 also had 2-3 diesel rice mills which were faster than the traditional water-mills, they were also more expensive to use; the rice mill workers would have to pay 50% higher rent to the mill-owner, and the diesel-mills also produced a higher proportion of broken rice.

Pay and Working Conditions in Laghman

In 1975, the pay and working conditions of the Musallis differed from area to area, but there may well have been a uniform system in the distant past. Professional grain-cleaning is carried out either individually or jointly by father and son , or by brothers. Where several Musalli households live in the same village, they will frequently work jointly and share their pay equally. Most households have several able-bodied men working jointly, normally sons working with their father. The sons begin to assist in the work when they start brooming from around the age of 7-8 years. When they are 10-12 years, they begin to take part in all the work processes and are counted as actual "workers" while from 14-15 years they participate fully in the work, at least in Laghman. The situation is different in the bigger workgroups in Kabul (see below).

The payment of Musallis today assumes two forms in Laghman. Depending on the locality, they either get a fixed proportion of grain measured by weight, or they get what is estimated to be their traditional share. The latter system is called *chuta'ī* and was probably the custom everywhere in former times.[44] The amount of grain paid as *chuta'ī* may vary annually as well as from one peasant to another. Whether *chuta'ī* is the same all over Laghman is hard to tell, as the estimates are rather imprecise, but it appears to be approximately 6% of the cleaned grain (5 *sēr* per *kharwār*).

In the *chuta'ī*-system, the Musalli himself after cleaning the grain, sets aside what he considers to be his proper share of grain. In addition, he receives the waste materials from threshing: the empty spikes and the left-over from sifting which is grabble mixed with a little grain (*sangchil*). The Musalli brings home both spikes and *sangchil*, and it is the job of the women of his household to extract whatever grain is left. The empty spikes may subsequently be used as fuel, which in these treeless parts of Laghman, is everywhere in short supply.

When the peasant comes to approve the division, he invariably reduces the Musallis' share, accusing them of being greedy. The Musallis cannot argue their case, they tell, since they may risk their share being further reduced. Instead, they take certain precautions beforehand and rely on their luck and the decency of the peasant. A Musalli explains:

> "We will normally put twice the amount we expect to get in the *chuta'ī* knowing that it will be cut in half. We don't put more than the double – that would be too much. He [the peasant] will say that we are not fair and simply not give it to us."

In addition, the Musallis also make sure to put their pile of *chuta'ī* in a hollow in the ground so it appears less, or simply leave extra grain in the chaff and *sangchil*. These "tricks", however, are known by both parties and the bigger the piles of chaff and *sangchil*, the more the peasant tends to reduce the *chuta'ī*. A wealthy, absentee landowner describes the system with these words:

> "Some grain they [the Musallis] steal away in threshing, some in the chaff and of course they have their *chuta'ī*. They are better off than many landowners. In a wheat stack which in size is 1 *kharwār* [approximately 565 kg], they for themselves will get 7-8 *sers* of wheat [approximately 49-56 kg]. If the wheat stack is bigger than 1 *kharwār*, they will normally get 3-4 *sers* per *kharwār* as they can't cheat so much at a big stack. Most of what they get from the wheat stacks are by cheating."

Another landowner says:

> "Quarrels about the payment to Musallis have always existed. They have such *chādurs* that if we let them fill them, they would take all the stack."

The *chādur* referred to by the landowner is the big cloth which men in rural Afghanistan frequently carry on one shoulder. It is used for many purposes: to wear as an overcoat, to sit on, to carry things in, etc. The Musallis would typically carry their *chuta'ī* back home in their *chādur*, and the bigger the *chādur* the less the *chuta'ī* appears.

The other system, payment by weight, has been introduced by the peasants in many villages during the last few years. In this system,

3,19 The Musalli family's share of grain is being cleaned on the roof top by the women of the household.

the Musallis normally receive around 4 *sēr* per *kharwār* of wheat and 2 *sēr* per *kharwār* of paddy, and then they cannot claim chaff and *sangchil.* In some localities, however, the pay is even lower. The Musallis are against this change, as it invariably reduces their own pay.

In some of the places where *chuta'ī*-payment exists or has existed until recently, the Musallis perform for the village community a number of tasks besides threshing. These may include running errands in the bazaar, carrying messages, and serving guests at feasts, while the village barber does the cooking. Like the barber, the Musalli is considered the servant of the village and neither of them is paid separately for the above-mentioned jobs.[45] Both the Musallis and the peasants see a connection between these servant functions and the *chuta'ī*-payment, although their conceptions differ at certain points:

> Rich landowner: "It is for the extra services we pay them."

> An old Musalli man: "All year long we serve these people. At midnight they would knock at my door to go here and there, to run this or that errand for them. But at harvest time they would first be hesitant to give us their wheat stacks for cleaning. And when they do it, they would give us very little and would still think that they are charitable to us."

The landowners are thus of the opinion that they pay the Musallis *extra* at harvest time in order to

3.32-3 The wheatstack is cleaned, the crop divided, and the straw being loaded on donkeys and carried home (Kabul, Sept. 1985).

be able to demand their services during the year. For the Musallis, on the other hand, it is a question of supplying a number of *free* services during the year in the hope that they will be allowed to clean peoples' grain stacks at harvest time.

Although the Musallis, to a certain extent, supply these free services to everybody in the village, they have originally only had obligations towards the landowners. When others enjoy these services, it is more a matter of mutuality, and it is stressed that the village professionals do not demand payment from each other for ordinary services.

The services rendered by the Musallis are comparable to those which the barber supplies in addition to his professional work:[46] For example, the barber performs circumcision while his wife works as a midwife. In those villages where the Musallis supply additional services, there exists a division of labour between Musalli and barber:

> Rich landowner: "Other than cleaning our wheat stacks for which they are well paid, they [the Musallis] run errands in the bazaar, informing people in time of the dead and the living. And also at offerings they will serve

3.33

[the meal] together with the barbers. But their duties are separate. The barbers will mainly do the cooking, while the Musallis serve the guests, for example, giving them water and also holding the hookah.[47]"

Like the Musalli, the barber is not paid for his specific services nor for his haircutting. Instead at harvest time he will receive a certain amount of grain according to the number of males in each family in the village, irrespective of the actual amount of work performed. Both the Musalli and the barber, after assisting in connection with celebrations, would often receive for example the head or intestines of the animals slaughtered at the occasion. However, this is considered a gift rather than payment for their services and does not alter the fact that they are obliged to assist.

As *Table 3,1* indicates, it cannot be definitively concluded that the *chuta'ī*-system and the accompanying position of Musallis as village servants have existed throughout Laghman in the past (i.e. in the areas where Musallis were tradi-

Table 3,1: Systems of Payment and Community Services in Laghman

Village	I. Pashtun domination II. Tajik domination*	No. of Musalli households	Payment before Wheat *sēr/kh.***	Payment 1976 Wheat *sēr/kh.*	Obligation to perform community services
Ali Khel	not known	3	4	3	not known
Diwa	not known	2	2	2	no
Chardehi	I.	3	not known	not known	yes
Karawoo	II.	not known	*chuta'ī****	2	not known
Sangtuda	II.	2	*chuta'ī*	4	yes
Near Sangtuda	II.	6	not known	4	not known
Parman Khel	not known	4	*chuta'ī*	1	yes
Qala-i Sardar	II.	1	*chuta'ī*	2	yes
Deh Sharana	not known	3	not known	1	not known
Qala-i Sufi	not known	not known	*chuta'ī*	not known	not known
Dand	not known	1	4	3	yes
Mohammad Khel	I.	2	*chuta'ī*	2.5	yes
Nimnani	I.	9	*chuta'ī*	2	yes
Qala-i Khan	not known	3	4	2-3	not known
Manjuma	I.	5	not known	not known	not known
Omarzai	not known	3	not known	not known	not known

Explanatory notes:

* The division into Pashtun and Tajik dominated villages is according to Warburton's distinction (Adamec 1985: 487-93).

** One *sēr* = 7.66 kg. One *kharwār* = 80 *sēr* = 565.28 kg.

*** *Chuta'ī* = the Musallis' traditional share of grain (unmeasured) after cleaning the stack.

tionally found). In some areas, payment by weight has existed for many years, and it is difficult to obtain information on former systems. Among the Musallis themselves, there is a certain hesitancy to discuss their servant position too much, since this would further underline the already inferior social status of their profession. This is clearly reflected in the contemptuous reference by one Musalli to these services as, "boot-licking" (*būt-pākī*). However, it seems likely that *chuta'ī* and the Musallis' role as village servants represent the traditional system, which has disappeared with varying speed in different localities. This will be discussed further on.

From *Table 3,1* it also appears that the tradition of community services by the Musallis is unrelated to the division into Pashtun and Tajik dominated areas of Laghman. However, most of the Musallis who claim descent from the prayer rug carrier of the Prophet appear to have the servant functions vis-à-vis the local communities, while many among the Persian-speaking don't. This fact is used by the latter group to underline that they have superior origins. As an elderly Persian-speaking Musalli man states:

> "I am not inferior to you ... I can do anything. Why should I take your child for shitting? But the Musallis do it. From the time of the Prophet until today, the Musalli has been a servant."

Migrant Threshers in Kabul

After cleaning the spring wheat in Laghman, the Musallis have for generations migrated to the agricultural areas around Kabul to clean the grain there. It has not been possible to assess when the Musallis began to go to Kabul for summer labour, but they have apparently done so for at least a century.[48] Hence, their seasonal migration pre-dates the rush of poor labour migrants who have come to the Kabul area, mainly from the eastern provinces, over the past generation. The Musallis were probably attracted by the extensive grain areas around Kabul which created a particular need for additional manpower at harvest time. The relative proximity of Kabul to Laghman and the difference in altitude meant that the Musallis could manage to clean the grain in Laghman and reach the Kabul area in time to clean the grain here. Travelling by foot and donkey they would not have been able to reach more distant provinces, where the harvest period would in any case be the same as in the Kabul area.

While they live in houses in Laghman, the Musallis stay in tents during their two-month stay in Kabul. The tents are of the type most commonly used by itinerant groups in Afghanistan: plain, white, normally Pakistani-manufactured canvas-tents. They are triangular in shape, held up with a pole at each end and occasionally also a horizontal top-pole. Low mud-walls are often built around the foot of the tent to provide protection from wind and rain-water.

In the past, the Musallis travelled by foot with their belongings loaded on oxen and donkeys. They would travel together in large groups of many familys, sending word to other Musallis regarding the date of departure for Kabul. They would then gather in Shegi Qala if they were to go via Badpakht. In case they were to cross the

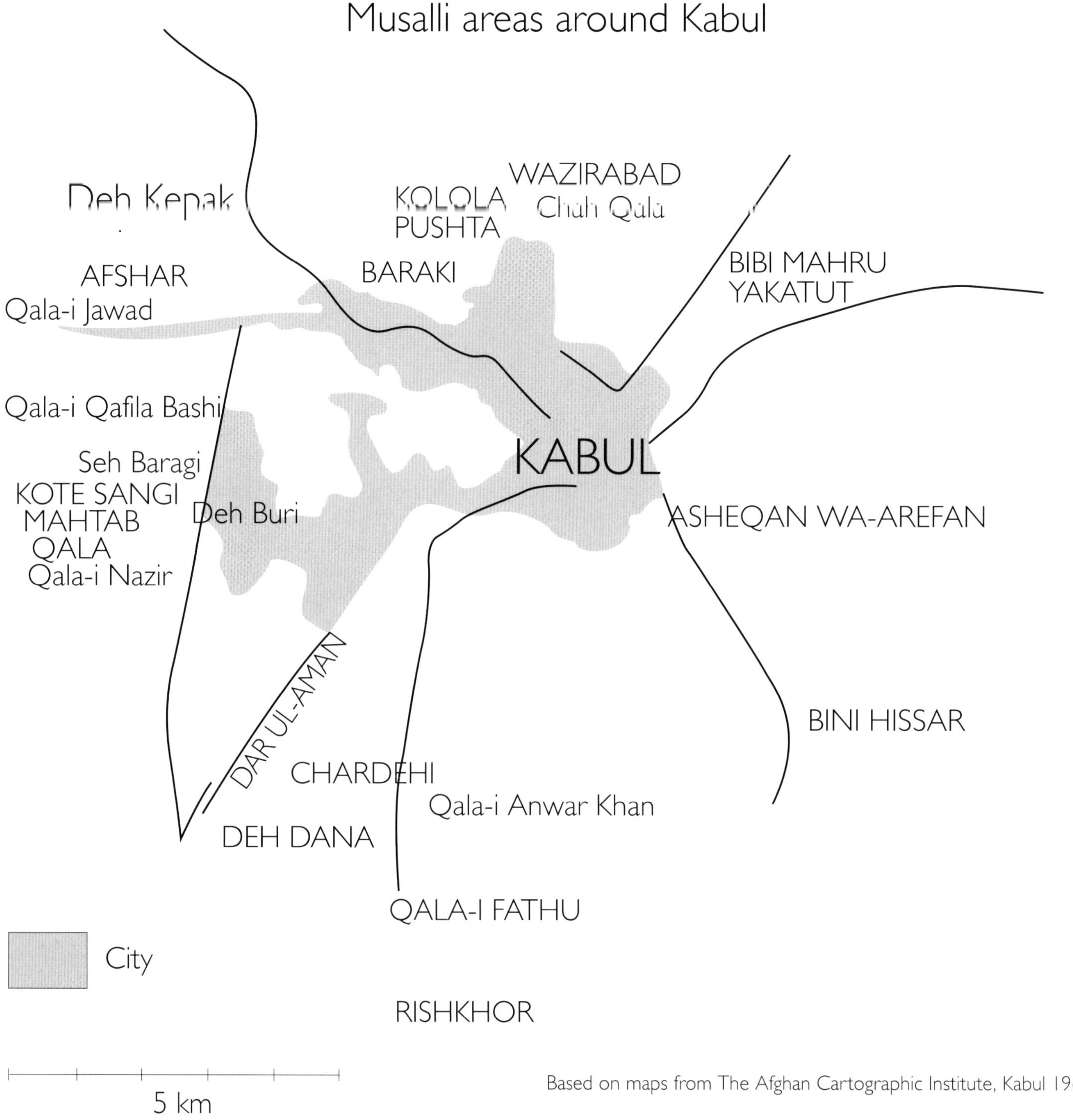
Musalli areas around Kabul
Deh Kepak
KOLOLA
PUSHTA
WAZIRABAD
Chah Qala
AFSHAR
Qala-i Jawad
BARAKI
BIBI MAHRU
YAKATUT
Qala-i Qafila Bashi
Seh Baragi
KOTE SANGI
MAHTAB
QALA
Qala-i Nazir
Deh Buri
KABUL
ASHEQAN WA-AREFAN
DAR UL-AMAN
BINI HISSAR
CHARDEHI
Qala-i Anwar Khan
DEH DANA
QALA-I FATHU
City
RISHKHOR
5 km
Based on maps from The Afghan Cartographic Institute, Kabul 1968

river at Darunta or by *zhāla/jāla* (a raft of inflated hides), they would take off from Mandrawar and pass through Kulala. These routes were used before the Lataband road was constructed.

The trip to Kabul normally lasted some 10-12 days; the actual travelling time was only some 8 days but the Musalli families would sometimes spend extra time on the way enjoying themselves. The whole group, for example, would slaughter a sheep or some chickens in common and eat jointly, and after arriving in Kabul, the families from different localities would remain in contact with each other. Today, however, when travel is by car, everybody goes on his own or at most a few families together. The large groups of former times presumably had their origins in security considerations. Today the Musallis regard these travels as representing the greater internal unity which is said to have existed among them in the past.

In Kabul the Musallis work in groups of 10-20 men. The groups are relatively stable over time, commonly consisting of close relatives from neighbouring villages in Laghman. They go to the same area of Kabul every year, staying there with their families throughout the two-month stay, whereupon they return to Laghman for the autumn harvest.

Since the Musallis in Kabul work jointly in comparatively large groups, the work is directed and organized by a foreman, called *kalāntar* (lit. elder). In principle the *kalāntar* is elected by the work group, but he tends to be the same person year after year. The function of the *kalāntar* is primarily to secure work for the group and direct and organize the work. During the first days following the group's arrival in the Kabul area, the *kalāntar* contacts the various landowners of the locality to contract for the cleaning of their grain stacks. To achieve the desired number of stacks for the group, the *kalāntar* frequently bribes the landowners with small gifts of various products brought along from Laghman, such as beans, threshing-trays, etc. Once work is secured, the *kalāntar* organizes the schedule for his group to start cleaning the various stacks of the locality and makes sure that each person performs the job for which he is best suited. During the actual threshing of the stack with flails the men are placed in two opposite lines, and the *kalāntar* directs their beating with the flails.

The benefit of the cooperation by larger work groups in Kabul appears mainly to be that the cleaning of each stack can be carried out faster, which is important in view of the fact that the grain-stacks are frequently double the size of those in Laghman; i.e. 10 *kharwār*, because of the larger land-plots around Kabul.

The *kalāntar*'s position and the tasks he performs means that it is up to the *kalāntar* himself to determine how much he will participate in the manual cleaning work. His share of the total payment equals that of the others, but he enjoys certain privileges which enable him to earn more than the other members of the work group. Hence, it is the *kalāntar*'s privilege to sweep up the cleaned stack of grain and decorate it nicely with patterns and flowers. The decoration might also include some Musalli implements and a container in which incense would be burned. Finally, the *kalāntar* carries out the weighing of the stack for the peasant. For this he receives a certain payment (called *kalāntari/tulana/tarāzū-dārī*) consisting of uncleaned grain (*chukak*). A Musalli explains that the amount of *chukak* payment may be influenced by the peasant's sense of affection and aesthetics (*shawqī*), so that he can appreciate the *kalāntar*'s efforts in decorating the stack.

Table 3,2: Composition and location of work-groups in Kabul

Laghman villages	No. of households	No. of workers	Location in Kabul	Additional non-Musallis present in the work-group
Qala-i Qazi, Maskurah, Bagh-i Mirza, Qala-i Sarwar	5	not known	Mahtab Qala	yes
Mandrawar	not known	not known	Qala-i Qazi	not known
Qala-i Sahib, Chunduk, Parman Khel, Qawal Khel	8	not known	Qala-i Fatu	yes
Chardehi, Karawoo, Gulkari	15	25	Kolola Pushta	yes
Qala-i Sardar, Diwa	9	18	Dar al-Aman	yes
Qala-i Sardar	7-8	18	Dar al-Aman	yes
Ali Khel, Pashai, Deh Sharana, Qala-i Sahib, Qala-i Sufi, Madad Khan, Mohammadpur	18	not known	Baraki	not known
Parman Khel	6	not known	Chardehi, Rishkhor	not known
Gumain, Qala-i Khan	8	not known	Bibi Mahru	not known
Pahlawan Bibi	not known	not known	Yakatut	not known
Qala-i Khan, Omarzaî, Sangtuda	9	not known	Afshar	not known
Mohammad Khel, Dand	3	14	Qala-i Qafila Bashi	no
Nimnani (Niazi)	9	15	Bini Hissar	no

The *kalāntar* thus has the role of representing his group vis-à-vis the employers, i.e. the landowners or peasants. This position provides him with a degree of power over other members of the work group; however, in the smaller groups of closely related people this power differential is of little practical consequence. All members have come to the same area for a number of years and are thus also acquainted with the landowners and might therefore replace the *kalāntar*. Moreover, kinship relations prevent the *kalāntar* from exploiting the situation. In the smaller groups, the *kalāntar* is normally the eldest person, while in the larger groups, the position is more dependent upon his personal qualities, but even then, a son may often inherit the *kalāntar* position from his father.

As *Table 3,2* shows, the Kabul work-groups used to consist of closely related Musalli-families, while several work groups now add non-professionals (i.e. non-Musallis). These non-Musallis are mostly poor people from Laghman, some of them rice mill workers, who because of their own profession are acquainted with threshing. This situation has affected the *kalāntar*'s position. Without his guarantee, the landowners would not allow non-professionals to clean their stacks, both Musallis and the non-professionals tell. Hence, in the large groups the *kalāntar* single-handedly decides who and how many non-professionals will be included in the group. He alone can expel people from the group if he is dissatisfied with their work performance or behaviour. A *kalāntar* explains: "Yes, a *kalāntar* can expel a man from a camp if he is a man of bad deeds or if he is an idler, a gambler, a liar, a homosexual, or if he is spreading gossip about others everywhere."

In these large groups, the *kalāntar* to a great extent assumes the role of a labour broker or "employer", and among the non-professionals of the group he is also looked upon as such. He may even be able to expel Musallis from the group, but the excluded Musalli has the possibility to go to another *kalāntar* and try to be included in his group. Endowed with such authority, the *kalāntar* may come into conflict with other members of the group. This is apparent in the following description by a non-Musalli who worked under a *kalāntar* in Kabul:

> "While we were having lunch he would turn it into poison by asking us to leave immediately for a certain wheat stack. And then he would go ahead of us with a scowl on his face and would take us there to the stack, would order us to start working, and would himself be sitting on his arse. When the time came for the division of payment [at the end of the season] and everybody was to get his share, he suddenly becomes like a dead snake. He is gentle with everybody and asks whether they have been annoyed. And he explains that he has behaved as he has for their own good, so that they could do more work [*gharîbî* – and hence earn more money in there]."

While the work groups in Kabul are relatively stable, in that the Musallis from specific villages in Laghman return to the same locality in Kabul each year, changes in group composition occur. When the group becomes too big for the available work it may split up. The problem, however, is that most of the area is already divided up between various Musalli groups. Internal quarrels or disagreements with the *kalāntar* may also cause families to join another *kalāntar*. Some Musallis state that it is internal quarrels which have resulted in the inclusion of non-professionals, who are given stack work provided they work under a Musalli guaranteeing their performance.

The authority of the *kalāntar* in Kabul has no bearing on his position in Laghman, where each Musalli family has its own traditional area, and the *kalāntar* is just an ordinary man or, as one informant noted: "There [in Kabul] he is *kalāntar*, here we make him a *kalān khar* [i.e. large donkey]."

In Kabul the Musallis of an area work and get paid collectively. Payments from the various landowners or peasants are pooled by the entire camp and then divided equally among all workers at the end of the season. However, when the young men start to participate in the work groups, about the age of 16, they will obtain a half share for some three years until they have proven themselves able to work competently. The same system applies when non-professionals are included in the group: they receive only a half share the first 2-3 years, until they have become skilled in the job. A *kalāntar* explains:

> "I might broom a field in one hour or more, but he [the novice] might not be able to do it in a whole day. ... I may clean some 20 *sērs* of wheat in a short time ... he can't do 3 *sērs* in that time. He may move his winnowing tray and his arse, but he can't clean the wheat. A man may be strong, but when it comes to threshing with a flail he might kill somebody if he hasn't got the skill. If he makes just a small mistake, he will break somebody's head."

The payment in the Kabul area is everywhere an unmeasured portion of the cleaned crop, *chuta'ī*, and in addition the Musallis are allowed the empty spikes and the left-over mixture of grain and stones, *sangchil*. Unlike in Laghman, no other services have ever been associated with the system of *chuta'ī*. The Musallis stay in the area for a comparatively short time, during which they have no other contact with the local community than their specific work relation. It is unclear whether *chuta'ī* in Laghman and Kabul used to be the same proportion of the cleaned crop, but it appears that *chuta'ī* in Kabul has remained more constant over recent years than has been the case in Laghman. This may be because of the comparatively smaller landholdings in Laghman, where the Musallis' payment thus is a bigger strain on the peasant's economy and where he actually can manage the grain dealing himself.

Threshing: a Threatened Profession

The social and economic changes in agriculture within the 1950s and 1960s have severely reduced the Musallis' occupational niche and threatened the viability of their livelihood. Since the 1930s, a general impoverishment of the small peasantry has taken place in Afghanistan (see Ch. II), while at the same time big landlords and merchants have increasingly invested in land.

The Kabul area and the north are characterized by the commercialization of agriculture, which has led to an increasingly uneven distribution of land. In Laghman, on the other hand, there are few big landowners; population growth and the constant division of land through inheritance have reduced the size of landholdings to uneconomical size. Moreover, changes in consumption patterns have caused the peasants to depend increasingly on market economy. Already in the 1960s, Hahn had pointed out that agricultural products, due to price controls were keeping pace with the general increase in prices (1965: 68). The result was an ever-growing debt among the peasantry. Today, the 14 years of warfare has left Afghanistan's agricultural economy in ruins due both to the destruction of irrigation systems, and to the population having fled to Pakistan.

In 1975-76 with a deteriorating economy, more and more peasants chose to clean their grain themselves or try to reduce the Musallis' wages. In the case of sharecroppers, the Musalli is paid *before* the grain stack is divided between landlord and cultivator, which means that the Musalli's share also reduces the sharecropper's part. Where there are leaseholders, a category on the increase, the Musalli is paid entirely from the tenant's part. With changing consumption patterns causing a growing proportion of the crop to be marketed, the employment of Musallis directly reduces the cultivator's marketable surplus, thus causing a bigger strain on the economy than earlier, when peasant households were more self-sufficient. A Musalli informant is well-aware of this process:

"People now know the value of money. Earlier they would just want enough to survive. Now they want a better standard of living. Until some years ago, there was some land which people would not dream of cultivating, but now they have become so eager for wealth that that land is cultivated, too. So they try to keep as much as possible to themselves!"

The economy of the Musallis depends on a traditional distribution of rights and duties within the village; that is, the recognition of the Musallis' *right* to clean grain.

As those landowners with large holdings increasingly leave the village community to settle, for example, in Kabul and invest in trade or join the bureaucracy, they lease their land to small peasants, either as sharecroppers or more often as leaseholders.[49] This new class of cultivators feel no special obligation towards the Musallis. Their economic situation forces them to disregard the Musallis' customary rights. They turn from the system of *chuta'ī* to paying by weight, or by cleaning the grain themselves. Furthermore, Musallis state that in some places internal competition has developed among them, as the following example illustrates:

"Last year a land-owner asked me to clean the stack which my father-in-law's brother was supposed to clean, for less pay. I said: 'No, we have agreed not to take each other's stacks'. Instead another man took it, and the brother of my father-in-law came and took my stack. This year, I will do the same to him."

Payment by weight has paved the way for competition between Musallis and non-professionals. Rice mill workers in particular are challenging to the Musalli monopoly on threshing, as they are familiar with the work from their own profession. Threshing is a much-welcomed additional source of income for these workers, the more so as their own work of paddy shelling occupies them only after threshing has been completed. In many villages the rice mill workers offer to thresh at a lower fee than the Musallis.

Rice mill work is no longer an ethnic monopoly occupation either. Various groups of poor people, including Musallis, work at rice milling in order to earn an extra income. In some villages competition for rice mill work has become so sharp, that the professionals offer to clean the stacks for free so as to be allowed to shell the paddy afterwards.

Yet another factor threatens the occupation of *muṣallī-tūb*: the introduction of new, high-yielding varieties of grain, mainly Mexipak wheat.[50] Apart from its higher yield, it is easier to clean, and the Musallis claim that their services have partly become redundant due to this. As one of them explained:

"The new variety of wheat has made work much easier. The peasant threshes it, the peasant sifts it, too, in a sieve. There remains the grain on the ground; if we manage to reach it and glean it, we will get something out of it. Otherwise he will glean himself and take everything away. Nothing is left for us because the new variety [Mexipak] hardly needs any work anyway."

While the situation varies from village to village, all Musallis have suffered an economic set-back. Traditionally, *muṣallī-tūb* was inscribed in a system of mutual rights and obligations reminiscent of the Indian jajmani system, which provided security and continuity of labour for the landowners and a guaranteed livelihood for the specialists. The landowners' main interest in the system lay in ensuring labour in times of shortage, where the recognition of the Musallis' right to a share can be seen as the cost of securing a steady and loyal labour force. However, the reciprocity in the system was not rooted in equality between the parties but was based upon uneven access to productive assets, as well as being inscribed into the generalized system of political patron-client relations. Hence, today, when the agricultural sector is characterized by a steady increase in seasonal and permanent wage-labourers, the Musallis are unable to maintain their traditional rights. The ethnic division of labour is breaking down and both peasant cultivators and specialized occupational groups in the village are suffering, competing among themselves in order to secure a meagre existence.

The different groups in the local communities vary in their conception and interpretation of this situation. A peasant close to Mohammad Khel provides the following explanation:

> "The Musallis started not only rice mill work but also *dihqānī* [cultivation]. Rice mill work is closely related to their occupation, and it was accepted that they started on that, but the peasants got angry when the Musallis started doing *dihqānī*. The peasants would say that they [the Musallis] should stick to their own occupation and that they were spoiling people's lands, as they didn't know *dihqānī*. So the peasants, in retaliation, refused to give their wheat stacks to the Musallis and cleaned it themselves. They [the peasants] had thought that as *muṣallī-tūb* is the Musalli's livelihood and as they rendered other services as well, it would only be fair to give them the wheat stacks to clean, and so everybody did so. But then, when they had earnings in Kabul as well as here, they became greedy and grabbed for rice mill work and for *dihqānī*."

In the Kabul area, the Musallis face competition from non-professionals, some of whom were introduced to the occupation of threshing by Musalli *kalāntar*s. However, it is the reduction of areas under grain cultivation which forms the major threat to their livelihood. Reduction of grain land is caused by the growing cultivation of vegetables as cash crops for the Kabul market and by the expansion of residential areas of Kabul city which have, considerably decreased available agricultural lands in traditional Musalli areas such as Kolola Pushta, Afshar, Bini Hissar, Baraki, Qala-i Fathullah, Qala-i Qafila Bashi, Mahtāb Qala, and Dar al-Aman. Lamenting the loss of summer earnings, one Musalli explained:

> "Earlier a person's share was 120 *sēr*s. Now it is around 40 *sēr*s. The agricultural land decreased as Deh Afghanan, Afshar, Deh Kepak, and Wazirabad all became residential areas, all became buildings."

Another Musalli commented upon the peasants' situation:

> "Earlier a person would get 50 *kharwār*s from his land. Now he only makes 10 *kharwār*s. Agricultural land has diminished. Buildings and people have multiplied."

One of the Ali Khel Musallis explained that while earnings from stack-cleaning in Baraki previously amounted to 80-120 *sēr*s, this sum had now decreased to 20-25 *sēr*s "because of all the orchards and buildings". As a consequence, rather than migrating to Kabul for the summer, he chose to stay in Laghman and bought some donkeys, with which he collected firewood in the mountains for sale.

Cultivation of vegetables had begun only in 1960, when Hahn carried out his research, but already then, the tendency was clear in areas like Bibi Mahru, where vegetables were grown on more than 50% of the land, leaving some 35% for grain cultivation (Hahn 1965: 19-23). Horticulture gradually spread to other areas around Kabul, and ultimately it will leave the Musallis jobless.

By 1975, the HYV wheat had also been introduced in the Kabul area, greatly diminishing the need for the Musallis in grain-cleaning. In spite of this, one *kalāntar* claimed that the new varieties necessitated the inclusion of non-professionals in the work-group, not to cope with more work, but to speed up the work. With the new varieties, all the wheat stacks "appear at the same time", and the Musallis cannot afford to let the peasant wait for their services, as he might choose to clean the grain himself.

Additional Incomes

In the past, Musallis could augment their earnings from threshing by doing transport work, inasmuch as there existed considerable regional price differences on agricultural products, caused by the poor infrastructure. The Musallis were able to exploit their familiarity with the regions through which they travelled on their seasonal migrations and could benefit from the fact that they owned a few oxen, which they used as transport animals. Apart from transporting rice, the Musallis were also engaged in other forms of small-scale trade in agricultural products in the region.

This transport work is referred to as *gāw-rānī* (i.e. cow driving), and consisted mainly in carrying rice for other people from Laghman to Kabul for sale.[51] If the Musallis had any of their own surplus rice this, too, was brought along for sale. Since paddy was not grown in the Kabul area, rice prices here were well above those in Laghman, where paddy is one of the main crops.

It is possible that only some of the grain-cleaners engaged in this activity, as is indicated by this account about the transport work of the past, told by an elderly man from the Persian-speaking Musallis:

> "Earlier we were transporters [*gāwrān*], when cars were not there. And we were traders. These Musallis [Pashto-speakers] can hardly load a cow, they would put the halter on its back rather than on its head! ... I myself, for example, I would finish stack-cleaning, [and] Sangar Saray, the Mullah Akhund village, Deh Bala, and the sands region in Kunar were the places from where I transported maize, and I would bring rapeseeds [*sharsham*] from Chashdar at the end of the [Panjshir] valley. Not only rapeseeds, but also clarified butter [*rughan*] and dried curds [*qurūt*].[52] We carried out this trade ... . We did not go to Nuristan ... the cows couldn't go there ... but we brought cumin [*zīra*] from Farajghan and Chashdar ... . Now we can't afford it [i.e. lack sufficient capital]... . Now the cars have appeared. Earlier, rice was transported to Kabul on cows. I myself have sold 8 *khānī*[53] for 28 Afs ... . We abandoned *gāw-rānī* many years ago. Earlier those Hussain Khēs and Hazarmeshis and Tarra Khēls and some others were *gāw-rānī*s, but now *gāw-rānī* has disappeared. Now everybody uses cars, and the poor can't afford it [i.e. lack capital to ensure a remunerative business]. ... We went to the

3,35 The wholesale market of grain.

> valley, to Kabul. From here to Kohistan [the Alishang valley] we took unrefined cane sugar [*gurr*], salt, and we would sell it for wheat, for maize, and *latirī* [a yellow pulse]. And from there we would take walnuts and carry it to Kama. ... We also transported cottonseeds from the valley. We carried our own things and traded in them. Yes, we were exchanging it in kind; for example maize or wheat in exchange for salt. ... Wheat was expensive while maize was cheap. If you would give them 1 *sēr* of salt, for example, you would get 2, 2.5, or 3 *sēr* of maize, or 1 or 1.5 *sēr* of wheat. From this side we would bring rice to Kabul, from there we would bring nothing."

Each family would have a few cows, but they might be unable to spare a driver. Hence, they would therefore send their cows loaded with rice with somebody else, asking him to sell the rice along with his own in the wholesale market (*manda'ī*). With such cooperation, each family was able to engage in several sale trips between Kabul and Laghman during the summer months.

Today (in 1976), one Musalli family is still engaged in rice trade between Laghman and Kabul. The others say that they lack the necessary capital. With the introduction of trucks, this form of trade is only profitable on a larger scale. Some Musallis have instead turned to middleman activities of a smaller scale in Kabul in order to supplement their income from threshing. They bring samples of rice from the wholesale grain stores of Kabul to the peasants of their work area; the peasants place orders with them for bigger quantities. In this way, the Musallis may make a profit of some 5 Afs per *sēr*, each customer buying some 10-30 *sēr*. Their profit is derived from buying in bulk at a wholesale price. For the peasants, the attraction may be that the rice is delivered to them and presumably also that the Musallis, by force of their profession, are supposed to be 'connoisseurs' of rice.

Another source of income for the Musallis is to engage in *'allāfī*, i.e. buying wheat from the peasants, cleaning it at home, taking it to the mill, and ultimately selling the flour in the bazaar.

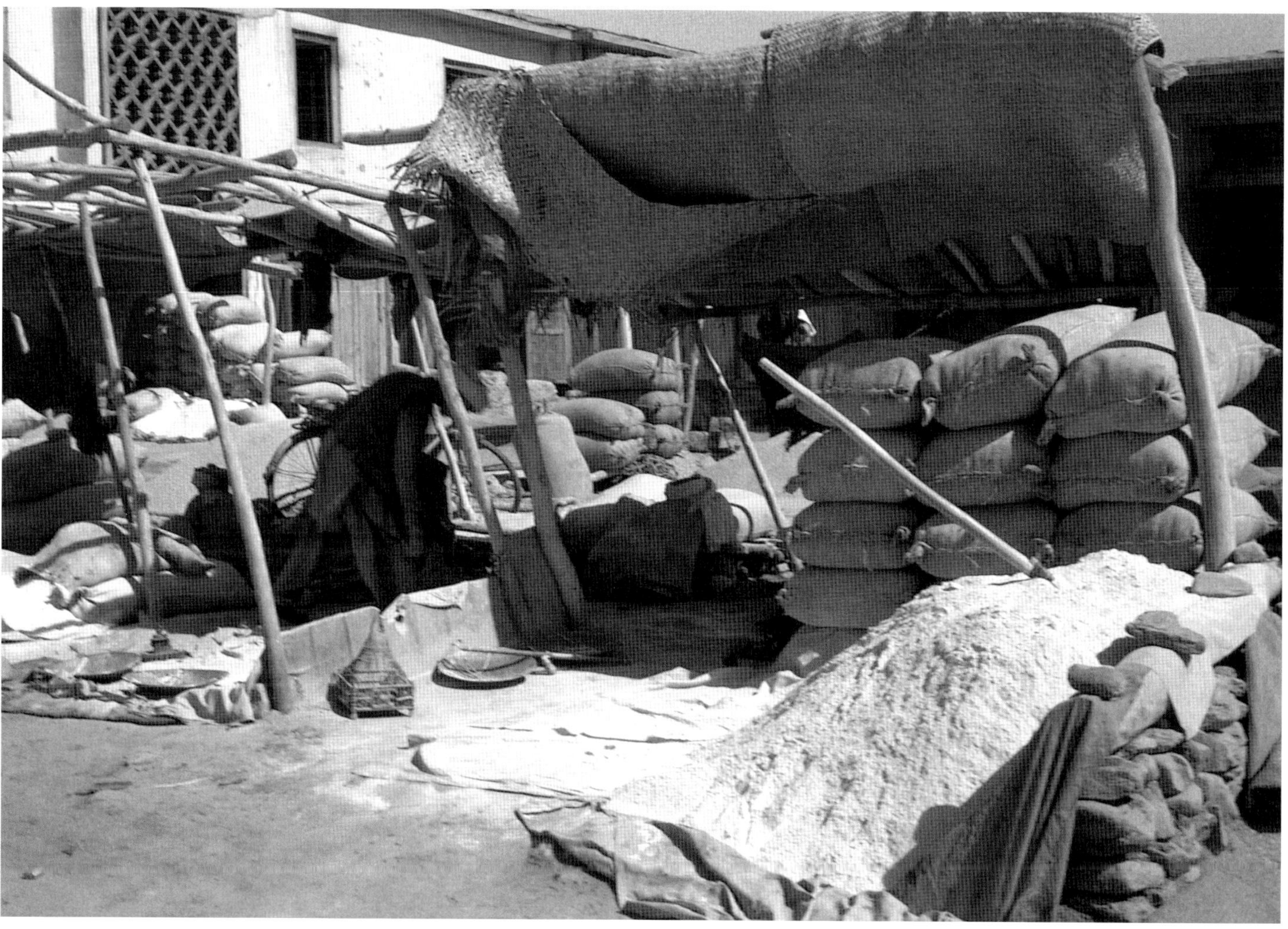

3,36 A stall at the wholesale market of flour.

For most Musallis today, however, additional income in the Kabul area is of a more humble character and requires no initial capital investment. When the threshing has been completed, many Musallis engage in construction work or in local transport work (see *Table. 3,3*). For those who migrate to areas where demand for grain-cleaning has diminished, these additional jobs have become more remunerative than *muṣallī-tūb*.

In larger households with several working members, the father remains in Laghman for the summer doing rice mill work while the adult sons migrate to Kabul doing *muṣallī-tūb*. The household's women will also remain behind to participate in rice mill work, since part of the work process, i.e. the par-boiling and drying of paddy, normally takes place next to their house.

In pursuing ordinary wage work, the Musallis must compete with the many other poor and landless villagers who migrate to Kabul during summer in the hope of finding work. The wages for ordinary day labour is so low that some Musallis do not see it as an alternative to thresh-

Table3,3: Economic resources (1975)

House-hold No.	Ratio of producers: No. of persons in household / No. of working males in household	Livestock	Wages from grain-cleaning in Laghman/in Kabul	Other sources of income
1	6 / 3	2 cows 2 donkeys	wheat: 2 *kh*./ - paddy: 2 *kh*./ - corn: 1 *kh*. / -	4000 Afs from transport work
2	9 / 3	3 cows donkeys	wheat: 5-6 *kh*./40 *sēr* paddy: 3 *kh*./ -	rice trade, *iǰāra* (2 *ǰarīb* for 200,000 Afs)
3	6 / 1	3 donkeys	wheat: 1 *kh*./- paddy: 1 *kh*./-	transport work
4	3 / 1	-	wheat: 1.5 *kh*./115 *sēr* paddy: 2 *kh*./-	rice trade
5	2 / 2	-	wheat: 50 *sēr*/50 *sēr* paddy/corn: 90 *sēr* / -	-
6	6 / 2	-	wheat: 1 *kh*./1 *kh*. paddy/corn: 180 *sēr*	-
7	9 / 2	-	wheat: 1 *kh*./1 *kh*. paddy/corn: 180 *sēr*	-
8	8 / 3	6 donkeys	wheat: 1.5 *kh*./1.5 *kh*. paddy: 3 *kh*.	transport work
9	9/ 4	-	wheat: 1 *kh*./1 *kh*. 40 *sēr* paddy: 1 *kh*.	3-4000 Afs from flour mill work
10	13 / 4	3 cows	wheat: 3.5 *kh*./2.5 *kh*. paddy: 6 *kh*. corn: 4 *sēr*	singing
11	6 / 1	-	wheat: 100 *sēr*/60 *sēr* paddy: 2 *kh*. corn: 20 *sēr*	-
12	4 / 1	-	wheat: 60 *sēr*/50 *sēr* paddy: 1 *kh*. corn: 30 *sēr*	-
13	6 / 1	-	wheat: 1 *kh*./none paddy: 100 *sēr*	singing

House-hold No.	Ratio of producers: No. of persons in household / No. of working males in household	Livestock	Wages from grain-cleaning in Laghman/in Kabul	Other sources of income
14	3 / 1	-	wheat: 1 *kh.*/40 *sēr* paddy: 1.5 *kh.* corn: 20 *sēr*	-
15	3 / 2	-	wheat: 50 *sēr*/40 *sēr* paddy: 1 *kh.* corn: 20 *sēr*	-
16	6 / 2	2 cows 2 calves 2 donkeys	wheat: 100 *sēr*/50 *sēr* paddy: 1.5 *kh.* corn: 40 *sēr*	transport work
17	12 / 3	3 cows 2 calves 2 donkeys	wheat: 100 *sēr*/50 *sēr*	transport work, rice trade
18	6 / 1	-	wheat: 100 *sēr*/20 *sēr* paddy: 40 *sēr*	-
19	4 / 1	1 cow 1 calf	wheat: 70 *sēr*/50 *sēr* paddy: 1.5 *kh.*	-
20	6 / 2	3 cows 2 calves	wheat: 1 *kh.*/1.5 *kh.* paddy: 2.5 *kh.*	shop in Laghman
21	5 / 1	-	wheat: 60 *sēr*/1.5 *kh.* paddy: 1 *kh.*	construction work in Kabul and Laghman
22	18 / 3	2 cows 1 donkey	wheat: 3 *kh.*/3 *kh.* paddy: 3 *kh.*	rice trade in Kabul
23	9 / 2	2 cows 2 calves	wheat: 1.5 *kh.*/2 *kh.* paddy: 2 *kh.*	-
24	5/ 1	-	wheat: 1 *kh.*/1 *kh.* paddy: 1 *kh.*	-
25	6 / 3	3 donkeys	wheat: 30 *sēr*/ - paddy: 30 *sēr*	transport work
26	8 / 2	3 donkeys	wheat: 10 *sēr*/ - paddy: 25 *sēr*	transport work

ing and prefer to remain in Laghman during the summer. The work possibilities are somewhat similar there, but the wages even lower. However, since many Musallis own a donkey or two, they collect firewood from bushes in the mountains and sell it in the bazaar. The profit is small, some 2.5 to 3 Afs per *sēr*. Even here, however, the competition from truck transport has increased since the beginning of the 1970s when the road was extended all the way to Dawlatshah.

Poverty and Dependency

The vast majority of Musallis are poor people who supplement their declining income from *muṣallī-tūb* with poorly paid wage labour or some transport work with their donkeys. A few Musalli households with several able-bodied members are doing reasonably well especially where they have additional sources of income. (see *Table 3,3*). This is usually indicated by a house of their own, investment in rice trade, and in one case the leasing of land (*ijāra*).

Ideally, the Musallis' payments in kind from grain-cleaning, in rice and wheat, should be enough to cover family consumption, and leave a surplus to sell on the market. In this way, they would obtain money to buy cloth, tea, salt, sugar, cooking oil, etc. By 1975-76, however, many families were complaining that their payment in kind hardly covered their consumption, and basic necessities had become unattainable luxuries.

Table 3,3 shows the income of 26 families during 1975. They earned an average of 181 *sēr* of wheat and 136 *sēr* of paddy, i.e., 1,448 kg and 1,088 kg, respectively, from grain-cleaning in Laghman and Kabul. One-third of the families had no additional income and had to manage exclusively on these earnings. For the sake of comparison, it should be mentioned that Kanne has calculated a minimal budget for a family of five persons in Kabul. Even though a Kabul family derives its income largely from wage labour, it gives a rough estimate of a family's consumption needs. According to Kanne's estimate, such a family requires 56 kg of wheat flour per month for bread and 1.5 kg of rice per month (Kanne 1974: 585). The Musalli households comprise in average 6.7 persons, who have at their disposal 120 kg wheat and 90 kg paddy per month. Apart from rice and wheat, Kanne estimates the value of other necessary consumer items – e.g., kerosene, cooking oil, clothes, etc. – to be about 721 Afs a month, a sum which the Musallis have to acquire either from selling part of their payment in kind or from additional wage work. The Musallis obtain the greatest surplus on paddy, but even if they process and sell all of it, paddy amounts to only about 60 kg of rice, and obtains no more than 4,800 Afs on the market. According to Kanne's budget, this sum covers around half the family's annual cash need for consumer items.

It is little wonder, then, that many Musalli families are desperately short of cash before the end of winter, and their only alternative is to approach the money-lender in order to borrow money on rice or wheat. According to a Musalli trapped in debt, the system operates as follows:

> "If rice is 80 Afs per *sēr*, they [the money lenders] would say, 'If you want money at the rate of 50 Afs per *sēr*, then it is OK. Otherwise no deal'. And since I am hungry, I will agree to the terms: 50 Afs per *sēr*. And I will buy tea, sugar, cooking oil, salt, and such things. ... We will pay back when we earn [the rice] on the stacks. And then, putting our hope in God, we wait for the next harvest,

Table 3,4: Comparison of *hamsāya* and house owner households in terms of labour power and space:

	No. of households	Average size of household	Average number of rooms per household	Average number of workers per household
Hamsāya	23	6.1 pers.	2	1.8
House owner	10	8.1 pers.	2.4	2.3
Total	33	6.7 pers.	2.1	1.9

and then we borrow more and more. Again we weigh our grain and pay him all of it ... only dust [*khāk*] remains for us."

That Musallis experience poverty as a humiliating condition is demonstrated by the following incident, related by a poor widow living with her son's family:

"I once asked my son to go and buy one *paw* of *gurr* [unrefined cane sugar] as we had no more money anyway.[54] The shopkeeper looked at the face [of my son] and said: 'Look at your stature and look at your moustache. You have come here to buy one *paw* of *gurr*!' Out of shame, my son told him that he was not buying it for himself but for his donkey. He got the *gurr* ... and gave it on the spot to the donkey, and came home empty-handed, blaming me for having let him suffer the shame."

Like other poor people, most Musallis do not own their own dwellings, but live as tenants in the homes of better-off people. Tenants are called *hamsāya*, which literally means "common shadow" but also carries the connotation of "neighbour". The word is used euphemistically about the kind of tenants who do not pay rent in money but in the form of services.[55] A house owner provides a few rooms for a poor family, who in return provides free services for the landlord and his family. A Musalli described the relationship as follows:

"For us, being a *hamsāya* includes the running of errands, doing mud work for the house owner, cleaning his wheat stack, covering his roof with *kāh-gil* [mud mixed with straw] so that the rain will not get through. At weddings we sweep the place, and the head of the slaughtered cow will be given to us."

In daily life the major part of the *hamsāya* duties fall upon the women in the tenant family who will assist in the arduous or dirty household chores such as cooking, cleaning, and washing clothes, cleaning the grain in the house, etc. While the servant position is generally considered socially degrading among the equality conscious Afghans, the *hamsāya* situation in particular reinforces social inferiority, as it implies that the women of the *hamsāya* household have to work for strangers. In the male-dominated Afghan ethos, the chastity of women is the measure of family honour and with his wife and daughters working for strangers, a *hamsāya* man reveals his inability to protect his women's privacy, and hence, his family's status.[56]

Among the 26 families in *Table 3,3* as well as among an additional seven families closely related to them a total of 33 families 23 live as *hamsāyas* and 10 own a house of their own.

Both the *hamsāya* rooms and the private houses consist in almost all cases of small, dark, frequently windowless, mud-rendered rooms, with a hard, compacted mud floor. In case the family owns animals, these may be in one of the rooms or in a shed next to the house. Cooking takes place outside under an awning or shade. The *hamsāya*-families have, on average, 2 rooms per household, the house owners 2.4 rooms. It turns out however, that while the average household size for the 33 families is 6.7 persons, those who own their house tend to live in household units with an average of 8.1 persons per household. In spite of having more living space, they in fact live more congested than the *hamsāya*-families. The households of the house-owners are in 7 out of 10 cases extended families, while this is true for only 8 out of 23 cases of the *hamsāya*-households. The number of workers per household is higher among the house owners, 2.3 as compared to 1.8 for the *hamsāya*-households, but there are also more stomachs to fill, and with virtually identical proportion of workers to dependents, the houseowning households are not necessarily better off just because of their higher rate of workers.

Organizing the Community

For generations, the traditional patron-client system of Laghman has secured the Musallis both a livelihood and protection, albeit at the bottom of the social ladder. With the landowners' growing neglect of their obligations towards the village poor and with the internal competition among these, the Musallis feel insecure about their future. They blame the landowners for exploiting them or for disregarding their traditional rights, and blame themselves for lack of unity.

In 1974, such sentiments led to an initiative among the above mentioned 33 closely related Musalli families from among the Persian-speaking group to develop more internal unity and solidarity. The immediate background of their initiative was the misgivings of some families over failing *qawmi*-participation in connection with the funeral of a girl. This situation was skillfully exploited by a relative of the family, Ainullah. A poor widower, he was himself acutely aware of the predicaments of the Musallis and had for some time awaited an opportunity to mobilize his kinsmen to stand up for their occupational rights and interests. Ainullah had considerable rhetorical talents. The uncle of the deceased girl, Abdur Rahim, had not, but he was the most well-to-do of all the Musallis, living comfortably in a big house of his own. After the funeral, Ainullah contacted Abdur Rahim, and convinced him that the best response to the lack of participation by the *qawmis* in the funeral would be to invite all the close kinsmen to a dinner. Reluctantly and somewhat bewildered, Abdur Rahim consented. Ainullah gave the following account of what subsequently happened:

"After we had dinner, I started talking and I said, 'Everybody has got a *qawm* of their own. They have elders, *kalāntar*s – even the bazaar has a *kalāntar*, and that is only a bazaar. But we have nothing. What shall we do about it? I think we shall choose somebody as our *malik* [i.e. representative]. We are scattered in every village, and everybody can crush us, and we don't know about each other. Suppose there is a village where there is only one family of us, while they [the other villagers] are all of one *qawm*. They will beat us and in the government imprison us, too, because they are a whole village. If each one of you contribute some 5 Afs, it will make a lot of money, so you should help him in the government and also when the time of the stick comes [i.e. fighting breaks out]. When somebody dies or somebody gets married, you should sympathize with each other and help with some money [i.e. to cover the expenses for weddings and bride-price]. If it is me today, it is you tomorrow. We should be lenient with one another. You should have compassion for a person who is young but poor and who can't get married because of the expenses.' When I brought up these issues, they agreed that it was to the benefit of all. Then there was the question of who should become the *malik*. I said: 'Whoever you old men choose among the young should be the *malik*'. You know, King Zaher became too old and the control went out of his hands and his ability to think was impaired. It was a kingdom and it became a republic.[57] It was the old [who ruled], and the young took over, those whose brains functioned properly. The old men have lost their reason. They are still moving in the past. They don't know what is happening now. I told them that 'we, the young people will accept your decision as long as you choose one of us'. So finally, after some other choices, it came upon Abdur Rahim ... I seconded it, and everybody raised their hands [in prayer]."

"So, the next morning he [Abdur Rahim] called me to his place and told me that 'You put such a burden on my shoulders. I can't carry it'. I said 'Why'? He said, 'For one, I don't have the tongue and can't talk, and second, I am not here all the time. Who will then be doing the *malikī* here?' I told him that 'When it comes to talking, I would do it. When you are here, you know your work. If there is something, then you call me, and even if we are sitting together, I will talk and you say 'Amen''. So I convinced him and he said 'OK, if you want me, I will be your *malik*'. The next Friday, I went to Jalalabad and bought a turban for him for 500 Afs, and I also bought a bag of sweets for him. Again the *qawmi*s gathered, and we tied the turban on his head."

In a subsequent interview, Ainullah's account of his own back-stage role in the foundation of the *malikī* was not directly confirmed by Abdur Rahim himself, but it appeared obvious that Abdur Rahim was not the man to foster such ideas on his own, let alone implement them. It is little wonder then that even Abdur Rahim initially wanted Ainullah, as the driving force behind the *malikī*, to accept the position as *malik*. But as Ainullah explained to him:

"I don't have a house of my own, and I can't afford to have 10 people meeting in my place. How can I honour the 10 or 20 people who would be gathering in my honour? Suppose I could afford the tea and the food, I can't provide the accommodation. But you [Abdur Rahim], thanks to God, have a house and

3,37 The widower, Ainullah and his two children (Qala-i Sardar, Dec. 1986).

> enough food, so you do the *malikī* and we follow you '. He said: 'But I can't talk'. I told him: 'Leave the talking to me, and let the *malikī* be in your name.'"

The establishment of the *malikī* was formalized in a document specifying that in case of internal conflicts, the *malik* and five assistants should act as arbitrators, and their decision would be binding on both parties. If a member became involved in conflicts with somebody outside the community, the other members were obliged to help him, even if the case went to the government. And if anybody violated or deviated from the word of the *malik*, all the *qawm* would gather and impose a fine on that person. It was agreed that fines may amount to one sheep and 10 *sērs* of rice. All *malikī* members signed the document and their identity-card numbers were listed. Ainullah explained, moreover, that the local Laghman *maliks* of the villages where the members of the Musalli-*malikī* lived, signed the document in recognition of Abdur Rahim's authority as *malik*. Although not the same as a *malikī* officially recognized and registered with the authorities, the *malik*'s authority was nevertheless recognized by the population.

The 33 families of the *malikī* were divided into 7-8 work groups during their summer migrations to Kabul. Encouraged by the formation of the *malikī* in Laghman, the Kabul work group for which Ainullah was *kalāntar* formulated a document in which all participating Musallis agreed to exclude non-Musallis from the work group. They also obtained a written agreement from the four local *maliks* of their Kabul area to the effect that in the future the grain-stacks would be cleaned only by these Musallis, i.e. it was an exclusive agreement with their employers. Later on, the group attempted to extend this organizational work to Laghman, but the dispersed settlement of the Musallis there complicated this task. The long-term goal of this initiative was to obtain the recognition by local authorities of the Musallis as professional threshers in order to end competition from non-Musallis. Ainullah, who fostered the whole idea explains:

> "There is only one way it could be achieved, and that is if the government, after examining our ancestry, takes down our names and issues us work permits, and in this way confines the profession to our group so that others could not take up the occupation. And we will pay income tax. But now, we are neither

3.38 Most Musallis irrespective of whether they own their houses or stay as tenants live in very humble circumstances. Here is seen the little courtyard in front of the two small dark rooms where a Musalli family resides (South of Mehtarlam, Dec. 1976).

recognized as a *qawm* nor do we count for the government."

The formation of the *malikī* by the Musallis was an attempt not only to promote internal solidarity, but also to provide themselves with a political identity, to constitute themselves as a *qawm* equal to other communities rather than as social inferiors. The initiative was also aimed at protecting the Musallis' employment possibilities, i.e. as a sort of trade union. However, the means to achieve this goal were traditional, as they were based upon the reestablishment of the ethnic division of labour, which over the years had kept the Musallis at the bottom of Afghan society.

In this sense, the establishment of the *malikī* was self-defeating. In addition, it was highly unlikely that any Afghan government would endorse such an ethnic monopolization of a profession, as it would run counter to all the official "nation-building" and de-tribalization efforts of this century. The future prospects for the Musallis and similar groups of poor, landless people consisted rather in being recognized as eligible for land-allocation. Here the Musalli *malik* could be instrumental in forwarding a collective application. Although receiving land grants was known to be a long and difficult process, it had been tried before and had proven at least partly successful for a considerable number of Musalli families in Laghman.

Musallis in Helmand

A large number of Laghman Musallis managed to realize their dreams of a better future, and thus indirectly nourished the hopes among those left behind. Since the late 1950s, successive groups of Musallis had been given land by the government within the Helmand settlement scheme.[58] The Musallis in question came from areas such as Dand, the southern part of the Alingar valley and Kach, i.e. from areas where Musallis still could be found in 1975-76. In addition, around 40 families of Musallis from the areas of Chilmati, Gumain, Alishang, and Dand were supposed to have settled some years ago in the Baghlan province.

Application for land could be made individually or collectively. In the Musallis' case, several hundred families were settled over the years through collective applications forwarded by representatives (*wakīls*), while a smaller number of families acquired land through individual efforts. The first and most successful initiative was taken by Sayid Jan, a Musalli from Charbagh who had managed well as a singer and even opened a shoe shop in Tirgarhi. He gathered his *qawmis*, convinced them to apply for land in the Helmand scheme, and was elected their representative for that purpose. Each family paid him some 600 Afs as compensation for his work and trouble.

Wakīl Sayid Jan, who in 1975 lived as a settler in Nad-i Ali, told how his *qawmis* had contacted him, requesting him to manage their land applications, as he was better off and supposedly had better connections with the government than they. He had, for example, met Prime Minister Daoud *Khān* when the latter was still governor of Nangarhar. The Musallis' initiative did not pass unnoticed in their home-villages in Laghman. All the involved families came from areas where Musallis traditionally had done "community service", and the landowners became angry when they learned about the settlement plans, accusing the *wakīl* of taking away the people who used to serve them. In *wakīl* Sayid Jan own words:

3,39 In the mid-1970s it was still common to use camels for local transport in the dry, hot Helmand province (Babaji, Nov. 1976).

"The *khāns* in Laghman at that time had more power than the government. ... When I went to Kach, there was a very powerful *khān*, Ismatullah *Khān*, always carrying a machine gun. The *khān* ordered that I should be captured because of my attempt to settle the Shāhi Khēls. But I just managed to cross the river in a *zangu* and in that way saved my neck.[59]

"The *khāns* of the Kach area went straight to the Prime Minister [Daoud *Khān*, to complain about the settlement of the Musallis]. Among them were such prominent people like [members of parliament] Gul Pacha Ulfat and also Ghulam Hassan Safi. But Daoud *Khān* rejected their petition, saying, 'Do you want them [the Musallis] to be your servants for the rest of their lives?'"

It was, however, a major decision for the Musallis to leave Laghman, to leave their homeland, their *watan*, as *wakīl* Sayid Jan's account illustrates:

"A man came and told me, that he had decided that he could not leave Laghman, he could not leave his dead behind. I said OK and removed his name from the list. But the following morning he returned and wanted to be put back on the list. I got angry and asked what the hell it was all about. ... The

3,40 Musallis from Manjuma in Laghman settled in Babaji, Helmand (Nov. 1976).

> man said that the preceding night he had changed his mind. He had only been married for three days. He was living as *hamsāya*, and the preceding night the house owner had told him that he had a guest and wanted the Musalli to go and sleep in the guest room so that the guest should not be left alone during the night. The Musalli did so, but when the guest had fallen asleep, he could not bear that he, so newly married, should sleep apart from his wife. So he got up and went back to his home. Here he found, that the house owner was sleeping with his young wife! After that he decided that it was getting too much, and that he had better leave [Laghman]."

A landlord has no claim on sexual favours from tenants. The above case simply illustrates how a landlord could abuse his powers in view of the economic dependency and general social inferiority of the Musalli which prevented the latter from defending his honour by retaliating.

In the late 1950s, *wakīl* Sayid Jan managed to obtain land in Nad-i Ali for some 45 Musalli families from the Dand area, plus for some eight families of landless peasants. Two years later he acquired land in Nawa for an additional 50 Musalli families from Alingar (between the *Vilāyat* and Pul-i Shahi). After another two years 47 Musalli families from the Kach-i Aziz Khan area were settled in Garamsel, and 27 families in Babaji, Basharan.

The Musallis settled at that time all received 30 *ǰarībs* of land – 27 *ǰarībs* of agricultural land, 1 *ǰarīb* for the houseyard, and the rest to grow trees for firewood.[60] The government had built houses for all the settlers; these were distributed among them according to kinship so that relatives could settle next to each other. In addition, the government provided each family with 50 *sēr* of wheat and 3,000 Afs to be repaid over 12 years.[61] Being new settlers, however, meant unexpected hardships not only for the Musallis, but for all settlers in the Helmand scheme: According to Sayid Jan, during the first ten years the crops were very poor because of soil salinity, and at times they even had to eat alfalfa and "sell

3,4 / The flat land of Helmand with its desert-like climate offers a stark contrast to the narrow, fertile river valleys of Laghman (Now-i Naqil, Nov. 1976).

their women's trousers", an expression which indicates their state of destitution. The first year he himself harvested 12 *kharwār* of grain on his 30 *ǰarībs* of land. Next year the yield fell to 6 *kharwār* and the third year it was as low as 1.5 *kharwār*. As a consequence of the bad harvests, the government nullified the initial loan, but the hard conditions still forced about two-thirds of the Musalli settlers to leave the scheme for wage-work in Laskargah and Kandahar. Ultimately, the predicament of the settlers came to the notice of the government, according to Sayid Jan in the following way:

"Prime Minister Daoud came here to see the situation, and the officials wanted to deceive

3,42 *Wakīl* Sayid Jan in front of his house in Nad-i Ali (Nov. 1976).

> him and show him Marja rather than Nad-i Ali, as Marja was better off. But Daoud *Khān* insisted on going to Nad-i Ali, and when he saw the plight of the people, he got angry with the officials – and drainage work was thereafter undertaken, which improved the situation."

The Musallis' difficulties, however, were not only caused by the quality of agricultural land but also by their neighbours. Next to the Musallis were settled some former pastoral nomads, *māldār*s (i.e. cattle owners) whose animals would break into other peoples' land and eat the crop.

In spite of the hardships in Helmand, new vistas opened for the Musallis and *wakīl* Sayid Jan claims to have been instrumental in getting the government to build schools in the area, and, from the start, to get 40 Musalli children to attend school, which is "more than the *māldār*s today have managed to send to school".

3,43 Settler houses within the Helmand project area (Nov. 1976).

"At that time the governor was Dr Kayum Khan. He came here every Friday, asking what people needed. All the people asked for wheat, cooking oil, rice, and such. Everybody talked, but I didn't. The governor knew me and asked, 'What do you people [i.e. Shāhi Khēl] need?'[62] I said, 'We need a school. Even in Laghman, I sent my children to school'. The *māldār*s, the Kharotis, and others got so angry at me: 'A school – up my arse!'. I got scared but repeated the proposal to the governor."

Sayid Jan also encouraged the initiative of starting a girls' school, and he sent his five daughters there. As a consequence of high school enrollment, the Musallis can boast of a comparatively high proportion of public employees who earn important additional income for their families. Since the agricultural yields have remained low, other families supplement the household income with jobs as drivers and unskilled labour.

Another 50 Musalli families, from Badiabad, Zalingar, Qasaba, Mandrawar, and Dand, were settled in Darweshan, and in the place of *Ḥaǰǰi* Mohammad Sharif Khan through the efforts of a *wakīl* Nabi Jan, who himself was from Qasaba of Laghman.[63] These settlers each received 15 *ǰarīb* of land and had to build their houses themselves according to a government design. They had to pay for the land, some 10,000-12,000 Afs on installment, as well as for an initial loan of cows, tools, 30 *sēr* of wheat for seeds, and another 30 *sēr* for eating. The land, however, was of a better quality than in Nad-i Ali, but now drainage problems are also causing salination here.

Yet other *wakīls* obtained land in Marja for some 30-50 Musalli families originally from Manjuma and elsewhere in Laghman, and there were also families who during this time managed to settle on their own in Helmand.

One of the main concerns of the government was to ensure that the settlers actually stayed on the land and undertook the cultivation themselves. Hence, as the settled Shāhi Khēls explained, during the first years government officials frequently turned up to take attendance, and if a settler was absent during three consecutive visits, he lost his right to the land. Later on, government controls were taken only once a year. Apart from the actual property document, the settler also had to sign a document stating that he would cultivate the land himself to the best of his ability, and would not let it on lease. In addition, he guaranteed not to cultivate prohibited crops or to violate the agricultural programme which included cultivating the crops demanded, such as cotton, which is the major cash crop in Helmand. Finally, he also promised to live on the land with his family and build a house according to the maps issued.

When President Daoud assumed power in 1973, he proclaimed a land reform, and the Musallis in Laghman were among the first to apply for land. But the reform turned out to be largely a paper reform, and the Musallis experienced deep bitterness and disillusionment as well as a renewed realization of social injustice. One Musalli man expressed these feeling to me in 1976 in the following way:

> "We send our men to the army and will give our blood for our country. But the landowners, whom we have served all our life, will not even give us their wheat stacks any more. We see how much land some people have, and we cannot see any justice in it."

However, some land was in fact being allocated to landless during the 1970s, although slowly and gradually. In 1976 in Helmand I met a couple of Musalli families whom I had met the previous year in Laghman. One of them had just received land in Helmand, and the other was going to try to push its case locally.

After the Saur Revolution in 1978, the government again proclaimed a land reform, and during the first months of 1979 thousands of poor, landless people received land.[64] However, while the confiscated land was mainly in the west, the excess population was mainly in the east. The redistribution of land thus involved a veritable mass migration. Thousands of landless peasants were moved in trucks from the east and dumped on their future plots. For the Musallis, the Helmand province was their destination this time. However, the Ministry of Agriculture and Land Reform was unable to deal with the situation and had neither tents to shelter all the settlers, nor capacity to keep up with marking the land plots to be distributed. Hence, the Musallis and countless other landless people, surviving on World Food Programme food supplies, packed their few belongings and returned to the east, more disillusioned than ever.

Social Organization

Whatever the original descent structure of the Shāhi Khēl/Musalli groups of Laghman, in 1975-76 the main factors in their social organization were close kinship relations and geographical proximity. A few informants mentioned a subdivision into *khēls* (i.e. descent-segments), but this was not generally recognized. Among the Musallis, *qawm* turned out to be subjectively defined, including/excluding various families according to the informant's own position in the kinship network. Hence, a *qawm* could neither be co-terminous with "ethnic group" nor "occupational group" in any objective or absolute sense. Rather it referred to the recognized group of living kinsmen, matrilateral and patrilateral alike, with whom one shared obligations and solidarity. Both groups of Musallis practiced *qawm*-endogamy with a preference for cousin-marriage, and a person's recognized *qawm* thus included many people who were simultaneously matri- and patrilaterally related. Although patrilineality was predominant in virtually all communities in Afghanistan, among the Musallis the picture was ambiguous due to the multiplicity of relations among *qawmis*.

Social contact was primarily maintained between close relatives and with Musallis of neighbouring villages, two categories which would often be identical. Close kinship and spatial proximity were also the major recruitment principles for the Kabul workgroups. When geographical or kinship distance increased, contacts grew increasingly scarce.

Most Musallis lived in nuclear family households, but extended families of different composition were almost as common. The latter might consist of three generations, either a married son living with his wife and children in his parental household, or a widowed mother living in the household of her married son. Just as responsibility for an elderly parent normally would rest upon the (eldest) son, an elder brother was responsible for fatherless, underage siblings, as well as for orphaned children of his own siblings. In the before-mentioned group of 33 Musalli households of the Persian-speaking group there were 17 nuclear families, 8 three-generation households, 5 extended households with widowed mother/siblings, 2 households where a widower lived with his children, and one household containing two orphaned nephews. Household composition would change over time: nuclear families would by the marriage of a child and birth of a grandchild develop into three-generation households, three-generation households might split into nuclear segments with the death of one or both of the parents, and a widower with younger children would most certainly try to reestablish a nuclear household by a new marriage. In this latter case, economic factors such as wedding expenses and bride-price would be the major factor in delaying the reestablishment of the nuclear family.

A section of the Pashto-speaking Musallis illustrate some of the possible variations from the nuclear family household (see 3,44). (I do not have sufficient quantitative data to assess whether the household composition varied between the two groups of Musallis, but my impression is that nuclear households were less common among the Pashto-speaking Musallis than among the Persian-speaking immigrants).

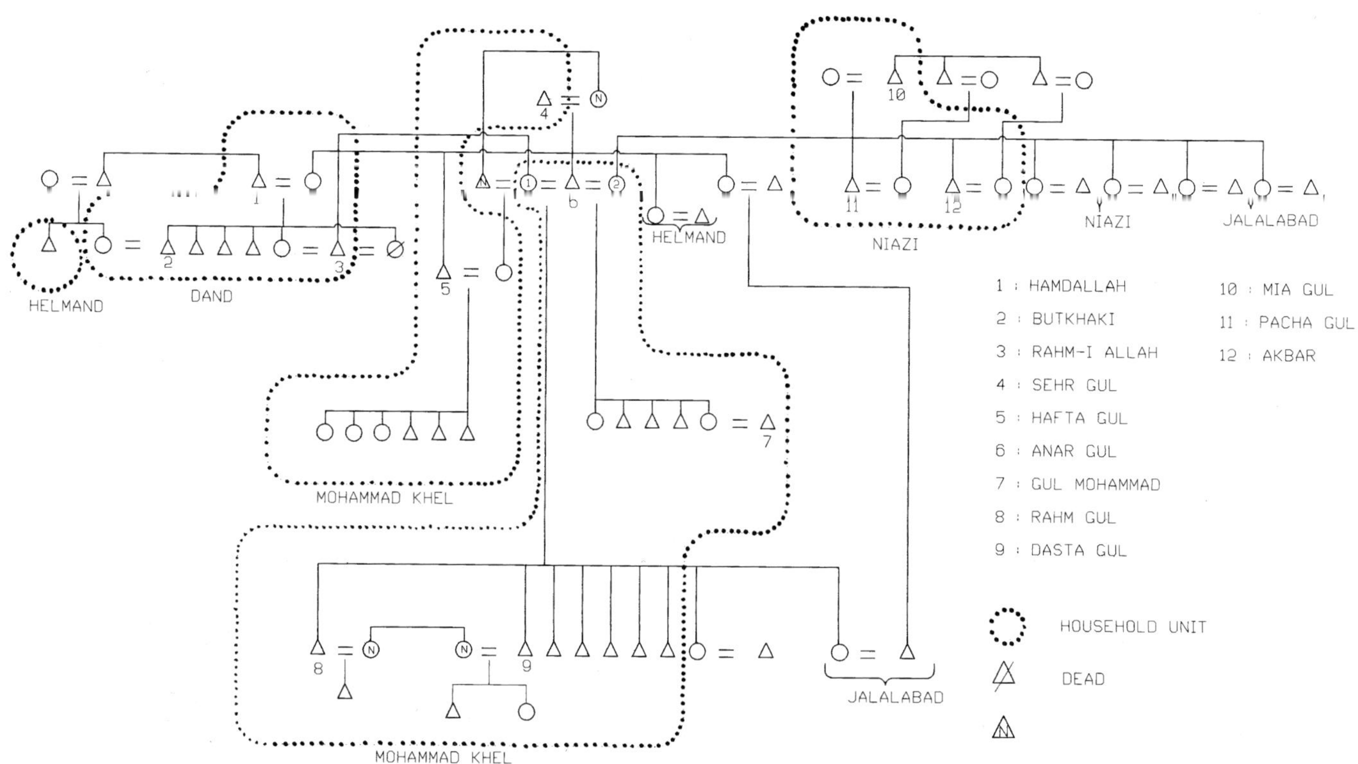

*3,44*The households of Hamdullah, Anar Gul, Mia Gul, and Hafta Gul were all three-generation households. While three-generation households in most cases consisted of married sons living in the parental household, under special circumstances married daughters living in the parental household were also found. Hamdullah's household, for example, contained both his married son, Butkhaki, and a daughter, married to Rahm-i Allah. Rahm-i Allah grew up in Hamidullahs household after his own parents died, and his father's brother had refused to have him. He married a daughter of Hamidullah, and when she died, Hamdullah gave him another daughter as wife. After his marriage, Rahm-i Allah remained in Hamdullah's household as a *khāna dāmād*.[65] Living within the same household would normally mean forming one economic unit, "sharing one cooking pot" as it was phrased. However, this was not the situation in Rahm-i Allah's case. While the four adult sons of Hamidullah, including Butkhaki lived and worked jointly with their father, sharing incomes and expenses, Rahm-i Allah had formed his own economic unit: "he has a separate cooking pot." He did not get along with his wife's brothers. He had twice tried to move away from them but could not find another place to live.

The three-generation households normally contained just one married son or daughter. Segmentation of the household in most cases took place when the next child married. The oldest married child would then set up an independent household. There might be several reasons for this: one would simply be lack of space, since each married couple usually got their own room to ensure a measure of privacy under the congested conditions. Another reason for segmentation might be, as pointed out by the Musallis, the frictions which arose when two daughters-in-law occupied the household, or as in Rahm-i Allah's case, friction between the adult brothers-in-law.

Anar Gul, however, was an exception. He lived with his

two wives and their respective children, but also with two of his married sons from his first wife, Raham Gul and Dasta Gul, and the son-in-law (*khāna dāmād*), Gul Mohammad, who had married a daughter from his second wife.

Mia Gul's household was another exception with two married sons in one household. The sons of Pacha Gul and Akbar explained that they had not split because, "if I make a mistake, my brother will forgive, and if he makes a mistake, I will forgive." In this case, an additional reason to stay together might be that since their father, Mia Gul, was ill and unable to work, the two sons were obligated to support him.

Hafta Gul, who lived next to his brother Anar Gul, took care of their widowed father Sher Gul. Anar Gul's first wife had been the widow of his mother's brother. He subsequently married off her daughter (from the first husband) to Hafta Gul. Hence, Hafta Gul was both a brother-in-law and a son-in-law to Anar Gul's first wife.

Anar Gul and Hafta Gul lived in the village of Mohammad Khel, while Hamdullah, who had married their sister, lived in Dand. During summer, they all went together to Kabul, where they worked jointly in the area of Qala-i Qafila Bashi. Since the three households had a labour force of no less than 12 adult men, they did not need to invite any outsiders to join their work group.

Mia Gul's household, which was located in Niazi in the Alingar valley, migrated for the summer to the Bini Hissar area, where they worked jointly with 10 other Musalli households from Niazi. They had no outsiders in their work group, either.

Among all ethnic communities in Afghanistan, marriages tend to be contracted between people belonging to the same community; i.e., the marriages are *qawm*-endogamous. This was also seen in the case above, where marriages were contracted with other Pashto-speaking Musallis from other villages of Laghman or from the Jalalabad area. A similar pattern is found among the Persian-speaking Musallis, as illustrated in the following case.

An old, knowledgeable woman from this group, by the name of Nurani, gave an account of her close relatives (see *3,45*), which covered 71 marriages. Of these, no details were given in 24 cases, but we can assume that most were exogamous. As regards the remaining 47 cases, 25 of the marriages took place among members of the same *qawm*, and 22 were exogamous, i.e. between Musallis and non-*qawmi*s. Hence, taking only the known cases, 53.1 % of the marriages were *qawm*-endogamous, which is low by Afghan standards. This rate would be even lower if we add the 24 cases where details are lacking, probably due to exogamy. Among the *qawm*-endogamous marriages with first, second, or third cousins were frequent, though apparently without any preference for maternal or paternal cousin marriage. Consequently, within both groups of Musallis, people were closely related, often patrilaterally and matrilaterally at the same time, as indicated on the chart.

Since Musallis generally have no material assets worth mentioning, economic considerations could hardly create a preference for paternal cross-cousin marriage, as is the case, for example, among landowning Pashtuns (see Christensen 1982). While I do not have data concerning bride-prices, in general, there appeared to be a tendency towards lower bride-price among close relatives. In case of "exchange" marriages (*badal*), bride-price can virtually be done away with, for which reason *badal* has been attractive for Afghanistan's poor people.[66] In the present context, however, only one case of *badal* was registered, and this was in connection with an exogamous marriage (see below).

In case a relatively young person becomes a widow or widower, the in-laws frequently provide a new spouse, either directly by marrying off a brother or sister of the deceased to the

THE QAWMIS OF NURANI

INFORMANT

NON-MUSALLI

NOT DOING MUSALLĪ-TŌB

DEAD

PATRILATERAL RELATIVES

MATRILATERAL RELATIVES

PATRI- AND MATRILATERAL RELATIVES

3,45 The *Qawmis* of Nurani

widow/widower, i.e. levirate or sororate, or by marrying this to another close relative. This was illustrated in the case above, where Anar Gul had married his mother's brother's widow, and Rahm-i Allah married his dead wife's sister. Similar cases can be seen in the second case of Persian-speaking Musallis, where the levirate is seen to extend beyond marrying brother's widow to also include marrying FaBr's and FaBrSo's widow.

Multiple marriages were common in both groups (17 out of 71 marriages in *Fig. 3,45*), but polygamous marriages would normally take place only in cases of childlessness or levirate, when securing the livelihood of a brother's widow was the main concern. Most multiple marriages were probably consecutive, perhaps caused by the fact that many men and women died at a comparatively young age. One consequence of these multiple marriages was that many persons have step-parents and half-siblings, and some cousin marriages were in fact between step-cousins rather than between real cousins.

In Afghan society, it is generally not considered proper to give girls in marriage to persons of inferior status, but only to those considered as one's equals or superiors. This pattern is associated with the tradition of patrilineality, whereby at marriage the rights in a woman are transferred from her father to her husband and offspring are counted in his descent-line. Hence, the honour of a family will be tainted in case a daughter or sister marries socially "downwards", while receiving a girl from a socially inferior family is not considered harmful to one's honour. The *qawm* endogamy of socially low-ranking groups such as the Musallis is supposedly reinforced by the reluctance of other groups to marry them. This fact is reflected in the following statements, the first by a wealthy landowner and the second by a poor, landless Pashtun:

> "It is rare to see marriages between Musallis and the settled population. ... These marriages are rare because nobody wants to marry them as they are so ugly dark ... and maybe because their profession is considered inferior. ... But the villagers will never marry barbers as they are considered more inferior than the Musallis."

> "*Muṣalli-tūb* ... is not a good profession. Somebody would shout at them: 'Hey, Chungar, come and clean my wheat stack', and the name 'Chungar' is disrespectful. ... They are not looked down upon [but] people don't intermarry with them. Some orphan would marry them, someone fatherless or motherless. And according to the Book [the Qor'an], marriage with a Musalli is forbidden because he was a slave. ... From the beginning to the end he is a slave, God has created him to be a slave. For example, if somebody asks for a daughter from another person, he would reply: 'Go away, you cuckold – you have married your daughter to a Musalli'. Because they are afraid of other peoples' spite [*ta'na*], they don't intermarry with those Musallis."

Nevertheless, the above *Fig. 3,45* shows 46.9% exogamous marriages among the Farsi-speaking Musallis, contracted with the following groups: rice mill workers, Kohistanis (i.e. from the upper Alingar or Alishang valleys), the Pashto-speaking Musallis, and Tarra Khēl (a nomadic Pashtun group spending winters in Laghman; see Ferdinand (1978)). In 9 cases the Musallis have given away girls and in 12 cases received girls. Hence, these figures reveal no general pattern of inferiority/superiority relations in the exogamous marriages. Nevertheless, the above obser-

3,46 Musallis settled in Now-i Naqil visited by relatives from Dand, Laghman. The Dand-relatives had applied for land, too, and were in the process of being allocated land plots (Now-i Naqil, Nov. 1976).

vation, that "only orphans will marry a Musalli", was confirmed in the sense, that those Musallis who intermarried with other groups did so with poor and landless people who had no other prospects in life than a continued struggle for their living.

As described above, the rice mill workers were specialized rural craftsmen like the Musallis, and the two groups increasingly competed for work. Consequently, although Musallis originally ranked below rice mill workers, the status differential between the two began to disappear. The Kohistanis and Tarra Khēls contained many poor households who had little chance of demanding or paying high bride-prices, and for whom marriage with the Musallis might be and acceptable option.

Since the preference was to marry a *qawmi*, the decision to contract marriage with a non-*qawmi* was based on a broader range of considerations. An old woman from the Persian-speaking Musallis, whose daughter married a rice mill worker, expressed her own concerns as follows:

> "We usually intermarry with Musallis, but the fact that the rice mill worker married my daughter was because somebody had praised

3,47 Musalli children in the courtyard of their house (Qala-i Sardar, Laghman, Nov. 1976).

> her to him. I didn't get a single penny [in bride-price] for my daughter. The rice mill worker brought me 6,000 Afs, but I gave it back to him, telling him to spend it on his household. People were laughing at me, saying 'Look at that woman – all day doing *kalpī* and now she refuses to take 6,000 Afs!'[67] ... I didn't really want to give my daughter to that rice mill worker, as I was afraid that she could not cope with the mill work [i.e. assisting her husband]. But then it was her fate, and also because my sister's son praised that man to me ... "

I have no systematic record of bride-prices among the Musallis but was told that bride-prices are normally 2,000-10,000 Afs, which sounds reasonable compared to other communities. In view of the Musallis' poor economic conditions, this is as low as could be expected.

Among the Pashto-speaking Musallis, Anar Gul explained how his two sons got married to a couple of non-Musalli sisters:

> "He [the girls' father] is a poor man, who comes often to visit his two daughters. He gave one of his daughters to one of my sons, and we paid him a bride-price of 10,000 Afs. All of us combined efforts to earn the money and gradually paid him the 10,000 Afs bride-price. After seeing our good behavior towards his daughter, he agreed to give his second daughter to my other son, also for 10,000 Afs. Otherwise, nobody gives two of his daughters to the same family. He was poor like us, and he gave us his daughters. A rich man would never dream of marrying his daughters to us Musallis."

In this case, paying two bride-prices of 10,000 Afs each must have put great economic strain on the family, but then the comparatively high cost also reflects the higher prestige of non-Musalli rather than Musalli wives. This was further illustrated by a case where a Musalli widower, the above-mentioned Ainullah who initiated the *malikī*, wanted to marry one of his relatives' daughters, supposedly for a bride-price of 15,000 Afs, but the father wanted to marry his daughter to a Laghmani peasant, i.e. a non-Musalli. Marrying a "Laghmani", was considered as marrying a superior, and although endogamous marriages were the norm for the Musallis, exogamy carried more status and might in this sense be called "preferential".

Fig. 3,45 from the Persian-speaking Musalli household is a graphic illustration of the people whom the old woman Nurani mentioned, when asked about who constituted her *qawm*. As the diagram indicates, the majority of her *qawmi*s are descendants of two brothers, but since one of these was her maternal grand-father as well as her paternal great-grand-father, most of her *qawmi*s were simultaneously her matrilateral and patrilateral relatives. While her matrilateral and patrilateral relatives were equally represented as *qawmi*s, a number of people were included with whom Nurani was not biologically related. These could be offspring whom a widow/widower had brought along into a second marriage with one of her relatives, or children born from a new spouse after being widowed. A case in point is Nurani's step-brother Ainullah: Nurani's mother died, whereupon her father took a new wife. Some years later, Nurani's father also died, and her step-mother remarried. Nurani's step-mother and her new step-father had a son, Ainullah. Although Nurani and Ainullah were step-siblings, i.e. not biologically related, they were nevertheless *qawmi*s.

In Nurani's list of *qawmi*s no attempt was made to define all Persian-speaking Musallis as relatives. Membership of the *qawm* was defined solely according to a person's kinship with her. In everyday life, the question of obligations and solidarity, however, was more pertinent in relation to one's neighbours and co-villagers than to some distant kinsmen. As described earlier, the Musallis were economically and politically part of their respective Laghman villages, and they took part in the social life of the villages, albeit at an inferior level. One Musalli expressed their sense of belonging to a certain village and solidarity towards their non-Musalli fellow-villagers by noting that, "Their death and living are our death and living". Similarly so, in case of need, the Musallis would borrow money from co-villagers rather than from more well-off relatives. A Musalli explained:

> "My *qawm* is Ali Khel as I live here, although my [real] *qawm* are these 12 families. But we are scattered. My *qawm* is Ali Khel, and I borrow money here. Yes, we [Musallis] do have some unity. When there is an incident or event in the community, we will inform each other, gather in one place and discuss it. [But] what can I borrow from community-people [other Musallis]? A Musalli has no property. Here [in Ali Khel] we can borrow from somebody who has something."

The above statement again reveals the ambiguous meaning of *qawm*. On the one hand, *qawm* refers to the group of known kinsmen, and on the other hand, *qawm* may also mean a local group of people with whom one shares everyday life. In this sense, the Musallis' sense of belonging and loyalty were split, just as their work, social life and marriage were divided between their kin-based *qawm* of Musallis and their village based network in Laghman.

Summary

Like all itinerant communities, the Musallis were dependent upon the larger economic system. In their seasonal migrations, the Musallis followed the agricultural cycle of their employers, the cultivators in Laghman and the Kabul area, to whom they offered their specialized services. Their economy was contingent upon the elaborate division of labour in the settled communities and the high population density of these areas, which provided the clientele for specialized services. This was amply illustrated by the distribution of Musallis in the lower, fertile river-valleys of Laghman and their absence in the higher, thinly populated uplands. Unlike many itinerant communities, however, Musallis were also fully integrated into their respective villages in Laghman, albeit with unequal social, political, and economic relations to the settled community. Hence, their relations to the settled community was characterized by powerlessness and dependency, which was reflected in the Musallis' weak negotiating position in economic matters and their impotence in the face of social abuse. Within the traditional socio-economic organization, this powerlessness was partly countered by paternalistic protection by their patrons, but the breakdown of these structures and traditional systems of rights and obligations left the Musallis exposed in their economic dependency and inferior social and political position.

The Musallis constitute an ethnic minority group of Indian origin. Barth has pointed towards the features of ethnicity and endogamy as prerequisites for intergenerational succession and acculturation in the peripatetic lifestyle (1987). However, the case of the Musallis illustrates how ethnicity, here formulated in terms of *qawm*-membership, is a highly variable and certainly negotiable phenomenon, so that the distinction between ethnicity and occupation may not always be so clear. While the settled community equals occupation (*kesb*) and *qawm*, the Musallis in their struggle for social mobility, strive to disassociate the two. Some of the threshers thus claimed to be members of the dominant Pashtun community, and those settled in Helmand disassociated themselves completely from their former *qawm*-name and occupation.

Endogamy may be another feature in the maintenance of itinerant communities, which Rao has argued is a reflection of the social marginality of such communities (1987). *Qawm*-endogamy is a tradition among both settled and nomadic communities in Afghanistan, but the frequency of endogamy among the Musallis was lower than among many non-itinerant communities in the country. It is thus questionable to single out endogamy as being particularly related to itinerancy. On the other hand, it is arguable whether the comparatively low frequency of endogamous marriages among the Musallis can be seen as part of a conscious strategy for social acceptability or as a reflection of the gradual dissolution of ethnic occupational structures among the poorest strata of society.

The Musallis apparently originate from the Muslim, menial castes of the Indian Subcontinent, be it Chuhras or Changars. As rural professionals, they presumably have never been part of any guild organization as such, although they relate all the legends of religious initiation of the occupation and of protecting *pīr*s typical of guild structures throughout Central and West Asia. In addition, at least one part of the Musalli community were disciples (*murīd*s) of the late *pīr* Shams Tabrizi of Multan. While sacralizing one's occupation by claiming prominent religious origin is common among settled, menial craftsmen (Centlivres 1972), the concept of an "Original Sin" followed by a divine curse as explanation of their present deprived position, may be peculiar to itinerant communities, as pointed out by

Casimir (1987). Despite their migratory lifestyle, the Musallis' close attachment to and integration into the settled communities of Laghman means that they have continued to share the religious folklore associated with the guilds, just like the settled, rural craftsmen.

This association with settled populations raises the following question: To what extent has the Musallis' itinerancy, their seasonal migrations, significantly shaped their lifestyle as compared to that of the settled specialists? While the available information may be insufficient for a conclusive answer, two main responses are possible: on the one hand, in their economic and social relations with the settled population in Laghman, the Musallis did not appear to be any different from the settled specialists of the villages. Their lifestyle, habitation, and problems seemed primarily to be conditioned by their poverty, but not in a way which distinguished them from other poor villagers. On the other hand, their seasonal migrations to Kabul, where they temporarily joined and worked together with fellow-Musallis, defined them as a separate community and were a recurrent reinforcement of *qawmi*-relations as well as of the interconnectedness of occupation and *qawm*. Although the legendary tales of the Musallis', so central to their identity formation vis-à-vis the surrounding society, were framed within the cultural tradition of the urban crafts, their particular importance among the Musallis might be attributable to this recurrent overlapping identity between occupation and *qawm*. Hence, the migratory lifestyle might be essential in the maintenance of Musallis/Shāhi Khēls as a distinct *qawm*, both in legends and at a more mundane level.

NOTES:

[1] See, for example, Wiser (1936).

[2] Musallis were found south of the village of Nimnani in the Alingar valley and south of the town of Alishang in the Alishang valley. Hence, it is in the most fertile and densely populated areas of the river valleys that threshing constituted a specialized occupation, as well as in similar areas around Jalalabad and in the southern part of Kunar valley.

[3] Kabul is located at about 1,800 m above sea level, 800 meters higher than the lower parts of Laghman.

[4] Laghman, according to local legends, owes its name to Lamech or Mehtar Lam, father of Noah, whose ark is said to have rested on the Kund mountains after the deluge. At that time Laghman was occupied by *kāfir*s (infidels), against whom Lamech/Mehtar Lam and his brother fought. While the *kāfir*s suffered a severe defeat, both Lamech and his brother Nur Lam were killed in the fighting. Lamech/Mehtar Lam's tomb has turned into a shrine, *zīyārat*, and so has that of Nur Lam. Sultan Mahmud of Ghazni is believed to have had the place of Mehtar Lam's grave disclosed in a dream, upon which he erected a tomb over the body, and named the country Lamak-an (Adamec 1985: 477, 485). A less flattering legend relating to Laghman is presented in *Amīr* Abdur Rahman's memoirs: "it is generally believed in Kabul that the Devil was thrown into the Valley of Laghman when expelled from Paradise. This is the reason, according to the statement of the Kabulese, why the people of Laghman are so clever in deceiving and taking in other people" (S. M. Khan 1980(1900), I: 247, note).

[5] Of the approximately 25,000 ha of cultivated land in Laghman, a third of the total area, around 95% is irrigated. Virtually all the rainfed areas are located in the northern Nuristan part of the Laghman province (Adamec 1985: 476-500).

[6] *Kāfir* had been the common reference to the original, non-Muslim, Dardic-speaking population of the area.

[7] For comparison, see the outline of the settlement history in neighbouring Kunar, described by Christensen (1980).

[8] According to official Afghan statistics, the average size of landholding is 4.2 *ǰarīb* (approximately 0.8 ha), which can hardly sustain a family.

[9] The hottest months being June-July with mean temperatures ranging from 22.5 C (night) to 38.7 C (day), while January is the coldest month with mean temperatures of 1.1 (night) to 18 C (day). Annual rainfall is 334 mm, of which around 40% falls during March (Dupree 1973: 18). According to Adamec the elevation of the inhabited parts of Laghman ranges between 2,200 and 9,000 feet (approximately 730-3,000 m) (Adamec 1985: 477).

[10] This parallels Barth's material from the Swat valley in North-west Pakistan (Barth 1959, 1962) and Ahmad's (1977) from the Punjab.

[11] For a comparison, see Ahmad's study of the Punjabi village of Sahiwal and his division of the various artisan communities into "agricultural *kammis*" and "general *kammis*" and the accompanying dependency relations between the *kammis* and the landowning group. Occupational specialization in Punjab is more developed and the social structure more stratified than in east Afghanistan, but the parallels are obvious. Ahmad also discusses the extent to which the *kammi qawms* can be compared to the Hindu castes (Ahmad 1977).

[12] See also a number of short articles (in Pashto) on Laghman in Nangarhar Magazine (1974-75/AH(Sh) 1353-54)), where Z. Safi describes the crafts of blacksmithing, goldsmithing, soapmaking, potterymaking, carpentry, and leather-work (tanning, shoemaking, and repairing).

[13] Christensen also points to the obvious parallels with the jajmani-system of the Indian Subcontinent.

[14] This group is found in the following locations: Nimnani/Niazi (9 families), Dand (1 family), Aghabad (1 family), Mohammad Khel (2 families), Omarzai (3 families), Khan Qala (3 families), Manjuma (5-6 families), Sangtuda (3 families). In addition, they report about having relatives in Kach-i Aziz Khan, Banda-i Sappo Khel, Kamalpur, Maidani, Sangdar, Sahingar and Qasaba in Laghman, as well as in the Behsud and Surkhrod areas of Nangarhar and in Sheva and Kama areas of the Kunar province.

[15] Presently, this group can be found at least in the following locations: Qala-i Khan, Gulkari, Haiderkhani, Gumain, Chunduk, Diwa/Palwata, Tashkari, Narenj Bagh, Qala-i Mansur Khan, Pul-i Jogi, Bagh-i Mirza, Qala-i Qazi, Karawoo, Mohammadpur, Pashai, Qala-i Sufi, Deh Sharana, Madad Khan, Qala-i Pahlawan, Gonkur, Deh Ziyarat, Bolan, Parman Khel, Qala-i Hamisha Bahar, Logarlam, Maskurah, Ali Khel, Qala-i Sahib, Mandrawar, Chardehi, Qala-i Akhund, Qala-i Sardar, Qala-i Sarwar Khan.

[16] Those Musallis who speak mainly Persian are found around the *Vilāyat* (provincial centre) and from there southwards towards the bridge of Surkhakhan at the "entrance" to Laghman, with the exception of the Dand area, which is Pashto-speaking (observation by my interpreter M. Azim Safi).

[17] Lit. Ethiopians, used in Afghanistan as a reference to black people, and it carries the connotations of "wild" or "barbarian".

[18] *Rak'at*, a section of the daily prayers. *Nafl*, a voluntary act of religion, the observance of which is not prescribed; a work of supererogation. In this context, it entails enlarging the prayer beyond what is directly prescribed.

[19] Shīsh, identical to the biblical Seth, the third son of Adam, to whom it is said that God revealed fifty small portions of scripture (Hughes 1982(1885): 569). Being a prophet, the name of Shīsh is followed by the invocation *Alai-hi 's-salām* 'Peace be upon him!' This phrase is added after the name of any prophet and enlarged upon in various ways after that of Muhammad (Steingass 1973).

[20] Sana, in his article "Le vocabulaire du fait ethnique en Afghanistan" explains *sīyāl* as a counterpart or individual whom one considers as an equal in terms of family or tribe and with whom one consequently may engage in relations of equality (1988: 280). In the specific context here, my interpreter suggested "religiously worthy" as covering the implications of *sīyāl*.

[21] *Khwāja*, title given to patrilineal descendants of Abu Bakr, the first caliph. *Walī* refers to a saint or holy man.

[22] This may refer to the *zīyārat* of "Khowajah Safa" in "Ashokan-o-Arefan" in Kabul, mentioned by Einzmann (1977: 165-6). The tomb consists of a comparatively elaborate structure – albeit without the decorations mentioned by the Musalli informant. There are three versions regarding the origin of "Khowajah Safa": (1) he was a close associate of the Prophet and came as a soldier with the first Muslim armies to Afghanistan; (2) he was a servant in the Islamic army and fell in the battle of Kabul; (3) he was a son of the famous Khowajah Abdullah Ansari (and thus uncle of Ashokan-wa-Arefan) (ibid.).

[23] However, the Musalli was not the only one to provide an improper answer to the Prophet. The story continues with the Prophet asking the same question to the blacksmith: "The blacksmith answered: 'Shit'. Then the Prophet said: 'Let that be your lot for ever'. And ever since the blacksmith's iron stopped rusting into gold, so what he now got was shitty rust".

[24] *Bābā*, used as "father" but also as a title of respect and endearment toward the head of a religious order.

[25] In Northern India, Shams Tabrizi is counted among the so-called *Panj Pīrs*, one of five original saints of Islam. While these would normally be the Prophet, *Ḥaẓrat* Ali, Fatima, Hassan, and Hussain, in India the term *Panj Pīr* usually comprises the leading saints Shah Shams Tabriz of Multan, Baha ud-din Zikariya of Multan, Shah Ruqa-i-Alam *Ḥaẓrat* of Lucknow, *Shaykh* Jalal Makhdum Jahaniyan Jahangasht of Uchcha in Multan, and *Bābā Shaykh* Farīd ud-din Shakkarganj of Pak Patan (Crooke 1978(1896), I: 202-3). However, other *pīrs* may be included, and as Crooke comments it is impossible to find a generally recognized list of saints.

[26] *Ṣāḥib*, in Afghanistan and the Indian Subcontinent, is a title of courtesy equivalent to "Mister" and "Sir".

[27] *Pīlaw*, the national rice dish of Afghanistan.

[28] Villages in the province of Laghman where Shāhi Khēl presently live.

[29] *Ḥaẓrat*, honorific religious title.

[30] Masson states that "north of the town (i.e. Multan) is the magnificent and well-preserved shrine of Shams Tábrēzī, of whose memory the inhabitants are now proud..." (Masson 1974(1842), I: 396).

[31] *Faqīr*, an itinerant dervish (*faqīrī*, the profession of a *faqīr*).

[32] *Sēr*, local measure of weight equal to 7.66 kg.

[33] See note 25.

[34] *Chugak* presumably should be *changak* which is a hook used for guiding elephants.

[35] Denzil Ibbetson wrote the chapter "The Races, Castes, and Tribes of the People" in the *Report on the Census of Punjab* from 1883, which was later published as a separate book (Ibbetson 1974(1916)). Westphal-Hellbusch stresses the quality of this work, which still earns Ibbetson a position as key source and authority in contemporary research on Punjab (Westphal-Hellbusch 1980: 9).

[36] Among the Pashto-speaking Musallis, some of whom claim Pashtun origin, *khēls* are also mentioned, although it has been denied by most people. Here Shahī Khēl is mentioned as the *khēl* of all Laghman Musallis, with other *khēls* being Dargai Khēl, Kabuli Khēl, Natu Khēl (those settled in Helmand) and Mir Ali Khēl. Kabuli Khēl should indicate that the first person to take up the occupation of *muṣallī-tūb* came from Kabul to Laghman, while Dargai Khēl "were those going from door to door, i.e., from place to place (*darga* meaning 'door')". No further details could be obtained, and most Musallis rejected the whole idea of any *khēl*-division.

[37] For. and Pol. Dept. Sec. F, Proceedings. Feb. 1892, Nos. 265-80: No. 3, 6-8 Jan. 1892

[38] As used here, "peasant" may refer to the actual cultivator, who may be a smallholder, sharecropper, or tenant.

[39] Apparently the word is derived from the verb *sipardan* in the sense of something being trodden upon.

[40] According to Steingass (1973) *siwāra* means "sweepings".

[41] Elphinstone, who wrote his famous Account of the Kingdom of Caubul around 1808, remarks that "the use of the flail is unknown for separating the grain from the straw; it is either trodden out by oxen, or forced out by a frame of wood filled with branches, on which a man sits, and is dragged over the straw by cattle. This seems to be the way in Persia, too. It is threshed by being thrown up to the wind with a large shovel" (1972(1839), I: 400).

[42] 1 *sēr* = 7066.0 grams. 1 *kharwār* = 565 kg. Lit. *kharwār* means an ass-load. There are 80 *sērs* in one *kharwār*. These local measures have historically varied between different regions.

[43] *Māsh* is *Phasaeolus radiatur*, a small, round, and green pulse resembling lentils.

[44] *Andākhtan* = to throw. *Chut andāz* = to throw at random.

[45] From the Punjab, Ahmad refers to the "Mussali", who apart from threshing grain, for which he is paid separately, is also employed by each landlord and "keeps the *dera* clean, waits on guests, keeps *hooka* ready, etc." In return for these services, the "Mussali" receives "1 *topa* from each of the landlord's *patti*" (Ahmad 1977: 69).

[46] All Laghman barbers are said to be interrelated.

[47] Hookah (*ḥuqqa* or *chilam*), a cone-shaped pipe with a long, flexible tube by which the smoke is drawn through a vessel of water and thus cooled.

[48] As previously mentioned, Musallis are known to have been in the Kabul area in 1892, where they were engaged in threshing (For. and Pol. Dept. Sec. F, Pros. Feb. 1892, Nos. 265-80: Kabul Agency Diaries: No. 3, 6-8 Jan. 1892.

[49] The leaseholding system called *ijāra* involves a predetermined rent in money or grain paid to the landowner, with the cultivator bearing all the risk. "Die Festpacht ist in den allermeisten F#llen auf das Land stadts#ssiger Grundeigentümer und des Staates beschr#nkt. Absentismus der Grundbesitzer und 'ejara' sind demnach fast stets miteinander verknüpft" (Grötzbach 1972: 217).

[50] The HYV was an important element in the government's attempt to create a Green Revolution. Initially, the price of the required chemical fertilizer was subsidized to encourage the peasants to cultivate the new varieties. Subsequently, however, the price of fertilizer increased, and it is reported that the cultivation of HYV has consequently stagnated as the peasants cannot afford to buy fertilizer.

[51] Ferdinand describes similar trading activities for the Tarra Khēl pastoral nomads, who were eventually out-competed by trucks. (1962: 113).

[52] *Rughan*, Hindi ghee or clarified butter, but also used in a general sense to refer to cooking oil.

[53] Old measure of weight. Elphinstone refers to the "*Maund Khaunee*" of the Kabul area as equal to about eighty pounds (1972(1839), I: 391).

[54] *Gurr* is so cheap that one normally would buy a couple of kilos at a time and not as little as a *paw*, i.e. 441.6 grams.

[55] Writing of Sahiwal, Punjab, Ahmad states that "like the tenants, *kammis* live in rent-free houses provided by the landlords, in return for which they are obligated to contribute *bigar* or free labor on demand . ... The demand for labour may be very brief or lengthy but is usually only for one or two days, and includes at least one free meal. Refusal can have detrimental consequences" (Ahmad 1977: 66).

[56] For a provocative discussion of the social dimensions of religious puritanism and "defensive sexism" associated with the status of women in Afghan society, see Neale, who points out that within the honour-obsessed Afghan society, the poor man has "to eat shame" (Neale 1981).

[57] King Zahir reigned from 1933 until 1973, when he was toppled in a coup d'état staged by his cousin and brother-in-law, the former prime minister Daoud *Khān*, who proclaimed Afghanistan as a Republic and himself as its president. In 1978 President Daoud was killed during the coup d'état carried out by the Peoples' Democratic Party of Afghanistan (PDPA).

[58] The Helmand Valley Project was initiated in 1946 through American assistance. It was an ambitious attempt to rejuvenate the Helmand desert through the construction of two dams; an extensive canal system was to harness the waters from the Helmand and the Arghandab rivers for irrigation purposes. Thousands of landless people and former nomads have over the years been allocated land in the new Helmand settlements. The Helmand Valley Project was far from successful. For many years the settlers suffered from social and technical problems, as well as from increasing soil salinity which resulted in steadily decreasing yields (for a more detailed discussion of the HVP, see, for example, Dupree 1973).

[59] *Zango*, suspended wooden chair to be pulled across a river.

[60] According to *wakīl* Sayid Jan, the land was only given for free in Nad-i Ali, while in other places like in Marja and Nawa the settlers were charged 120,000 Afs for 10-12 *jaribs*, to be paid over 20 years, the first three years being free of instalments.

[61] In this area, the land measures differ from those of the east: 1 *kharwār* = 100 *sēr* = 1,000 *paw*.

[62] The governor knew that the *wakīl* was from Laghman and that the Shāhi Khēls were poorer than the others.

[63] All 50 families used to go to Chardehi near Kabul during the summer.

[64] I have discussed the Saur Revolution and the popular response to it in Olesen (1983 and 1991).

[65] *Khāna dāmād*, a son-in-law (*dāmād*) living with his wife's family.

[66] *Badal* literally means "exchange", and in case of marriages it means, that two families exchange daughters.

[67] *Kalpī*, gleaning the harvested field for additional grain.

CHAPTER IV

THE SHAYKH MOHAMMADI PEDLARS

Introduction

About 150 families of Shaykh Mohammadi pedlars live in Maskurah village, in the Alishang valley of Laghman. They form around half of the population, the remainder are landowners, small peasants, and landless families of mainly Tajik and Pashtun descent. All the Shaykh Mohammadis are related and according to their own accounts of the past they have been itinerant pedlars within and outside the region. Today (1975-76), the majority of Shaykh Mohammadis sell their wares in the villages of Laghman, and undertake seasonal migrations to the Koh-i Daman area north of Kabul where, throughout the summer, they stay in large camps in four locations. Most Shaykh Mohammadi men, and a few women, earn a living by peddling thread, needles, hairpins, and other petty trinkets for a payment in kind. Others sell cloth at weekly markets, and the poorest manufacture winnowing trays for sale. Among the better-off, a few own a bazaar shop in Mehtarlam, the provincial capital of Laghman, and a few other well-to-do Shaykh Mohammadis have settled as shopkeepers in the city of Jalalabad, about sixty kilometres from Maskurah, but have maintained close contact with the families there.

Research was carried out among the Shaykh Mohammadi of Maskurah, although there are several other occupationally specialized communities which also call themselves Shaykh Mohammadi. These include cotton codders (*nadāf*), riveters of china ware (*patragar*), and religious mendicants (*malang/faqīr*), as well as a number of wealthy cloth traders in the Siyahsang quarter of Kabul.[1] These groups are apparently unrelated, and even though they may not recognize each others' claim to be "real" Shaykh Mohammadis, they share an eponymous ancestor, *Shaykh Ruhānī Bābā*, and replicate the legendary tales about him. Moreover, they agree that knowledge of a special language, *Ādūrgari*, is a defining criteria for being a Shaykh Mohammadi.

As with the Musallis, Shaykh Mohammadis' oral accounts constitute the only information on their past. While their tales of the miraculous powers of *Shaykh Ruhānī Bābā* and of the *pīr* of petty traders have mythical components, they nevertheless offer some evidence as to the origin and development of this group. Many questions remain unanswered, of course, but the picture emerges of a spiritual community, originally constituted by unrelated disciples of the pious *Shaykh Ruhānī Bābā*.

In this chapter, we shall first examine the mythical and historical origins of the Shaykh Mohammadis. This will be followed by an account of the trading activities of the Maskurah Shaykh Mohammadis during the past century. It will be shown that by exploiting price differences on various products between the regions of Kohistan, Kafiristan, and Laghman, the Shaykh Mohammadis' trade and migration activities continuously adapted to the expanding road and transport network. Ironically, improvements in transport have made regional trading beyond the economic capability of most Shaykh Mohammadis, and for many pedlars their livelihood consists of a combination of barter and trading based on price fluctuations between adjacent areas in the Koh-i Daman market. Adaptability and flexibility have been typical of this type of trading during the last 100 years, and are also seen from the seasonal and individual changes in trade activities during the year. The seasonal character of their trading means that the summer's earnings are exhausted during winter, such that many Shaykh Mohammadis are at the mercy of moneylenders each spring, before trade activities resume.

The latter part of this chapter describes the internal social organization of the Shaykh Mohammadis, including household composition and marriage patterns. In this context, it will be shown how the Maskurah Shaykh Mohammadis, originally defined by their membership in an open spiritual fraternity, have over the years apparently developed into a closed, kinship-based community.

Conflicts and group solidarity are prominent features of the Shaykh Mohammadis' everyday life, both internally and in their encounters with other groups. An important factor in the Shaykh Mohammadis' relations with outsiders is their numerical strength. This has had a bearing as well upon their integration in the political structures of Laghman. These issues will be discussed at the end of this chapter, when the Shaykh Mohammadis will be compared to other itinerant and settled communities in the region.

Mythical and Historical Origins

Shaykh Mohammadi communities are found all over northern and eastern Afghanistan.[2] According to their own estimate, there may be a total of some 10,000 Shaykh Mohammadis in the country, with the highest concentration in the Siyahsang and Kote Sangi zones of Kabul.[3] While the name of Shaykh Mohammadi covers a number of diversified and unrelated communities, the respective legends about their common eponymous ancestor, *Shaykh Ruhānī Bābā* add pieces to the same overall picture: the Shaykh Mohammadis seem to have originated as a spiritual brotherhood constituted by the followers of a *pīr*, *Shaykh Ruhānī Bābā*, which gradually evolved into several separate but internally kinship-based Shaykh Mohammadi communities. We can obtain one account of their origins from tales related to me by three different Shaykh Mohammadi groups: the pedlars in Maskurah, a family of rich and settled cloth traders in Siyahsang (Kabul), and an itinerant riveter of chinaware in Jalalabad.[4]

The account begins as follows: At the time of Nasruddin 3-400 years ago, *Shaykh Ruhānī Bābā* lived in East Afghanistan. The *shaykh* was companion (*mujāwir*) to a holy man.[5] Apart from being a descendant of the Prophet (*sayyid*), the *shaykh* was also a religious mendicant (*malang/faqīr*), with his own special powers.[6] The following story is told to illustrate why

4,1 Maskurah village in the Alishang valley.

he was considered a *ruhānī* (a "spiritual" person):

"He was called *Ruhānī* because one day, the day of a market [in some versions it is referred to as the *ḥajj* or pilgrimage to Mecca], while other people rode on horses, he asked his father to fetch him a donkey. But his father told him, 'I am a poor man; where would I find a donkey?' So the *shaykh* simply mounted a wall and went away on that. When he came back to his home, his father told him, 'You have disgraced me, go away.'

"His abode was Pishin, near Kandahar and around Quetta and Chaman. From there he went to Zurmat in the *Junubi* province He was doing *shaykhī* [i.e. acting as a dervish] and was worshipping God. The people [in Zurmat] called him *Shaykh Ruhānī Bābā*.

"He asked those people in Zurmat to pay him homage [*shukrāna*]. The people told him, 'First you shall show your greatness, then we will pay you homage.' The *Shaykh* said, 'What do you wish?' They told him that they had no water, and that they would like water to flow as they were digging a *kārīz* [underground water-channel]. The *Shaykh* prayed to God,

4,2 View over the roof tops in Maskurah.

and wherever those people went to dig a *kārīz*, the water flowed. Now the court of *Shaykh Ruhānī Bābā* is as high as that of *Sakhi Shāh-i Mardān* [lit. the king of men, i.e. *Ḥaẓrat-i* Ali]. His tomb is in Gardez."

The special powers of *Shaykh Ruhānī Bābā* were passed on to his descendants, as illustrated by a riveter's account of one Mira Shah Laghar:

"At the time of some king, all the people calling themselves *sayyid* were assembled [presumably by the ruler] and sent to Mecca to prove their identity. In Mecca, there was the tomb of somebody, I have forgotten his name. They were asking all the people calling themselves *sayyid* to [go to the tomb and] shout the name of the person buried there. They were told that all those who got a response were true *sayyids*. Many people went there and called out without getting any reply from the tomb. But one Shaykh Mohammadi, Mira Shah Laghar, uttered the name of that person buried there, and got a reply from the tomb, 'Yes, Sir'. In the beginning people would not even give him a chance to call, as he was walking only with a piece of cloth wrapped around him. He was almost naked,

1,3 Shaykh Mohammadis in the Ghulam Ali summer camp (Oct. 1976).

but he proved himself the true *sayyid*, and hence, the Shaykh Mohammadis are the true *sayyids*."

All of *Shaykh Ruhānī Bābā*'s descendants are supposed to enjoy his protection, and the riveter of china ware relates his own dramatic experience of this:

"Once I was buying a tin of snuff, but bargained over the price. ... There was an argument, followed by a quarrel. The *ḥākim* ™locally elected leader® of the place was either a relative or a friend of the seller, so they tied my hands with my turban and others attacked me. My waistcoat was lost and with it 700 or 800 Afs and a small bottle of diamonds for cutting glass. So they took me to the *ḥākim* and said that I was a pickpocket. Then I prayed to *Shaykh Ruhānī Sāhib*: 'If there is any holiness in you, you should save me from this disgrace.' A *sayyid* had arrived to that place and was the guest of the *ḥākim*. They called him *Pāchā Sāhib*, and he himself had an important position. When they told him that I was a pickpocket, *Pāchā Sāhib* asked who I was by *qawm*? I told him that I was a Shaykh Mohammadi and not a thief. He said:

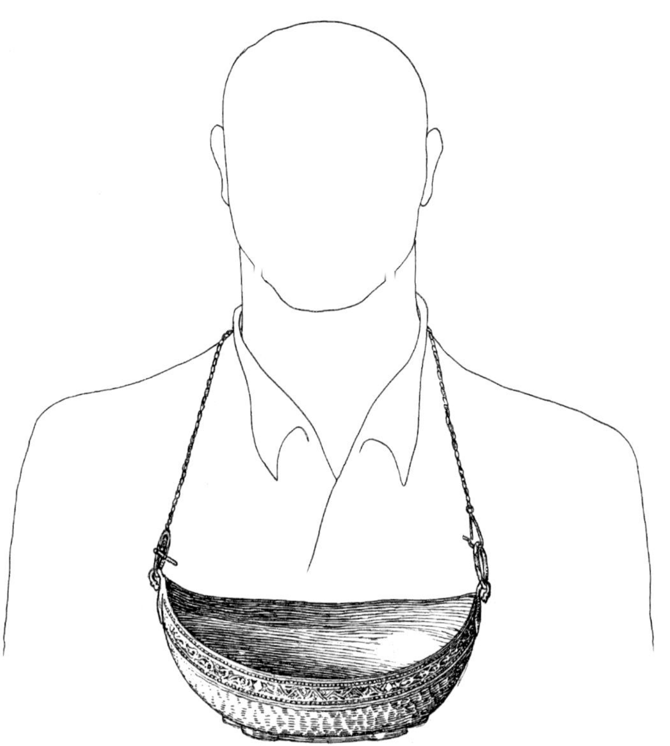

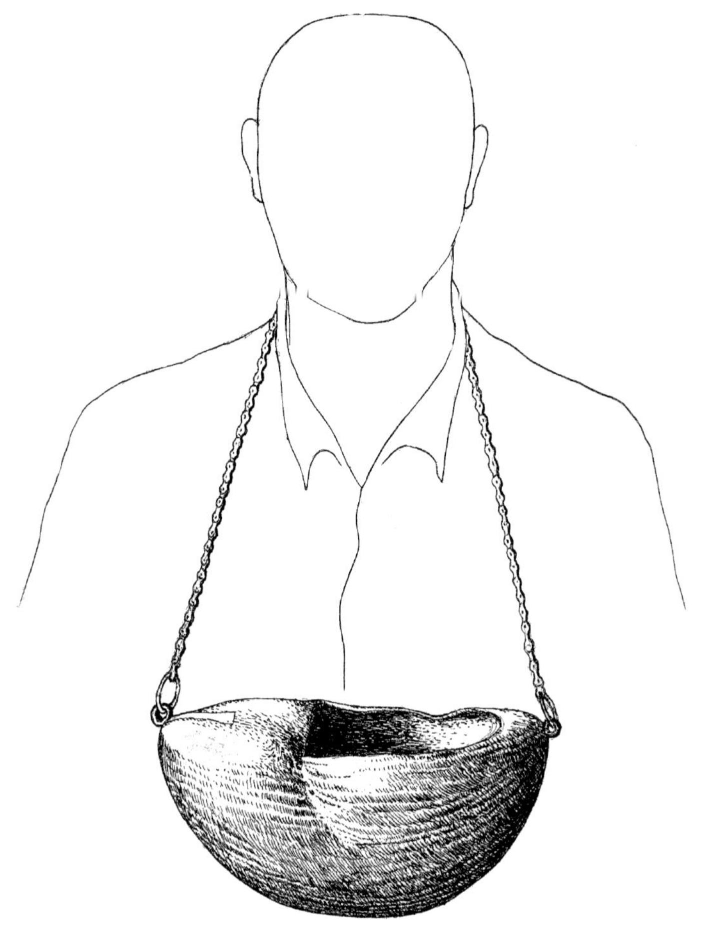

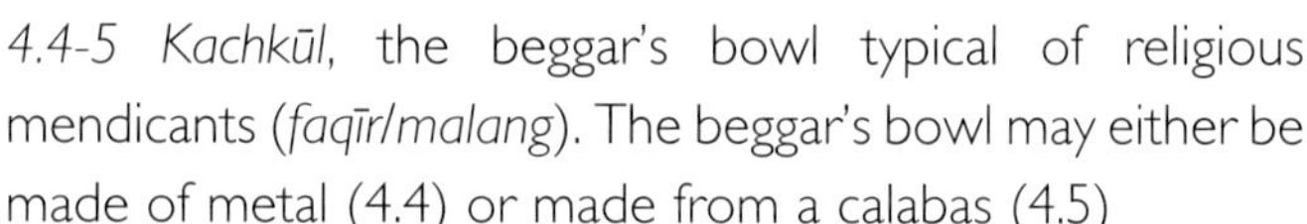

4.4-5 Kachkūl, the beggar's bowl typical of religious mendicants (*faqīr/malang*). The beggar's bowl may either be made of metal (4.4) or made from a calabas (4.5)

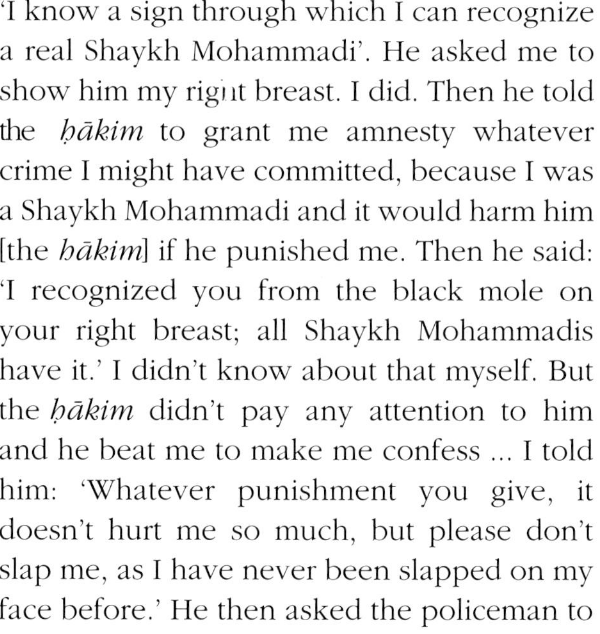

'I know a sign through which I can recognize a real Shaykh Mohammadi'. He asked me to show him my right breast. I did. Then he told the *ḥākim* to grant me amnesty whatever crime I might have committed, because I was a Shaykh Mohammadi and it would harm him [the *ḥākim*] if he punished me. Then he said: 'I recognized you from the black mole on your right breast; all Shaykh Mohammadis have it.' I didn't know about that myself. But the *ḥākim* didn't pay any attention to him and he beat me to make me confess ... I told him: 'Whatever punishment you give, it doesn't hurt me so much, but please don't slap me, as I have never been slapped on my face before.' He then asked the policeman to slap me on the face, but as the policeman stretched out his hand to slap my face, I shouted 'Yā, *Pīr*!' at which the policeman's hand broke at the joint! Then the *Pāchā Sāhib* kicked the poli ceman in the arse and started cursing the *ḥākim*, telling him: 'Didn't I tell you beforehand not to beat this man!'"[7]

The Maskurah Shaykh Mohammadis go even a step further, hinting that descendants of *Shaykh Ruhānī Bābā* are not only blessed by his protection but that they themselves have inherited some of his special powers. Their statements in this regard are ambiguous, as they also joke about it, implying that they do not believe in these special powers themselves. Yet as long as

4.6 In the Kandahar bazaar the cotton codder or 'fluffer' re-fluffs the cotton stuffing inside quilts, matresses, and cushions (Photo: Klaus Ferdinand).

others believe in them, they will actually work. I was told the following three stories, which on the one hand illustrate the Shaykh Mohammadis' reservations, but also their recognition of the strength of other people's faith in them:

> "We are called *Badmār*, too, and *Chahārtagān* ['the four *Tag*', a *Tag* being a charlatan]. For example, I may consecrate some soil and give it to a man telling him that it has the blessing of the King of Saints. Well, I have never seen the King of Saints myself!"
>
> "So you see, we are a blessed people. And when we go to Wardak, they say, 'Oh, may I die for you', and we take threads out of our mouth and tie the horns of their cows with it. If the cow is sick, it will soon recover. If it is barren, and they believe in us, then it will bear calves. And if I do that, and if God doesn't give him children, then I will slaughter myself. By the will of God and the blessing of that ancestor of ours."

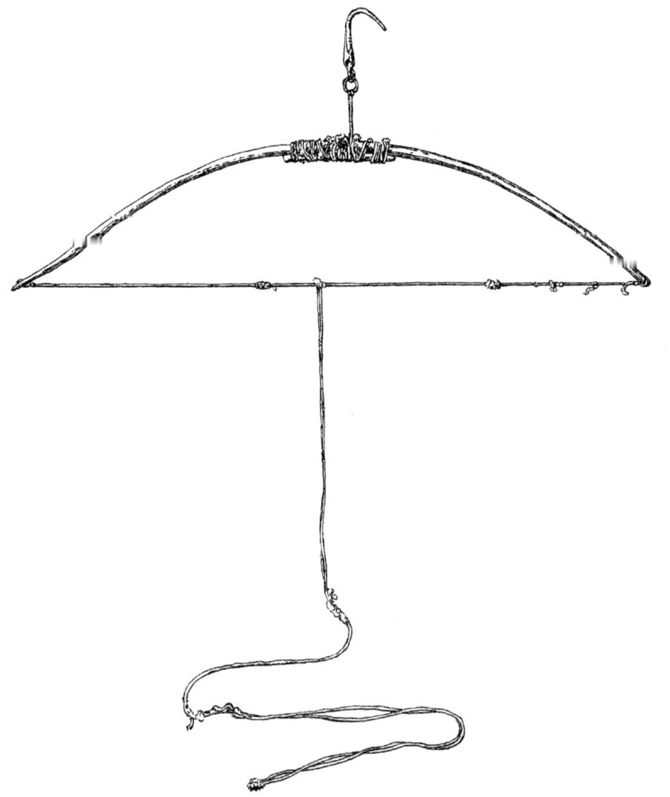

4,7 The wooden bow across which a string is strung. The bow is hung at a beam or from the ceiling; its function is to suspend the main instrument (*Fig. 4,8*) just above the floor by means of a line of raw-hide

"Some years ago, somebody came to Gul Agha [a Shaykh Mohammadi] and asked about his help in curing a disease. Gul Agha just ridiculed him, telling him to bring a rope and a pitcher. He made a hole in the bottom of the pitcher, put the rope through it and asked him to carry it around his neck every day for a week. The old man did so and was cured after a week! So people find we are holy people like the *sayyid.*"

Shaykh Ruhānī Bābā's descendants split up into various sections, although nobody knows when or how it happened. It is unanimously recognized that the true descendants of the *Shaykh* are the *Faqīrs*, who continued his profession as religious mendicants with the *kachkūl* of *malangi* (beggar's bowl, typical of the wandering medicants) hanging on their shoulder and who took up *tawafi*, which is the selling of Greek medicine. The various Shaykh Mohammadi groups also readily admit, that the Shaykh Mohammadis have been joined by many outsiders, which on the other hand also results in a

4,8 The *kamān* is more than 2 m long. Stretched between the board and the top of the pole is a single strand of raw-hide. The wooden mallet is used to strike the string, causing it to vibrate, and thus stretch the cotton.

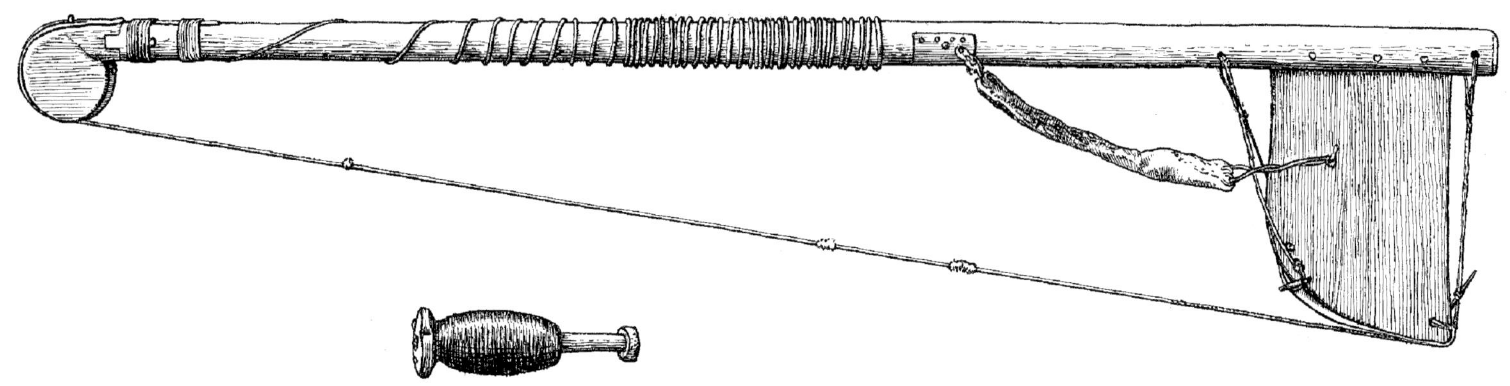

4,9 The *Nadāf*, the cotton codder squats at the floor, holding the *kamān* with one hand so that the string barely touches the pile of cotton. The *kamān* is hung about 40 cm above the floor. Holding the mallet in his right hand, the cotton codder strikes the string of the *kamān*. The vibrations fluff up and stretch the cotton

general disagreement about whose claim to be Shaykh Mohammadi is real or fake.[8]

The Shaykh Mohammadis of Maskurah are convinced that *Shaykh Ruhānī Bābā*'s descendants split into at least three groups, the Balatumani, the Tela Khēl, and the Faqir. They claim that they themselves belong to the so-called Balatumani, a word which is said to mean either "those living above" (*bālā*) or "those above twenty."[9] People who want to curse the Maskurah Shaykh Mohammadis, call them *Siyāhpāyak*, meaning "those with black feet." The Maskurah Shaykh Mohammadis also indicate that the group known as Tela Khēl (*telā* meaning "gold") is superior to the others, apparently because they are descendants of an elder brother, although this is not unanimously recognized.

Cloth traders in Siyahsang argued that, apart from the Faqirs, the Shaykh Mohammadi consisted of the following eight sub-groups: (1) the Tela Khēl, which had incorporated outsiders like the Zaku Khēl of Kandahar and the Jajis; (2) the Nadaf Khēl, located in Kote Sangi and Mandrawar of Laghman; (3) the Maskurahi Balatumanis so called because their ancestors came from Kohistan, i.e. from "up (*bālā*) the mountains"; (4) the Babar Khēl; (5) the Charbaghis, who are Zaku Khēls, coming from the village of Charbagh in Laghman; (6) the Kolukhi; (7) the Karang; (8) the Buzak. These names refer in two cases to a locality, in one case to an occupation, and the remainder to physical appearance, like *bābār*, meaning "fuzzy" or "mangy". Nadaf Khēl, however, is not the name of a group of professional cotton codders (*nadāf*), but refers to shopkeepers and cloth-sellers, while the Tela Khēls are cotton codders. The names are said to have been given to the Shaykh Mohammadi groups by *Sayyid* Mir Ali Shah of Laghar, Shamsapur.[10] He was apparently

4,10 An itinerant *patragar* with his equipment in the bazaar of Diwanqol, Behsud area, Central Afghanistan (Photo: Klaus Ferdinand, Aug. 1954).

4.11-18

The equipment of the riveter of china ware, the *patragar*

4.11 A teapot repaired by a riveter. In the broken pieces of china, the riveter drills tiny holes by use of the bow-drill which is fitted with a diamond point (*4.12*). Through these holes, small metal staples (*4.13*) are inserted to keep the pieces in place. The spout of the teapot has been repaired with a metal top, and the pot itself has been reinforced by metal rings at top and bottom between which a number of metal "ribbons" are suspended, including a ribbon to hold the spout in place

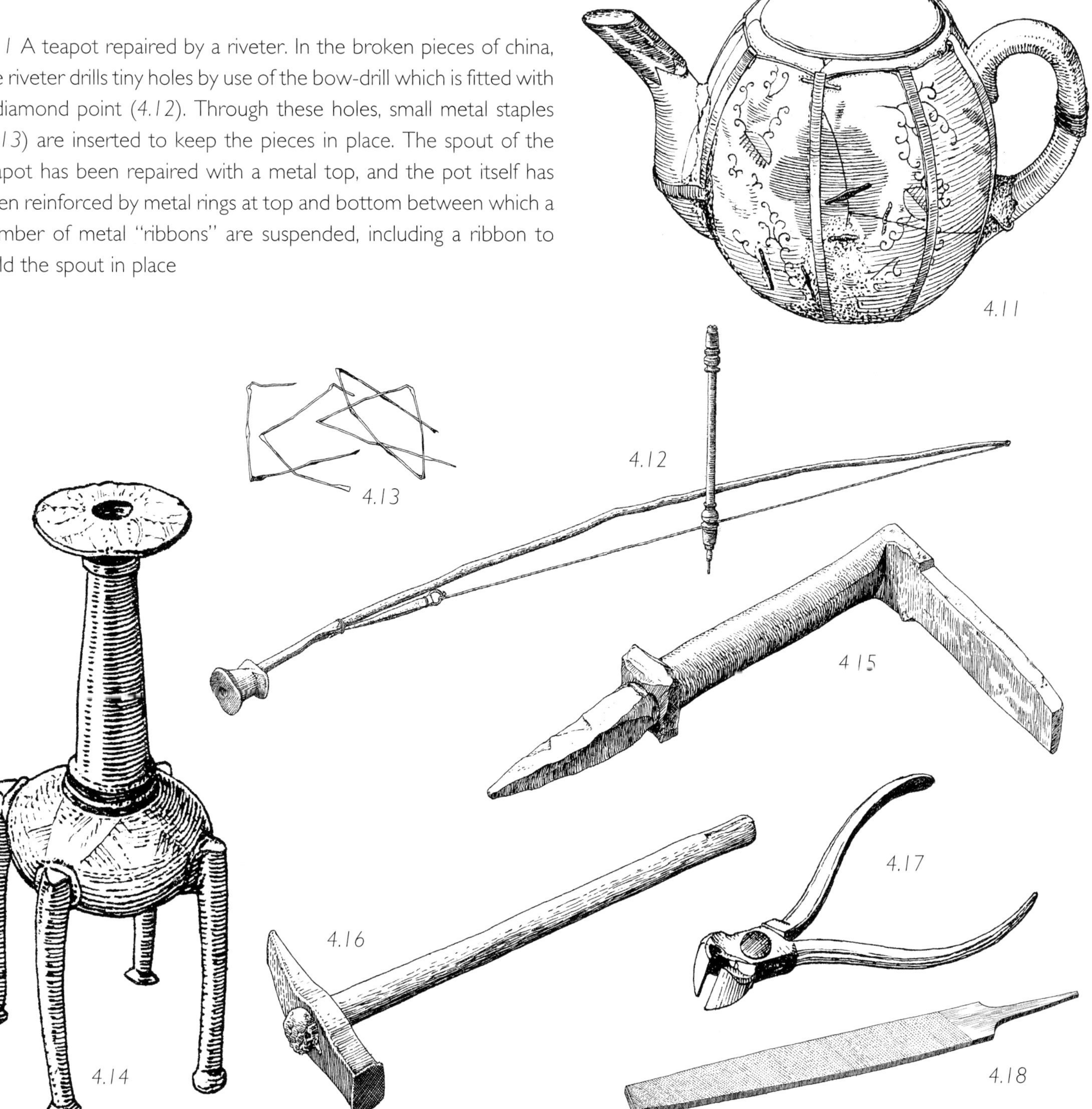

4.14-18 The rest of the riveter's equipment: A small brass burner (Fig. 4.14) for heating the staples and small metal pieces used in the work of repair . An anvil (*Fig. 4.15*), a hammer (*Fig. 4.16*), a pair of tweezers (*Fig. 4.17*), and a file (*Fig. 4.18*)

their *pīr*, collecting tribute among them. The wealthy cloth trader in Siyahsang, *Ḥajjī* Nabi Jan explained to me that:

> "When they [the *sayyid* and his company] went to Babar Khēl, they were reapers. They had very long hair, so the *sayyid* called them Babar Khēl."

And Ḥajjī Nabi Jan's son told:

> "When they [the *sayyid* and his company] came to our village in Laghman, the people were reapers and had built some huts from mud, which looked like a lump of earth [*kolukh*]. So they called them Kolukhis. ... But when they came to the real Shaykh Mohammadis, they had their medicine and good clothes on, so they called them Faqirs. In that way, the Shaykh Mohammadi *qawms* became about twenty-five."

Shamsapur apparently has been the traditional centre of the Shaykh Mohammadis' *pīrs*. A riveter of chinaware from Siyahsang of Kabul relates that descendants of their *pīr*, *Sayyid* Jafar Agha, who is buried in Shamsapur, come twice a year to collect tribute from them. Presumably, the above *Sayyid* Mira/Mir Ali Shah was spiritual successor to *Shaykh Ruhānī Bābā* and *Sayyid* Jafar Agha, a more recent descendant and successor. While the Shaykh Mohammadis in Siyahsang, who are rich cloth traders or riveters of china ware, apparently still pay tribute to the *pīrs* of Shamsapur, the Maskurah Shaykh Mohammadis did not mention any such connection in 1976.

The scattered and diversified character of *Shaykh Ruhānī Bābā*'s descendants is explained by reference to the *Shaykh* cursing his sons for their disobedience:

> "Then he had children. His sons became villains, gamblers, deviants. So he cursed them all and said: 'May you never be together'. So they dispersed and went on dispersing in many places."

Unlike what is the case among many other low-status groups, the curse occupies no prominent position in these origin myths. As illustrated above, the Shaykh Mohammadis consider themselves a blessed rather than a cursed people. The original curse may serve to render the diversification of the Shaykh Mohammadis understandable to themselves, although they readily offer more historical and matter-of-fact explanations; i.e. that the diversification is the result of a political situation in which many different people saw their benefit in claiming to be Shaykh Mohammadis. One explained to me that:

> "During the reign of *Amīr* Abdur Rahman [1880-1901] there was a Karim *Khān* of Jabar Khēl, who was the *khān* of Kach [Laghman], and who levied taxes on the people. He exempted the descendants of *Shaykh Ruhānī Bābā* when they came to him with their beggar's bowl on the shoulder, as religious mendicants [*faqīrs*]. When that happened, you became a Shaykh Mohammadi and I became a Shaykh Mohammadi, because they were exempted from the tax. Some of them were runaways from Farajghan in Kohistan, some came from Mangal, some from Wardak, and some from Kandahar. When these Kohistanis and others came, they spoke this language, *Ādūrgari*, among themselves and the Shaykh Mohammadis learned it. This language is a

mixture of twenty languages – Kohistani, Nuristani, and others – so they stole [words] from everybody. With the increase in number, noisy and brash [*qawālī*] behavior spread among the Shaykh Mohammadis."

It is said that none of the *Shaykh*'s sons left any offspring, and that only his daughter remained, so it was to her that all the 'runaways, outlaws, thieves and bastards' turned, in order to be exempted from tribute (by being recognized as followers of *Shaykh Ruhānī Bābā*).

Unfortunately, I have not collected any material on the *Ādūrgari* language. The Maskurah Shaykh Mohammadis claim that it sets them apart as Shaykh Mohammadis. It appeared to be used as a defining criterion, since it was only when we spoke this language that the wealthy cloth trader, Ḥajjī Nabi Jan allowed us into his home in Siyahsang. Among the Maskurah Shaykh Mohammadis, *Ādūrgari* is used only as a trading language. Until the age of six to seven, children speak Persian, after which they are taught *Ādūrgari*, which is used "when strangers shall be prevented from understanding what we talk about", as an old man explained. Secret trade language is a well-known phenomenon in this part of the world, but *Ādūrgari* is apparently more than a trade language. It seems to be an argot associated with all Shaykh Mohammadis irrespectively of their occupation and origin.

Today, Shaykh Mohammadis may be engaged in various occupations such as trade (from small-scale peddling to export-import), cotton codding, riveting china ware, and *faqīrī*, but it appears that the selling of petty trinkets, *banjaragī*, has a long history among various groups of Shaykh Mohammadis. The abovementioned riveter of chinaware, for example, was also born into a *banjaragar*-family, and learned the profession of riveting in a dream. The Maskurahi refer to *banjaragī* or *sawdāgari* as their original occupation, as do the Siyahsang cloth traders, although they changed to cloth trade during the time of King Amanullah (1919-29) and ultimately became shop-owners. While the profession of *faqīrī*, being religious mendicant, is inherited from *Shaykh Ruhānī Bābā*, peddling holds a special position, since the first to engage in this occupation was *Khwāja Tār-i Walī*, who according to some descended from *Shaykh Ruhānī Bābā*, although others refer to him as the *pīr* of the peddling only:

> "When the world was created and the various professions, too, *Khwāja Tār-i Walī* was the first to engage in this business.[11] So this profession has existed from the time the prophets were doing it, and *Khwāja Tār-i Walī* has put his hand into the sack. You see, the sack [in which the pedlars carry their merchandise around in the villages] which contains needles and threads is not light, it is heavy. When they [the Shaykh Mohammadi pedlars] take it out of the their houses, they are carrying small portable loads; but when they return, they shuffle along under the heavy weight [of barter goods]. *Khwāja Tār-i Walī* has put his hand into the sack, so it will never be light. It will always be heavy, and so that one *paw* in it will bring forth four *sērs*".[12]

Another reference to peddling as their traditional occupation comes from a story about "Mir *Ḥajjī* Shah *Ṣāḥib* [presumably the above Mir Ali Shah of Laghar], who gave the Shaykh Mohammadi pedlars the name of *ādūrgar*" (*ādūr* being the term used by them about their peddling activities, and *Ādūrgari* the name of the Shaykh Mohammadis' "secret" language).[13]

To sum up, it appears that there exist no kinship connections between the various Shaykh Mohammadi communities, and in most cases no genealogical connection between them and *Shaykh Ruhānī Bābā*, either. There is nothing unusual in an ethnic group or community being joined by outsiders, but the scale at which this has occurred among the Shaykh Mohammadi seems extraordinary. It is also unusual that the inclusion of outsiders is not subsequently glossed over by kinship mythology. Compared to the general occupational specialization along ethnic or community (*qawm*) lines in East Afghanistan, it is also noteworthy, that although Shaykh Mohammadis have typically had diverse occupations such as religious mendicants (*faqīri/malangi*), cotton codders (*nadāfi*), riveters of chinaware (*patragari*), and petty traders (*sawdāgari/banǰaragī*), there does not appear to be any connection between the subdivisions of the Shaykh Mohammadis, their names, and their occupations. Nor have I encountered myths explaining how specific groups obtained their occupations. Only *Khwāja Tār-i Walī*, the *pīr* of peddling petty things is comparable to the other mythological *pīrs* of various artisan communities, while *Shaykh Ruhānī Bābā*'s position is based neither on occupational nor genealogical relations.

The question of the historical origin of those who consider themselves Shaykh Mohammadis thus remains open. One possible hypothesis, which appeared only after I had left Afghanistan and thus could not be tested empirically, is to consider the "Shaykh Mohammadis" as simply a spiritual community. *Shaykh Ruhānī Bābā* had been a Sufi *pīr* who attracted devotees (*murīds* and *mukhliṣ*) from various communities, and those who today call themselves Shaykh Mohammadis are the descendants of these devotees, albeit, perhaps, with a core of his biological descendants, i.e. those of Faqir descent.[14] A spiritual origin would explain the absence of relations between the groups, in spite of their shared heritage of myths related to the *Shaykh*. Today, some if not all Shaykh Mohammadi groups are devotees of the Shamsapur *pīrs*, whom we may assume to be the heirs to *Shaykh Ruhānī Bābā*'s spiritual legacy. The picture which emerges is that *Shaykh Ruhānī Bābā* was a "maraboutic" *pīr*, and his followers were devoted to him at a collective level, implying that the individual devotee, *mukhliṣ*, did not have to actively partake in the devotions of the order (*ṭarīqāt*) (Roy 1985: 57-8). Rather, the *pīr* performed religious practices on behalf of his followers, who benefitted from his special powers via blessings, cures of diseases, miraculous deeds, etc. The followers of such maraboutic *pīrs* prove their devotion to him through annual visits and offerings, just as the Shamsapur *pīrs* today; in return, the *pīr* provides hospitality and protection to his adherents. This type of maraboutic Sufism flourished in East-Afghanistan during the 19th and beginning of the 20th century (Olesen 1994).

What is particularly interesting in connection with *Shaykh Ruhānī Bābā* is the fact that membership in his spiritual fraternity became the most significant marker of identity, overshadowing other primordial loyalties and affiliations. The Shaykh Mohammadis explain that it were "the outlaws and runaways" who became devotees, and this, perhaps explains why they sought membership in the spiritual community.

The Trade of the Past[15]

The Maskurah Shaykh Mohammadis have experienced a considerable change in their trade activities since "the time of the grandfathers," or

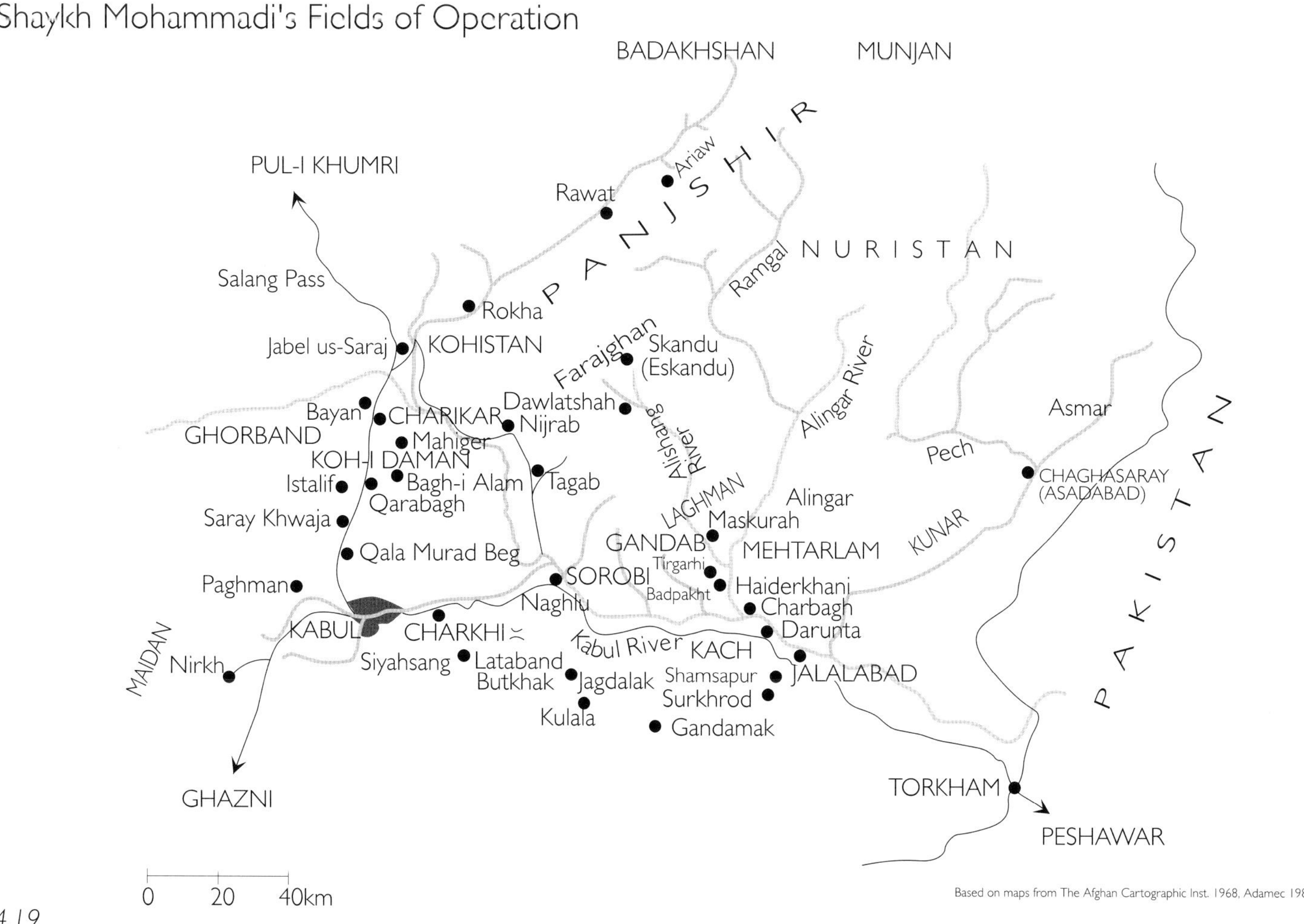

4,19

he reported barter trade still common in the Waigal valley (1974: 27). In fact, this type of trade has been widespread all over the country, as also Ferdinand (1962) describes in Central Afghanistan, where it was mediated by pastoral nomads. With the expanding road network and communication, the marketing of goods was gradually taken over by small, local bazaars in most parts of the country, which were regularly supplied by trucks from the larger trade centres. Hence, the shopkeeper replaced the pedlar in most areas.

In the mountainous areas of Nuristan this change has come relatively recently. In his *Historical and Political Gazetteer of Afghanistan*, based on 19th century British-Indian sources, Adamec provides the following description of the situation in Kafiristan at that time:

> "The main roads of communication, if roads they can be called, are almost invariably along the river banks, so narrow and so steep are the valleys. Although they vary very greatly, the one from the other, they have this quality in common, that they are almost always extremely difficult. [Apart from the Bashgul valley above Chabu and nearly the whole of Presungul] ... all other known Kafiristan roads

are simply abominable ... .The bridges over the rivers are sometimes extremely well built, but are high above the water, and often not more than 18 or 20 inches wide in the middle, with parapets only a few inches high, so that the whole structure looks far more like an irrigation trough than a bridge. If this is the case with the good bridges, it may easily be conceived how extremely bad the inferior ones are. ... No horses can be used in any known part of Kafiristan, except in the upper Bashgul and the Presungul valleys" (1985: 346-7).

After the conquest of Kafiristan in 1896, the Afghan government attached much importance to the construction of roads into the area. Three main roads were built, connecting Badakhshan with the Kunar and Laghman valleys through Kafiristan (Chaghasaray to Munjan, Asmar to Badakhshan, and Laghman to Munjan). These roads were usable for loaded ponies, horses, and mules (Kakar 1971: 205). However, even up to the middle of this century, Nuristan remained relatively inaccessible. In recent years, the roads have been widened so that trucks may reach some of the villages, with the result that the pedlars in these areas have been unable to survive as small-scale middlemen. Just as the Musallis had to renounce their transport work with oxen, the Shaykh Mohammadis have had to give up part of their trade activities as being unprofitable. An old Shaykh Mohammadi pedlar describes the situation thus:

"I would buy a lot of rice, 8 *sēr* for 24 Afs. I would buy it in Laghman ... and then I would carry it all the way through Gandab, Badpusht, Naghlu, Tagab ... We would sell it in Jamalagha, all of it for 32 Afs ... In the past, we used to go to Panjshir each year, but certainly not any more. Now one *sēr* of rice costs 100 Afs in Laghman itself, so why should I take it there?"

Even today, however, in many parts of Kohistan and Nuristan, roads have not yet been constructed. Around 1970, the road was extended to Dawlatshah, but from Dawlatshah to Farajghan, there is still no road, and by foot the distance takes 1-2 days. Traders of Alishang have now established shops or rented rooms in Dawlatshah bazaar, where they store the products they have bought higher up in the valley, and later on bring it for sale to Kabul by truck. Beyond Dawlatshah, goods have to be borne on the back, as even a donkey cannot pass on the paths. However, most of the trade, it is told, goes from Panjshir, Ghorband into Nuristan, although there is no road here either.

Today, when the Shaykh Mohammadis go to Farajghan, they will sell their goods for cash or for pine nuts and cumin. These products will be stored in the respective villages, while they proceed further on their sales trip, *ādūr*. On the way back to Maskurah, they will either rent a donkey and transport the products, or they will hire someone to deliver them in Maskurah. When the pedlar returns home, he checks the amounts delivered, and this is why he does not send the products to Maskurah until he himself is on his way back. Otherwise, his family in Maskurah would not be able to control that the correct amounts have been delivered.

Pine nuts are still an important trade item in Nuristan, but as an export item (for example to India) subject to price fluctuation, pine nut trading may result in either great losses or gains for the trader. A Shaykh Mohammadi, who four years earlier had bought pine nuts in Nuristan for 80 Afs per *sēr* told me that on his return to the provincial capital, pine nuts were bought up by commissioners for the export traders at a rate of 350 Afs per *sēr*. His partner expected the price to rise even further and did not want to sell until it had reached 400 Afs per *sēr*. In a few hours, however, the price dropped to 300 Afs per *sēr*, and then they sold their load; they were fortunate, for the price soon fell to 80 Afs per *sēr*.

Not only do Shaykh Mohammadis trade in Nuristan, but also other Laghmanis. They sell cloth, which fetch double the price in Nuristan as compared to the central parts of Laghman, in exchange for animals such as goats. The animals are brought back to the provincial capital of Laghman and sold there. Such trips often last a couple of months, but "the Shaykh Mohammadis don't have the patience for such *ādūr*", as they explained themselves.

A Shaykh Mohammadi pedlar who recently had traded in Farajghan maintained that in spite of the improved infrastructure, the subsequent sharp competition from other traders, and the generally lower profit rate, the Shaykh Mohammadis' total earnings from trade in that region have remained more or less constant. The reason, he pointed out, was, that the demand in those areas had increased; not only had the population increased, but so had peoples' expenses: "Now they make new clothes every day", he said. Cloth trade is what pays the best, and he would travel with goods worth 20,000 Afs and make a profit of 2,000 Afs, while he would earn only half that amount in the provincial capital of Laghman. However, in others' opinion, improved infrastructure has made trade in Nuristan more dangerous. "Earlier, those people felt besieged by everyone around them, and if they robbed one of us, they would be beaten when they came to Laghman. But now, they can just get in a car and go all the way to Kabul", he explained.

Abdul Ghani, a middle-aged man, told of his first expedition to Nuristan a few years earlier. He had just earned good money by buying up 'Mashadi coins' (an old currency) in Laghman, and when that market was exhausted, he decided to try his luck in Nuristan. The hardships he and his group encountered, the way the transactions were handled, and his account of their relationship with the local people offer insight into the life and profession of these pedlars in this not-so-distant past:

Abdul Ghani's cumin trade in Nuristan

"We were eight persons altogether. One day and one night we travelled by foot. When we reached the bottom of the pass, we spent the night there. In the morning, as we were about to get moving, somebody told us that there were bandits on the way, but we thought, after all, since we were eight people we could do it. But these six tough men got scared and decided to go back, and only I was left with Inzar Gul. We went [about 100 metres] but then Inzar Gul said to me: 'Oh, Ghani, the money is not mine – mine is only my life, but these six tough men got scared and went back. Why should you go – have you got your money from the water?' When I thought about it, I found that he was right. Why should I go to Nuristan for those Mashadi-coins? So we returned, but we said to ourselves: 'Oh, God, what a shame for us to go back to our home. How can we face the villagers, without bringing back any money?' So then we decided to go to another valley [Farajghan]. But I found no Mashadi-coins there, either.

"A friend of my father recognized me and asked how come I was looking for Mashadi-coins, while my father had been buying cumin, pine nuts, and walnuts. I said: 'I have not been doing such things, although my father might have done it'. He said: 'Then do it now'. I decided to buy cumin. The price was 100 Afs per *sēr* ... I bought 100 *sēr*s of cumin. It was like gambling, as I didn't know the market-price myself. I hired porters, who carried it for 5 Afs per *sēr*. Donkeys and horses couldn't go there. The strong [porter] could carry 5-6 *sēr*, the weak 3-4 *sēr*s. I lined up some 24 porters, men and women. I came down to a place where mules could be used as means of transportation. ... I rented mules for 5 Afs per *sēr* and loaded them with some 20 *sēr*s ... and sent Inzar Gul along with it. I told him to carry the cumin to the *Vilāyat* [provincial centre of Laghman] and send me some 8 mules on which to carry the remaining *kharwār* of cumin. I remained another night there and the next day the mules arrived. [Arriving in Maskurah] I found Inzar Gul, who told me that he had already made a deal to sell the cumin for 240 Afs per *sēr*. I criticized him for having made such a deal, as he was not sure the cumin would reach the *Vilāyat* in the first place ... . So as we reached the *Vilāyat* with the cumin, some [Pashtun] Pakistanis came and offered to buy the cumin for 280 Afs per *sēr*. The Hindu [with whom Inzar Gul had made the deal] said: "You can either give up your 20 *sēr*s of cumin or else sell the whole for 240 Afs per *sēr* as agreed. I slapped him two or three times on the face and told him that he could buy the 20 *sērs* for 240 Afs per *sēr*, but not the remainder. But as five or six traders gathered they told me, that such were the ways of trading: Once you agree upon a price ... you have to stick to your own agreement. I yielded to their judgement and sold the cumin for 240 Afs per *sēr* to the Hindu, who without losing much time sold it immediately to the Pakistanis for 280 Afs per *sēr* – while I was weighing the cumin for him. So the Hindu made 6,000 Afs profit, while I made 8,000 Afs profit."

Encouraged by the profits from the cumin trade, Abdul Ghani and Inzar Gul decided along with a few other traders to go to Nuristan to buy up more cumin. Just as they reached the foot of the pass to Nuristan, they came across some people who told them that the price of cumin had risen to 350 Afs per *sēr*.

"We were five people. We reached the other side of the pass the next evening – one whole day we used just to cross the pass. There was a village called Skandu. When we reached there, we found out that some other people from Alingar had gone there to buy cumin, so we didn't find any cumin there. For two days and two nights, we travelled until we reached Nilan [northwest Nuristan, upper Alingar-Ramgal valley], and there when we became hungry, we only got some bread of barley, and there were feathers in the bread. Those people don't make good flour, but we were eating it, and because of hunger we were eating apricots, as we could not eat the barley bread. For seven days and nights we travelled ... When we reached Nilan, people told us that there we could find cumin, and it was a very good cumin, like rice, very clean. They told us that they would sell it for 100 Afs per *sēr* although the market price was 350 Afs per *sēr* ... the transportation was also 100 Afs per *sēr* [i.e. from where they came]. I said: 'Why not through Charikar – through Desht-i Rawat and Ariaw?' They said 50 Afs per *sēr* on this way ...

"For those people cumin is free – they just cut it from the mountains, then they thresh it and sell it for 100 Afs per *sēr* ... So I bought some 60-70 *sēr*s of cumin ... I told the *malik* [of Nilan]: 'You charge 50 Afs per *sēr* for transport. Now, can you provide me with some porters?' They were speaking in another language, and I knew a little of that language ... there was an uncle of mine, who ... was acquainted with that region: they will give you something for 10 Afs but will ask 20 Afs to carry it for you, so then you can either carry it yourself or throw it away. So the *malik* arranged it in such a way, that they gave us cumin for 100 Afs per *sēr* and demanded 200 Afs per *sēr* for carrying it, because he knew that we could neither carry it ourselves nor throw it away, and they would not take it back. But I outwitted him and I told him 'You first find me the porters so that before everything, I pay them. He said: 'Don't worry,' since porters could be found. I said: 'No, there is neither a car here nor donkeys nor cows, who will carry it for us'. He told me: 'My son, have you ever done this business before?' I said: 'No, I haven't done it, but my father and grandfathers have done it.' He just tapped me on my back and said, 'Bravo, you are very clever!' I said, 'I am not so clever, but any fool can see that with this lack of any means of transportation, it is better to think twice before buying anything, especially if it is a matter of 60-70 *sērs* of cumin.' He called some people who owned horses and asked each of them how much their horses could carry ... . Before paying the price of the cumin and weighing it, I paid the porters ... . I bought 60-70 *sērs* [of cumin] for myself, [and] my wife's brother-in-law bought some 60 *sērs*, too. We were at the end of Nuristan, and it was quite a place, you know. I saw some stones which were green, some others yellow like apricots in those mountains. And I saw some others like glass, like crystal. But we didn't know what those stones were.

"So we got moving in the afternoon ... . We reached the pass in the evening ... . In the night it started raining and we found shelter under some big rocks. It was very cold. We used some stones as pillows. At the time of the morning prayers, we told the porters to load the horses. There were ten or twelve porters. We got moving. Just as we reached the entry to the pass, the horses got tired. Each of these Nuristanis was pulling the horse from the tail, but then I asked them, 'Why are you so cruel? The horse is carrying a load of 20 *sērs*, climbing the mountains, and then you are pulling it back, too!' They got angry, and those people are murderers and don't care about peoples' lives. They said that it was none of our business and 'that if we let them [the horses] go freely, they are like *Deos*, they will go up and up and their heart will break.[22] I am holding it by the tail so it will hold a rest after each few steps.' We were holding our knees while climbing. It was such a high mountain. We reached a place where there were some nomads from Alingar. We told them that we were hungry. They brought us some yoghurt and three or four maize breads and then we just thanked God for having reached a place of Muslims. After passing the Nilan pass, we reached Ariaw. There the Nuristanis decided to spend the night ... . We spent the night there and in the morning we got moving again ... . They [the porters] wanted to take us through the Panjshir river, it would have taken us two more nights. But we had heard earlier that there was another way to Desht-i Rawat which was closer. So we just took that way. As we reached the peak of the pass, we saw the river flowing below like the Nile. And after coming down, there was a path on which one person could walk with difficulty, because the sand had covered it. The Nuristanis decided to unload the horses, claiming that they [the horses] couldn't pass. So we were in trouble. There is no government in there, and we were five against twelve. But we told them, that 'if one horse can pass then we will go; if not, then you unload the horses.' I went ahead and started removing the sand from the path into the river. The four other people behind me did the same so we made some way for the horses. The horses passed. It was only about 100 meters which was bad and through all that, we were praying for the safety of the horses. At Desht-i Rawat we reached the road, but only one car went to Kabul daily from there, not more. We came to an orchard, there was a young man ... who came to ask for cumin for 20 Afs. I told him that he could not buy cumin for 20 Afs, it would be about 1/4 *paw* ... . But later on I called him and ... I told him: 'Stretch your *dāman* [frontlap of the long shirt]' ... and then I put a lot of cumin in his lap. He was surprised and said: 'You were not giving me cumin for 20 Afs and now you are giving me a lot more'. So he was happy with me. ...

"Suddenly as we had camped, ... I saw some five Nuristanis beat my wife's brother-in-law. So I ran and joined the fight. As there were more of them, they beat us. Suddenly I saw the man whom I had given some cumin for free appear, and he asked: 'What is going on?' Then my brother-in-law explained that he had given 500 Afs as rent on a horse to one of the Nuristanis who had gone back as we reached that pass. Now the man's brother also demanded the price [for the same horse]. He wanted 500 Afs more. The young man went and put on his uniform. He happened to be a police officer, and he brought four soldiers and started beating the Nuristanis and beat them hard and was telling them: 'You were once *kāfirs* and we made you Muslims by force; you are still going on the path of the unfaithful.' And he told that man to go to Nuristan and bring back that brother: 'If those Shaykh Mohammadis have not given him his fare, then I would take the double amount from them. But if they have paid him, then I will take double from you.' Now of course, that man could not walk two days' travel to Nuristan, so they said: 'OK, let us forget it, whether they have paid us or not.' The police officer then said:'No, I am going to put you in jail.'

"There were two teahouses. We spent the night in one, the Nuristanis in the other. So one of them came in the night and asked me to play *dambura* [drum] for them. I went there and played it for them, and my God, they were dancing and dancing all the other eleven, until midnight. Some of them had beards, some were young, but all of them were dancing in the teahouse. After that I took my leave. ... So in the morning we loaded our cumin on a bus and paid 5 Afs per *sēr* till Kabul ... . We left the cumin in a *sarāy* and asked the *sarāydār* [care-taker of the *sarāy*] to take care of it, and we went to Laghman.[23] Even at that time the price of cumin was 350 Afs per *sēr*. We didn't sell, as we were worried about our families in Laghman. Of 500 families only four had remained [i.e. the others had left for their summer areas in Koh-i Daman]. They might be eaten by wolves, or attacked by thieves. So we went there [and brought the families to the summer camp in Saray Khwaja] ... . And I had hardly spent two days here, when my stomach started swelling ... . My mother and my friends were all visiting me and crying and the cumin was still in

Kabul. I was telling my friend and others to go and sell the cumin while I was sick. They would not sell it and told me that only I could do such dealings and they were not accustomed with that trade. I said, 'What shall I do with this stomach?' So I went to Qarabagh, where there was a doctor who had just come from abroad. He gave me some injections. Some ten people had gone with me, as they were not sure I would come back alive. So I was cured and I went back to Kabul ... and while I am shaking the [cumin] sack it begins to tear apart: about one month had passed and the sacks are all rotten and it had rained, too. I took a sample of the cumin and displayed it in the wholesale market [*sarāy*] to see if somebody would buy it. They would not, not even for 200 Afs per *sēr*. Finally I found a man ... who was the uncle of another man to whom I earlier had sold cumin. I told him that his nephew had told me to take the cumin I had brought from Nuristan to him in Kabul. He called up his nephew in Laghman and asked him if he had ever bought cumin from Ghani. The nephew said: 'Yes.' He asked if he had told me to go to him and sell it in Kabul. The nephew said: 'Yes.' I played a trick on him, although he was a nice man. I told him that the cumin I brought could be sold for 350 Afs per *sēr*, and then I fell sick. The *Ḥajjī* said: 'Forget about the 350 Afs per *sēr*, I will buy it from you for 300 Afs per *sēr*.' I agreed. Then I just hurried up to weigh the cumin for him and finish the deal ... . It amounted to 2 *kharwārs* of cumin altogether. The *Ḥajjī* took another 2 *kharwārs* of anis buds [*bādiyan*] ... and mixed these with my 2 *kharwārs*. He had bought the anis buds for 40-50 Afs per *sēr* [the green cumin of Nuristan and anis buds resemble each other] and exported it. He gave us our money and said: 'Go!'"

In the past as today, the Shaykh Mohammadis would trade in anything that may generate profit, no matter whether in Nuristan, Laghman, or Koh-i Daman. Prior to his Nuristan expedition Abdul Ghani, as mentioned earlier, had earned good money by buying up 'Mashadi-coins' (an old currency) in Laghman. One day, when he had returned from cloth-selling, his mother told him that some silversmiths had been around to buy up 'Mashadi-coins'.

> "Then I thought that there must be something to it. When I went to the *Vilāyat* [provincial centre], I saw that the same coins which these silversmiths had bought for 20 Afs they now were selling for 30 Afs. But then I thought, that I have the same feet and hands as these people, so I had some 4,000 Afs in my pocket, sitting in a bus to Jalalabad to buy cloth, but I changed my mind and got out of the bus ... I came back ... and for 5-600 Afs, I bought some 'Mashadi-coins'. When I went back to the *Vilāyat* and sold them, I made some 600 Afs profit. I returned and until I reached Maskurah, I made some 400 Afs *gharībī*. So that one day I earned 1,000 Afs *gharībī*. I just got involved in that trade – after 10-20 days of working, all of the village after they saw me started doing the same ... . For about 20-30 days this work continued, and as 100 families started doing the same, everything was finished in one month. So I made some 8,000 Afs *gharībī*."

Shaykh Mohammadi Trade Today

Since the beginning of this century the Shaykh Mohammadis have carried out seasonal migrations with their families, where until the end of the 1950s they travelled by foot with their belongings loaded on donkeys. All the Shaykh Mohammadis started out jointly from Laghman in the spring, heading for Maidan province, later on proceeding together to several localities in Koh-i Daman, north of Kabul, and returning to Laghman in the autumn.

Today they no longer travel by foot. Instead, a few families jointly rent a bus or truck, and they go only to the Koh-i Daman area, where they remain in the same locality throughout the summer. In the beginning of July they either go directly from Laghman to Koh-i Daman, or they stop over in Kabul, staying for a few nights in the outskirts of the city, in Yakatut, for example. After buying supplies in Kabul the families proceed to their respective summer areas, which, though not fixed are fairly constant. When they travelled by foot, the Shaykh Mohammadis stayed in one big group, but in recent years they have split off into four localities in Koh-i Daman, from where the men ply their trade: in Saray Khwaja (approximately 45 families), in Ghulam Ali/Mahigir (approximately 50 families), Bayan (approximately 10 families), and in Bagh-i Alam (5-10 families), where a few also have invested in orchards. At the end of November, they return to Laghman.

Nowadays, the Shaykh Mohammadis' merchandise mainly consists of 'petty wares' (*sawdā*) bought in the wholesale shops of Kabul and Jalalabad, including plastic bangles, hairpins, threads, balloons, and pills, mostly imported from Pakistan and India. The better-off pedlar may invest in cloth, while the poorer pedlars manufacture and sell winnowing trays (*chaj*). A pedlar's choice of merchandise – i.e., cloth, petty wares, or winnowing trays – directly reflects his economic situation, since the available capital affects the types of goods one can invest in. In order to engage in the most profitable item, which is cloth, a pedlar needs an initial capital investment of around 10,000 Afs to obtain a sufficiently varied supply. It is cheaper to invest in petty things, where an ample supply can be obtained for about 2,000 Afs. Those who can afford neither investment will need only about 100-200 Afs to buy reeds for making winnowing trays, but here the daily earnings will be very limited.[24] With the very small capital investment required for surviving on manufacturing winnowing trays, even the poorest family is able to remain within the community and maintain the migration pattern.

Pedlars of petty wares normally go by foot into the villages and hawk their merchandise from door to door at a distance of up to 10 kilometres from the summer camp, thus avoiding spending money on bus fares, etc. They rarely attend the local weekly markets, as their supplies are too limited and the competition too great. The cloth traders, on the other hand, would load their goods on a donkey and apart from selling in the villages, would frequently attend the weekly markets of the region. Those who make winnowing trays may try to sell these either at the weekly markets or to shopkeepers. The Shaykh Mohammadis do not sell their merchandise on credit, and while the pedlar of petty things would prefer barter payment in agricultural products rather than money, the cloth traders would mostly be paid in ready money. With their expensive merchandise, barter payment would be heavy and impractical.

Since their customers are rural people, the best market time for the Shaykh Mohammadis is just after harvest. Hence, their trading and migrations are closely adapted to the agricultural

4,20 Two young Shaykh Mohammadis, their wares on their backs, on a peddling trip in Koh-i Daman.

4,21-2 The winnowing trays (*chaj*) are made from reeds tied together and reinforced on the reverse side with reeds and, for larger trays, a thin stick tied across (see *Figs. 3,17-8*).

4,22

cycle of the various provinces. In Laghman, the spring wheat is harvested in May-June, and for about one month the Shaykh Mohammadis hawk their merchandise in the villages there. They are paid mainly in wheat, since people are short of cash, and grain is plentiful at that time. Leaving Laghman, the Shaykh Mohammadis reach Koh-i Daman just after the wheat harvest, which occurs later there owing to the altitude of the area (approximately 1,000 m higher).

However, the southern part of Koh-i Daman, including the Saray Khwaja area, is not primarily a wheat area, but one of the main grape areas of Afghanistan. Trade there is rather limited until the grapes ripen in August-September, and trading is most intense after the grapes have been processed into raisins. The Shaykh Mohammadis are also paid in kind here, mostly in grapes and raisins. The traders keep some products for themselves and sell the rest, with profit, to big raisin traders in the local markets. In the beginning of December the trade declines, and as the winter approaches the Shaykh Mohammadis leave for Laghman.

Once back in their houses, the Shaykh Mohammadis resume trade. The paddy harvest has just ended, so the buying power of the Laghmani people increases. The approaching winter dampens the market, however, and it is not as good as after the spring harvest. From the summer trade most families have saved up 7,000 to 10,000 Afs, which they hope will bring them through the winter.

The poorest pedlars continue on several days of *ādūr* to Kohistan; others sell their merchandise from the sidewalks of the provincial capital, while the most well-to-do among them just live off their summer earnings. For the average Shaykh Mohammadi, trade during the winter time amounts to no more than sixty to seventy Afs per day, and profits are said to be as small as ten to fifteen Afs, which is much less than the daily expenses of a family. In the early spring, trade virtually ceases, and everybody looks forward to the coming harvest, which will bring new income to all households and restore the market for the Shaykh Mohammadis.

The seasonal variations in the trade and income of the Shaykh Mohammadis is also reflected in the merchandise of the individual pedlar. Not only may he shift from trading winnowing trays to petty things or cloth over the years, but he may even do so during one season, depending upon his finances and upon the immediate market situation. A pedlar formulated it this way:

> "One day I am a *chaǰ*-maker, another day I am a cloth-seller, depending upon my fortune. Even right now we cannot tell. Yesterday this man was one, today he is the second and tomorrow he may be the third."

Among the 66 economically active Shaykh Mohammadi pedlars in the Saray Khwaja camp, 21 were making and selling winnowing trays, 44 sold petty things, and 14 persons were engaged in cloth trade. However, the total figure for people trading in the various commodities exceeds the number of economically active persons, which illustrates the fact that a person during one season may change from one trade item to another.

A number of the poorer Shaykh Mohammadis start in spring to make winnowing trays; by the time of the grapes and raisins, they will have saved up 1,500-2,000 Afs, which they can invest in petty things and thus benefit from the improved market situation. A similar process can be seen with people changing from petty things to cloth, when the grapes and raisins start. Dur-

4,23 Shaykh Mohammadi cloth trader displaying his wares at the Qarabagh weekly market (Oct. 1976).

ing the grape season the market for cloth improves compared to the market for other goods. The reason is that cloth is a much more expensive product and also has to be bought in larger quantities, and that it is to a certain extent a necessity in all households. Petty things, on the other hand, can be considered as cheap luxuries. A Shaykh Mohammadi explains:

> "Suppose I bring cloth now [September]. It will not be marketable. Since the grapes are not dried into raisins, these people [in Koh-i Daman] will not buy cloth, because they will not yet have sold their fruit. ... But [in the raisin season] one man will sit and ask me for cloth for 2,000 Afs; just one man will buy cloth for his blankets and mattresses, for his children, for his woman."

While peddling petty goods is the main economic activity in the Saray Khwaja summer camp, the other big summer camp of Ghulam Ali contains a majority of cloth traders and hardly any manufacturers of winnowing trays. This may indicate that the Shaykh Mohammadi families there are better off. However, this difference in

4,24 This Shaykh Mohammadi from the Saray Khwaja camp has invested in china ware, which he trades at the weekly markets in the region, as china is too heavy to peddle from house to house.

trade does not necessarily mean that marketing conditions are significantly better in Ghulam Ali than in Saray Khwaja. If that were the case, one would expect an increasing number of pedlars going to Ghulam Ali until the differences were levelled out. This is far from the case: in fact, some years ago all the Shaykh Mohammadis went to Ghulam Ali, but now the two summer camps are of almost equal size, and the composition of the summer camps has remained stable, despite minor changes. But there are clear differences between the two areas. Ghulam Ali is mainly a wheat-growing area, while Saray Khwaja has vineyards (see Allan 1976, 1978). For the Shaykh Mohammadi pedlar, this difference in crops means that the general market situation favours cloth in one place and petty goods in the other. This point will be discussed below, as we look into the question of barter.

Apprenticeship

The Shaykh Mohammadis' peddling activities do not require any form of cooperation among households or among persons within one household. The individual pedlar buys his merchandise wholesale in the *sarāys* and travels about selling it without involving anyone else in the household. There is neither a division of market nor an organizational specialization of merchandise within the group. This individualization of trade was aptly expressed by an old Shaykh Mohammadi: "Everybody is for himself – king of his own head". Any internal economic variation in the community is thus the result of the financial capacity of the individual pedlar and the existing market situation.

The training of young boys is done by letting them join their fathers or an elder brother on the sales trips, *ādūr*.[25] They start around the age of twelve, when they are big enough to carry home one or two *sēr* of wheat (7-14 kg) as barter goods. The most important part of the trade is to learn to make calculations, not to be cheated. The young follow the elders until they are fifteen or sixteen years old. Apprenticeship includes not only management of business transactions but also self defence, as one has to stand up against the harassment of other boys on the streets and hold-ups, which lonely pedlars are exposed to mainly in the summer area. When trained, the boys start working independently, but remain in the parental household. They do the buying and selling themselves, and at the end of the economically active summer season, their earnings are added to the family's joint winter reserves. This means that even with several economically active members in a family, consumption is the only joint activity.

Although a young man is potentially economically independent at the age of sixteen, he is not considered old enough to marry and establish a new household. Normally this happens only after a man has completed his two years of national service.

Activities of the women

The work of the Shaykh Mohammadi woman normally consists of the daily housekeeping, which means cooking, cleaning, washing, serving, and looking after the children. In the summer camp, women's work also includes collecting straw from the nearby fields to use as fuel for the bread oven, as well as for building the kitchens and bathrooms adjacent to the tents.

Some women have also taken up peddling petty goods. It is mostly the poor widows who earn their living in this manner, but among poorer families the wife may also go peddling, although this is considered degrading for her husband. The husbands of such women are called *kakul* (cuckold), a word implying that they do not care about the chastity of their wives. One Shaykh Mohammadi puts it this way:

> "Some women do it [work as pedlars] out of necessity and others out of greed. Those women who are selling, although they have sons and husbands, are not highly respected."

In a conflict between two families, which ended up in court, the fact that the wife of one of the combattants was a pedlar was a sign of the family's lack of honour:

> "What else can one expect from such people, where the wife goes peddling although they have two adult sons and the husband is still alive. It is unacceptable. They are not decent people."

Among the 43 Shaykh Mohammadi households in the Saray Khwaja camp, at least 5 women

were pedlars: two were widows and three were married. Women are considered successful pedlars since it is easier for them to enter peoples' houses and sell merchandise to female customers. Women do not sell cloth because cloth is considered too heavy for them to carry to more distant locations, and "if they in such villages carry cloth around for a lot of money, they could be killed and the cloth stolen", as one male Shaykh Mohammadi explained.

Beyond the household chores, many women also maintain an income by stitching clothes on request by people from inside and outside the community. In the Saray Khwaja camp some ten women owned sewing machines. With a sewing machine two sets of clothes can be made in a day. For friends and relatives the stitching charge would be 15 Afs, and for others some 20-25 Afs per set. More women are involved in embroidering skull caps with gilded thread. It takes 6-10 days to embroider a cap, and it yields a profit of 30-40 Afs.[26]

In the summer locations women earn extra income picking grapes. Every morning vineyard owners announce that such and such a vineyard needs grape collectors. Older women, girls, and boys all work as grape collectors. They work in groups, and only in nearby areas. The daily payment consists of 15 Afs and an amount of 1/4-1/2 *sēr* of the sorted out grapes removed from the bunches during packing. These sorted out grapes are dried in the camp and subsequently consumed or sold as raisins. In Koh-i Daman, nomad women would also work as grape collectors.

4,25 Young Shaykh Mohammadi family in Ghulam Ali summer camp. For most women, their main work is as housewife and mother (Oct. 1976).

The Saray Khwaja Summer Camp

Every year some 40-50 Shaykh Mohammadi families migrate to Saray Khwaja for the summer, where they camp at some harvested fields northeast of the town, with a nearby *kārīz* (underground water channel) ensuring the water supply for the camp.[27]

Most of these families live in white canvas tents, but some prefer to build small mud-rooms to stay in. Close relatives camp next to each other, and 3- 4 families share a bread oven (*tandūr*). Sometimes, a couple of families take turns providing the fuel (straw collected from the fields or bushes), as the required amount for heating the oven suffices for the baking of the daily bread of two families.

Since the camp is located in the middle of a field, there are no trees or other shade or protection from heat, wind, and dust, which during the summer time can be extreme. Most people therefore build a mud-wall (about 0.5 m high), over which the tent cloth is pulled, or, alternatively, dig out the floor of the tent some 1-2 feet, obtaining the same effect.

On arrival at the camp site the women build small circular rooms for kitchens, as well as an approximately 1.5 m high, uncovered circular room about 1 m^2, to be used as a bathroom especially by themselves. I have not seen anything similar in tent camps of other communities, and it may reflect the fact that the camp is so big that unrelated people also live close to each other (hence necessitating the observance of more formalities regarding the decency of women). The fact that the Shaykh Mohammadis during most of the year live in houses of their own and can afford to be more particular about their women may also play a role. While most of their houses in Maskurah would have some

4,27 Cleaning food grains for impurities before cooking is one of the many tasks of a housewife. The small circular room to the right is used as kitchen (Saray Khwaja summer camp, Sept. 1975).

4,26 Bread-oven in front of one of the few temporary built-up houses in the Saray Khwaja-camp. The oven consists of a a large, round clay container sunk vertically into the ground. The flat round breads are placed at the sides of the oven to which they stick until baked.

kind of toilet, these are not constructed in the summer camp. For the men, who are away most of the day, this is not a problem, but the women basically have to restrict themselves and go after sunset to a nearby hollow in the field. Since the Koh-i Daman area, as previously mentioned, is believed to be ridden by robbers and highway men, the women cannot go very far away in the dark, and frequently go two-and-two.

4,29 The summer camp at Saray Khwaja. Low perimeter mud walls provide protection from wind, dust, and rain.

Barter and Profits

The very same merchandise which the Shaykh Mohammadis peddle in the villages is also found in the rural bazaars, but in greater variety. One may therefore wonder whether the pedlars survive by selling their merchandise at a lower price than the bazaar shopkeepers. Although there is no fixed price system in Afghanistan and bargaining is part of most trade, there exists among traders a sort of informal, general agreement about the 'proper' price of various commodities. This is true for shopkeepers and pedlars alike, but the latter are able to sell more cheaply than the shopkeepers, as they have no expenses of renting a shop, or paying taxes. The example below illustrates the minute margins on which the pedlar may base his economic activities:

4,30 The Saray Khwaja camp. In the background can be seen women carrying firewood on their heads

> In the small bazaar of Mehtarlam, the provincial centre of Laghman, a Shaykh Mohammadi pedlar bought cloth from a local shopkeeper at a wholesale price, paying for it in cash. Then he sat down on the opposite sidewalk and sold this cloth at a price lower than the shopkeeper's retail price. The pedlar and the shopkeeper were both making a profit on this deal: selling wholesale to the pedlar, the shopkeeper made 1-5 Afs per metre in profit, while in the retail trade he would make 5 Afs per metre profit.

4,28 Shaykh Mohammadi woman with sewing machine on top of her house in Maskurah (Dec. 1976).

4,31 The summer camp in Ghulam Ali is also located on a harvested field in the outskirts of town. It is about the same size as the Saray Khwaja camp (Oct. 1976).

> Within this margin of 3-4 Afs per metre, the pedlar could still sell at a competitive price and make a profit. Although the pedlar in this case competed directly with the shopkeeper for customers, the latter still earned a profit (albeit reduced) by supplying the pedlar.

Discussing the Qarabagh bazaar in Koh-i Daman, D. G. Norvell (1973: 21) implies that pedlar and shopkeeper serve different markets. The pedlar may sell cheaper than the shopkeeper, but he offers no credit, nor can he offer customers the assurance that they will be able to return and purchase additional pieces of matching cloth for repairs and alterations.

Three factors are of special significance for most Shaykh Mohammadis' trading activities: (1) they market their goods directly at peoples' doorsteps, (2) their customers are mainly women, and (3) the barter character of their dealings renders the barter products more significant than the primary commodities, both in terms of migration pattern and profit-making.

The shopkeepers' greater supply of merchandise protects them from competition, to the extent that Shaykh Mohammadi pedlars dealing in petty wares do not even bother to attend the weekly markets in the Koh-i Daman area. Instead, they go directly to the customers in the villages and, being alone with them, can sell at prices which may be higher than in the bazaar. Apart from the lack of comparability of prices, trading directly at people's doorsteps has an additional advantage. The Shaykh Mohammadis themselves emphasize most of their trade in petty goods is aimed at female customers. Afghanistan is a rather conservative Muslim country, and most village women are subject to purdah restrictions and therefore rarely go to the bazaar to shop themselves. This is done by the men. Only when the pedlar goes from house to house women are able to choose for themselves and buy. An old pedlar explained how this affects the cloth trade:

> "And the women, even if they have only worn cheap clothes, will ask us for 'the kind of cloth which makes the *khān* sad and his wife happy' [i.e. expensive cloth]. They will say, that somebody else's wife has such a nice one [dress], and 'I do not want to be inferior.' No longer do they wear the cloth from the Gulbahar Textile Factory [cheap cotton cloth made in the local factory]".

Although women subject to strong purdah norms are not supposed to be seen by any man outside the close kinship circle, these restrictions generally do not apply when it comes to male pedlars. The reason for this may partly be the pedlar's low social status – he is not considered a real threat, since social inferiority reduces a man's claim to honour and manhood. Hence, a dependent or socially low-ranking man is considered sexually comparatively harmless by people of higher social standing.[28] This reflects the unequal distribution of power inherent in all social relations, and in this sense the socially inferior man is actually more harmless than a higher-ranking person. The assumption that the pedlar will not ruin his means of livelihood by misusing his contacts with women may also play a role.

Secluded in their homes, the women often have no money to spend, but since the pedlars are ready to engage in barter, a deal can still be made. Payment in produce has the extra advantage for the women that their husbands are unlikely to discover in case they have taken grapes or raisins to pay for new bangles, fancy hairpins, and balloons for the children. An old pedlar describes the situation in the following words:

> "I go to the villages and some women surround me and I tell them secretly 'Oh my sister, I can even buy raisins. So if you will not buy anything [from me], I can still buy raisins from you.' So those raisins, which cost 120 Afs per *sēr*, she will give me for 60 Afs per *sēr*, so I make 100% profit, because she is doing it secretly."

By trading with women in their homes, the Shaykh Mohammadis exploit a market which the local bazaars cannot reach. However, this hidden market is not the complete explanation for the profitability of their trade. On an annual basis, the pedlars' earnings in the sale of petty things do not exceed 100-150 Afs per day, and with an average nominal profit of 20-25%, this would mean a daily profit of 20-40 Afs. An income at this level cannot maintain the Shaykh Mohammadi families at their present standard of living, i.e., with decent food and clothing, a few expensive consumer items, etc.

However, while the nominal profit may be 20-25%, the actual profit is far greater. The profitability of hawking petty things derives from the further sale of the bartered goods. Two examples on p. 170 from September 1975 will illustrate this.

Owing to the widespread use of barter, the actual profit on petty things is not 20-25%, but rather 100% or more. Barter is thus highly profitable for the pedlars because the customers are unable to keep track of the exact market value of barter products. In addition, the highly fluc-

Example 1:

Wholesale price of merchandise bought by a pedlar:	42 Afs
Payment received from customers:	
4 *paw* of wheat:	approx. 20 Afs
1 *sēr* 2 *paw* raisins:	approx. 63 Afs
Payment in money:	10 Afs
Total payment:	93 Afs
Profit:	51 Afs (121%)

Example 2:

Wholesale price of merchandise bought by a pedlar:	35 Afs
Payment received from customers:	
400 walnuts:	approx. 60 Afs
Payment in money:	30 Afs
Total payment:	90 Afs
Profit:	55 Afs (157%)

4,32-4,40 Qarabagh market

Many small towns of Koh-i Daman have a weekly or bi-weekly market or bazaar day, which the Shaykh Mohammadi cloth traders frequent. In September 1975 I was present at a market day in Qarabagh, a little town along the Kabul- Charikar road. On such days, Qarabagh is filled with thousands of customers visiting the traders and pedlars. These weekly bazaars have a distinct resemblance to the permanent bazaars: the market area is divided such that similar goods are sold in the same place. Most traders simply put their commodities on the ground, but even then, everybody has a specific place. Although it is not formally registered, it is generally recognised by other traders and by the authorities. The traders pay a fee to the local authorities every market day; the amount depends on the type of commodity, irrespective of the amount transacted; cloth traders for example pay a fee of 5 Afs for each market day.

In Qarabagh, the bazaar was located on either side of the main road bisecting the town, and it branched out on both sides. Immediately along the main road, the fruit market was found. To the west side of the road, a fairly big animal market was held with sheep, goats, donkeys, cows, and camels (*Fig. 4,32*). A section of second hand clothes sellers was also to be found on this side, as well as a sizeable cloth market. About ten Shaykh Mohammadi traders from Saray Khwaja and Ghulam Ali were present, but they formed only a minor part of the cloth market (*Fig. 4,33*). Adjacent to them were a number of tailors (*Fig. 4,34*) and a seller of Greek medicine (4.35). On the east side of the road was the meat market, the photo shows camel meat for sale (*Fig. 4,36*). Beyond the market, i.e. farther from the main road, was the vegetable bazaar, with onions, garlic, tomatoes, potatoes, eggplants, chili peppers, etc. (*Fig. 4,37*). Close to the meat market were a number of knife-grinders and also a Shaykh Mohammadi riveter of china ware from Siyahsang, Kabul. On bazaar days, he would sell repaired, second hand china. He stated that broken china was imported from Pakistan, repaired by riveters in Afghanistan, and resold.

To the west side of the main road was a small square with a large section of petty traders: they were sitting in one long row offering a more or less identical supply of merchandise – hardly any of these were Shaykh Mohammadi (*Fig. 4,38*). Also on the west side of the road were sellers of dried fruit, e.g. raisins and mulberries (*Fig. 4,39*), as well as flour-sellers (*Fig. 4,40*).

4,32

4,33

4,34

4,35

4,36

4,37

4,38

4,39

4,40

tuating prices of fruit on the local market creates possibilities for additional profits. In September 1975, the raisin price in Koh-i Daman was 40 Afs per *sēr*, but a month later had increased to 70 Afs per *sēr*. Equally so for almonds, which in a short period rose from 240-260 Afs per *sēr* to 400 Afs per *sēr*. The pedlars, naturally, store their barter goods until they think the price has reached its maximum. A Shaykh Mohammadi explained the transactions in these terms:

"When we sell petty things bought for 1,5 Afs, we can sell them for raisins worth 3 Afs, in accordance with a raisin price of 48 Afs per *sēr*. We will later sell the raisins for a price of 60-70 Afs per *sēr*... For 5-6 rolls of thread, we are paid 1 *paw* of prunes at a price of 5-6 Afs per *paw*. We will be selling the prunes at 8-9 Afs per *paw*, which is the market price."

The pedlars thus have a limited interest in cash payments. They directly request the customers to pay them in goods. Literally anything will be accepted as payment: At times they are even paid in worn out plastic shoes and sandals which are accepted at a price of 80 Afs per *sēr*. Subsequently, the pedlar re-sells them in Kabul for 160 Afs per *sēr*, and from there the shoes are exported to Pakistan where they are recycled.

4,41 Production of wooden crates for grape export (Saray Khwaja, Oct. 1976).

4,42 Raisins spread on the ground to dry (Ghulam Ali, Oct. 1976).

4,43 Small-scale raisin-buyer at Saray Khwaja market (Oct. 1986).

Because of the relative importance of agricultural barter items in these dealings, the migrations of the hawkers of petty goods should be seen as determined by the season for potential barter products rather than by the market for petty things. Petty goods trading becomes merely a means of obtaining desireable barter products, primarily the agricultural produce which is subject to great seasonal or local price variations. That agricultural products are considered the essence of the barter comes out clearly when pedlars describe their trade, not in terms of what they sell, but what they receive, or to use their term 'collect':

> "Last year at this time, I was mainly collecting *sāyagī* [raisins dried in the shade] and almonds. In June and July I was collecting wheat."
>
> "If I see my profit in pine nuts, almonds, and ghee, I just run for that."

Yet, why do the Shaykh Mohammadis bother to sell petty goods, when these are obviously of only secondary economic importance? The answer may lie in a complex set of factors: (1) As illustrated above, a profit of more than one hundred percent is earned through selling petty goods. It is not likely that the Shaykh Mohammadis could buy up agricultural products directly at the same low prices they obtain via barter. Generally speaking, barter deals involve small amounts of produce from each customer, who certainly would not sell larger quantities of agricultural produce below existing local market price. (2) Since the profit of more than 100% is realized through a chain of transactions, the invested capital need only be small; for petty things around 2,000 Afs. Obtaining the same amount of profit from buying up raisins, for example, would involve higher risks, a slower turnover of capital, and a larger capital investment, the latter being one of the Shaykh Mohammadi pedlars' greatest problems. (3) The petty wares provide the pedlars an income during the months when there is no agricultural produce. By hawking petty wares around in the region, the pedlar acquires intimate knowledge of the local market which enables him to exploit the price fluctuations. (4) Finally, only the pedlar can approach women as customers, and the petty trading is the means by which barter contact is established in a legitimate way.

Earning a living by hawking petty goods thus involves a lot of haggling, an intimate knowledge of the market for a range of agricultural products, and, to be really profitable, utilizing price fluctuations on the market. The grape and raisin markets in the Saray Khwaja area certainly display such price fluctuations. Being among the biggest export products of the country, the domestic market prices of grapes and raisins are highly dependent upon international market conditions. A raisin trader explained the hazards of this trade in the following way:

> "Two years ago I bought raisins for 160 Afs per *sēr*, but couldn't sell them due to lack of demand. So I stored the raisins for a whole year and then sold them for 78 Afs per *sēr*. Last year, the prices had fallen to 60 Afs per *sēr*. But this year, we hope things will improve as the government announced the minimum price for red [i.e., sun-dried] raisins. This means that export contracts have been signed with foreign countries.[29] Only the rich, big traders never lose in this trade, as they can afford to store raisins until the prices rise again, while we small traders will have to dispose of our supplies at any cost."

The raisin market is dominated by big private traders and joint-stock export companies, who buy the fruit through brokers (*ǰalābs*) and smaller private traders.[30] There are no contracts between the cultivators and the export companies, nor with private traders. The big traders and company brokers sign individual contracts for delivery with the biggest producers. In the local bazaars a number of middlemen buy up limited quantities of raisins from the smaller producers, reselling them to the bigger traders. At the beginning of the season, before the big traders and brokers have arrived, many producers will have to sell limited quantities cheaply to the small traders because of an acute shortage of cash to pay the day-labourers who pick the grapes. As soon as the big traders appear, the price will reach a considerably higher level.[31]

Consequently, the vagaries of the market, localised and individual dealings, and a network of middlemen make the market situation very confused. The large number of local markets, their uneven supply of products, and the daily variation of supply and demand provide ample opportunities for speculative enterprises. It is such enterprises that the Shaykh Mohammadis engage in, at a very minor scale.

In spite of the relative profitability of hawking petty things to female customers for a barter payment, the Shaykh Mohammadis claim that for those who can afford the investment, the biggest part of their trade is the sale of cloth for mattresses, clothes, etc. This market would appear after the vineyard owners have received payment for their grapes and raisins, and those deals of a large scale are conducted with the pater familias, and mostly for payment in cash.

The peculiarities of the grape and raisin market also explain why the Shaykh Mohammadi camp of Saray Khwaja is dominated by hawkers of petty goods, while it is mainly cloth traders who remain in Ghulam Ali. Some ten of them do not even peddle their goods in the villages, but have specialised in the weekly bazaars. Ghulam Ali is located in a mainly wheat-growing area, and the local and seasonal price fluctuations of grain are far less than in the case of fruit. Consequently, the profits to be made by reselling bartered goods would be much smaller here, rendering it difficult to make sufficient absolute profit from the small amount of capital invested in petty goods. Hence, the tendency is for those who can afford to invest in cloth to go to Ghulam Ali for the summer, while Saray Khwaja holds possibilities for both categories.

Economic Conditions

In most Shaykh Mohammadi families, summer earnings are eaten up during the winter, and many people are left without sufficient capital to resume trade activities in the spring, and hence, forced to borrow the necessary capital. These loans must be arranged in various ways, all of which serve to conceal the taking of interest, which violates Islamic Law. These systems of borrowing include:

(1) *Borrowing money on rice*, or borrowing rice on money, from the big landowners in Maskurah, most of whom are Shaykh Mohammadis themselves. The borrower receives an amount of cash from the lender and has to repay the loan in produce, normally rice (although wheat may also be used). The loan is generally taken in May June, the time of the wheat harvest, and is due in November-December when the Shaykh Mohammadis return from Koh-i Daman.

The actual transaction operates as follows: A borrower receives, for example, 4,000 Afs in springtime and must repay in the autumn with 80 *sērs* of rice, i.e. at a price of 50 Afs per *sēr*. However, the rice price never falls below 70-80 Afs per *sēr*, so the creditor will in fact get some 5,600-6,400 Afs worth of produce in return for a loan of 4,000 Afs. Through this arrangement, based on an artificially low rice price, an interest rate of 40-60% is obtained over a six month period.

If the loan consists of borrowing rice on money, the rice price will instead be fixed artificially high. The individual family will most often borrow a couple of *kharwār* of rice, which means that a loan of some 8,000 Afs has to be repaid with 11,200-12,800 Afs from the summer's earnings.[32]

(2) *Buying cloth on credit* from the Shaykh Mohammadi cloth traders in Jalalabad. The pedlars dealing in cloth can buy on credit from these relatives for 5,000-10,000 Afs, the credit period also being May-June to November-December. However, pedlars must buy the cloth at a price which exceeds the normal retail price by 0.5 Afs per metre. The pedlar will have to sell the cloth at the ordinary market price and thus actually lose the above-mentioned 0.5 Afs per metre. This solves his immediate liquidity problems of course. By selling the cloth, he obtains cash so that he can buy wholesale later on and make a real profit. The actual interest is camouflaged through the manipulation of prices.

(3) *Small and short term loans* given within the Shaykh Mohammadi pedlar group. These loans amount to approximately 500 Afs. They are given in Laghman and repaid in raisins in Koh-i Daman. The

principle is the same as when borrowing on rice, but as raisin prices can vary dramatically, the loan is a gamble for both parties.

(4) *Buying on credit from camp shops.* In the beginning of the 1970s, some families took the initiative of starting individual camp shops which sold petty goods on credit to others in the camp. The shopkeepers buy wholesale in Kabul and sell the merchandise in the camp at a profit of 10-12 % – as compared to selling directly to the villages where the direct profit would be 20-25 %. The credit term is not fixed, but the debt must be paid before returning to Laghman. This is the cheapest way for a pedlar in petty goods to get started on the summer trade and to make a profit, although this profit is reduced right from the beginning. The importance of the camp shops is mainly in the beginning of the season because of the credit given; later on, they function primarily as an economic reserve for the traders.

In 1975-76 three such camp shops were found in Saray Khwaja, each serving around ten families, normally of the shopkeeper's relatives. The customers would buy on credit for 600-1,000 Afs each. The invested capital in the shop was around 10,000 Afs, and the daily sale in the beginning of the season would be around 1,000-1,200 Afs.

One of the shops was owned jointly by a man and his son-in-law, until they parted because of a disagreement. Both were ordinary pedlars as well. The busy time in the shop was between 6 a.m. and 8 a.m., before the pedlars went on *ādūr*; for the rest of the day, their wives took care of the shop. Informants stated that the shop brought less profit than the pedlars' cloth trade.

(5) *Buying reeds for winnowing trays on credit.* The poorest families buy reeds for making the winnowing trays on credit in the spring time. At one time they themselves harvested the reeds in Samarkat, located in the mountains of Laghman, but since the 1972 drought, the straw has almost disappeared, they say.[33] A wealthy Shaykh Mohammadi shopkeeper in Jalalabad has therefore started to import reeds from Pakistan, selling them on credit at very high prices to his poor relatives. Nobody else imports reeds.

Most Shaykh Mohammadi families from the Saray Khwaja summer camp are, or have been, involved in these credit and loan systems. The consequence of the usury paid here is that although a family has earned enough to survive through the winter, the repayment of debts will be such a heavy burden that in the following spring they will again have to borrow. Thus, many families see no improvement in their trade activity over the years, and they start right at the bottom each spring.

The big loans are given by a small group of 5-10 landowners and shopkeepers, most of whom are Shaykh Mohammadis themselves. Kinship relations have no influence on the terms of credit and loan. Usury persists despite kinship ties because "even your brother will lend you money for profit ". The individualized character of the Shaykh Mohammadis' economic activities thus extends to all financial matters, where the main aim is to earn a profit. As crudely formulated by a pedlar: "When one gets poor, the other will be happy about it, because the former may borrow money on rice from him."

The establishment of camp shops has considerably eased the financing of petty trade, and many are taking advantage of them. As a result, informants state that fewer people have taken large loans in recent years.

Despite the risks and hazards involved in their trade activities, the Shaykh Mohammadis appear to be better off than most other non-pastoral, migrating communities in eastern Afghanistan. The men in particular are well dressed, which of course can be associated with their specific trade. However, many families possess expensive items such as watches, radios, sewing machines and pressure cookers.

In addition, with the exception of three families, all the Maskurah Shaykh Mohammadis have houses of their own in Laghman, while most of the other migrating communities have no permanent settlements. Among the poor, settled, rural communities, many are forced to live as tenants (*hamsāya*), in which their free housing is paid for by performing services to the landlord household, as with the Musallis. While most Shaykh Mohammadi houses are inherited from earlier generations, there are also families among the present generation who can afford to buy/build new houses and to invest in or lease land.

An elderly pedlar in petty goods gave me an outline of his monthly budget which confirms the above impression. This family, consisting of the pedlar, his wife, and adult son, could not be considered well-off, but still he calculated the family's monthly expenses as about 2,010 Afs.[34] In addition, the family spends some 1,000 Afs per person annually on clothes. Flour and rice may partly be obtained through payment in kind, which leaves a monthly expense for this 3-person family of 1,350 Afs per month. The comparable (minimal) budget formulated by Kanne (1974: 585) for a 5-person family in Kabul amounts to 721 Afs per month (excluding rice and flour). Hence, the living standard of the Shaykh Mohammadis would be considerably better. In the previous chapter it was demonstrated that the Musallis fall well below this level.

It was argued earlier, that poverty would not force people out of the community, because even the poorest could make winnowing trays and maintain the migratory pattern. Wealth, however, ultimately leads to an interruption of the migratory lifestyle and in some cases also to settlement away from Maskurah. This is the case for a few Shaykh Mohammadi families who have shops in the provincial capital of Laghman or in Jalalabad. A couple of these families were in 1976 engaged in importing, and possibly also smuggling.

Another break with the migration pattern of the community has occured in the case of some 3-5 wealthy families who have given up trade completely and invested in bigger areas of land in Maskurah: 20 *ǰarīb* or more, which is considered large landholdings in Laghman.[35] Like other big landowners, they let land to local peasants and supplement their income with moneylending activities. A poor Shaykh Mohammadi explained:

> "Trade is most profitable, but if they [the Shaykh Mohammadis] get enough money, they will buy land – it is like your roots; while trade is like a hat – it can blow away."

Other well-off families have leased or bought a couple of *ǰarīb*s of land in Maskurah village (at least seven in Saray Khwaja and apparently several more in the three other summer camps). Since a couple of *ǰarīb* is not enough land to sustain a family, these people have continued their seasonal migrations and trading while renting the land to local, non-Shaykh Mohammadi share-cropping peasants. One family had applied for and had just received land from the government in Nangarhar province, and a non-Shaykh Mohammadi relative was tilling the land while the actual owner continued his peddling activities.[36] Others have land inherited through generations, back "from the time of *kāfiri* [heathendom], when Laghman and Alishang were all *kāfir*, and in Tirgarhi, their king Sharan, was a *kāfir*."

During the 1960s and 1970s, many rural specialist and small peasants in Laghman and East Afghanistan were becoming increasingly dependent upon seasonal labour migrations and on occasional day labour to earn their living. The Shaykh Mohammadis, on the other hand, deny that a pedlar can be so poor that he is forced to take up daily wage work. Only during the 1972 drought did some Shaykh Mohammadis engage in harvest work in Laghman, work which most other rural people are forced to take up as a matter of course. The Shaykh Mohammadis are thus in general faring better than most other rural, landless groups, and migrating, non-pastoral communities.

Social Organization

We have seen that the Shaykh Mohammadis' economic activities are organized on an individual basis, and this is paralleled at the social level by the predominance of the nuclear family household. Among the forty-three households in Saray Khwaja summer camp, only four comprised married sons living with their families in the parental household.[37] For these extended families, it appeared that the sons had married prior to their entering national service and, since their wives and children had to be supported during those two years, it was not practical to form separate households.The composition of households and number of working members (excluding women's home handicraft production) in the Saray Khwaja summer camp was as follows:

Table 4,2: Household composition in the Saray Khwaja summer camp:

Family type:	Households:	Working members:
Nuclear family	27	39
Extended family (+ married son)	4	9
Extended family (+ widowed parent)	5	8
Widow(er) w/ children	4	5
Siblings *	2	4
Single (deaf-and-dumb man)	1	1
TOTAL	43	66

*In both cases, the family has split for the summer, the father remaining behind in Laghman to cultivate land, while the adult sons and daughters had gone to Saray Khwaja for the season.

When a male head of family dies, the widow maintains the household if there are unmarried sons to support her, or she takes up peddling herself to sustain the family. Eventually, she may also remarry; in three cases widows with children had remarried. In one case, the second husband was the FaBrSo of her first husband; in another case the husbands were unrelated, but the second husband was the FaBrSo of the widow; and in the third case, the widow was an unrelated non-Shaykh Mohammadi whose first husband was not a Shaykh Mohammadi, either. If the widow is elderly, she may join the household of one of her married children, most frequently that of a son. A widower will maintain the household, and he will either remarry or household chores will be given over to an unmarried daughter, sister, or even an elderly mother.

Apart from three-generation extended families, other variations from the nuclear family norm are caused by death, remarriage, and divorce. It is primarily the economic resources which determine whether or not independent household units will be established. Three cases will serve to illustrate the point.

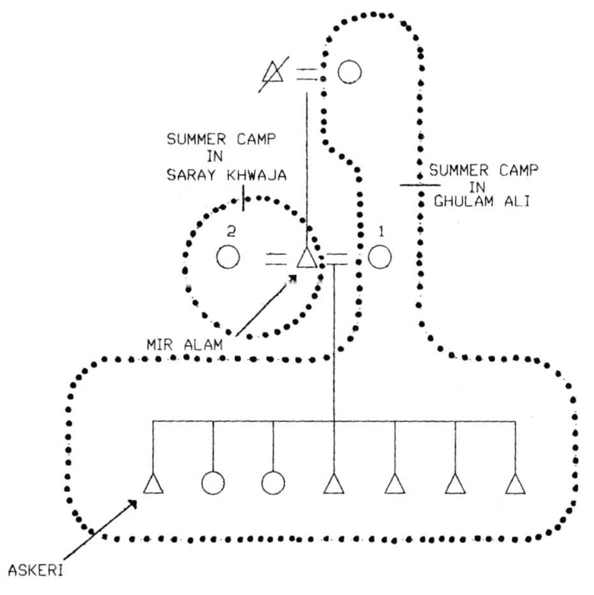

4,44

Case 1: Grandmother as breadwinner: Mir Alam has divorced and left his first wife and seven children in order to marry a peasant girl from Laghman. His widowed mother and his eldest son Askeri support his first wife and the children by petty trade. They go to Ghulam Ali for the summer, where the relatives of his first wife stay. Mir Alam lives with his second wife, and pays short visits to Saray Khwaja. He earns his living by smuggling cloth and tumeric from Pakistan.

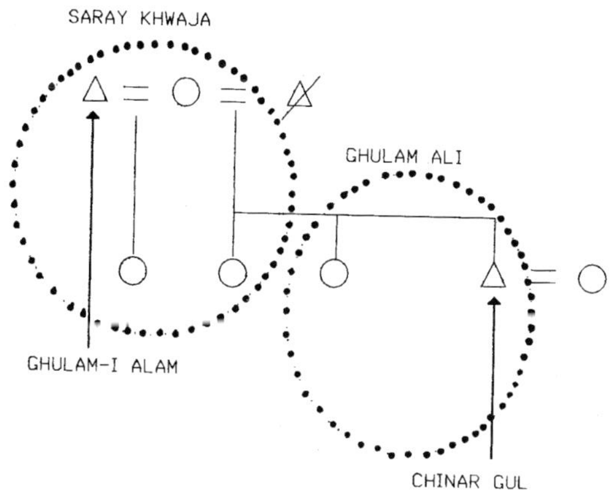

4,45

Case 2: Brother as breadwinner: Ghulam-i Alam has married his paternal cousin, a widow with three children. Ghulam-i Alam's household comprises, besides himself, his wife, one step-daughter, and one daughter. Chinar Gul, the wife's son from her first marriage, is a widower and has formed a household with one of his sisters. Ghulam-i Alam's household travels to Saray Khwaja for the summer, Chinar Gul's household goes elsewhere.

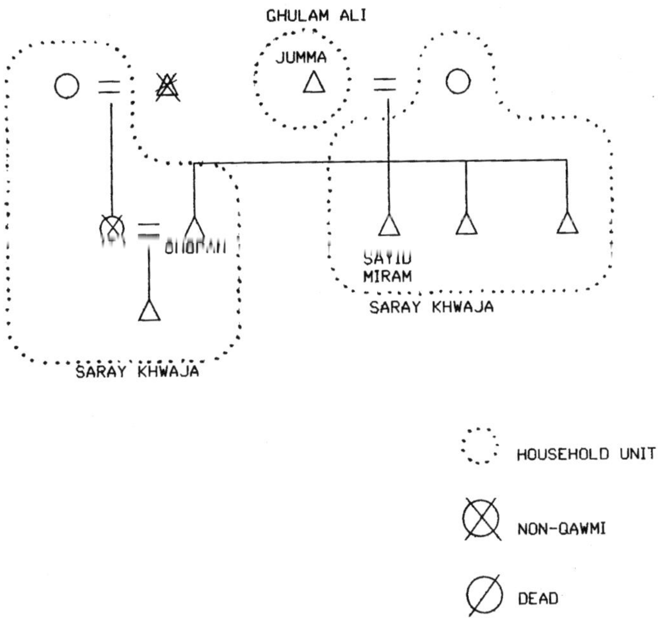

4,46
Case 3: Son as breadwinner. Jumma has divorced his wife and is now living alone. He went to Ghulam Ali for the summer. His eldest son Chopan has married a non-Shaykh Mohammadi and lives with his wife, one son, and his widowed mother-in-law. Jumma's ex-wife lives with their remaining three sons, and the household sustains itself by trade in petty wares undertaken by the eldest one, Sayid Miram.

The above examples illustrate however, that close kinsmen do not necessarily migrate to the same summer location. While differences occur from year to year, the composition of the summer camps remains relatively stable: in 1975, of the 43 Shaykh Mohammadi households in Saray Khwaja, 38 had also been there the previous year, two households had been in Ghulam Ali, two had not joined the summer migration at all, and one family only used to come for shorter stays.

A kinship diagram of the inhabitants of the Saray Khwaja camp reveals the following structure (see *Fig. 4,47*): The majority of the families are closely related although three groups, composed, respectively, of three, two, and one families, had no immediate relations which could be traced to the rest. The importance of kinship is also demonstrated in the physical structure of the summer camps, where close relatives – if on good terms – camp close to each other. In spite of the apparent importance of kinship in the composition of the summer camp, many households also had close relatives in one of the other summer camps. There is no indication that paternal relations are more preferable than maternal ones in the choice of summer locations. Since there are no economic or other factors favouring one or the other type of relations, one may assume that the final choice of settlement is determined by personal friendship and business considerations.

The kinship chart from Saray Khwaja, which covers about 2/3 of the Shaykh Mohammadi community from Maskurah, also gives important information on the Shaykh Mohammadis' marriage pattern: A total of 117 marriages (dead and living alike) were recorded, in which *qawm*-affiliation and kinship details were obtained in 79 cases. Out of these 79 cases, altogether 25 marriages were between Shaykh Mohammadi and non-Shaykh Mohammadi, i.e., 31.6% exogamous marriages. This is a comparatively high frequency of exogamous marriages in view of the fact that literally all communities in Afghanistan practice preferential endogamy, and that the Shaykh Mohammadis propagate this norm as well (see below).

As far as the 54 endogamous marriages were concerned, 14 of these were between first cousins, of which 7 were with FaBrDa, a marriage choice which is generally supposed to be preferential in this part of Muslim West Asia. If second

KINSHIP RELATIONS IN SARAY KHWAJA SUMMER CAMP

⊗ Non-Shaykh Mohammadi

∅ Dead

— Present in Saray Khwaja summer camp, 1975-76

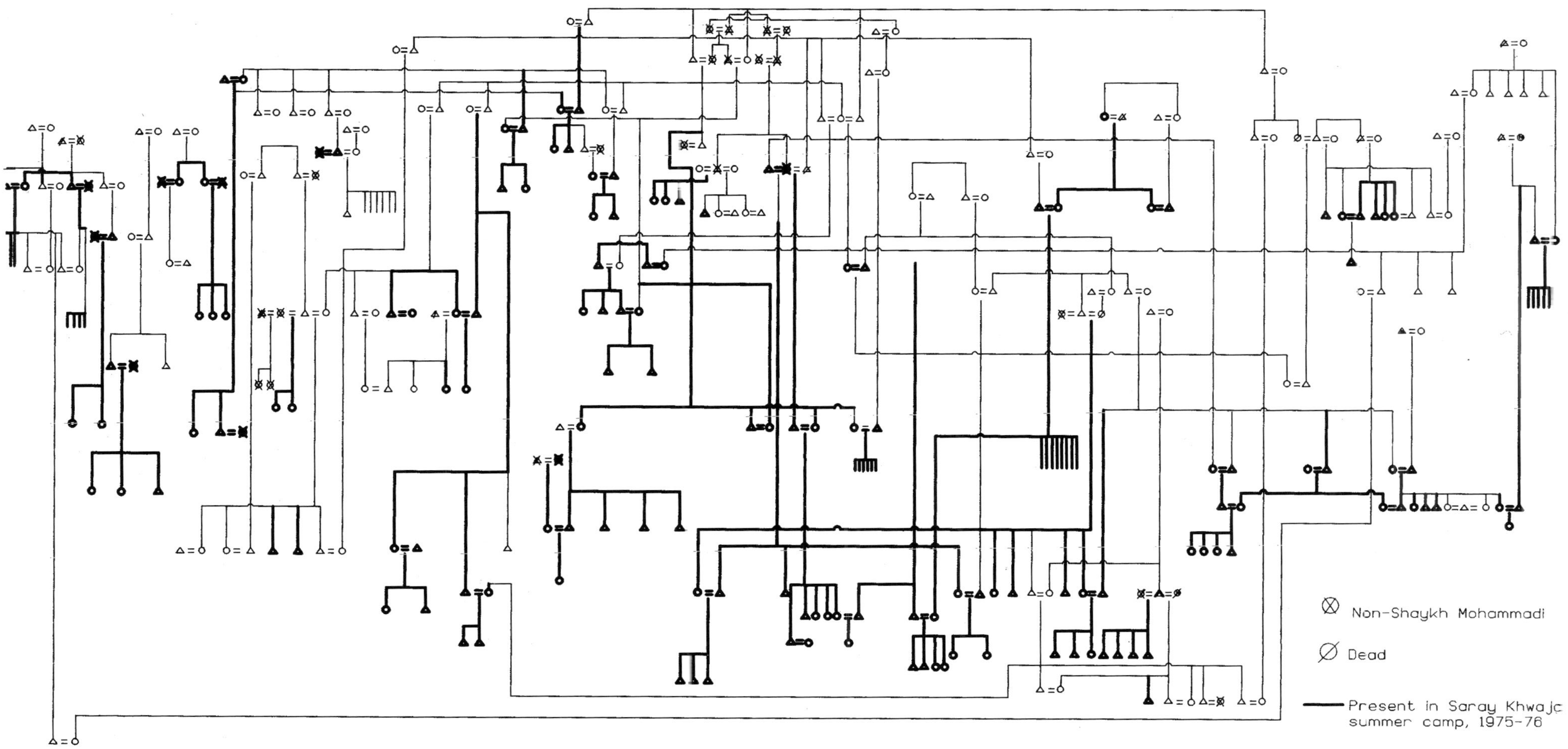

and third cousin marriages are added, the figure is 21 cases. Hence, there is a preference for cousin marriages among the endogamous marriages, but the frequency is not very high.

Three *badal* (exchange) cases were identified, as well as a case of levirate (FaBrWidow) and one of sororate (WiSi), so these practices occur, but apparently without being very frequent. Polygamy was not found among this section of Shaykh Mohammadis, but there were two cases of divorce, one followed by remarriage. In both cases, the mother had kept the children and set up a household of her own. Obviously, no conclusions can be drawn from the two divorce cases and the absence of polygamous marriages, but in general, polygamous marriages seem to be far less frequent in contemporary Afghan society than a couple of generations back. However, one may assume that the potential economic independence of Shaykh Mohammadi women tends to discourage polygamous marriages. In the case of Mir Alam, described above, his widowed mother and a son supported his divorced wife and smaller children through peddling activities, and in the other case of Jumma, his unmarried son Sayid Miram supported the mother and younger siblings while the father lived alone.

Of the total 117 cases, only 10 were successive, multiple marriages which is far less than that recorded among the Musallis (17 out of 71 cases). The reason may be that the Shaykh Mohammadis are better off; consequently, fewer men and women die at a young age, where remarriage would be the natural option for the widow(er).

As far as exogamous marriages are concerned, it is interesting to note that of a total of 25 cases, the Shaykh Mohammadis have given girls in only 8 cases, and have received girls in 17 cases. Even granted that the number of girls given may be higher (in that the girls have been "forgotten" when they have left the group) it seems clear that the Shaykh Mohammadis are wife-*receivers* far more often than they are wife-*givers*. This is confirmed by the Shaykh Mohammadis' own reluctance to marry girls out of the community, an attitude underlined by the culturally defined "inferiority" of wife-givers, which is a general phenomenon in Afghan society:

> Shaykh Mohammadi-woman: "...our people find it humiliating when a Pashtun has sexual intercourse with a woman from our community whom the community considers *khwāharzāda* [sister's daughter, i.e. expression of the feeling of close kinship inside the community]."

> Shaykh Mohammadi-man: "All men curse their wives, but if an outsider marries one of our girls, it curses all of us."

The Shaykh Mohammadis state that the only girls they can accept marrying off to outsiders are girls "who are either crippled [and thus unable to go on the summer migrations] or girls who have lost their virginity", in both cases girls who would be among the least attractive brides.

However, the endogamous tendency among the Shaykh Mohammadis is also a result of the settled community's reluctance to marry them, as the Shaykh Mohammadis are considered quarrelsome and somewhat lacking in piety and decency, in spite of the fact that they consider themselves good and pious (Sunni) Muslims, who pray and keep the fast throughout the month of *Ramazan*.[38] A Laghmani Pashtun, whose aunt and uncle are married to Shaykh Mohammadis and who himself joined the Saray Khwaja camp, expresses the reluctance of the settled community towards intermarriage with the Shaykh Mohammadis in the following words:

"Nobody will marry from these *Jats*, *Qawāls*. Even if a person can't find any other girl he will not marry one of them ... . It is only their own people who will marry them."

Nevertheless, intermarriage between Shaykh Mohammadis and outsiders is quite frequent and can be arranged for various reasons. Mutual acquaintance and friendship are mentioned as one important factor. An old Laghmani peasant woman of non-Shaykh Mohammadi origin who married Shaykh Mohammadis in two successive marriages tells her own story:

"My father's paternal uncle's son was a wrestler (*pahlawān*) a long time ago. And there was a wrestler from the Shaykh Mohammadis, too. They were wrestling one day – my mother was telling me this – in Diwa they were wrestling. They had bet their sisters on the match ... . What happened is that first my father's cousin beat the Shaykh Mohammadi, and in the next match he himself was beaten. So they exchanged sisters. Actually they should have tried three times ... . So my father's paternal uncle's daughter got married to a Shaykh Mohammadi. When I was born, my father, being from Diwa, started working as a peasant in [the neighbouring village of] Maskurah. My father's paternal cousin wanted me for her own community, for the Shaykh Mohammadis. So she arranged my marriage. Otherwise I would not have gotten into the community."

This case also illustrates the general preference for marrying relatives, whether *qawmi* or not: subsequently, the old woman's brother also married a Shaykh Mohammadi. With the exception of two girls, who married peasants, the offspring from these four exogamous marriages have all married Shaykh Mohammadis and identify themselves as such. The son of the old Laghmani woman explains the circumstances around his own wedding with a Shaykh Mohammadi some 20-25 years ago:

"After my father died, I lived with my maternal uncle. When I reached adulthood, my maternal uncle went to my father-in-law and asked for his daughter to me. My maternal uncle was a peasant. He is not from our people, but my father-in-law [a Shaykh Mohammadi] said, 'I don't want my daughter to be carrying rice and food to the fields.' My maternal uncle said, that he would agree to any conditions – dowry, money, cows – 'You impose it on us.' My father-in-law said, 'No. Not unless he separates from you, not unless he takes up his late father's occupation [as a pedlar].' So I separated from my maternal uncle, and my father-in-law gave me some 120 Afs of petty goods. I took the 120 Afs to the [Kohistan] valley and made 240 Afs out of it. So my father-in-law took the 240 Afs and gave me petty things worth that amount. I took it and turned it into 480 Afs. So when these people were coming to Kabul, I remained in Laghman and when they were coming back, I had made some 3,000-4,000 Afs. And then my maternal uncle with some other people said, 'He remained in Laghman and made so much money. Will you now give your daughter to my nephew?' My father-in-law agreed and took only 1,000 Afs from me. For that money he bought clothes for his daughter, 3-4 *sērs* of rice, 1-2 *paw* of cooking oil [*rughan*]."[39]

A common justification for choosing close kinsmen or at least *qawmis* as marriage partners is that it creates less conflict within the family when husband and wife are related beforehand: "She will not curse my family, as that would be cursing her own family". For the Shaykh Mohammadis, this argument is further underlined by their summer migrations, which for a settled girl would appear as a considerable hardship. I was told of how upset some settled in-laws became, when visiting their daughter in one of the summer-camps. Hence, while the above Shaykh Mohammadi did not want to see his daughter "carry food to the fields", a peasant would not like to see his daughter live in a dusty tent-camp. In both cases, a higher bride-price may smooth over the problems.

Not surprisingly, it appears that the bride-price tends to be higher for exogamous than for endogamous marriages, no matter whether the Shaykh Mohammadis are wife-givers or wife-receivers. Bride-price will probably tend to be lower among close relatives. However, various considerations are involved in a family's choice of marriage partner for a son/daughter. Not only actual *qawm*-affiliation, but also the economic and social conditions of the potential in-laws and the character of their son/daughter play important roles both for the choice of bride and for the subsequent bride-price; in the above case, for example, the prospective son-in-law had to demonstrate his ability as a pedlar.

Generally speaking, in the patrilineal Afghan context, a woman normally becomes a member of the husband's household and local kingroup at marriage. A married couple would reside virilocally and children counted as belonging to their father's *qawm*. This is also the case when Shaykh Mohammadi men marry outside their community, but in the case of Shaykh Mohammadi women there are differences. Virtually all non-Shaykh Mohammadi men who marry Shaykh Mohammadi women join their wife's community and gradually take up her *qawm*'s peddling and migratory life-style. In spite of having married a Shaykh Mohammadi herself in two consecutive marriages, an old Laghmani woman explained that, "it is only outsiders who are good for nothing who marry these people. They are people without an occupation of their own who marry with the intention of taking up the Shaykh Mohammadis' business."

Both the men and women who have married into the community from outside are mainly from poor landless families in Laghman or Kohistan. The three outsider men in the Saray Khwaja camp are, respectively, a peddlar of petty things, a transporter who works with a donkey, and a seller of pickled chickpeas (*nukhūd*). Although the three men live with the Shaykh Mohammadis and take part in their summer migrations, they are not considered "equal" members of the community. Only their children are counted as "real" Shaykh Mohammadis. A young man whose father is of Laghmani peasant stock expressed this reservation towards outsiders:

> "I will not have as much respect for the newcomer as for the Shaykh Mohammadis. A Laghmani remains a Laghmani, and a peasant remains a peasant."

The above-mentioned old Laghmani woman, married to Shaykh Mohammadis for nearly 40 years, spoke most of the time as a member of the community, but occasionally distanced herself from the Shaykh Mohammadis, and expressed the settled community's spiteful attitude to these noisy and quarrelsome people (*qawāls*). In practical terms, this "split loyalty" operates in such a way that towards outsiders, she would identify with the Shaykh Mohammadis, while within the community she might invoke her status as non-Shaykh Mohammadi. This is in perfect congruence with the attitude of the Shaykh Mohammadis themselves, the background of an outsider will always be used against him/her in the numerous internal con-

4,48 The old Laghmani woman with her youngest grandchild.

flicts in the community. The old Laghmani-woman explains, "I am always told while quarreling that I am a Laghmani-*larmun-khūr* [i.e. one who eats intestines]."

The Shaykh Mohammadis', social status is thus ambiguous. On the one hand, the settled society considers them of low social standing due to their migratory lifestyle and behavior, which is associated with 'noisy and quarrelsome' behavior. In spite of this, many outsiders do marry into the group and join their community. For their part, the Shaykh Mohammadis do not

4,49 Cloth trader in Ghulam Ali camp.

4.50 Young men in Saray Khwaja.

consider themselves inferior, as underlined by the fact that they receive more girls in marriage than they give, and that they turn those outsiders who intermarry with them, into Shaykh Mohammadis. In fact, the Maskurah Shaykh Mohammadis are deemed low not because of, but in spite of their descent, since their eponymous ancestor *Shaykh Ruhānī Bābā* is generally recognized as a pious and holy person. Consequently, settled and wealthy Shaykh Mohammadis do not attempt to change their identity but rather boast of it. The Laghmani Pashtun with Shaykh Mohammadi relatives expresses the ambiguity in the following way:

"These people [Maskurah Shaykh Mohammadis] may be quarrelsome, but they are certainly different from *J̌at*s. These people are Shaykh Mohammadis, but do not know themselves [what that means]. The real Shaykh Mohammadis are pious people – always saying their prayers, having a good life in Kote Sangi and Siyahsang – a better life than the Mohammadzais [i.e. the former royal family]. But these Shaykh Mohammadis [the Maskurahis] are bastards. A real Shaykh Mohammadi would not shave his beard [i.e. sign of a holy person, a Sufi] ... *These* people are mixed. Their wives became Laghmanis, their men became *Qawāl*s, *J̌at*s, and sellers of bangles. They became children of five fathers..."

4,51 Women gathered for an afternoon chat, Saray Khwaja camp.

It was argued initially, that the Shaykh Mohammadis originally constituted a spiritual community, the followers of *Shaykh Ruhānī Bābā*. This explained the lack of genealogical connections between the various groups, the free absorption of outsiders into their ranks, as well as the notions held both by themselves and outsiders that they were a blessed people. Among the Maskurah Shaykh Mohammadis studied in 1976, the spiritual core of their identity seems to have disappeared, and they have turned into a kin-based community (*qawm*) on a par with other ethnic/genealogical communities (*qawms*) in East Afghanistan. Outsiders are still integrated into the community, but now it is via the institution of marriage rather than via religious devotion to *Shaykh Ruhānī Bābā*. However, the Shaykh Mohammadis' self-assertion and pride in their holy "descent", together with a comparatively high rate of community exogamy and their tendency to "absorb" outsiders, male and female alike, may still be reminiscent of their past, when "Shaykh Mohammadi" was a chosen identity and not only an inherited one. This may also explain why poor, settled people still find it attractive to marry into the Shaykh Mohammadis.

Conflicts and Solidarity

The Shaykh Mohammadis' summer camps are permanent for four months, and with the large number of pedlars in Saray Khwaja and Ghulam Ali the risk of saturating the local market with petty things and cloth is obvious. When trade turns bad, close kinsmen may break out and proceed to a new location. Some years ago, all the Maskurahi Shaykh Mohammadis went to Ghulam Ali in summer, but then some families started going to Saray Khwaja instead, so these two camps are now of almost equal size (40-50 families). Subsequently, about 10 families began to migrate to Bayan and 5-10 more to Bagh-i Alam. The Shaykh Mohammadis themselves explain the fact that they are scattered over four summer areas in terms of economic necessity.

Ideally, the Shaykh Mohammadis ply their trade in a radius of some 10 km from their summer camp. In spite of the individualisation of the trade, however, living in a large group is preferred. They would rather go away for several days, hawking their merchandise in more distant areas, than having to separate from the community. In Saray Khwaja, the Shaykh Mohammadis state unequivocally that for the sake of peddling the optimal size of the camp would be ten to fifteen tents instead of the present forty-three, but that they will "eat less in order to be together."

Historically, the big groups were a security guarantee during migrations. This is still partly true, since the neighbouring, settled community in the summer area does not welcome the presence of itinerant people, and particularly not in such large camps. In Saray Khwaja then, there is an ongoing conflict with the settled population regarding Shaykh Mohammadis' use of a nearby under-ground water channel, *kārīz*. The local people claim that Shaykh Mohammadi women pollute the water by washing their clothes next to it. My own presence in the Shaykh Mohammadi camp became another issue to which the local people objected, but in this, as in other cases, the Shaykh Mohammadis were unyielding, insisting that they would rather "fight it out" with the locals. Equally so Shaykh Mohammadis who walked through the bazaar of Saray Khwaja were frequent objects of hostile comments from local people, comments which the Shaykh Mohammadis never left unanswered!

The large size of the Saray Khwaja camp may well explain the hostile attitude of the settled population. In the small Shaykh Mohammadi camp in Bayan, the situation was quite different: for the last 6 years, 6-7 households including 2-3 Laghmanis from Maskurah, have left for Bayan to sell pickled chickpeas and other produce. Relations between this small camp and the local villagers are cordial, despite the fact that the Shaykh Mohammadis have not been more accomodating there. A man from the Bayan camp describes the situation:

> "When we went there, we liked those people, who were such that if we cursed them 10 times, they would not be provoked. We are on very good terms with them. They are very nice people. If we curse their children or adults, they will not be provoked. We trespass on their orchards and their vegetable fields [and they will not be provoked]."

Although the Shaykh Mohammadis prefer to live in a large settlement it does not guarantee a peaceful, harmonious co-existence; on the contrary, *jang* (fighting, skirmishing) occurred daily also within the Saray Khwaja summer camp. Both as a community and individually, the Shaykh Mohammadis are very assertive and unyielding regarding what they consider as their right, almost to the point of being aggressive. Their social life was marked by frequent quarrels, with verbal and physical conflicts among both men and women. The relatively strong position of the women, who may earn their own living by peddling, is born out by their free participation in internal camp quarrels. This reduces Shaykh Mohammadis' reputation inasmuch as the surrounding, settled society prescribes chaste and subdued behavior for women.

The Saray Khwaja camp, which was located on a harvested field, was divided into two sections, an upper and a lower, but immediately adjacent to each other. Close relatives pitched their tents next to one another, provided they were on speaking terms. Between the upper and the lower sections, however, there was hardly any social contact. In one case where close relatives of the upper camp were fighting, one family removed its tent to the lower camp. The objects of conflict, both inside the community and with non-Shaykh Mohammadis, are frequently money or women, as the following cases illustrate:

(1) One of the rich cloth traders in Jalalabad supposedly lent 1,000 Afs to a poor family. When, on 'Eid day he came to collect his dues in the camp, the family denied ever having borrowed the money[40]. The brother-in-law of the cloth trader, whose daughter was married to the poor man's son, got into a fight with the poor man over the loan. The fight evolved into a family brawl. After several members of the poor man's family had been beaten, they went to the police, complaining that they had been assaulted by a number of people (all were close relatives). As a consequence, 20 people were arrested and imprisoned from morning until 3 p.m.. The attacking party was ultimately fined 800 Afs and the poor man 400 Afs.

The Shaykh Mohammadis carry the culture of *ǰang* so far that they also fight at weddings – with stones, "so that the children can become tough." The bride's party will start the fighting, and it is claimed that this is not simply a mock fight, but a real one. People may be injured, and once even a rifle was used. The following story is told with considerable excitement and no trace of regret:

(2) "We brought a bride to Alishang ... Those people offended us and our bridegroom, too. Those people of Alishang were potterymakers and also peasants and transporters who used donkeys [*kharkār*]. A Shaykh Mohammadi had gotten into a fight with them and had blinded somebody, throwing a stone in his face. ... The boy is still alive [and] it was actually me who blinded him. So they attacked us. ... We were about 250 people. They were about 3,000 families. ... We put the litter [*dulī*] down in a safe place, turned back, and the fight started.[41] Fight, fight, fight. So we fought until we drove them into their village and we followed them there, fighting and breaking all their pottery with stones. So we took the *dulī* and proceeded on our way. The next day they went to the governor and sued the bridegroom, accusing him of having encouraged his men to attack the potterymakers."

(3) "There was another wedding. A Shaykh Mohammadi had married a Laghmani but the girl's family would not hand over the bride to him. They went with all the singers and the rest. They were asking for an additional sum of money. They said, 'unless you give us so much additional money [as bride-price], we will not put the bride in the *dulī*'. So they fought each other from the morning till late evening. At the end of the fight, some 5 or 6 from their side and some 4 or 5 from our side were injured. Finally, more than 500 more people had joined on our side. There was *malik* Sher Ali Khan from Maskurah, he went on horseback and as he went there he won the quarrel and brought the bride. As these people were hit quite hard, they did not dare go to the government [and complain]."

Another example of a fight with non-Shaykh Mohammadis:

(4) "Eight or nine years ago, we beat up some ferrymen [*ǰālawāns*][42]. At that time there was no dam in Naghlu, and it was our turn to ferry our things [across]. And then other people carried

4,52 A couple of young cousins on a roof-top in Maskurah. The Shaykh Mohammadi men are normally well-dressed, which at least in the case of the cloth traders is both natural and perhaps necessary for the business (Dec. 1975).

4,53 Roof-top view of Maskurah (Dec. 1975).

their things [on the ferry] before we did, although it was our turn. ... . We were on our way to Kabul, coming on donkeys. Cars were not there ... . There was an Ahmad Jan among us. He had a bag of rice on his back and wanted to put it down on the fleet. But the ferryman began to hit him with a stick and he hurt him a lot. And then Ahmad Jan called on his brother-in-law, who was *Ḥajjī,* Sharif, an important man. He called on others, on everybody, to beat that ferryman. He had hardly closed his mouth when everybody, about 6, started beating the ferryman and pushing him into the water and taking him up again. About 5 or 6 people beat him. The son of Ahmad Wali Sahibzada went to the village and brought some 100 people, and we beat them all. They were around 45 people."

However, it is not only their numbers which makes the Shaykh Mohammadis somewhat belligerent. Individual families are also ready to pick a fight if necessary, as the following case illustrates:

(5) A landless Shaykh Mohammadi family had been allotted 12 *jarīb*s of land in Qala-i Gul Jan in Nangarhar. Rather than building their house on the land itself, they chose to build it on a nearby hillock. That hillock was government land intended for the construction of a school or a hospital, but the Shaykh Mohammadis didn't like the idea of having schoolboys roaming around so close to their home, so they occupied the land. Subsequently, a group of former nomads from Kunar settled next to the Shaykh Mohammadi family, and they objected to the house of the Shaykh Mohammadis on the hillock, presumably because its higher location was felt to jeopardize the privacy of their women. Quarrels broke out between the Shaykh Mohammadis and the nomads on this point, and although the Shaykh Mohammadis' "head was broken twice," they had not been entirely innocent, since the son was fined 6,000 Afs for beating one of the nomads and drawing a knife. But still, the Shaykh Mohammadi house remains on

the hillock, and one of their wealthy relatives is building a *qal'a* next to it.

In spite of the Shaykh Mohammadis' assertive, and at times agressive behaviour, it is quite common that outsiders be allowed to camp with them for the summer. For the individual outsider, the attraction may be the increased security from staying in a large camp, since the Koh-i Daman area has from ancient times been considered an area of robbers and highwaymen. For the Shaykh Mohammadis, already so numerous, one more family hardly matters, and in view of their own account of their mixed origin, there may even be a tradition for tolerating outsiders. In 1975, in addition to the 43 Shaykh Mohammadi households, the camp contained a household of a poor Pashtun with his wife, child, and a younger brother. The Pashtun was earning his living by catching snakes and curing snake and scorpion bites, while the younger brother learned petty trade from the Shaykh Mohammadis. The reason for their joining the Shaykh Mohammadi summer camp, and for being accepted there, was that their maternal aunt had married a Shaykh Mohammadi. There were two additional outsider households, unrelated Shaykh Mohammadis from Kabul who lived from cotton codding, riveting china ware, and making winnowing trays. They had joined the camp for the first time and were tolerated for their one month's stay "because they were Shaykh Mohammadi anyway."

However, with a large and self-assertive community like the Shaykh Mohammadis', outsiders will be allowed only as long as "they know their place," a process thus described by a Shaykh Mohammadi:

> "... [the outsider] will be tolerated and treated well for the first year like a guest. But the next year, he himself would get snobbish as he got rich and would start quarrelling with us. So in the end he will find life difficult inside the community and leave. We will not kick him out; he leaves by himself."

A touchy point seems to be if outsiders take up petty trade and become competitors to the Shaykh Mohammadis. A Shaykh Mohammadi explains that some years ago, four Laghmani brothers were introduced to the summer camp by a wealthy Shaykh Mohammadi trader who presumably had lent them money to start petty trade. As they became successful pedlars, trouble began:

> "For the first year, they were treated well, but as they did good business here that year, the next year I kicked them, you kicked them and everybody kicked them [i.e. quarrelled with them]. And the third year, the Shaykh Mohammadis just kicked them out and now they live in another village. ... They come with us and go back with us to Laghman, but they don't stay with us here in the camp, as the Shaykh Mohammadis will not let them."

The situation is different for outsiders who join because they have relatives married to Shaykh Mohmmadis. For example, the two Pashtun brothers who had an aunt inside the community counted on the aunt's relatives and in-laws to support them against attacks from others. But the aunt stressed that this would be the case only as long as she was alive. Afterwards, the brothers might well be kicked out of the summer camp.

While the Shaykh Mohammadis are divided amongst themselves and have little cooperation in business or economic affairs in general, there is a strong esprit-de-corps. Community solidarity is quickly activated in conflicts with non-Shaykh Mohammadis. Not only does everybody willingly participate in a fight to defend the rights of a Shaykh Mohammadi, but everybody also contributes economically in such a situation, either to pay a fine/compensation or to raise money for bribing the authorities. In such cases, all Shaykh Mohammadi households, irrespective of internal quarrels and divisions, would contribute a fixed sum. In the previously described fight with the ferrymen an example of such solidarity is given:

> "So after we had beaten those ferrymen, they went to the government of Sorobi, to the governor himself and complained that they had been beaten by the Shaykh Mohammadis. ... But we collected 10 Afs per family, which altogether made 2,000 Afs. ... We gave the 2,000 Afs to the governor [as bribe]."

Similarly, in the before-mentioned case, where the bridegroom was sued for the fight with the potterymakers, the Shaykh Mohammadi community collected the money among all the households and paid the fine imposed on the bridegroom.

This type of all-embracing community solidarity is invoked only in conflicts with outsiders say the Shaykh Mohammadis, but not in criminal cases if somebody is sued of theft or murder. Weddings, funerals, 'Eid-celebrations, and other rituals do not involve the whole community either, but only immediate relatives and acquaintances.

In the past, when conscription to the army was on a community basis according to the so-called *haft-nafarī* system, such that one man (*nafar*: person) out of each seven (*haft*) in a community were conscripted, the Shaykh Mohammadis say, that the whole community would collect money and pay compensation to whoever would volunteer for national service. Such compensation was essential, as doing the obligatory two-year national service constituted a significant economic burden on a family.[43]

As petty traders, the Shaykh Mohammadis compete with each other and are frequently involved in internal quarrels. They have neither the mediating institutions nor the leaders who could help them resolve those conflicts. In disputes with outsiders, however, they display a strong esprit-de-corps and in-group solidarity, involving not only economic but also physical support to an extent which seems greater than among other specialized communities in Laghman. This partly explains the Shaykh Mohammadis' "quarrelsome" reputation. In this sense, the Shaykh Mohammadis exert a pronounced marking of community boundaries. This may appear curious considering the number of outsiders absorbed into the community by marriage. Whether this boundary-maintaining behavour is a remnant of their past as a spiritual fraternity, where esprit-de-corps and honour traditionally have been central values, is impossible to confirm. However, this tradition has no doubt had a positive bearing upon their position within the traditional political structures of Laghman.

Political Structures

Historically, there are no traces signifying that the Shaykh Mohammadis of Maskurah have had any autonomous political organization; instead, they have been part of the general political structure of the Laghman region.

Until the reign of *Amīr* Abdur Rahman (1880-1901), the central power was weak and entirely dependent upon the tribal leaders, and political unrest and succession strife were rife. Common people had to look to their local leaders, *khāns* for political and military protection. In Laghman, the situation was further aggravated by raids from the *kāfirs* of the north, i.e. from the independent, non-Muslim areas of present-day Nuristan.

The economic and political integration of tribes and local communities into the Afghan State was until the centralisation of the State by *Amīr* Abdur Rahman mediated principally through tribal elders and *khāns*, who were usually big landowners as well. Apart from representing their tribes and communities vis-à-vis the government, the *khāns* frequently acted as local revenue collectors, paid by the government. Sometimes they would use other means to directly enhance their own incomes. It was also an old practice in Afghanistan to realise part of the state revenue through contract or farming, and such contracts were also taken up by the *khāns* and by well-to-do people in general (Kakar 1979). Locally, the *khāns* had immense political and economical power. As the representative, protector, and intermediary between the population and the government, local people were at his mercy, and he would exploit the situation to amass even more personal wealth. An elderly Shaykh Mohammadi gives an example of how the common man was exploited:

> "The straw tax would be about 40 *sēr* per *ǰarīb*. Many would leave their land, as they could not deliver the straw. As there were no cars, government transportation [i.e. military transport] was on animals: horses, donkeys, mules, elephants. They would camp on the fields of one or another *khān*, with 40 or more horses. The *khān* would normally graze the horses on the fields of small landowners and would also collect most of the straw from them. To the small landowner, the land would soon become more of a liability than an asset, and they would therefore leave it for the government, which was not interested, and therefore the *khān* would add it to his own land."

Hence, the *khāns* as local political leaders profited greatly from their relationship with the State.

The Shaykh Mohammadis were subject to the *khān* of Alishang, and an old Shaykh Mohammadi provides the following description of one of their old, big *khāns*, Hamza *Khān*, who lived during the last century:[44]

> "His ancestors were Pashtuns from Kandahar, but he lived with the Tajiks. He was a big *khān* in Laghman and the Jalalabad area. ... He was from Alishang himself but could order people to work as far as Jalalabad. He built a *qal'a* in Alishang and is supposed to have buried three masons as punishment for having dropped a brick. He was that powerful! He owned the land of Alishang and Maskurah, perhaps 500 *ǰarīb*, while another 500 *ǰarīb* were owned by the local people ... He collected taxes from the people, and everybody had to go to him to settle disputes. He would keep half of the tax for himself and give the other half to the government."

Since Laghman is ethnically mixed, with Pashtun- and Tajik-dominated areas, there were both Pashtun and Tajik *khāns*. During the 1929-Civil War under the brief rule of the Tajik rebel *Baccha-i Saqqao*, the loyalties of the Laghman residents were thus divided between the supporters of *Baccha-i Saqqao* and his Pashtun opponent and subsequent king, Nadir *Khān*.

Pashtuns and Tajiks fought each other, and the Shaykh Mohammadis counted themselves as Tajiks in this connection. It is said that when the victorious Pashtun (Safi) Akram *Khān* invaded Tajik-dominated Alishang, where Sher Ali *Khān* ruled, some 200-300 people were killed.[45]
When the Tajiks had surrendered the throne of Kabul to the Pashtun Mohammadzai dynasty under Nadir *Shāh*, peace was reestablished in Laghman by the marriage of Sher Ali *Khān's* daughter to Akram *Khān*'s son.[46]

The Shaykh Mohammadi community was subject to the local *khān*, who protected them vis-à-vis other groups and handled any disputes they had with the government; in return, his decisions and authority were binding on everybody, as one Shaykh Mohammadi explained:

"In marriages nobody would go against his [the *khān*'s] will, nor in the buying of land. Whatever they had decided, nobody could object. If you killed a man and somebody reported it to the government, the *khān* could go there and flatly deny that anybody had ever been killed. The *khān* would go to the government and say that it was all a lie, return to the village and reconcile the parties. ... And when somebody received his notice of conscription into the army, the *khān* would just report him dead and take some money from the person in question. Nobody would dare go to the government and say that the man was in the village. Nobody could defy the *khān*'s will. Moreover, he could also go to the government and testify that somebody who was 30 years old was only 20 years old. He could also certify him as 10 years old. So to his face, the commandant and governor could say nothing. He [the *khān*] would be cursing the governor while the latter would be hearing him".

When the last big *khān* of Alishang, Sher Ali *Khān* died, his subjects and area of authority, *khānī*, were divided between his brother Nabi Jan and his son, Sher Mohammad *Khān*. The Shaykh Mohammadis fell under Sher Mohammad *Khān*'s domain, or as they phrase it, they "were in the foot of" Sher Mohammad *Khān*.[47]
The following account is told by a Shaykh Mohammadi to illustrate that while the subjects or "followers" of a *khān* were at his mercy, they also had a claim on his protection. Only a poor *khān* would fail to take care of the interests of his followers:

"One of my cousins was arrested for theft. ... There was a gambler who was arrested and at the police he would give the name of anybody, so he had given the name of my cousin. And when they took the people to the government, the old would not be beaten but the young would be beaten severely. At that time [i.e., approximately one generation back] we were living under feudal conditions. ... We went to Sher Mohammad *Khān* and told him that 'we have been 'in your feet' from father to grandfather. You are our *khān*.' ... He [Sher Mohammad *Khān*] mounted his horse and went to the government, cursed the commandant and also his wife and told him: 'Have you caught that man in bed with your wife that you are beating him so hard? If the person from whom something has been stolen will not report him as thief, what right have you got, just because somebody has reported him involved? What kind of man are you? Are you a weaver or what?'[48] He [the commandant replied] 'I have not imprisoned him, but the vice-governor [*ḥukmrān*] has.' The *khān* asked where the vice-governor was. The commandant answered: 'He has gone to Alingar to dig a ditch.' The *khān* told me, that he would give me a letter so I could take it to the vice-governor: 'He will release your cousin'. I told him that 'I did not come to you in all this heat so you could give me a worthless paper in my hand'. He said: 'My letter will work'. But I provoked him by saying 'Go back to your house'. He returned and asked me to ride his horse while he himself was riding in a *gawdī*.[49] We went to the place where the governor was working. ... Then the *khān* shouted some obscenities so that the vice-governor could hear him. The vice-governor heard him, upon which he started running towards him out of fear, asking him: 'Why are you angry with me?' The *khān* told him about the matter. The vice-governor denied having beaten or imprisoned anybody, but the *khān* told him: 'Yes, you have. This is an orphan boy who has inherited some wealth from his father and his mother, has done some *gharībī* and collected some money. Some devil has given his name as accomplice, and you are beating him like a devil'. ... The vice-governor ordered him [the cousin] released immediately."

As tradesmen within the traditional political structures of Laghman, the Shaykh Mohammadis have been economically independent of the local landowners and thus not subject to patron-client relations at village level. By living together in one village as a group, the Shaykh Mohammadis formed a large, strong community, and became direct political clients of the *khān* of Alishang. While the *khān*'s power was immense, the above example illustrates that political clients also had a certain leverage with which to manipulate the *khān* to live up to his position and reputation as protector of his clients. By comparison, other specialized communities, such as the Musallis, who at an individual level were economic clients of the local landowners, had no political identity of their own vis-à-vis the dominat *khān* of the area. Other communities formed part of the overall political structure only as dependents of the local landowners (who were themselves clients of the dominant *khān*). Thus, unlike the Shaykh Mohammadis, these other groups have neither individually nor as a community a voice of their own.

With the growing influence of government officials in administration, tax-collection, together with the extension of education and communication since the time of *Amīr* Abdur Rahman, the power of the *khān*s has decreased considerably. High up in the river valleys there are remnants of traditional political and economic patronage, while in the plains of Laghman this has largely disappeared.[50] Instead, a representative system of elected *malik*s has been introduced: in Maskurah in 1976 half the Shaykh Mohammadis are officially represented by, and hold their identity cards in the name of the locally biggest landowner (a non-Shaykh Mohammadi), while a poor, non-Shaykh Mohammadi peasant, who is dependent upon the big landowner, represents the other half.[51]

Summary

In their migration patterns and general spatial mobility, the Maskurah Shaykh Mohammadis exploit social resources in their summer and winter areas, resources which are determined by both the agricultural cycle of their customers and by the infrastructure development and peculiarities of the existing market situation in the respective areas.

Historically, the Shaykh Mohammadis have displayed a considerable economic adaptability by shifting their commercial activities between the exploitation of various economic niches. Individual families continue to demonstrate considerable economic flexibility today. Hence, occupation as such is not a defining criterion for Shaykh Mohammadi identity. While the Shaykh Mohammadis have traditionally held certain occupations, they in no way hold a monopoly on these. The occupational variation between the different Shaykh Mohammadi groups is indicative of this.

The peculiarity of Shaykh Mohammadi identity is the lack of genealogical, ethnic, and occupational connection among the various groups claiming Shaykh Mohammadi identity, despite the existence of a common language serving as an ultimate marker of this identity. Apparently the Shaykh Mohammadis originally constituted the spiritual community of *Shaykh Ruhānī Bābā*'s followers, in such a way that membership in this fraternity overshadowed prior differences in ethnic and other primordial affiliations. It also means that while all Maskurah Shaykh Mohammadis consider each other as *qawmi*s, this term cannot, like segmentary lineage systems, be extended ultimately to embrace all other Shaykh Mohammadi communities; thus, the category of Shaykh Mohammadi is composed of a number of unrelated *qawm*s, who derive from members of the same spiritual fraternity and share the associated (secret) language. In this respect, to the best of my knowledge, they are unique in an Afghan context. And the Maskurah Shaykh Mohammadi's subsequent gradual development into an "ordinary", albeit very open, kin-based community only serves to underline the complexity of the question of ethnic identity and origin.

The social reproduction of the Maskurah Shaykh Mohammadi community, particularly its endogamy, thus acquires quite another significance as compared to other itinerant communities. The frequency of exogamous marriages is rather high among the Shaykh Mohammadis. They are predominantly wife-receivers, and non-Shaykh Mohammadi men tend to join the community upon marrying a Shaykh Mohammadi girl. It has been argued that endogamy among itinerants or peripatetics is a precondition for intergenerational succession (Barth 1987) and a mark of social inferiority (Rao 1987). However, the present case displays some peculiarities: the comparatively high frequency of exogamy among the Maskurah Shaykh Mohammadis is counteracted by the uniform practice of affines joining their community, assuming their migratory lifestyle and gradually taking up the same economic activities. Hence, intergenerational succession is hardly affected by the exogamous marriages. This practice also illustrates the complexity of the Shaykh Mohammadis' social position. On the one hand, their comparatively low social status as an itinerant community discourages exogamous marriages, while on the other, the Shaykh Mohammadis' group cohesion and political strength render them attractive marriage partners for poor settled people, despite their migratory lifestyle.

The inclusion of outsiders into the community accords with the originally and recognized formation of the Shaykh Mohammadi at a national level. Shaykh Mohammadi identity was achieved via membership in a spiritual fraternity and not by virtue of ethnic or kin-based identity. This fact leads to another way in which the Shaykh Mohammadi differ from many other itinerant communities: their comparatively low social status is solely associated with their lifestyle and not with their identity as Shaykh Mohammadis, which is recognized as implying respectability and piety.

Finally, itinerant commmunities have also been characterized by unequal economic and political relations to the settled society (Rao 1987). Economically, Shaykh Mohammadi peddling activities may be marginal in relation to the overall economy of the respective regions, but in their adaptation to and exploitation of various niches in the market, their marginality and social inequality become assets. Politically, the Shaykh Mohammadis have been clients of the dominant *khāns* of their part of Laghman. However, in relation to other settled groups in Laghman, their very number, group cohesion, and internal solidarity have rendered them a force to be reckoned with, as they have not been easily subdued in conflicts. Even today, this factor is of importance in the formation of their summer camps in the Koh-i Daman area and for their relations to the settled community there. Hence, being itinerant, the Shaykh Mohammadis are considered politically inferior by both the authorities and by the settled society. Yet by force of their sheer numbers, they manage to assert themselves and force the settled community to acknowledge and tolerate them. The importance of physical force is clearly recognized by the Shaykh Mohammadis themselves in all their accounts of successful fights. It is reflected in the fact that a Shaykh Mohammadi boy is considered a fully-fledged pedlar by the time he can manage the necessary calculations and physically defend himself against attacks from robbers and thieves along his peddling route.

While the Shaykh Mohammadis share a number of basic characteristics with other itinerant communities, they also add new dimensions to this discussion. As regards social status they illustrate the contradictory effects of an itinerant lifestyle, "respectable" origin, occupation, and the significance of physical power and external political relations.

NOTES:

[1] For a description of the technology of the *nadāfi* in Afghanistan, see Wright (1982). For a short description of the *patragari*, see Charpentier (1972: 126-7).

[2] Besides Laghman and Kabul, Shaykh Mohammadis supposedly are found in towns of Khanabad, Taluqan, Aibak, Kunduz, Kandahar, Ghazni, Logar, Jalalabad as well as in Peshawar and Quetta, Pakistan. In Laghman, the Maskurah Shaykh Mohammadis explain that another group of 25-30 Shaykh Mohammadi families lives in Chilmati, with whom they have no contact. In summer, the Chilmati Shaykh Mohammadis migrate to the Siyahsang area in Kabul, where they earn a livelihood as petty traders, fortune-tellers, and "charlatans."

[3] From the time of *Amīr* Abdur Rahman (1880-1901), a group of wealthy Shaykh Mohammadi cloth traders have been permanently settled in the Siyahsang area of Kabul. Here, as well as in Kote Sangi of Kabul, the cotton codders also live.

[4] Upon my continued probing, the Maskurah Shaykh Mohammadis ultimately suggested that I should get in touch with *Ḥajjī* Nabi Jan, an old and wealthy Shaykh Mohammadi cloth trader in Siyahsang, Kabul. They were not personally related to or acquainted with him, but he was reputed to be knowledgeable. Wealthy cloth traders were generally considered as prominent and pious examples of Shaykh Mohammadis. I finally went there and after my Maskurah companions had been identified as Shaykh Mohammadis by force of their knowledge of the *Ādūrgari* language, we were warmly received. The *Ḥajjī* himself, approaching 100 years of age, was very weak and had nearly lost the ability to speak. However, the information provided by him and his relatives confirmed and supplemented what I had already been told by the Maskurah Shaykh Mohammadis.

[5] *Mujāwir*, litt. adjacent, also used to refer to someone being employed in somebody's service, the man guarding or serving at a shrine.

[6] *Shaykh*, a title for the leader of a dervish (Sufi) order.

[7] Subsequently, the *patragar* recovered his lost waistcoat, money, and bottle of diamonds. In another quarrel about who could claim Shaykh Mohammadi identity, a religious mendicant (*malang*) had asked him to prove his holy descent by placing his hand under the boiling tap-water of a samovar. He did so without suffering any injury.

[8] The *Ḥajjī* and his family thus denied that the Maskurah Shaykh Mohammadis are "genuine" Shaykh Mohammadis. And subsequently, a group of Shaykh Mohammadi riveters of china ware (*patragars*), from Siyahsang of Kabul who spent winter in Jalalabad in tents, claimed that while his group were the "real" ones, the *Ḥajjī* and his family were *Nadāf Khēl*, i.e. not "real" ones, and the case was even worse with the Maskurah group: "The Shaykh Mohammadis of Maskurah we call *Siyāhpāyak*. ... are of the same ancestry as that of the *Jats*, the sievemakers are also *Jats*. The grandfather of *Ḥākim* Nabi Jan had gone to India and brought one man from the jungle back to Laghman. He taught him to speak, brought him up and got him married, from which these Maskurah-people and also the *Jats* appeared."

[9] 1 *Tumān* was equal to 20 rupees.

[10] Presumably Shamsapur near Surkhrod, in Nangarhar province. Mir Ali Shah is apparently identical to the above-mentioned Mira Shah Laghar, who had proved his identity as a true *sayyid* in Mecca in the cotton codder's account above.

[11] *Khwāja* – title given to male, patrilineal descendants of Abu Bakr, the first *khālifā*.

[12] 1 *paw* = 441.6 grams; 1 *sēr* = 7066.0 grams.

[13] The sievemakers, Ghorbat (see Ch. V) use the same term for their sales trips. The term (*ādūr*) is apparently neither Persian

nor Pashto, although I have been unable to trace its origin.

[14] *Murīd*, novice in a Sufi order, *ṭarīqāt*. *Mukhliṣ*, devotee.

[15] Most of the following data was collected among the Maskurah Shaykh Mohammadis in their Saray Khwaja summer camp, but visits were also made to the summer camp at Ghulam Ali. Additional data was gathered during a subsequent stay in Maskurah.

[16] Kafiristan, lit. Land of Infidels; the mountainous eastern region of Afghanistan inhabited by non-Muslim, Dardic-speaking peoples. After its conquest and the forced conversion of the population to Islam, the region was renamed Nuristan, "Land of Light". The Shaykh Mohammadi cloth-traders in Siyahsang mentioned several ancestors who had fought in the *ǰihād* (holy war) against the infidels (*kāfirs*).

[17] This type of trade was called "doing *ǰopa*."

[18] Among these traditional medicines were mentioned *chāhartokhum* (lit. four seeds), *tiz-i Hindu* (the fart of the Hindu), *shākh-i shutur* (the camel horn), and *kaf-i dariā* (the foam of the river), *pitali*, *khalastali*, *murdār sang* (death stone). *Kaf-i dariā* is the internal calcareous shell of the cuttlefish. Aitchison (1891: 187) states that it is usually brought to these parts of the world by pilgrims returning from Mecca, and hence cuttle-bone is looked upon as a most important and valuable medicine. *Murdār-sang* is the oxide of lead (*ibid*: 136). More exact information on the other medicines is unavailable.

[19] *Laltak* and *lawang* are plants from British India, the leaves of which have a pleasing smell. They were sold mainly in Kohistan. *Murwali* is "something green which the Kohistanis hang around their neck."

[20] *Sang-i basrī*, tutty, an impure oxide of zinc obtained from the exhaust pipes of smelting furnaces or a similar substance occurring as a native mineral; used chiefly as a polishing powder (Steingass 1973).

[21] In selling traditional medicines, the Shaykh Mohammadis have probably profited from the authority of their "holy" descent, which would have given the customers additional faith in the cures prescribed.

[22] *Deo*, lit. *dīw*, meaning devil or demon.

[23] *Sarāy*, dwelling for accommodating travellers and their pack animals, consisting of an enclosed yard with chambers around it. Can also refer to a wholesale market.

[24] The production cost and labour time for *chaǰ*-making should be as follows: 1 *sēr* of reeds: 100 Afs. Skin straps for stitching: 40 Afs. From this, 12 winnowing trays will be produced. These will be sold for 200 Afs, thus leaving a profit of 60 Afs. It will take some two days to make the 12 trays, resulting in a daily earning of only around 30 Afs.

[25] Professional training may even start earlier: one morning in Saray Khwaja I saw an approximately 5-year-old boy go around selling boiled potatoes inside the camp. He expected to make a profit of 5 Afs on 1/4 *sēr* potatoes.

[26] The production cost of a cap is 30 Afs: 10 rolls of gilded thread (20 Afs), 2 rolls of ordinary thread (3 Afs), plus cloth (5 Afs). The cap is sold for 60-70 Afs, with a profit of 30-40 Afs per cap.

[27] In 1975, when most of the quantitative data was collected, there were 43 Shaykh Mohammadi families in the Saray Khwaja camp and 3 "outsider" families. One of these "outsiders" had relatives among the Shaykh Mohammadis, and the two remaining tents were unrelated Shaykh Mohammadis from Siyahsang of Kabul.

[28] A somewhat similar observation has been made among the Rwala bedouin society by Lancaster and Lancaster (1987: 317).

[29] A representative from the Afghan Fruit Cleaning Co., a joint-stock company and one of thirteen such fruit exporting companies in the country, denies that there should be a connection between trade protocols and the increase in raisin prices: "The reason we have higher prices this year is solely due to the international market. The US has had a bad harvest, the raw material prices have risen in the international market, and so have the prices of raisins."

[30] The brokers get paid 1-2 Afs per *sēr* commission by the traders.

[31] In 1976 the Afghan government, in order to protect the producers, fixed a minimum price on raisins based on international prices. However, these minimum prices had no effect. Even if the producers had been properly informed (which they were not) economic pressures would have prevented them from holding out until the brokers of the joint stock companies bought at a better price. In addition, these companies have a reputation for being so late in paying the producers that financial problems would have forced the producers to sell part of the crop for cash payment below the fixed minimum price to private traders.

[32] 1 *kharwār* = approximately 565 kg.

[33] The reeds are called *tutani*, while the people of Samarkat, where the reeds used to grow, call them *chaǰwāna*.

[34] The monthly expenses of 2,010 Afs covered the following items: meat (800 Afs), tea and sugar (150 Afs), kerosene for lamps (60 Afs), brushwood for fuel (300 Afs), flour (600 Afs), rice (100 Afs).

[35] According to a local landowner, the land price in Maskurah is 80-100,000 Afs per *ǰarīb*.

[36] They received 12 *ǰarībs* of land, where 1 *ǰarīb* was meant as site for the house. The land was given freely, but they received no assistance regarding housing, seeds, or tools. The soil is very rocky and cannot be ploughed manually, so they hire a tractor for this work. The land yields two crops (wheat and *māsh*), but in 1975 the *māsh* was ruined by insects and the wheat was destroyed by hail.

[37] Three families were "outsiders", i.e. unrelated families not belonging to the community of Maskurah Shaykh Mohammadis.

[38] It can hardly be denied that the Shaykh Mohammadis are quarrelsome. During my stay in the Saray Khwaja summer camp, I experienced a number of outright fights involving both men and women. *J̌ang* (physical fight or heavy quarrel) occurred daily and was almost considered public entertainment. Quarrels involved accusations of the most base character, often in terms of obscenities, and women were no more restrained than men in this respect.

[39] The following account is given of wedding expenses in connection with a Shaykh Mohammadi who married a Laghmani girl: The brideprice was 17,000 Afs. The number of guests was 500, of which 300 were from the girl's side. The wedding itself involved the following expenses for the groom's family: 80 *sērs* of wood, wheat, 1 cow, 40 *sērs* of rice, 3 *sērs* of ghee, 1 goat, 2 *sērs* of henna, 10 *sērs* of flour, 5 *sērs* of salt, 2 *paw* of black tea, 2 *paw* of *gil-i sar-shūy* (lit. face-washing mud), 2 *paw* of red pepper, 2 *sērs* of peas, 4 *paws* of walnut-tree wood for cleaning teeth, 4 pumpkins, 8 *sērs* of raw sugar, 6 *sērs* of sweets, 10 *sērs* of walnuts, 1 *paw* of cumin, 2 *sērs* of potatoes, 5 dresses, 5 cakes of soap, 1 big

mirror, all sorts of hairpins, 2 bottles of hair oil, red and white face-powder, 1 lipstick, moulds, 1 veil, 2 pairs of shoes, 2 pairs of socks, and a special kind of handkerchief. In addition, a number of monetary gifts were paid to participating persons: 1,000 Afs went to the girl's maternal uncle for his officiating (*namāna*); 500 Afs was to go to the *malik* (= *malikāna*); 100 Afs to the barber, who cooked the meal; 100 Afs to the woman, who made the bride's make-up; 50 Afs to the blacksmith, who delivered the presents; 50 Afs to the carpenter, who was to bring a stand on which to put the lamp; 50 Afs to the goldsmith for plating the bride's hair (the goldsmith would also bring as a present a pin for parting the hair); 30 Afs gratuity to the village shopkeeper for bringing a plate of *nukhūl* (glazed almonds); 30 Afs for the painter who would bring a tablecloth; a gift for the barber's wife, for standing in the bride's house with an incense vessel; and 20 Afs to one of the bride's relatives for preparing a kind of syrup, into which the bride and groom dip a finger and taste.

40 The moneylender's complete disregard for the religious holiday and *qawmi*-relations were noted by several people in the camp: "While he is from our *qawm*, he has not given a single meal to anybody. When he came here, we expected that he was going to give a party...!" And "He came like a and everyone left the camp quarreling with each other".

41 *Dulī* is a Hindustani term for a litter, "consisting of a cot or frame, suspended by the four corners from a bamboo pole, and is carried by two or four men. ... As it is lighter and cheaper than a palankin it costs less both to buy, rent, and carry, and is used by the poorer classes" (Yule and Burnell 1986(1886): 313). In Afghanistan, the bride, on her wedding day, is placed veiled on a *dulī* and carried from the house of her parents to that of her in-laws thus signifying her transfer to the in-law family.

42 *Zhāla* or *ǰāla*, fleet constructed from empty containers tied together. *Zhālawān*, the person who sails the *zhāla*.

43 An old man thus states that his son's expenses while doing national service amounted to around 6,000 Afs; the servicemen are given no salary nor pocket money, and those who can afford it spend money on additional (better quality) food. It was also stated that while in the army the soldiers have to supply their own bedding.

44 The successors of Hamza *Khān* are said to be, in chronological order, Abdul Samad *Khān*, Jalad *Khān*, Jalil *Khān*, and then Sher Ali *Khān*, who took part in the Civil War in 1929.

45 Sher Ali *Khān* was here counted as Tajik, although his ancestors had supposedly been Kandahari Pashtuns. Actual ancestry was probably less decisive than the fact that Sher Ali *Khān*, who was *khān* in a Tajik-majority area, had apparently been supporting *Baccha-i Saqqao*.

46 This marriage was referred to as *bad*, which implies "compensation." While the marriage connection served the point of re-establishing good relations between the two *khāns*, it is also significant that it was the losing party which found themselves in the position of "wife-givers." This has been a well-established practice in Afghanistan, where preference is to marry off daughters to equals or superiors. Most Afghan rulers have used marriages to establish political alliances, and took wifes from conquered or subjected people.

47 An informant defines the expression in the following way: "To 'be in the foot' of somebody means every sort of dependence. It means that you can't piss without his permission. If a *khān* ordered him, a person will leave his wife."

48 Reference to the low status group of weavers is used here as a curse.

49 A *gawdī*, known as a *tonga* in the Indian Subcontinent, is a light, small two-wheeled horse-drawn vehicle with two cushioned seats placed back-to-back, and covered by a bonnet. Outside the major cities, *gawdīs* were the most common form of "taxis" in Afghanistan even in the 1970s.

50 This description from Alishang (November 1976) illustrates that the *khān*'s power is not completely finished: " Taj Mohammad of Alishang exacts tribute, a couple of *sērs* of wood per family, on those Kohistani villages in Karenj. The reason he can do this is that these people are hardly in contact with the government. They speak little Farsi and if they have matters to solve, they act through the *khān* as the official spokesman, or the *khān* resolves pressing issues. In weddings, the *khān* receives 300-500 Afs from the family, and he also gets money when people need his help as official spokesman, for example, in obtaining exemption from military service."

51 The power of the Alishang *khāns* was not only weakened due to the changing circumstances but also by internal feuds. According to one Shaykh Mohammadi: "There came a time where the *khāns* fought each other. He [presumably Shere Mohammed *Khān*] killed his son-in-law in broad daylight and also the latter's brother. They [the khāns] were put in jail. They were 4-5 brothers. They had to pay a lot of money to obtain release, but after that they became weak. And now everybody is *malik* for himself, everybody is a *khān*, nobody cares about anybody, as everybody became 'oily' [i.e. a rich person]."

CHAPTER V

THE GHORBAT SIEVEMAKERS

Introduction

Throughout Afghanistan, the traditional manufacture of sieves made from wood and leather straps has been carried out by an itinerant and endogamous community calling itself Ghorbat. The Ghorbats, who adhere to the Shi'a sect of Islam, claim to be of Persian origin. They state that they first took up sievemaking after their arrival in Afghanistan, probably a few centuries ago. The Ghorbats speak a language of their own called *Qāzulāgi.*

The Ghorbats were in 1976 divided into two major subgroups, the Farāhis, who subsist predominantly as animal traders at the Kabul market, and the Siāwuns, the only sievemaking community in Afghanistan and the group among which I conducted field research. The Siāwun community is composed of four sub-groups (*khēls*), Nasir Khēl, Mehrāb Khēl, Mostafa Khēl, and Qāsem Khēl, totalling some 300-400 families. While sievemakers are found in all the accessible and densely populated regions of Afghanistan, the four Siāwun *khēls* have traditionally been associated with localities in East Afghanistan. Most Ghorbats consider these localities as their summer homes: Nasir Khēl and Mehrāb Khēl in Ghazni, Mostafa Khēl in Kabul, and Qāsem Khēl in Charikar. Sievemakers are also found, however, in Kandahar and Herat, as well as in many localities in the north, Pul-i Khumri, Kunduz, Balkh, etc.

The four Siāwun *khēls* display great internal variation in occupational and settlement patterns: All the *khēls* contain families whose *main* occupation is sievemaking, others who are occasional sievemakers, and some who have found completely other occupations. In all the *khēls* there are households who are settled, households who live in permanent dwellings part of the year, and households who are permanent tent-dwellers. These differences are linked mainly to two factors: the relative poverty of the household and its principal occupation. The marketing of sieves requires mobility, and sievemaking families will therefore invariably be on the move during the summer months.

Sievemaking is primarily a male occupation, and although women may assist in the work, a large proportion of Ghorbat women are breadwinners for their families on equal terms with their husbands. The women hawk petty wares in the villages, serving primarily female customers just like the Shaykh Mohammadis. In the past, they also offered their skills of medical blood-drawing, cupping, and fortune telling. These economic activities necessitate that women move freely and unveiled in public places, significantly adding to the settled population's view of the sievemakers as socially inferior. In a (Sunni) Muslim society like Afghanistan, the hierarchization of occupations is in principle not sanctioned by religious notions of purity. The very low ranking of occupations such as barbers and leatherworkers is explained by reference to their work as being "dirty", "unclean", or "inferior", but those performing these occupations are not necessarily considered religiously "inferior" or "unclean". Nevertheless, the social stratification of occupational and endogamous communities bears resemblance to the caste system of the Indian Subcontinent (see Ch. II) although the underlying ideology differs. As sievemakers with an itinerant lifestyle, with non-Afghan origin, Shi'a orientation, and with unveiled, economically active women, the Ghorbats are one of the socially lowest ranking groups in the society.

The following description of the Siāwun Ghorbats begins with their mythical and historical origin.[1] Unlike most specialized communities, the Ghorbats in their myths concentrate far more on their auspicious, heroic ancestry than on the sacred origin of their occupation. The theme of an original curse occupies prominent place as an "explanation" of how people of such past grandeur have fallen to their present low state. Where other ethnic specialist groups find redemption in sacralizing their profession, the Ghorbats primarily find it in a noble ancestry of equally mythical nature.

The historical facts of the origin of the Ghorbats are obscure. Generally, itinerant or economically marginal peoples have been ignored in historical records, and this is also the case of the Afghan Ghorbats. However, the name Ghorbat and related forms are found throughout the Middle East, as is the occupation of sievemaking. There is neither evidence of a common origin of these groups, nor of a general association between groups having this name and sievemaking. Here I have attempted to piece together the more recent history of the Ghorbats in Afghanistan, according to their own, often vague accounts.

In the following sections, the production of sieves is described along with the division of labour within the household, which is the unit of sieve production. However, sievemaking is not the only and in many cases not even the most important economic activity of the Ghorbats, and women's peddling activities are discussed as well as the other income resources which the men exploit.

The four *khēls* follow different migration patterns. While the summer migrations are determined by the marketing of sieves, the choice of winter location is often influenced by the cost of living and of shelter. Subsequently, the economic stratification between the four *khēls* is discussed in view of their different migration patterns and markets, and in connection with the importance of alternative, i.e. non-sievemaking, economic activities.

Finally, the social organization of the Ghorbats will be discussed, to be followed by an outline of their internal political organization, which in the past, has kept them isolated from the political system of the settled society. Today, these structures are loosing their importance due to the gradual integration of the Ghorbats into the administrative system of the Afghan State. Ultimately, the maintenance of the Ghorbats as social "outcasts" is reconsidered in view of their origin, lifestyle, economic activities, and religious affiliation.

Mythical Origin

The Ghorbats are eager storytellers. Their favourite stories are fairy tales, accounts of religious and supernatural character – or, equally popular, tales of their own noble ancestry. A characteristic feature of the latter is the liberal combination of religious figures, such as Allah, the Prophet, the arch angles, and so on, with pre-Islamic mythical heroes of Iranian legends, ultimately linking the sievemakers' ancestry to the heroes of the Iranian national epic, the *Shāh Nāma*.[2] In this context, the Ghorbats' claim to be of royal origin, *shāzāda khēl* (i.e. Prince *khēl*), stating that "By nature we are not low – actually we are *Kayāni*s [i.e. of Iranian royal stock]). From mother's side we mixed ... ." Patrilineality is the norm both among Ghorbats and in Afghanistan in general. Hence, "mixing from mother's side" does not ruin the claim to the identity as "*shāzāda khēl*", if they patrilineally are of royal stock.

The claim to be *shāzāda khēl* and *Kayāni*s is matched by a high frequency of royal or aristocratic titles used as names – *Khān*, *Shāh*, *Āghā* – as compared to their general use in Afghanistan. An interesting parallel to this is found in Casimir's discussion of the adaptive strategies inherent in the peripatetics' legends of origin:

> "Noble ancestry, true remorse and destitution are, in many societies factors which contribute to the success of peripatetics in their spontaneous dealings with customers. Several 'Gypsy' groups migrating in western Europe in the fifteenth century made use of such a strategy: Calling their leaders Prince, Duke or Count, many such groups proclaimed themselves Christians going on pilgrimage to expiate their sins, and were well received by local authorities" (1987: 385).

Another parallel may also be seen in the Musallis' calling themselves *Shāhi Khēl* (King Khēl). However, to trace the legendary ancestry of the Ghorbats, one literally has to start with Adam and Eve, as it appears in the following version:[3]

> "Adam had a son called Shish (*alai-hi 's-salām*) ... Adam prayed for Shish (*alai-hi 's-salām*) for an angel [*hūr*] to be his mate, Archangel Jibrail [Gabriel] performed the wedding ceremony. Out of this union came Kay Murz ... Thereafter Kay Kobad, thereafter Kay Khusrow, thereafter Kay Kanus, thereafter Kobad-i Shaheriat, thereafter Nowshervan ... After some generations came Kayhan ... and Rustam was the son of Zal, Zal was the son of Sam and Sam was the son of Naraivan ..."

While the source or inspiration of this tale is doubtlessly the *Shāh Nāma*, both the genealogy and actual stories seem more mixed up. To link the above genealogy up with the present-day Ghorbats, the mythical lineage is set in a comparatively recent, semi-historical Afghan context:

> "One of the sons of Kay Khusrow ... was Siavush. He managed to escape [from Iran presumably] and in Herat he learned jewellery. He got into contact with some nomadic people from Baluchistan who did sievemaking and married into [their group]. When he could not earn enough money on jewellery he took up sievemaking – and came all the way via Kandahar to the other places [in the east]. And from him there appeared all the other *khēl*s [of Ghorbat]."

While the original mythical ancestors of the Ghorbats were the pre-Islamic Persian kings, other legends tie them directly to Islam, irrespective of historical chronology:

"Kay Kanus was one day dreaming and he saw Mohammad in his dream. The Prophet told him: 'In a short time a person, the Lion of God, Ali, who is my son-in-law, is going to come to your place [Tehran, Iran].' After a few days, two men came to the town. They sent a messenger to the elders of the town, who, headed by Kay Kanus, returned with him. One of the two men told them: 'I am the Lion of God, the son-in-law of the Prophet, the King of the Faithful, Ali. I have come to convert you to Islam either by the word or by the sword.' After this speech, the elders consulted each other about what to do. They went to Ali and said: 'If you are the Lion of God, the son-in-law of the Prophet and the *amīr al-mu'minīn* [Leader of the Faithful], Ali, you should be able to perform miracles to prove your identity. We want to see the Prophet here right now at this moment.' Ali agreed and holding up his fingers [in a V-sign], he asked the elders to look between his fingers. When the elders did so, Ali told them that they would see a man sitting in a mosque in Medina. Kay Kanus recognized that indeed this man was the one he saw in his dream, and thus he became convinced not only of the identity of Ali but also of the truth of his religion, Islam. Kay Kanus told Ali and his elders that they believe in the truth. Ali informed them what to do to become Muslims, and to recite after him: 'There is one God but Allah ...' He also told them to build a mosque and how to do it, gave them a volume of the Qor'an, and told them to behave in accordance with its precepts. They build a mosque and then there is a need for a mullah. The most learned and intelligent among them was chosen, a man by the name of Faiz Ali. Ali ordered a glass of water and asked Faiz Ali to drink it. When he drank it, he remembered every word of the Holy Book. From then on, the people sent their children to him for instructions. Before they became Muslims they had the Book of Ghorbat."

This legend elevates the Ghorbats to be original Muslims, converted at the time of the Prophet and even by *Ḥaẓrat* Ali himself. Since Kay Kanus, one of the mythical ancestors, is claimed to be among the first Muslims, Ghorbat and Muslim identities become inseparable. This is somewhat parallel to the Musalli claim to be original Muslims by being descendants of the prayer rug carrier of the Prophet, a theme also reported prevalent among the Pashtuns of Afghanistan (e.g. Anderson 1984: 274).

The Ghorbats' present state as a despised minority is a far cry from their alleged past grandeur, and many of their tales explain this painful situation by reference either to the Ghorbats as victims of some external developments or as being cursed due to some past misdeeds, as the following statement from an old Ghorbat illustrates:

"God first examines a person and then determines his fate – that is why He has made the sievemakers so wandering and restless and poor, because they are a very unruly and disunited people ..."

In the Ghorbats' self-conception the idea of being victims is so prominent that they even explain it as the origin of their name, i.e that *ghorbat* means "exiles", "dispersed", or "runaways". In spite of their claim to be original Muslims, one Ghorbat legend explains their curse as being brought about by their ancestors' lack of respect for the Prophet:

"Our ancestors have been telling us that we were actually kings and that we are the descendants of Kayhan *Pāchā*. There were some other kings at that time, too – like the king of Soviet Union. But Kayhan was a very proud man, so when the Prophet sent letters to all the kings, all of them first kissed it and put it on their head [in the turban]. But Kayān after kissing it put it on his leg [litt. foot, i.e. presumably put in his leg-wrappings for safekeeping, which, however, was considered a disrespectful place]. When the Prophet was travelling in all these countries, the king of the Soviet Union got the letter out of his turban. But when he came to Kayhan, he just got it out of his leg [wrapping] due to which the Prophet got angry and cursed him: 'Wherever you go, may your family and descendants be running after bread'.

"The Soviets were blessed and they will never be defeated.[4] We are the descendants of Kayhan, that 'cursed be his father' [*pidar la'nat*], and now the bread is ahead of us and we are running after it. If he had been respectful, we would have been the greatest *khēl* of kings, *Pāchā Khēl*."[5]

The idea of God punishing disunited or unruly people with material and social misery was also found among the Musallis and the Shaykh Mohammadis, but far less prominently than among the Ghorbats. Casimir argues that the theme of "guilt and punishment" recurs in the legends of origin among itinerant peoples, who generally occupy a socially inferior and despised position.[6] These legends thus have a consoling function, assuring the itinerants a decent genealogy and removing the blame on the present generation for their socially unacceptable lifestyle (Casimir 1987, see also Rao 1982: 42). On the other hand, Casimir also points to the adaptive strategy inherent in these legends; i.e. that they serve to get the maximum out of the peripatetics' dealings with the settled society. While this hardly can be argued in case of the Ghorbats' myths, the observation may well apply to the Shaykh Mohammadi *faqīr*s, who make a living from their supposedly holy ancestry.

The Ghorbats are keen to tell legends of their noble ancestry so as to disassociate them from sievemaking. However, like other craftsmen in this part of the world, they also have legends which sacralize their profession, and tell of how it was given to them by the Prophet or by one of the archangels:[7]

"This profession has been picked from the Prophet. One of the women in the harem of the Prophet was eating uncleaned barley flour in a bread, and it stuck in her throat. She complained to the Prophet who sent four angels along with Jibrail [i.e. the archangel Gabriel] down to make sieves. They only had problems in sawing the wood. But in the mulberry tree there was a demon who told them that if they would make him partner, he would show them a trick. The leaves of the mulberry tree resemble a saw, and he told them to make an iron tool like these to saw the wood.

"This is told in the *ḥadīth*, and Siāvush learned it from there.[8] One of the reasons that sievemaking does not pay more is because a demon was partner in the original occupation."

The demon's involvement in trade has the same explanatory value as the initial guilt or fatal mistake of Kayhan in the above legend. Another version of the religious origin of the occupation was told by Ghorbats in Kandahar:

5,1 Sievemaker camp (Mehrab Khēl) in the outskirts of Ghazni (Nov. 1976).

"The metal tools for making sieves were made by Dawud (*alai-hi 's-salām*).[9] The wooden parts were made by Shish (*alai-hi 's-salām*).[10] The actual weaving was done by Jibrail". "When God created Adam, He needed a sieve to sift the dust from which Adam was made.[11] For that purpose a sieve was made. Then God ordered the soul to enter Adam's body, but the soul would not enter as it was afraid of the dark well which was the human body. So God promised the soul that he would take it out/release it from the body if it felt uncomfortable in it. God also ordered some music to be played – flutes and drums – so the soul would feel pleased. Then the soul entered the body. This is why we feel pleased whenever we hear music."

Whereas Ghorbat origin myths centre upon pre-Islamic figures – mythical heroes of ancient Persia who like Kay Kanus are rendered Islamic – legends of the Musallis and Shaykh Mohammadis remain entirely within Islam. Nevertheless, the combination of pre-Islamic heroes and Islamic holy men seems to be a common feature of the legends found among the artisan guilds of

5,2 Group of Qāsem Khēl sievemakers in Kote Sangi, Kabul (May-June 1975).

Westasia.[12] The lack of legends connecting sievemaking to the community of Ghorbats seems significant, however. In the tradition of the artisan guilds, sievemaking as an occupation is sacralized by an alleged religious origin of the most prominent kind, i.e. initiated by the order of God during Creation. In contrast, the Ghorbats' introduction to sievemaking is not religiously ordained but presented as a historical and mundane, rather than a mythical event. That is, the Ghorbats became sievemakers after their exile and downfall from royalty, either through the mythical ancestor Siavush's or some later ancestor's intermarriage with sievemakers – or due to economic need (see below).

The lack of inherent connection between the Ghorbats and sievemaking at the mythical level may be explained by the fact that sievemaking is a comparatively recent occupation for these people, as claimed in their historical accounts. The legends relating to sievemaking may in that case be seen as an assimilation to the general pattern of sacralizing occupations found among artisan guilds in West and Central Asia generally. Moreover, sievemaking is considered socially so low that sacralization of the occupation is not sufficient to

5,3 Qāsem Khēl sievemakers in their winter camp at the outskirts of Jalalabad, making wire-mesh sieves for sale to shopkeepers in the city (Dec. 1975).

counteract its low status. Instead, the Ghorbats claim royal origin, and sievemaking is reduced to a circumstantial rather than a religiously ordained condition. A similar situation although far less pronounced than in the Ghorbat case was found among the Persian-speaking Musallis.

Historical Origin

The name "Ghorbat" and related forms are widespread in the Middle East, Central Asia and even in the Balkans. Generally, the term or its derivative forms are applied to "Gypsy-like" groups, including people who practice sievemaking as a source of income (Rao 1982, 1983), and it is claimed that the term is found wherever Ottoman dominion once held sway (Arnold 1967). According to Amanolahi, the names applied to Gypsies in Iran vary from one province to another, where in Fars, "Ghorbati" is one of them (1992). Arnold claims that the Iranian Gypsies refer to themselves as Ghurbed (1967). "Ghorbati" is used by Barth to refer to a group of tinkers and smiths who are clients of the nomadic Basseri tribe in Fars, South Iran (1964: 91-2). Apart from their metalworking these

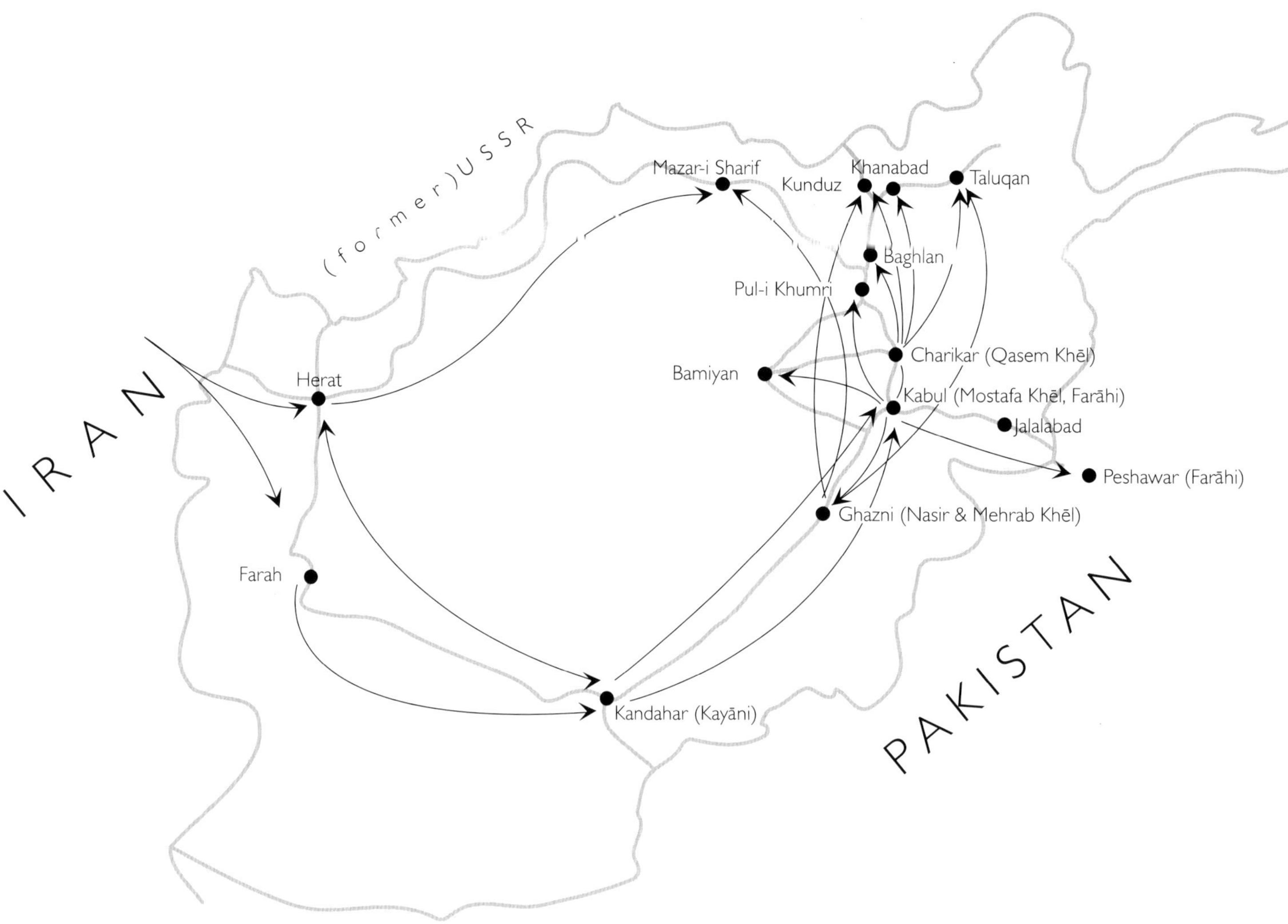

5.4 Historical dispersion of Ghorbat

Ghorbati men and women also produce large sieves of perforated gut. The technology is apparently different from that used by the Afghan Ghorbat, but it tallies with Arnold's information on Gypsy sievemakers in Iran (1967: 117). Wulff, on the other hand, in his comprehensive study of traditional crafts of Persia, describes the manufacture of sieves identical with that used in Afghanistan and Turkey – but these sieves are manufactured by Koulī-women (Wulff 1966).[13]

In Khuzistan and Luristan respectively, Gypsies may be referred to as "Kuli" and "Kowli", the latter terms often being used in Tehran and other major urban centers as well (Amanolahi 1992).

Are these various Ghorbat communities originally related? Is sievemaking their traditional occupation? And are the Ghorbats really Gypsies? With the Afghan Ghorbats' claim to Iranian origin, supported by their Shi'a faith, language, musical tradition, etc., it may safely be assumed that they originate from one of the so-called Ghorbat groups in Iran. There are, however, no further indications regarding the locality or circumstances of their Iranian past.

5.5-9 In 1948, Lennart Edelberg encountered a group of sievemakers in Sar i Chesma. He took photographs, but collected no further details of their whereabouts. Note the wooden sieve-frames lying in front of the tents. (*Fig.* 5,5)

Another issue is that while "Ghorbat" in Afghanistan is an ethnonym, i.e. the sievemakers' name for themselves, this is not the case with regard to the term's wider regional usage according to Rao. Here, the label appears to be used as a joint term of reference for various itinerant communities, similar to the way "*Jat*" is used in Afghanistan (Rao 1983). Similarly, Amanolahi lists "Ghorbati" as one of the names given to Gypsies by the settled population. This observation virtually renders meaningless the question of whether the "Ghorbats" traditionally were sievemakers. Although occupations like sievemaking, certain forms of smithing, and tinking in West and Central Asia have long been performed by itinerant communities, this does not necessarily indicate any inherent connection between a specific ethnic group and a certain occupation. On the contrary, itinerant communities are characterized by high adaptability to the overall economic structures rather than by rigidity in occupational patterns – a case in point is the Shaykh Mohammadis, and the Afghan Ghorbats confirm this picture as well.

5,6 The skins are being pegged to the ground to dry in the sun (Photo: Lennart Edelberg, Sar-i Chesma, 1948)

What about the Gypsy origins of the Ghorbats? There is a long tradition for labelling itinerant groups in the West and Central Asia "Gypsies" irrespective of whether it can be substantiated that they actually are of Romani-speaking, Indian origin (Rao 1983).[14] Amanolahi writes that Gypsy musicians were imported to Iran by the Sassanian king Bahram-i Gur (AD 421-39) and that Hamz-i Isfahani (AD 927) refers to these people as "Kowli" or "Zot"; they are likewise mentioned in the *Shāh Nāma*. It is most probable, Amanolahi argues, that over the centuries successive groups of Gypsies came to Iran (ibid.). It is simply not substantiated that all itinerant groups in Iran are actually of Kowli or Gypsy descent. In the case of the Afghan Ghorbat, there is very little evidence that this was the case: legends point only to an Iranian (Sassanian!) origin, as does their *Qāzulāgi* language.

5,7 From the dried skin, a long thin strap is being cut. (Photo: Lennart Edelberg, Sar-i Chesma, 1948)

A distinction between history and legend cannot be drawn from the Ghorbats' accounts of their past, as mythical ancestors may figure in historical events supposedly taking place a few generations ago. However, a common thread in all these tales is their Iranian origin[15], followed at some point of time by their arrival in West Afghanistan, due either to migration or forced exile. The Ghorbats first settled in Herat where they claim to have worked as jewellers/goldsmiths (*zargar*). Rao thus related that the Ghorbats view their exile from Iran as the result of God's curse of Kay Kayhan, resulting in the Baluchis overthrowing his rule and killing all his family except one son and daughter who managed to escape to Herat, where they intermarried with some "Syāhun"/ "Syāwushān" and became goldsmiths (1982: 42). Ultimately, the Ghorbats were forced to leave Herat as well.[16]

5,8 The woman is twining the skin strap using a distaff. (Photo: Lennart Edelberg, Sar-i Chesma, 1948)

They took up a nomadic way of life, which implied the giving up of their profession, whereupon they turned to animal trade. Having left Herat, the Ghorbats reached Kandahar, where they became acquainted with some sievemakers (*ilksāz*), intermarried with them, and consequently took to sievemaking themselves. Another version, still pointing to Kandahar as the place where the Ghorbats took up sievemaking, is told by a Nasir Khēl of the Siāwun lineage:

"When our ancestor, Mullah Nasir was exiled from Siawn of Herat, he came to Kandahar. In those days, prisoners could be set free if their families paid a certain amount of money, depending on the severity of the crime they had committed. Once in Kandahar, he [Mullah Nasir] witnessed how all prisoners were released that way – except two persons who had no one to pay the money for their release. He, Mullah Nasir, took pity on them and decided to pay the money for their release – 30 Afs for one, 50 Afs for the other. They decided to stay with him. When Nasir asked them what their occupation was, they said: 'We make sieves and drums.' So from

5,9 Sievemaker family camping in Sar-i Chesma. (Photo: Lennart Edelberg, 1948)

them our ancestor, Nasir, learned this occupation. Earlier we were jewellers."

Another Nasir Khēl associated this story with the mythical ancestor Kayhan *Pāchā*, who supposedly lost his kingdom in the Herat area prior to Ahmad *Shāh* Durrani establishing the Durrani empire (in 1747). In other versions again, the exiled king-ancestor is referred to as Siawn *Shāh* – or the mythical Siavush:

"Our ancestors escaped from Siawn. There was a king called Nadir-i *Chism-Kash* [Nadir the Eye-puller]. He pulled the eyes out of anybody speaking Persian, or he would kill or slaughter them. Our ancestor Kayhan *Pāchā* escaped and became a tent-dweller. He had two daughters – he gave one to a sievemaker and the other to a goldsmith [i.e. to the very two prisoners he got released]. From the sievemaker the descendants are those Mostafa Khēl. Now we have taken up the occupation from them – we are no longer goldsmiths."

Regarding the Ghorbats' old trade of jewellery, most Ghorbats claim that it was given up in connection with their exile from Herat, but an old Nasir Khēl told me that he remembered that his father occasionally made jewellery such as earrings. Apparently no Ghorbats practice jewellery today, and most likely this trade was given up some generations ago.

Rao tells that in the period prior to their departure from Kandahar, the Ghorbats constituted a single group. After they began to migrate they henceforth split into three distinct lineages: the "Farāi", the "Kayāni" and the "Syāwun". I have only come across the terms "Farāhī" and "Siawun", and these lineage-names, I was told, are derived from locations in the Herat area: the Siāwun being from Siāwn near Herat (presumably the town of Siawushan south of Herat), the Farāhis from Farah.[17]

Today, Siāwun is divided into four sub-groups or *khēls*: Nasir Khēl, Mostafā Khēl, Mehrāb Khēl, and Qāsem Khēl. Each is a patrilineal descent group consisting of some 300 families.[18] A single, generally accepted genealogy cannot be established but one version states that Kay Kanus (or Rustam) had four sons, all of whom were mullahs.[19] The Nasir Khēl, Mostafā Khēl, Qāsem Khēl, and the Farāhis are descendants of these brothers, while the Mehrāb Khēl a few

Table 5.1

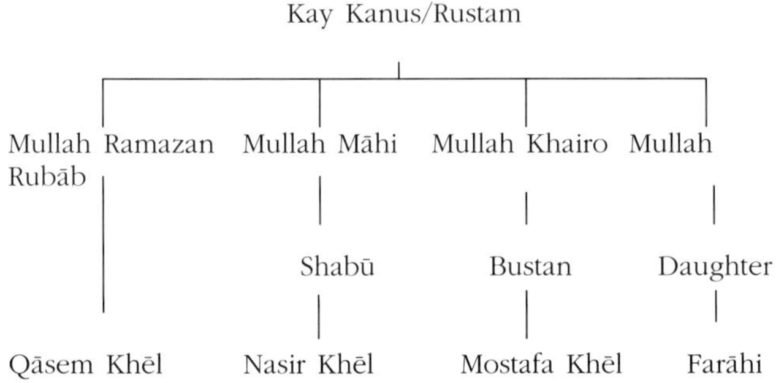

generations back split off from the Nasir Khēl (see below).[20] It should also be added that the Ghorbats of Kandahar, whom Rao classifies as Kayhanis, also mentioned Mullah Mahi and Mullah Ramazan as their ancestors.

The Farāhis apparently settled in Kabul during the reign of *Amîr* Abdur Rahman Khān (1880-1901), and more than half of them subsequently proceeded to Peshawar, where they became cloth sellers and animal traders (Rao 1982: 43). The Farāhis who remained in Kabul are not sievemakers either, but have largely taken to animal trade. A Farāhi married with a Siāwun told me, that the Farāhis have been horse-dealers ever since their time in Farah and that they now operate as middlemen at the animal market in Kabul. Although they have been settled for a long time, they still speak *Qāzulāgi* and occasionally intermarry with the other Ghorbat groups. The Siāwuns (and the Kayanis according to Rao), on the other hand, tell about other more or less voluntary emigrations.

As for the Siāwuns, they state that at the end of the last century they had their winter quarters in houses in Kabul. During springtime, they travelled in small groups to Balkh, Logar, and Ghazni, producing and selling sieves there during summer, and returning to Kabul for the winter (Rao 1982). Some Siāwuns also say that in the past they set out from Kabul in the springtime, travelled by donkeys all the way to Mazar-i Sharif, where they spent the winter, to undertake the slow journey back to Kabul the following spring. On the way, they camped for long periods of time at different places.

Subsequently, the Siāwun houses in Kabul were demolished by the government, presumably in the 1920s during the reign of King

Amanullah (Rao 1982: 44), and people had to find new winter quarters. Some managed to rent or buy houses in Kabul or Charikar, while the poorer among them became fully nomadic. Fate thus seems to confirm the Ghorbats' own claim of an original curse condemning them to eternal dispersion and migration.[21]

The Production of Sieves

From Afghanistan and Central Asia and westward to Turkey (and possibly North Africa) the technology of sievemaking has been unaltered, and remained in the hands of itinerant groups.[22] In Swat in Pakistan, where the occupational specialization is very similar to that of East Afghanistan, sievemaking is carried out by settled leather workers in the villages (Barth 1962). Sievemaking thus does not constitute an independent profession there, which seems also to be the case in the rest of the Indian Subcontinent.[23]

The traditional sieves consist of a rounded wooden frame over which a mesh of thin skin straps is woven. The skin mesh is manufactured in varying sizes and grades of fineness according to its use for cleaning grain or flour on the threshing ground, in the grain wholesale market, *manda'ī*, or in the household.

The manufacturing of sieves starts when the sievemaker buys a couple of tree trunks in the bazaar – either plane or willow tree. On a motor saw in the bazaar, he has the trunks cut into planks of a thickness of 0.5 cm (for sieves) or 1.0 cm (for drums). The planks are cut 5.0 cm wide and 7-9 hands long. After the cutting, the planks are left to dry for a couple of hours if they are to be used for sieves, and about four hours for the thicker drum-frames. The planks are then

5,10 Scraping the skin with the rounded knife (*Fig. 5,19*) to remove whatever may be left of fur and flesh (Kote Sangi, May 1975).

5,19 The skin-scraping knife

rounded by use of a special device called a *lurg* (Ql.). The principle of the *lurg* is like a rotary iron. The horizontal metal roller (*gulun-i lurg*), suspended between two wooden poles (*alāji*) in the ground, is turned by means of a stick

5,11 The cleaned skin is pegged to the ground to dry in the sun (Kote Sangi, May 1975).

inserted through the eye in its 'handle' by one person, while a second person passes the planks through the machine. The knotty surface of the roller breaks the fibers of the wood on one side of the planks, thus preventing the planks from splitting when they are rounded. In case the frame or hoop is for a sieve, holes are made with a drill (*kamāncha*) approximately 1 cm from the rim (and with 1 cm's distance in-between), while no holes are drilled in case of drum frames.

The mesh is made from skin straps, and the sievemakers buy raw sheep or goat hides from butchers, approximately 10 hides at a time. In camp the hides are soaked in water for some 12 hours, after which they are washed in clean water, folded four times, stacked, and covered with a cloth. The following day, the sievemaker checks if the fur is easy to remove. If not, the skin is rubbed with a piece of wood, hung up and scraped with a knife on the backside to remove remnants of flesh, and to make it thinner. This process is called *kalāch* (Ql.), and the instrument used is a semi-circular knife, *kard-i pusht-kalāchī* (Ql. 'the skin-scraping knife'). The skin is then washed again, folded, stacked and

5,12 The dried skin is cut into a long, thin strip from which the mesh will be woven. A specially formed knife is used *Awār Kūn*, is used to cut the thin skin straps. The old man is winding up the skin strap after cutting it.

Awār Kūn

covered. The skin is covered as it has to be hot and humid to make the fur go off. If this process is carried out in the morning, the fur may be loose in the afternoon. At this point, the skin is hung on a smooth wooden pole leaning on a tree or a wall. With a knife the fur is scraped off the skin. In case the fur still sticks, the skin may be rubbed with sand, too. After the fur has been removed, the skin is washed again. The scraping process (*kalāch*) may have to be done twice, in which case the skin becomes very soft and thin (and also larger) – and more suitable for use as drumskin. After a final washing, the skin is pegged to the ground and left to dry in the sun for a couple of days. The thinnest part of the skin is used for making drums, while the thicker parts are used for making sieves.

With a special knife (*awār kūn*), the dried skin is cut (preferably) in one long, thin strip (*tasma*) which is put in water to be softened up. The skin strip is now ready to be twined into a strong, thin thread using a distaff (*khrimtam*, Ql.). Strips to be used for the *chighil* or *katabīz* type of sieves, however, are not spun.

The sieves are woven in different ways, depending on the required mesh-size:[24] The *maydabīz* type is woven as follows: The skin strip is passed through the holes in the rim on opposite sides of the frame by means of a big metal 'crochet hook', called *kājek-e tanistāi* (Ql.) or *tasma kash* (Fig. 5,20a.), and fastened there with a loop around a skin strip wound around the rim. In this way the one-directional skin strips come to cover the entire frame. A square mesh of skin strips is then woven on top of the wooden frame: Initially, four strips are drawn to delineate a square inside the frame. The frame is then divided into four equal parts, which ensures that when an equal number of strips are drawn through each part, the mesh size will also be uniform. Two metal hooks (*sīkh-i gula* and *sīkh-i paigula*) (Fig. 5,20b) are

5,13 The planks for making the sieve- and drum-frames are cut in the bazaar.

5,14 The rounding of the wooden frames are done by the *lurg* (*Fig. 5,21*).

5,15 When the frames are rounded, small holes are made in the rim before the weaving can be made.

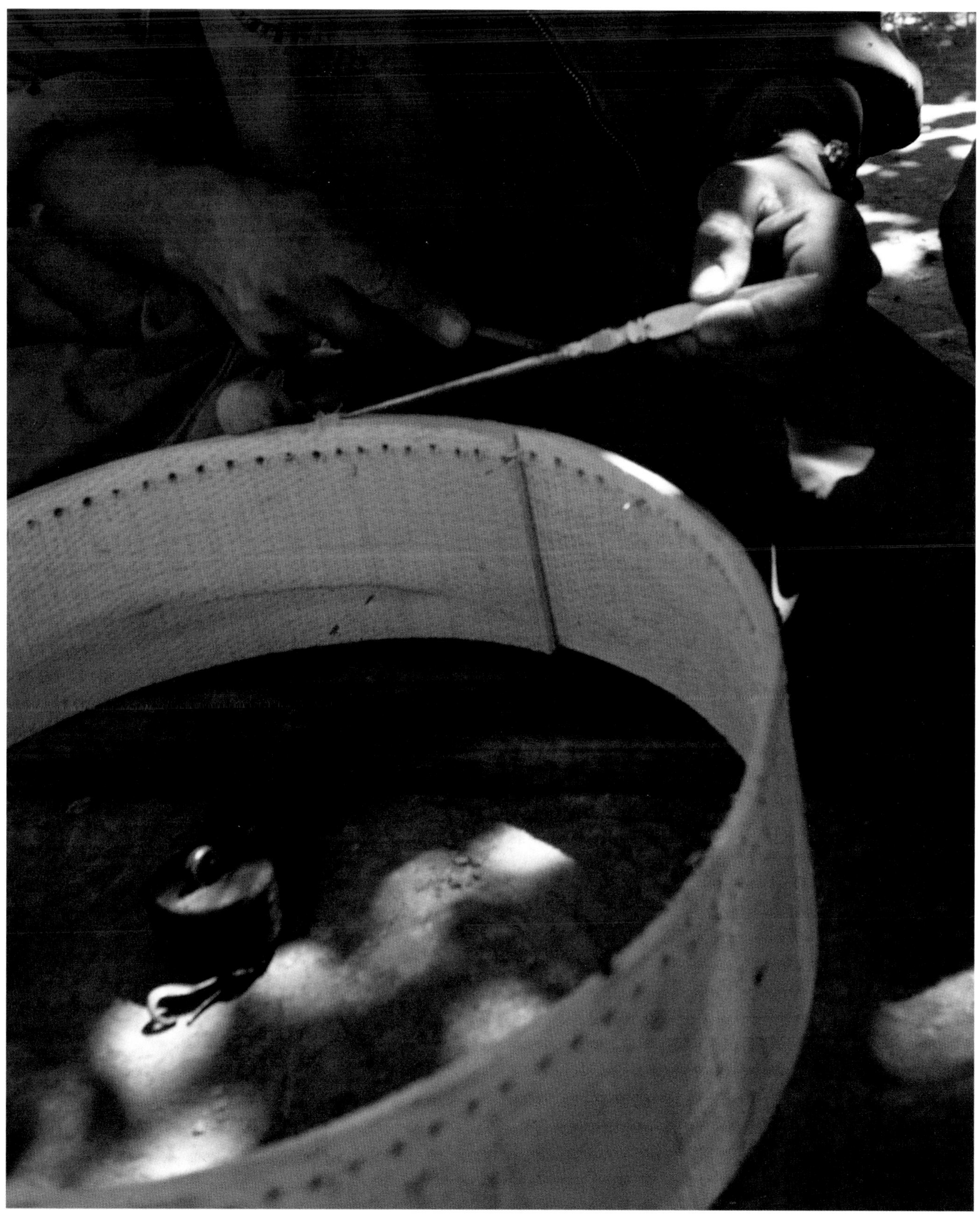

5.16-17 The *maydabīz* (*Figs. 5,23-4*) is woven by use of the wooden weaving frame (*Fig. 5,22*). During weaving, the skin strip is soaked in water to make it smooth and elastic. When the mesh is completed, the sieve will be left to dry in the sun, and the mesh will be hard and tight.

5.18 The one-sided tambourine is being decorated with colourful flowers on the drum skin. Two goblet-shaped pottery drums can be seen in the middle of the picture (Kote Sangi, June 1975).

then passed alternatively above and below the skin strips across the frame, each lifting every second skin strip up. The weaving frame, *sīkh-i tala*, is placed between the two metal hooks serving as a primitive loom, controlling the mesh size and keeping the weaving square, while the skin strip is passed by means of a big metal 'needle', *sīkh-i dast*[25] (Fig. 5,20c). This quadratic type of mesh called *tanistā* (Bahīn, ibid.), is used for the coarse *maydabīz* sieves used for grain cleaning, and also for the fine *ghalbel*, a hair-sieve used for sifting flour.[26]

In the other coarser type of sieve, *chighil* or *katabīz*, used for grain cleaning the skin strips are not spun and the mesh is braided rather than woven. Instead of a square mesh a three-directional braid is made: across the initial warp, two skin strips are diagonally braided by use of the 'crochet hook' (*tasmakash*), the 'needle' (*sīkh-i dast*) and the 'hooks' (*sīkh-i gula* and *sīkh-i paigula*).

Finally, the skin strips are crocheted around the internal rim of the sieve to cover the uneven holes which have appeared where the skin strips are fastened to the wooden frame. Throughout the weaving process, the skin strips are soaked in water to keep them subtle and

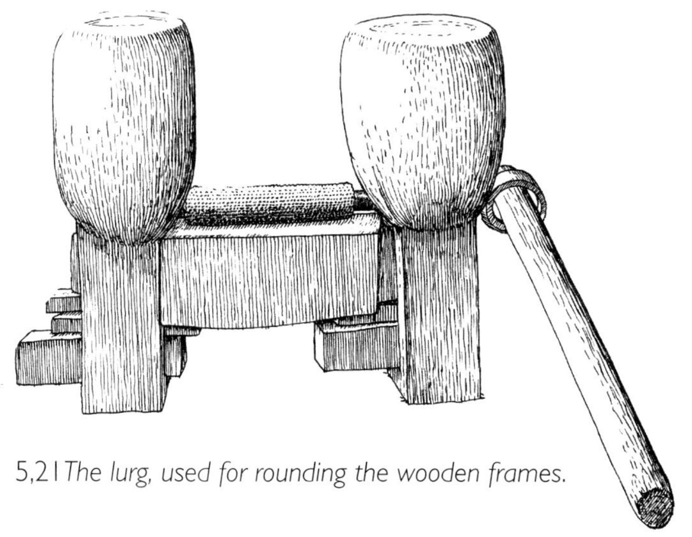

5,21 *The lurg, used for rounding the wooden frames.*

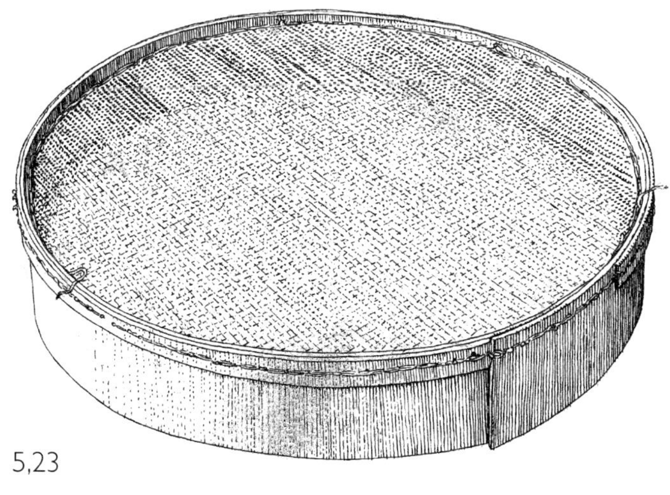

5,23

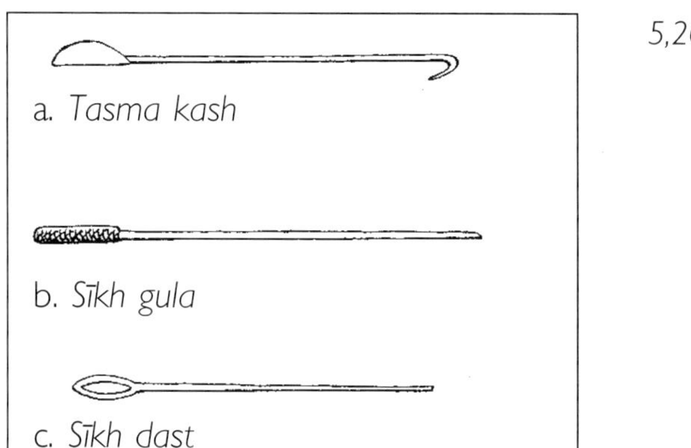

5,20

5,24

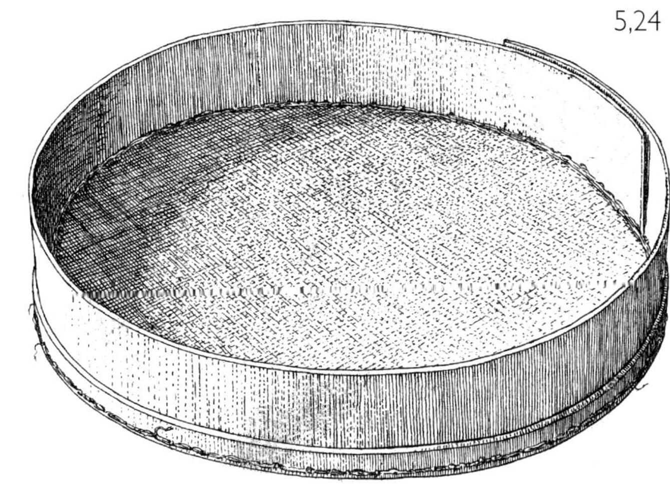

5,23-24 *Maydabīz type of sieve*

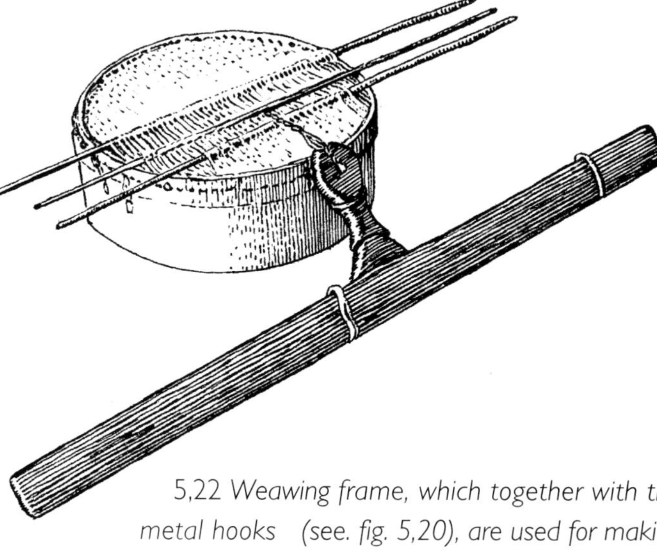

5,22 *Weawing frame, which together with the metal hooks (see. fig. 5,20), are used for making the maydabīz type of sieves.*

elastic, and the weaving will at this point be somewhat loose. When completed and dried in the sun, the mesh will become tight.

Since the 1960's, sievemakers have begun to manufacture flour sieves using a metal mesh called *ilak-i sīmī*. This metal mesh is purchased in large rolls in Kabul's bazaar and fixed with staples to the round, wooden frames.

Sieves are used for cleaning/sifting a variety of crops and materials, and the mesh size varies accordingly. In the countryside, the coarse *chighil* or *katabīz* type of sieves are used for sifting grains. The finer *maydabīz* type is used in the households for cleaning impurities from the grain, and the *ghalbel*, having the smallest mesh size, is used for sifting flour. Apart from the distinction according to mesh-type, the sievemakers also classify their sieves according to use.[27] For example:

(1) *chighil/ katabīz/ gundibīz* – used in wheat stacks to separate the chaff (*gundi*) from the grain.

(2) *chighil-i 'allāfī* – a large sieve used for both wheat and rice. 'The graincleaners at the flour mill (*'allāf*) buy it, the peasants buy it – everybody working on the grainfields buys it.'

(3) *chighil-i sharshambīzi* – used for sifting rapeseeds (*sharsham*). It is the most diffi cult to make presumably because of the very fine mesh-size. 'One can't make more than 1 of them per day – and they are sold for 200-250 Afs. Are made in the month of *Mizan*', I was told.

(4) *maydabīz* – used for removing dust from wheat.

(5) *ghalbel-i ard bīzi* (used for flour-sifting) -
(a) skin-woven (*ṭasma'ī*)
(b) wirenet type (*simiī*) – with a wooden frame, which can be made by the sieve-makers, or with a metal-frame made by local tin-smiths or in factories in Peshawar, Pakistan.

(6) *ghalbel-i birinjī* – used for rice (*birinj*)

(7) *ghalbel-i khāki* – used for sifting dust and soil (for example, by potterymakers)

(8) *zighirbīzi* – used for sifting oilseed(*zighir*)

(9) *shaftal-bīzi* -(*shaftal* is a spinach-like vegetable)

(10) *zughak-bīzi* – used for the cleaning of charcoal (*zughak*)

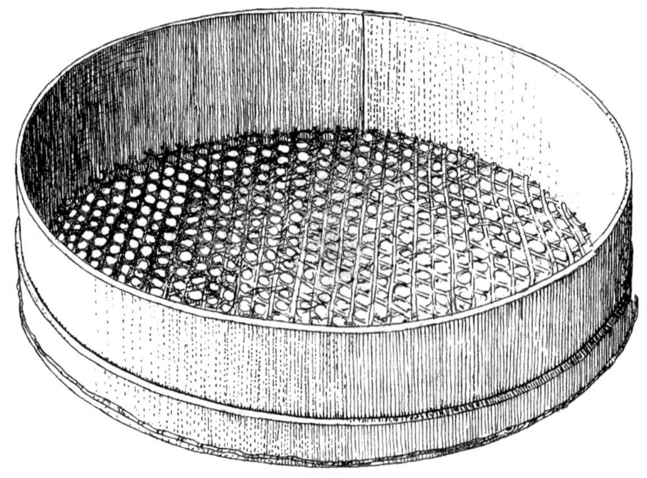

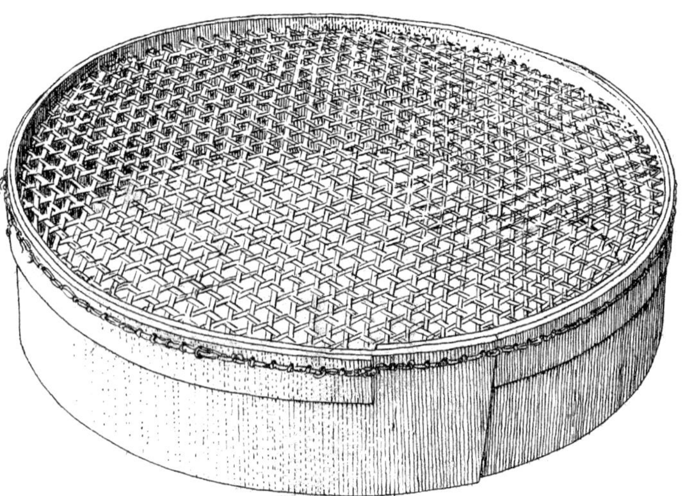

5.25-6 The coarse *chighil* or *katabīz* type of sieve used for grain cleaning. In this type of sieve the skin strips are not spun, and the mesh is braided rather than woven.

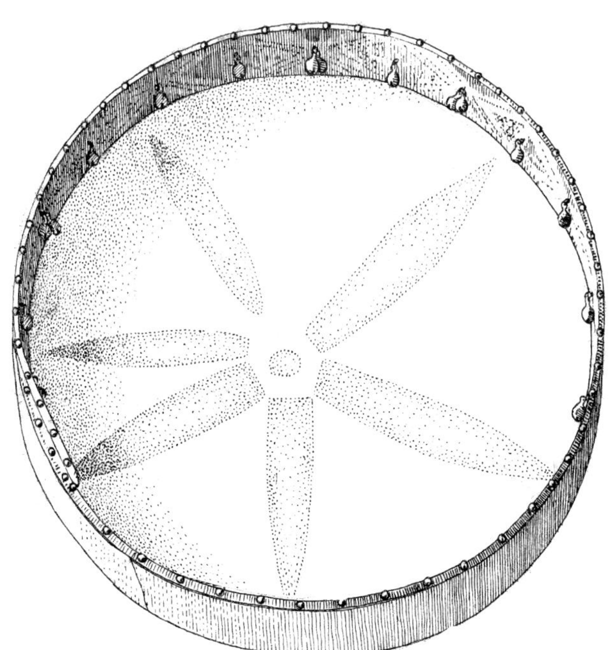

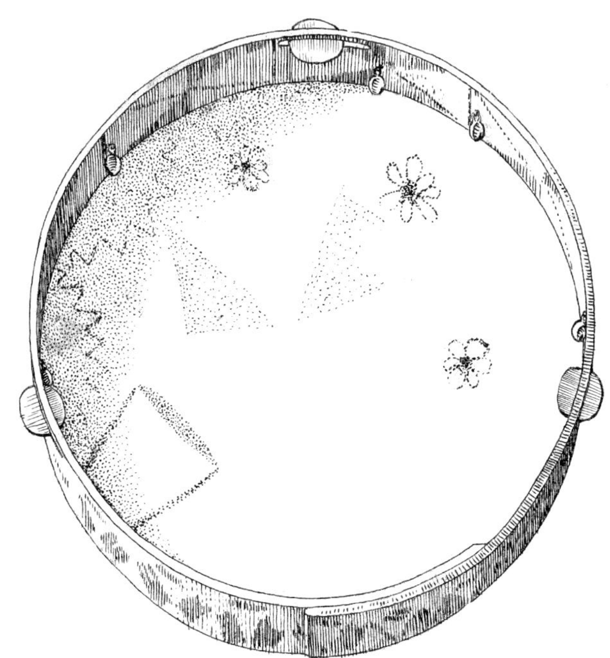

5.27-8 The one-sided tambourine. Small bells may be attached to the inside and round metal pieces inserted in slots in the frame. The drum skin may be decorated with painted flowers, and the frame may have a geometrical pattern painted in bright colours. As additional decoration, small studs can be inserted in the edge of the frame.

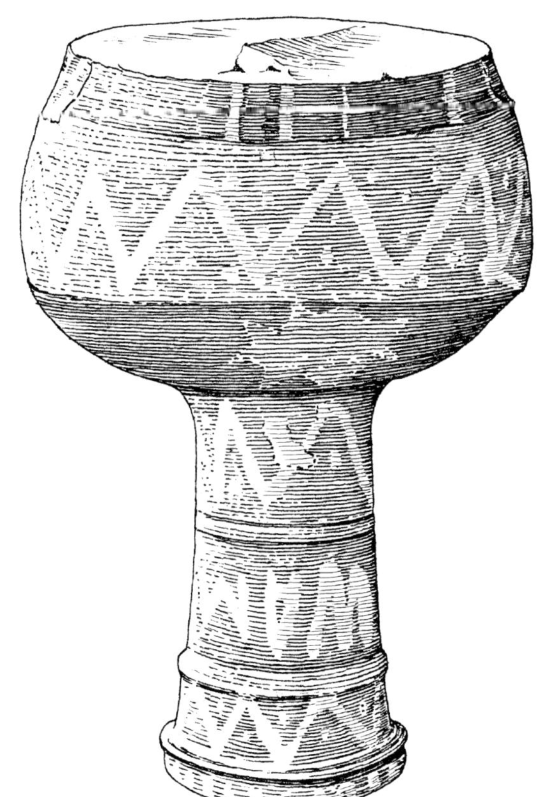

5,29 The goblet-shaped pottery drum *zīrbaghalī*. Here painted in bright turqoise-blue with a pattern in silver colour. The pottery body of the drum is made by a potter, and the sievemaker only fixes the drum skin.

The sievemakers also manufacture drums, but in far smaller quantities than sieves. Drums as mentioned, are made from the finest i.e. the thinnest part of the skin, which in wet condition is stretched over the round frame and fixed to it with resin and a piece of cloth. The drum is then dried in the sun. Both the wooden frame and the skin is decorated – the skin mainly with stylized flowers painted on the inner side in red, blue and green colours.

The most common drum is the one-sided *dāira* or tambourine which is used by women at festive occasions everywhere in Afghanistan. Round metal pieces fixed in slots in the frame, or bells attached to the inside of the tambourine, will jingle when the drum is used.

The Ghorbats also make a small two-sided drum, *naghāra*, used mainly by children. This drum has a handle and on either side are small wooden pieces attached in a short string. When the drum is turned from side to side by the handle, the wooden pieces hit the drum skin. Another drum manufactured is the goblet-shaped *zīrbaghalī*.[28] Its body is made by potterymakers, and the sievemakers only attach the skin-membrane with glue.

Apprenticeship

The manufacture of sieves takes place within the household, which is the production unit, normally consisting of a nuclear family with one skilled, male producer. Women and children in the household assist in the more tedious parts of the production process, but among the Qāsem Khēl I was told, that girls, too, may be taught proper sievemaking.[29] Adult women may be too preoccupied with their own economic activities as pedlars to assist in the manufacture of sieves. Young boys are trained in the occupation, either by their fathers or in some cases by uncles, from around the age of 12-13 years of age. A Mostafa Khēl gives this account of how he learned the skill:

> "In the beginning [up to the age of 16] I did nothing – I only assisted [my father] and did not do any weaving. Then I became my father's apprentice ... When I started learning the occupation I got my own tools, my father gave them to me ... I started by winding the skin straps for one month. Then for 1-1½ months I stretched the skins on the ground. After that I started to put the first round of straps on the sieves [*tānistā*]. Then I did the scraping of the skins for the same period of time. After that I made my first sieve, a *katabīz*, since that is the easiest ... The custom is to spend the money earned on the first sieve to make *ḥalvā* and give it to the poor.[30]
> "Then I learned how to make the straps, and after that I made a weave, *maydabîz*, and then the rounding of the wooden frames. Then the more difficult: the holes in the rim. Finally, I learned how to repair old sieves ... Nine years I stayed with my father making sieves. My father received all the money and I got only pocket money for myself. Then I married and my father told me to separate my house: 'You are free to work for yourself', he said".

A boy is supposed to be a skilled sievemaker by the age of 18-19 years, the time he is also considered old enough to marry. In fact, some informants stated that a boy is trained in earnest only after his engagement. This is not a rule, for the time of marriage depends on other factors, such as the economic situation of the family. The attitude to work, however, is influenced by the prospects of marriage. It is said that a young boy, even if he works as a skilled sievemaker, will give some of his earnings to his father and spend the rest on cigarettes and cinema tickets until he becomes engaged. Only then will he start saving for the future.

All sieve producers own the necessary tools, and the costs associated with sievemaking are insignificant - with the exception of those of the *lurg*, the implement for the rounding of the wooden frames. The *lurg* reportedly costs about 600 Afs, which is more than the total sum of all the other implements. Far from everybody owns such a *lurg*, but one can freely use those owned by others:

> "Our only expensive tool is the *lurg*, which can be enough for 13 tents. One person buys it and the others use it. The rest of the tools amount to around 300 Afs. Everybody can afford that, and everybody have them."

While the price of the *lurg* may prevent some of the sievemaker households from buying it, the explanation for not having one is more likely to be, that since they travel around in groups anyway, with free access to the machine, there is no reason for everybody to incur this expense.

Sievemaking is thus characterized by small, independent production units, usually identical with nuclear family households. The individual household buys the necessary raw materials, owns the work implements, sells the produce and consumes the surplus. There are variations in this general picture, but still with the household as the economic unit in terms of production as well as consumption. Exceptions occur mainly in the poorer households, where it may be difficult to save up enough money for the bride-price of adult sons. In these there may be more than one skilled sievemaker and these work jointly, even if each of them owns a set of the necessary work implements except the *lurg*.

There is no division of labour among individual households, either. They are all able to and actually do manufacture the different kinds of sieves. However, there is a tendency for the young to produce the sieves with metal mesh, possibly because it is easier and faster, and requires far less professional skill than the traditional woven sieves. As regards the latter, there may be cooperation *among* individual households. I found this in a Jalalabad winter camp, where three brothers from the Qāsem Khēl worked jointly to produce wire sieves together with the families of their two sisters. They were partners, so-called *sharīk*, sharing both the work and the profit equally among them.

The Marketing of Sieves

Sieves are used by all households, rural and urban alike, for sifting flour, lentils, and grains, but the main market of sieves is in the rural areas, where they are used for the still predominantly manual cleaning of grain and other crops. The best period for selling sieves is thus harvest time, where the sievemakers particularly sell the coarser types of sieves (*katabīz* and *maydabīz*) in the villages. In the towns and cities, it is mainly the finer flour sieves, *ghalbel*, which are sold, primarily through the shopkeepers in the bazaar.

Sievemakers may carry some 10-15 sieves on their backs, when they go around and sell them directly to customers in the villages.[31] Both barter deals and credit arrangements exist. A similar amount of sieves can also be brought to an urban bazaar and sold to different shopkeepers, who pay for the sieves in cash. Finally, the sievemaker may receive an order for a larger amount of sieves from a middleman who visits

5,31 The one-sided *dāira* is an instrument used mainly by women. Here it is accompanying women's songs at a Pashtun nomad wedding at Deh Sabz, near Kabul (June 1975).

5,30 The two-sided *naghara*, used mainly as a toy by children.

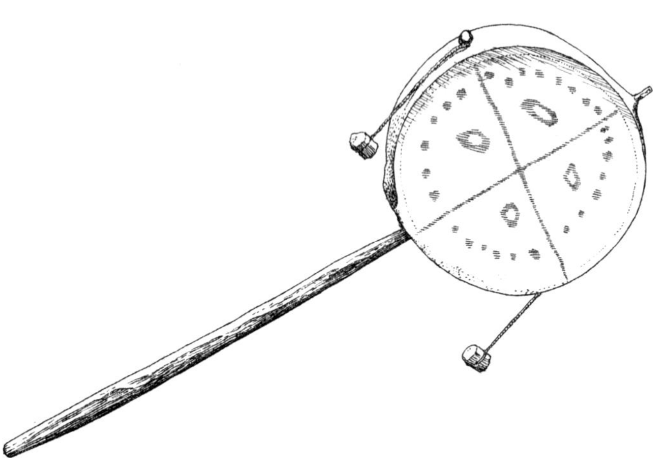

the camp. In this case the price paid per sieve will be 2-10 Afs below the retail price. The middleman will most frequently sell the sieves in areas where the sievemakers normally do not go themselves, such as the thinly populated region of Hazarajat. The smaller market there means that it would be too difficult for the sievemakers to earn a living on their mono-production; hence, middlemen supply these areas with sieves.

In case of wholesale dealings with urban shopkeepers, the sievemakers themselves contact the shopkeepers, bringing along a large quantity of sieves, or they go to receive orders for future supplies. The urban market for sieves is thus covered by the shopkeepers who also resell these to the more distant local bazaars. In Kabul, the grain wholesale market, the *manda'ī*, is the main place for selling sieves, but virtually every retail grain shop sells sieves as well. Three grain traders in Kabul were asked about their trade in sieves, and despite their regular contacts with sievemakers they referred to these not by their profession or as Ghorbat, but by the derogatory term *J̌at*:

The first grain trader stated that he bought some 400 sieves at a time. The price was settled in the month of April-May, and the sieves were delivered and paid in September-October. The trader bought fine wire-mesh sieves for sifting flour for 10-11 Afs a piece and sold them for 12-13 Afs a piece. He believed that the sievemaker was making some 3-4 Afs profit on each one. The skin-sieves were bought for 45-50-60 Afs a piece and resold for 60-65 Afs a piece. Before the onset of winter, the grain trader would buy large quantities (800-1,000) of sieves, mainly of the wirenet type. Altogether, during a whole year, he would buy some 2,000 netsieves and about 200 skin-sieves.

During the last two years, he had bought sieves from one person only, Barat, whom he considered his permanent supplier (*baypār*, Ql.). He dealt only with Barat, even though others would come and offer him sieves at the same price. Yet he did not want to break his word to Barat. Twice a week Barat checked whether the grain trader was short of any type of sieves, and filled up his stock. The second graintrader did not have a special supplier, but stated that he ordered sieves each 5-10 days – 100 wirenet sieves and 10-20 skin-sieves. The third grain dealer explained that he normally bought 500-600 small wirenet sieves at a time for 10 Afs, selling them for 11-11.5 Afs. He would also buy 200-300 big wirenet sieves for 40 Afs a piece and resell them for 43 Afs. "If the mice don't destroy the skin-sieves, they are better than the wirenet sieves". Sometimes he would order large quantities of sieves, and the sievemaker would demand an advance of 100-200 Afs as security.

5,32 Young Qāsem Khēl boy with a bunch of sieves for selling (Kote Sangi, Sept. 1976).

Around the time of the wheat harvest, middlemen (*baylākhar*, Ql.) turn up in the sievemakers' camp placing orders for larger numbers of sieves. These are sold directly to consumers in more distant rural areas with a considerable profit. Whether the middleman places the order with an individual sievemaker, or whether the order is shared among the members of the camp will most likely depend on the size of the order. Some middlemen request some 20-30 sieves, others as many as up to 200 sieves. A small order can be managed by a single family in a few days' time, while the middleman has to wait longer if a single producer is to supply him with a great many sieves. While retail trade in general tends to minimize the size of the migration group, wholesale dealings thus potentially work in the opposite direction, as bigger groups are able to effectuate large orders in shorter time.

During the summer months, the sievemakers' main business consists in such orders from middlemen and their own retail sale in the villages, while wholesale dealings with urban shopkeepers takes place largely during the winter. Retail sales directly to the villagers form the main part of the sievemakers' income. While middlemen always pay in cash, retail sales are frequently on credit and include payment in kind, such as wheat or dried fruit. A sievemaker explains:

> "Wheat is more profitable for us. We don't collect the wheat instantly on the spot, but sell our wares for wheat while it is still standing on the field."

The outstanding credits are collected after harvest or by the end of the summer season, and the profit is slightly higher than with cash transactions. The barter trade originates from the peasants' constant lack of cash. Barter is more profitable than cash, since the sievemakers, like the Shaykh Mohammadi pedlars, receive the bartered products at only half the actual market price. Payment in kind assumes such proportions that the sievemakers can normally cover their entire annual consumption of wheat via barter deals. And there might be a surplus to sell off at the end of the summer season, whereby a double profit is realized.[32]

Among the sievemakers themselves, there exist no agreements regarding the prices for their products, yet locally these are quite homogenous. A system of fixed prices hardly exists in Afghanistan; prices are negotiated in every transaction. One sievemaker's description thus has general applicability:

> "It is important [for the price] whether the person is easily cheatable or not, whether it is a wholesale deal or not, and whether he is a friend or not."

The price of sieves varies considerably across regions, however, depending on supply and demand, variations in prices of skin and wood and general economic conditions in the various areas. Those with considerable grain production are obviously better markets for sieves than are fruit-producing enclaves. The density of the agricultural population is another factor affecting the extent of the market; hence the attraction of the Parwan and Maidan provinces, the traditional summer area the Qāsem Khēl - and similarly of Laghman, the traditionel winter home of the Qāsem and Mehrāb Khēls (see below).

Those sievemakers who can withstand additional hardships and isolation from their kinsmen, can also find good opportunities in outlying areas. Three Mostafa Khēl families who stay in the Bamiyan region throughout

5,33 Thinly populated Central Afghanistan is supplied mainly with sieves by middlemen, as the sievemakers prefer to remain in less remote areas. In the middle of photo is a Hazara village (Summer 1975).

the year informed me that the demand for sieves here is high, mainly because the poor condition of the roads restricts the general supply of commodities and causes higher prices. In addition, they manage to buy wood comparatively cheaply there, but go through extra trouble by choosing the tree on the root and sawing the planks themselves, which in other areas is a phenomenon of the past.

Summer Migrations

Formerly, when the sievemakers travelled by foot with their belongings loaded on asses and horses, some 30-40 tents of the Qāsem Khēl would jointly leave Charikar, heading for their winter area in the east. First, they would reach Kabul, and from there proceed towards Laghman/Jalalabad, but on the way pass Tagab and Chah-i Mullah Omar. The direct trip from Kabul to Jalalabad with donkeys might take around a week. As with both the Musallis and the Shaykh Mohammadis, travel by foot in the past favoured large migration groups for security reasons and necessitated numerous stops en route. An elderly Farāhi, married to a Qāsem Khēl, explained the greater sociability of this form of travel:

5,31 Defying the isolation from kinsmen, three Mostafa Khēls have gone to Bamiyan and remain in that region throughout the year. They have pitched their tents just below the famous Buddha statues of the Bamiyan valley (Aug. 1975).

> "In those days, there was a lot of unity: Wherever we went, we had dog-fighting, cock-fighting and quail-fighting ... Everybody would cook the same things in one camp. If somebody said 'Let's have meat tonight', then everybody would cook meat, and so on."[33]

But Qāsem Khēl's migrations were not restricted to the east only. A few families migrated to Taluqan, where they sold 'one or two thousand sieves to these Uzbeks'. On their way back, they passed through Panjshir.

As a separate and independent occupation, sievemaking reflects the high degree of specialization traditionally found within the artisan sector in Afghanistan. Although sieves of different kinds are necessary for agricultural production, they are also a product that soon will saturate the market. Sieves last a long time, and once requirement has been met, demand drops. Specialization therefore necessitates a high degree of mobility among the producers in order to cover a sufficiently extensive market. It is not a simple sign of poverty that sievemakers are itinerant and live in tents, it also reflects the fact that their occupation requires geographical mobility to the extent that even those who have permanent dwellings are also itinerant (see below).

While sievemaking and economic considerations may bring individual families on migrations to most parts of eastern and northern Afghanistan, the Nasir Khēl, Mostafa Khēl, Qāsem Khēl and Mehrāb Khēl consider themselves as belonging from 'old times' to different areas of Afghanistan, although small numbers of families may go elsewhere.[34] Among the four sievemaking *khēls* in eastern Afghanistan, there thus exists a sort of market division due to their differing localizations during the summer months.

The Nasir Khēl are traditionally tied to Ghazni, where the majority of them dwell. Many families own houses there, but still migrate to Jalalabad for the winter, where some of them have second houses. About 20 years ago, some 50 families went to Turkestan, settling in Qataghan, Mazar-i Sharif, Kunduz, and Khanabad.

The Mehrāb Khēl are originally a sub-group of Nasir Khēl, and Ghazni has also been their traditional area. Most have permanent dwellings there, but the majority still migrate to warmer places during the winter. Earlier they went to Charbagh of Laghman, but for the last two years they have wintered in Jalalabad.

The Mostafa Khēl have retained Kabul as their traditional area. Unlike the other *khēls*, they have been more successful in maintaining houses here. Consequently, they spend the winter in Kabul. Some 30 years ago, a few families went to Pul-i Khumri, where they now own houses. Three families went to the Bamiyan area some 6-7 years ago, where they have remained. In the summer time these families travel to outlying districts like Kahmard and Sayghan and return to Bamiyan during the winter, where they live in the natural caves of that region.

The Qāsem Khēl have had Charikar and Kabul as their traditional areas. Since most of them do not own houses today, Laghman and Jalalabad have been their winter area, where they mainly live in tents. Some occasionally go to Turkestan

5,35 Qāsem Khēl tents in Kote Sangi, Kabul. They subsequently spread out in smaller groups in different places north and west of Kabul (June 1975).

instead. A number of Qāsem Khēls have migrated permanently to the north, to places like Baghlan, Khanabad, Taluqan and Kunduz.

Today, most of the Qāsem Khēl still undertake annual migrations between Laghman/Jalalabad and the Charikar areas. Travel between summer and winter area takes only a few hours by hired bus or truck, and the whole *khēl* does not migrate jointly, but splits in groups of 2-6 families. Within the summer area, they retain the smaller groups, since larger ones would saturate the market too soon and necessitate even higher mobility. In March-April, the Qāsem Khēl leave Laghman/Jalalabad and on the way to their summer area, like all the *khēls*, they make stop in Kabul to sell their products in the Kabul bazaar and obtain new supplies. Before the wheat harvest in the month of June-July, the migration groups scatter in the mainly grain producing areas of the Kabul river valley-system, i.e. the villages in the Kabul basin, in the Charikar area and in the Ghorband valley and Wardak (Maidan). In this area, they sell sieves directly to the peasants in the villages. A migration group normally remains in one place for 1-2 months, and the men take increasingly longer sales trips to reach more distant villages.[35] During the summer period, a family may thus have camped at four different places in the area. This pattern is

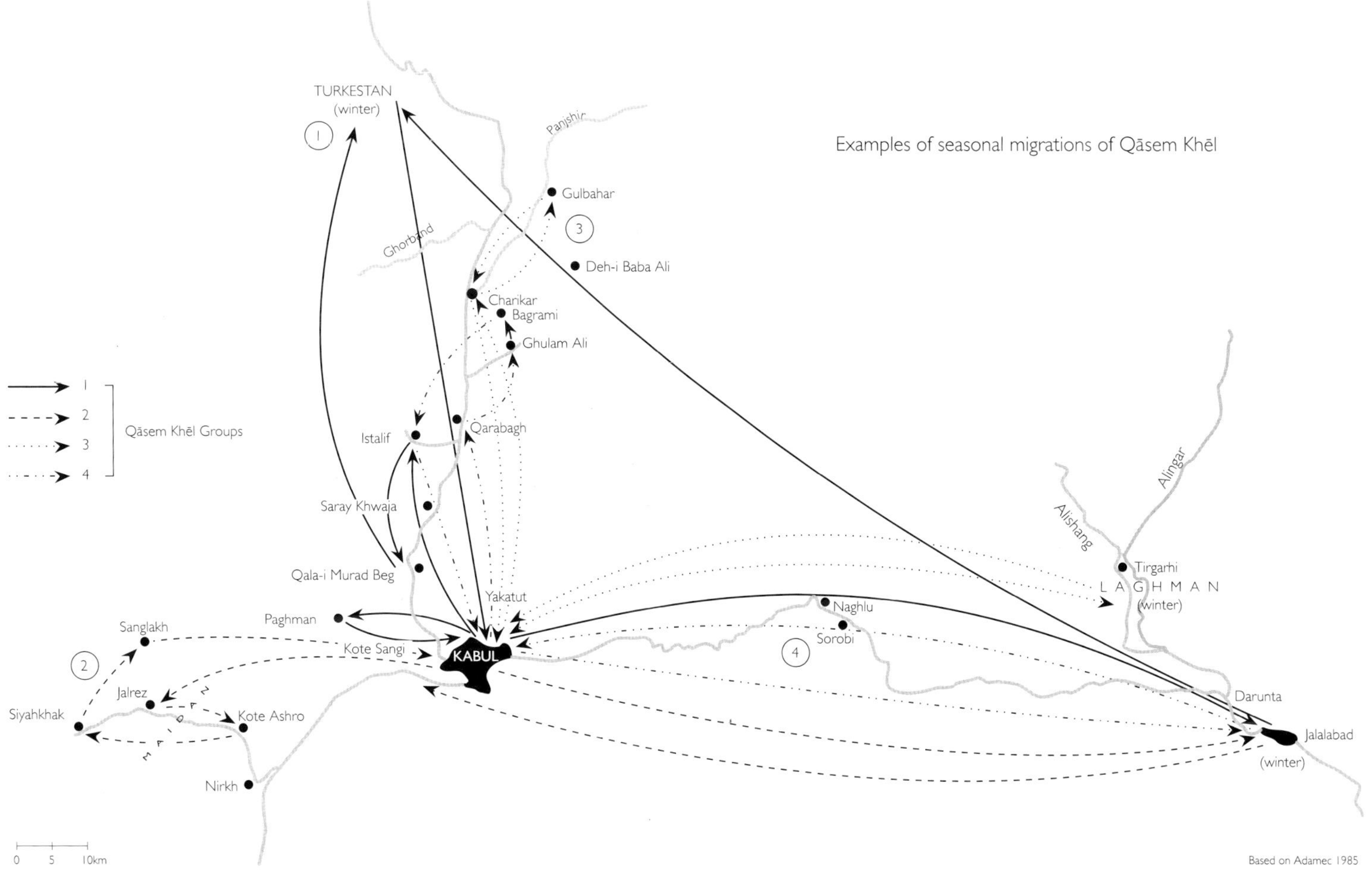

5,36 (Drawing: Elsebeth Morville).

illustrated by the following three examples from the Qāsem Khēl in 1975:[36]

(1) Two households consisting of a young man and his mother plus his two maternal cousins (unmarried) had spent the previous year in Paghman and Yakatut. During the winter, they had been in Jalalabad, but in the spring had traveled directly to Turkestan, then to Yakatut and subsequently to Istalif, where they spent 3 months. At the time of the interview (15th August), they were staying in Istalif and planned to go to Qala-i Murad Beg for some 20 days. Subsequently they would head for Turkestan again, where they intended to spend the winter.

(2) 5-6 households, who had spent the winter in Jalalabad, started their summer migrations by spending time in Kote Sangi of Kabul, acquiring the supplies for the summer etc. Their route took them to Jalrez (2 months), Kote Ashro, Siakhak, and Sanglakh.

(3) Three households, consisting of two brothers and their respective families, their widowed father, and the family of their father's paternal cousin. 14 persons altogether, came to Charikar on 31 March and stayed until August. Then they moved to Gulbahar, where they stayed in tents until November. At that point they returned to what is known as a *chār-dīwālī*, i.e. a walled-in

5,37 Two Qāsem Khēl brothers at work in the summer camp. The man to the left is weaving a *maydabīz*, while his brother is braiding the coarser *katabīz*.

future building site, in Charikar, but in December they rented a 3-room house in which they intended to stay until the end of May-June. They then planned to move into a *chār-dīwālī* again. During the last few years they had not gone east for the winter but had been able to rent rooms either in the Parwan or Charikar areas for the winter.

The migration group normally consists of closely-related families (sons, brothers, uncles, cousins). It may persist throughout the summer season, but this is not necessarily the case. Quarrels may occur which lead to temporary splits, or part of the group may split off but join the others again later in a new place. While the market situation thus determines the small group size in the summer area, kinship and friendship are decisive for group composition, since neither production nor marketing factors necessitate a permanent composition. In general, however, at least a couple of households travel together, presumably for social reasons as well as for security.

Within one *khēl*, the migration groups generally know the whereabouts of the others and individual households are thus able to join other groups. Although there is no formalized division of the market within the *khēl*, the sievemakers are able to ensure a certain informal coordination of their migrations, i.e. to avoid internal competition by going to locations already 'occupied' by others.[37] This was partly illustrated in Example (1) above, where the young men's maternal uncle stated that his nephews were supposed to seek his counsel before they could decide to winter in Turkestan.

Due to the mobility required to market sieves, most sievemakers in East Afghanistan live in tents throughout the summer – or part of the summer in case they own houses or temporarily rent a couple of rooms cheaply. Like most other migrating, non-pastoral peoples in Afghanistan, their white canvas tents are manufactured in Pakistan (Balland 1991), but the sievemakers buy them locally, either new or second-hand for 3,000-5,000 Afs, and they may then keep them for 5-10 years.[38] In spring and autumn, when the sievemakers arrive in Kabul on their way to and from the eastern areas, they frequently camp in Kote Sangi, which due to its empty lands and *chār-dīwālī* is the area of Kabul where the largest number of itinerant people from various communities, as well as poor pastoral nomads, gather. Outside of Kabul (and Jalalabad, see below) the sievemakers mainly camp in rural areas, either in the outskirts of smaller towns, as I have seen in places like Saray Khwaja, Jalrez, Istalif, and Paghman, or at shady camp sites along roads. For the sievemakers, a campsite is not only a place of habitation but also of production, and this makes some special requirements regarding its location. First of all, sievemaking requires the ready availability of water so sievemakers normally camp near a small stream or river. One drawback of such a location was, as I witnessed in Paghman, that it was only "by the grace of God" that the tents were not swept away when the river flooded due to rains in the mountains. Partly as a consequence of the location near a water source, and partly as a deliberate choice of a pleasant working environment for the outdoor activities, camps are often placed under shady trees, often fruit trees, the fruit of which at the same time can be enjoyed. My impression is that the sievemakers generally manage to find far more pleasant camp sites than most other peripatetic peoples; certainly better than the sites of the Maskurah Shaykh Mohammadis, who due to the large size of their camps must make do with a barren field; or the Musallis, whose choice of site is restricted by their need to be close to their wheat stacks.[39]

Wintering in Jalalabad

The majority of Siāwun sievemakers migrate to Jalalabad for the winter, where they arrive gradually during November and early December. At first, the winter cold in Ghazni forces the Nasir Khēl and Mehrāb Khēl to pack up and leave for the east and afterwards the Qāsem Khēl from the Parwan and Maidan areas gradually turn up in Jalalabad.

Here, the sievemakers stay at one place throughout the winter and tend to gather in larger groups than in summer time, with families from one *khēl* or sub-*khēl* camping together or sharing a house. As an explanation of why they do not form even bigger groups, the response is that "keeping distance maintains friendship" (*dūrī wa dūstī*). Practically, it would also be a problem to find sufficient space or accommodation for larger groups within the city.

While poverty and lack of housing force many itinerant people from all over East Afghanistan to gather for the winter in the pleasant sub-tropical climate of Jalalabad, rich people make the same choice, but out of comfort. The outskirts of Jalalabad are thus lined with shady avenues and here the huge villas with lush gardens protected by 2 m high walls are the winter residence of many a well-to-do family from other parts of east Afghanistan.[40] All around the city, in open spaces, in *chār-dīwālī* (4-walled enclosures), and in court yards, smaller or larger clusters of white tents can be seen, and from here the numerous itinerant peoples compete with each other for space and to eke out an existence.

In the middle of November 1975 my interpreter and I arrived in Jalalabad to search for our sievemaker acquaintances, who had told us that they could be found in the Reg-i Shahmard Khan area south of the city. During our search we encountered numerous other itinerant groups. The first we met were a group of snake-charmers and conjurers who had spent the summer in the Shahshahid-area of Kabul.[41] Further on, there were bangle sellers and Shaykh Mohammadi chinaware riveters from Siyahsang of Kabul, Shaykh Mohammadi cotton codders, Shādibāz performing with their monkeys, poor pastoral nomads and many others. The city of Jalalabad is thus a jumble of all kinds of people during winter, like a condensed image of people and lifestyles otherwise scattered in different areas.

Arriving in Jalalabad, the itinerant groups initially pitch their tents in some of the open spaces at the outskirts of the town, and from this base start their search for a more secure, protected and private place to camp. Some may rent rooms in the town, as already mentioned. There is a rapid turnover of people in these open spaces, but at any time some 20-30 tents may exist, belonging to various communities, hardly in contact with one another.

Those who cannot afford to rent a room for the winter will find it more attractive to camp inside a *chār-dīwālī*. These four-walled enclosures tend to be privately owned land plots on which nothing yet is built, but where the owner, in order to protect the property, has erected a 2 m high earthen boundary wall. The enclosure may also contain a wooden or sheet metal gate. The *chār-dīwālī* provides privacy for the tent-dwellers, particularly if they all belong to the same community, and a measure of security as well. If the tent-dwellers are familiar with the *chār-dīwālī*-owner, they may be allowed to camp there for free, but in most cases they will have to pay for the camping, in particular because of the competition for camp sites in Jalalabad. The rent may vary, but 50 Afs per month per tent is a normal sum.

The rush for *chār-dīwālī* is intensified by the local authorities' negative attitude to wild camping. As in Kabul, the local district police require a registration of all the households as well as a written guarantee from the "elder" of each camp group, who will be made responsible if something goes wrong. There is also a tendency among the authorities to demand that the itinerants should not be publicly visible, but hidden away inside *chār-dīwālī*. In 1975, the sievemakers stated that the local police would not allow anybody to camp outside *chār-dīwālī*. The explanation was that the previous year a bomb had exploded outside a police station in the Fourth District, and the police had argued

5,38 One of the many *chār-dīwālī* (enclosed plots) of Jalalabad. A group of sievemakers have pitched their tent with the intention of staying for the winter (Dec. 1975).

that "You are either harmed by such an incident, or you might have done it yourself. So go away!"

This complicated our efforts to find the sievemakers in Jalalabad, as it was impossible, when walking down the narrow lanes with their 2 m high boundary walls, to know whether they protected a fine house or a *chār-dīwālī* full of sievemakers and their tents. To enter a *chār-dīwālī* without knowing anybody inside was no easier than to enter a private house – which obviously is what makes a *chār-dīwālī* an attractive camping place.

Competition for good camping sites is hard in Jalalabad, so hard that even close relatives may come in conflict. Two households of Qāsem Khēl had agreed with a *chār-dīwālī* owner to live for free on his landplot, as they had done the previous year. However, the following day

5,39 One of the many open spaces in Jalalabad where people of different communities pitch their tents until they find a more protected camping site offering more privacy for their women (Winter 1986).

5,40 At the outskirts of Jalalabad, four Qāsem Khēl families have camped for the winter at the edge of a walled-in vegetable field which they have taken on lease (Dec. 1975).

he had rented out the *chār-dīwālī* for 400 Afs per month to another group of Qāsem Khēl. The two first families knew that if they paid more, they would still get the place, but since they were only two families, they could not afford to pay, for example, 500 Afs per month, while the others could well manage to pay 50 Afs per month each. The situation resulted in many bitter remarks between the two closely related groups.

In this case, the *chār-dīwālī* was small, and the sievemakers could rent all of it. In large *chār-dīwālī*, however, they may have to accept living next to people from other communities, something neither preferable nor without conflict. Thus, Gul Hassan from Mehrāb Khēl quarreled with a *chār-dīwālī* owner in Jalalabad because the latter had not only rented out rooms at the right side of the gate "to all sorts of people", but was also going to let more people into the *chār-dīwālī*. Gul Hassan had told him that "We have our *satir* and *nāmūs*" and they were going to move to another place. (*Satir* refers to the relationship between a man and a woman, where the woman is *satir* to the man if she will not sit unveiled in his company as she would in the presence of her close male relatives. *Namus* means family honour as embodied in the women of the family). The sievemakers stayed on, however, but conflicts constantly broke out between the various communities inside the *chār-dīwālī*. While visiting the camp one day, I experienced how a conjurer turned up to formally apologize for his daughter having called the sievemaker children *J̌at*, which had angered the sievemakers. Later on a quarrel broke out between the sievemakers and a group of bangle sellers, as the sievemakers threatened to report the bangle sellers to the police for prostitution, and according to some, for not having identity cards. The sievemakers gave me the following description of the banglesellers:

> "They are called *Chalasi* in Farsi and *Shāray* in Pashto. By origin they are Musallis, they speak *Inku*. Some of them are beggars, others sell water ... They are dirty people. Their men are engaged in smuggling, but most of the time they sit idle while their women carry on prostitution under the guise of selling bangles. They originally come from Pakistan, where their women are reported to be serving as 'masseuses', shouting 'Massage' on the streets. Some time ago, one of their pretty women danced in the house of a wealthy man. It is a disgrace for us to live as neighbours to them. We will never do it again!"

Numerous strategies are employed in the competition among groups for camp sites in Jalalabad. Rao describes how a group of Qāsem Khēl managed to chase away other itinerant groups from a camp site which they wanted for themselves. The Ghorbat women had stayed at home playing tambourine all day long and allowed the children to make as much noise as they pleased. The strategy had proven successful; after a few days of this unacceptable behavior, both the Laghmanis and the Shaykh Mohammadis left the camp. Only two Qawal tents remained, and they were henceforth left in peace. Rao notes that both the Laghmanis and Shaykh Mohammadis left without any quarrel or dispute, and she concludes that they probably thought that this was the sort of behavior one could expect from such people! (1982: 108-110).

Laghman had been the winter area of the Qāsem Khēl and Mehrāb Khēl, while the Nasir Khēl traditionally spent winter in Jalalabad. During recent years, however, the majority of Qāsem

5,41 A group of Qāsem Khēl families jointly manufacture wire-mesh sieves for sale in the bazaar of Jalalabad (Dec. 1975).

Khēl and Mehrāb Khēl have also wintered in Jalalabad. As new-comers, these two groups apparently encounter more camping problems than do the Nasir Khēl, who every year go to the Filwan Kocha area near the Hindu Dharam Sal. Filwan Kocha is an old sievemaker "stronghold" located on a hillock and altogether not a very inviting site. From the outside, only high walls are visible, and the only entrance to the area is a single, narrow lane, where any intruder is bound to be stopped and questioned. Inside Filwan Kocha, however, numerous sievemakers had pitched their tents, while the more well-to-do owned houses. I was told that in earlier times as many as 60 sievemaker families might be living here, while now only some 10 families lived in Filwan Kocha itself; another 6 families lived in a nearby building.

In the preceding chapters, it was argued that the Musallis' and Shaykh Mohammadis' annual migrations were geared to exploiting the difference in harvest periods due to the varying altitude between their summer and winter areas. For the sievemakers, the situation is somewhat different. While their migrations within the summer area are determined by the market for sieves, their travels between summer and winter area are not primarily geared to exploit the regional differences in harvest seasons and hence, market situation.

Migrations to the low lying sub-tropical areas to the east are set off by the climate in their summer areas, rather than by the harvest season in the east. Hence, the Nasir Khēl and Mehrāb Khēl who come from the comparatively cold Ghazni area, will arrive in the east earlier than the Qāsem Khēl, who come from Charikar. Moreover, those who own houses or can afford to rent a couple of rooms for the winter may choose not to go east for the winter at all, while the permanent tent-dwellers have to go to areas where a tent provides sufficient protection from the winter cold. Hence, it is not the market as much as the climate, or more precisely, the sievemakers' poverty, which determines the pattern of winter migration. A Qāsem Khēl explained the situation in the following terms:

> "It is only for the warm winter, that they [the sievemakers] go to Jalalabad. In other respects it is the most impoverished part of the country, where a person could starve without anybody helping with half an Afs (*Afghānī*), and where if we go with flour and ghee and five or six thousand Afs, we would return without money. And the prices of our products are lower. The population there is poor and stingy."

Obviously, there is a market for sieves in the Laghman and Jalalabad areas, since two main crops are grown there, but during winter the number of sievemakers is too big for them all to subsist by sievemaking alone. A sievemaker in Jalalabad told me that:

> "In summer time, the daily profit is 300 Afs. But in these days of winter, the best sievemaker cannot make 4 sieves daily, and he can hardly make as much money by selling it as he can make making it [i.e. the profit is zero]. He can hardly earn more than he daily spends on his stomach."

Under such economic conditions, around half the sievemakers who go to Jalalabad make no sieves here, but try to find alternative sources of income. The poorest take up shoe-mending in the streets or small-scale trading in fruit and sugar cane, while the more well-to-do lease vegetable fields and sell the produce.

However, the climatic factor probably also affects the alternative job opportunities. The late autumn and early spring harvests in the comparatively warm Jalalabad region probably generate more economic activities during the winter months than would be the case in most other towns in Afghanistan. Yet, for the sievemakers, as for so many other poor people in Afghanistan, the winter months are a period where reserves stored from the summer time are consumed. A sievemaker woman explains: "I swear by the oneness of God that for the past two or three weeks we have been here [Jalalabad], I have spent 3,000 Afs and I have not got any money left."

In Laghman, the Qāsem Khēl and Mehrāb Khēl used to be engaged in sievemaking throughout the winter, and being a predominantly rural area, Laghman does not offer the same possibilities for alternative occupations as the larger city of Jalalabad. Their partial shift from Laghman to Jalalabad may thus be explained by a search for better possibilities of survival in Jalalabad. In this context, the market situation for their primary products (the sieves) is of secondary importance.

The Qāsem Khēl state that there are no middlemen, *baylākhars*, in the Jalalabad area, so they have to sell their products directly to the consumers, or to the shopkeepers in the bazaar. Those sieves which during this time sell best are flour sieves for the urban market. When springtime comes, they go to various places in the neighbourhood of Jalalabad, such as Kukur Khel, Mama Khel, Nukur Khel, Chapriar, Kaja, and Bayar, the latter being rather distant. However, those Qāsem Khēl who have gone to Jalalabad may still go on short peddling trips to Laghman, where they stay with relatives who still chose this winter location.

With the Qāsem and Mehrāb Khēl's recent encroachment upon the traditional wintering area of the Nasir Khēl, there is no market-division between the *khēls*, as was the case during summer. Apparently, this has not led to major conflicts. An old Nasir Khēl explains:

> "Jalalabad has always been the place of the Nasir Khēl ... As the two other *khēls* moved to Jalalabad, we left Jalalabad for them. And we can't tell them not to come. They come because it is a big town. And myself, I go to the Shinwari region."

There may be several explanations for the Nasir Khēl's relaxed response to the other *khēls*' encroachments upon their traditional winter-area. Like the other *khēls*, the Nasir Khēl's choice of Jalalabad as winter location is not primarily determined by the market for sieves, but by its overall warm climate and the multitude of alternative income-possibilities. Hence, winter is a period of spending and exploiting alternative sources of income, irrespective of the number of sievemakers in Jalalabad. In addition, as will be discussed later, the Nasir Khēl is by and large better off than the other *khēls* and are therefore more able to utilize alternative income-possibilities.

In regions with less pronounced climatic differences than East Afghanistan, the sievemakers are not engaged in regional migrations. In Kandahar they live in houses all year round.[42] They told me that they peddle sieves for 2-3 months at a time, renting rooms in the different localities. They migrate a distance of "six *sarāys*" from Kandahar, reaching Lashkargah, Girishk, Mohmand, Morghan Kocha, Spinboldak, and Chaman, at the Pakistani border, and Panjwaii.[43]

The Herati sievemakers follow yet another pattern. They also live in houses throughout the year, and 2-4 men will go peddling, leaving the family behind. The men bring along 200-400 wooden frames, rent a room in the various places, weave the sieves jointly and share the profit. They may be gone anywhere from 2-8 weeks, depending upon whether they have somebody to look after their families. They travel as far as Murghab, Maimana, Obeh, Qala-i Naw, and up to what was then the Soviet Border, now Turkmenistan.

Women's Peddling

Ghorbat women have for generations maintained independent economic activities. In the past they practiced fortune telling and cupping, which was used as a cure for various ailments. If someone was, for example, hit by a stone causing some internal injury, i.e. a swelling, drawing blood was considered curative. Also in case there was "wind" in the body, this could be removed as foam by cupping. Had somebody a skin disease like small red spots and fever (*bukhār*), this was supposed to be caused by "impure" blood, which would then be extracted from the shoulder and the back. Infants were considered as too weak for having their blood drawn.[44] A few women are still supposed to practice cupping, but nobody wants to admit to it openly.

Today, many Ghorbat women work as pedlars (*sawdāgar*) in petty goods and cloth in rural areas, thus competing with other pedlar groups like the Shaykh Mohammadis. The petty wares may include hair pins, hair slides, rings, press buttons and a special kind of soap, manufactured by the women themselves. It is made by adding talcum to some kind of soap which they cut to pieces and boil in water. The fluid is then left to coagulate in cups. This soap is supposed to be good for cuts and scratches, and is called *ṣābun-i bukhār*. A cheaper version is also produced to which "Iranian plaster" or lime (*gutch*) is added instead of talcum (see also Rao 1982: 70).[45]

Unlike the Shaykh Mohammadis, the Ghorbats do not consider women too weak and vulnerable to be cloth traders. The women who trade in cloth carry some 20-30 units of cloth around on their sales trips (*ādūr*), each unit being of three metres, the normal length required for a set of clothes. From 20 to 30 units would normally sell in about one week, but selling time may range from 2 to 17 days. A female cloth trader may invest some 20,000 – 30,000 Afs at a time on such merchandise, sell these on credit, and collect the money after harvest time. Like in all credit transactions in rural areas, payment is due on the following harvest; these areas have two crops per year. In this way, the profit may reach 50%, or some 10,000 Afs. Has the woman too little capital to buy profitably on wholesale, daily profit may come to only 20-30 Afs. In such cases, she may only have invested 2,000-3,000 Afs, or in case of petty things even as little as 500 Afs. However, the women may also be able to buy their supplies on credit from shopkeepers who know them well; hence the Qāsem Khēl women buy from shopkeepers in Charikar and Kabul. Presumably, they do not buy any merchandise in Jalalabad but bring their winter supplies with them from Kabul. It is not clear whether the reason is that they can buy on credit in Kabul, or that the prices are lower there. A Qasēm Khēl woman explains about the credit dealings with Hindu cloth traders:[46]

> "The Hindus are very snobbish. The Hindu traders from whom the women buy cloth, would come to [the sievemakers'] camp either to sell them cloth or to collect their debts once a week. If the woman with whom he had dealings was at home, then they would do their business. But if not, he would sit there and wait, ask for some eggs and have these and tea, but not drink it of [the sievemakers'] cups. Instead he would take a cup out of his pocket, wash it and drink from it.[47]

> "Every woman from our camp owes the Hindu clothseller 20,000 – 30,000 Afs, and with the pretext of credit, those women who had just started their businesses and were not experienced would be cheated by buying bad quality cloth. The women themselves deal with the traders, going to his shop; or else he will come to their place. The woman will trade with him, but on the receipt would be written the name of her male guardian [husband, son etc.]. ... If the trader is acquainted well enough with them, there would be no signing or stamping. If not, [a receipt] will be signed, stamped or fingerprinted, and the address of our people would also be written, either a house belonging to one of us or to

one of our relatives would be given as places through which we can be found. But in many dealings this is not necessary, as the traders know us well."

Some women go peddling in groups of four, others in pairs. No woman goes alone, partly for security reasons, partly to protect her reputation. The women who go together may, for example, be two sisters, a mother and daughter or two sisters-in-law. Before a woman or girl can become an independent pedlar, she has to undergo an apprenticeship during which she accompanies her mother or another close relative to learn the trade. On the occasion of the girl's first independent peddling activity, her mother will prepare *ḥalvā* to be distributed among the women of the camp as celebration of the event (cf. Rao 1982: 61). This is similar to the celebration of the boy having completed his apprenticeship as a sievemaker as described above.

Women's peddling is a somewhat touchy subject, as in Afghan culture generally it is considered socially unacceptable and morally degrading for the whole family as well as for the community if women move about unveiled among strangers offering their merchandise for sale. The Ghorbats themselves pay lipservice to these norms, yet a great number of their women are pedlars – among the Qāsem Khēl, at least 75%. It is no doubt poor economic conditions which necessitate that the women go peddling. Yet among equally poor groups in Afghanistan, starvation would be preferred to the tainting of the honour of everybody. With improved economic conditions, probably all Ghorbat (men) would prefer to free their women from this occupation, if for no other reason than as a means of becoming more socially acceptable and respectable in the eyes of the wider society. As a consequence, many families are reluctant to admit that their women are pedlars, or they try to "explain it away". Some declare that during winter the men go peddling, while during summer it is the women who go, as the customers are rural women who are alone at home, and hence would not want to buy from men. This argument helps make women's peddling appear as an exception; however, Ghorbat women in fact carry out their peddling activities all year round and in all localities. Moreover, my observations among the Shaykh Mohammadi male pedlars show that rural women (in the very same localities) have no hesitation to buy from *male* pedlars.

The Ghorbats' argue that if women's peddling is necessary for the family, only the old women should be pedlars. When young married women indeed go, it is claimed that this does not include those women in the first couple of years after marriage. And finally, "unmarried girls will not go peddling;" however, in case a girl's father and brother agree to it, a girl may also go. Among the Qāsem Khēl in 1975-76, there were at least two cases of young unmarried girl pedlars and perhaps more. Regarding young girls, who as adolescents have been introduced to the trade, they would frequently abstain from peddling during the period between their engagement and the birth of their first child.[48]

Although the Ghorbats, as mentioned, pay lip-service to the larger society's condemnation of female peddling activities, it is nevertheless acceptable by their own standards. This situation may result in a conflict of values, or at least it appears so in communication with outsiders, who do not consider female peddling appropriate. A poor Mostafa Khēl thus tells about his reluctance to let his wife start peddling (out of concern for her honour and chastity), while his sister "always slights me by telling me that I am

5,43 In Kandahar, the Ghorbat women make embroideries for sale, like the woman at the photo. She shields herself out of shyness for the camera (Nov. 1976).

5,42 Elderly Mehrāb Khēl woman in camp outside Ghazni (Nov. 1976).

5,44 Well-to-do Nasir Khēl family in front of their house in Ghazni (Nov. 1976).

poor because my wife does not help me". However, women's peddling is also a question of honour among the Ghorbats, as is evident when the relatives of an unmarried Qāsem Khēl man contemptuously remark that "he will probably send his wife peddling the day after their wedding!", i.e. indicating that his greed exceeds his sense of propriety.

The settled Ghorbats in Kandahar told me that the women here did not hawk cloth or petty goods since they lacked the necessary capital. Nevertheless, the women were economically active. Old women practiced cupping and sold sieves in the country-side, while young women, in addition to their weaving of sieves, made embroideries and the like for sale. Among the settled sievemakers in Herat, on the other hand, the men said that their women "didn't do anything else but eat." Apart from the factual information of this message, it is noteworthy that such a spiteful tone is quite unusual for sievemaker men, who otherwise speak respectfully about their women, their wisdom, and their income-earning abilities. Local non-Ghorbats of the area stated that sievemaker women used to perform cupping, but that they had given it up "as they were ashamed of it" and that now their women were veiled.

The situation among the Herat sievemakers indicates that in case women's independent economic activities are renounced, their total situation and position in the community may also change. When women are engaged in peddling, they have to be away from home during the day, while the production of sieves ties men to the home. It appears that this situation, plus the income earning abilities of the women, creates different gender relationships than what usually predominates in Afghan society, despite the fact that sievemakers outwardly express their adherence to those norms. The women's comparative strength is reflected in the eastern sievemakers' social organization by the frequency of *khāna dāmād* marriages (bride-service, where a man spends the initial years of marriage in the parental household of his wife), the importance of maternal relations in social life, and the influence wielded by old women. Equally so, while household chores tend to be the women's exclusive domain in Afghan society, this is not necessarily the case among the Ghorbats, where women are economically active outside the home. A case in point was a formal dinner, to which I and my interpreter were invited by a Qāsem Khēl family. During the dinner, the husband explained that on this particular day the wife had stayed home from peddling in order to prepare the dinner herself, as "the guests may find it strange if the husband had cooked".

Rao also comments upon these differences in Ghorbat women's situation, but relates them to whether the family is nomadic (tent-dwelling) or settled (house-dwelling). The settled Ghorbats attempt to adapt to their neighbours' customs and attitudes, which invariably disfavours the Ghorbat women, rendering them economically dependent upon the men of the household. She also adds that while the comparative exposure of private life in a camp makes it virtually impossible for a man to beat his wife, several such cases were found to take place within the privacy of a house (1982: 127).

Generally speaking, settlement in houses requires a better economic situation than nomadic life in tents, as well as being the first step in achieving social respectability for the Ghorbats. Hence, house-dwelling would almost invariably be accompanied by restrictions imposed upon the women's mobility outside the house, since such outward signs of a woman's "morality" are probably the most important measure of the family's social position. Herat sievemakers in general have tried to renounce their Ghorbat-identity, claiming to be Pashtun or Tajik, and the imposition of purdah restrictions on the women was obviously an important step in trying to avoid being classified as *J̌at* by the settled community.

The connection between purdah restriction and upward social mobility, however, is neither restricted to the Ghorbats only nor to the difference between tent and house. While rural Afghan women in the first part of this century never used a veil, this practice has gradually spread from the cities to most of the countryside. In the mid-1970's, while the poorest women in town and countryside may not use a veil, as they had to be economically active, the ambition of the family was to increase their social position by relieving women of their work and to be able to afford keeping them veiled and unemployed. Only the most educated, well-to-do and liberal could socially afford to discard the veil and allow their women back in the labour market.

With the fall of Najibullah and the PDPA-regime and the subsequent establishment of the coalition government between the resistance groups in May 1992, one of the first measures of the new government was to issue a law demanding that all women in public have their hair covered. Hence, women's public appearance in Afghanistan is not only a question of honour, chastity, and social status, but has been a very touchy political issue.

Men's Additional Activities

Sievemaking is far from being Ghorbat men's only economic activity. Many sievemakers take up alternative occupations during winter, the slack season for sievemaking. For a few, sievemaking has become a way out if everything else has failed. In other words, while many sievemakers have tried other occupations they retain sievemaking as something on which they can always fall back. This was, for example, the case with two Qāsem Khēl brothers. They worked as carpenters for 15 years, but continued to migrate with the community, renting shops in the different localities. Today they are again mainly sievemakers, but carpentry, e.g. fixing new butts on rifles, provides an additional income. Other sievemakers have taken to making wooden cages for birds.[49]

Sievemaking's "dirty" character constitutes the principal basis by which the Siāwun are regarded as inferior. It is also in the face of such stigmatization, that they formulate their own social strategies. However, the Siāwun are in fact characterized by a considerable amount of occupational flexibility and adaptability both at individual and community levels. The case of Mohammad Ayub from the Mostafa Khēl can serve as an illustration:

> Until Mohammad Ayub was 28 years old, he manufactured sieves. Then he took up the production and selling of sweets (made from milk, sugar, and flavouring) as he started going to Jalalabad in winter time with his Qāsem Khēl in-laws. The following year he wanted to stay in Kabul for the winter where his father owned part of a house. He got a job as *sīmkār*, i.e. making the wire-netting to reinforce concrete pillars for house construction. However, he had to sign a two-year contract to get the work. In summer time, the *sīmkārī* wage of 1,200 Afs per month was less than the income derivable from sievemaking; hence, after work hours he supplemented his income with shoemending. This profession he knew since childhood, when his father had sent him to assist a shoemaker in order to learn another profession. When the contract for *sīmkārī* expired, he returned to sievemaking, continuing to supplement his income with shoemending in winter time (it was too cold for sweetmaking in Kabul during winter). For some time he also worked as a servant (*khāna zaman*) in the Ministry of Communication, serving lunch for the staff and making mail rounds. In 1975-76, he was mainly a sievemaker.

Like Mohammad Ayub, the poorer sievemakers may thus supplement their income from sievemaking during shorter or longer periods with other poorly paid jobs. Those who have accumulated a bit of capital have more remunerative options; they can lease land (*ijāra*) and cultivate cash crops while maintaining their occupation as sievemakers. This happens both in the winter and summer areas. A Nasir Khēl explains:

"In the former place [Nangarhar] we will take orchards of loquat [*lôkāt*][50] on lease for four, five, or six thousand Afs. If we couldn't get an orchard on lease, then we will buy loquat there, bring them to town and sell them for profit ...

"In the latter place [in Wardak], the prospects for lease are much better. There we take an orchard on lease for 5,000-6,000 Afs, the fruits of which may bring 8,000-10,000 Afs, making 3-4,000 Afs profit. However, until the fruit ripens we don't sit idly. We make sieves."

Others have completely changed occupation, and their sievemaker relatives take great pride in telling their success stories, since they prove that even a sievemaker "can make it". The following cases are examples of this:

(1) As a young man, Rahmatullah from the Mostafa Khēl became apprentice in a mechanic workshop in Kabul. After ten years of work, he wanted to start a workshop of his own. To raise the necessary capital, his father borrowed a total of 15,000 Afs from three close relatives. The workshop is going well, and Rahmatullah has managed to get a house of his own, too, in which his brother and his family also live during winter time. Although Rahmatullah's earnings are considerably higher than those of his relatives', he has remained socially integrated in the community and is willing to lend money to his relatives when needed.

(2) Another Mostafa Khēl, Qalandar, became a painter after having worked as a sievemaker for some nine years. Now he is working on his own, employing six apprentices, four of whom are Ghorbat. His economic situation is good, he owns four houses in Kabul and has managed to send his three sons to school until 9th grade.

Other Ghorbats, mainly Mostafa Khēl and Nasir Khēl, have become shopkeepers, and some of them continue sievemaking during the evenings, selling the sieves from their own shops.

In all the above cases, people have managed to improve their economic (and social) situation by changing from the traditional profession of sievemaking to other occupations. However, there are also people who have had to give up sievemaking and take on what are considered less remunerative jobs. The reason for this is not economic, since sievemaking requires very little investment capital, and production is more dependent upon the artisan skill than anything else. Nevertheless, sievemaking is considered a physically taxing job, and there are several people who are said to be too weak for the profession or have become too weak following illness. They have then changed to other occupations like shoe-mending, making cages for birds, etc., but have in most cases remained migrating with the rest of their community.

Among the sievemakers in Kandahar, the situation was similar to that in the east, but here sievemaking was supplemented by cagemaking, manufacture of nets for catching birds as well as making decorations for horse-carts (*gawdī*). In Herat, the settled sievemakers stated that they made sieves only and had no other occupation.

The view of sievemaking as a safety net if everything else fails, was also demonstrated among four well-to-do Mostafa Khēl brothers in Pul-i Khumri. They had settled there some thirty years earlier, had each bought land and a house, and one family even had a non-Ghorbat family living as tenant. They continued to make sieves but had also made good profit on reselling some residential land and a house. In one of the families, however, the sons did not want to take up their traditional occupation. One son said that

5,45 Two Qāsem Khēl brothers supplement their sievemaking with earnings from carpentry. Here they have been fixing new butts on a couple of rifles (Kote Sangi, Oct. 1975).

he "hated sievemaking and prayed that the profession may disappear quickly from the surface of the earth". Instead, they preferred to work in the factories of Pul-i Khumri, presumably to get rid of the social stigmatization attached to sievemaking. However, their father insisted that the sons at least learn the technology of sievemaking to have something to fall back upon.

Most of the Siāwun men's non-sievemaking activities are either culturally neutral, i.e. poor men's jobs that are not in themselves stigmatized like sievemaking, or respectable partly because of being economically remunerative, such as those as shopkeeper, mechanic, painter and leaseholder. However, some alternative occupations are considered less respectable even though they may pay well. This is the case with various forms of entertainment, which in Afghanistan have traditionally been associated with moral depravity and shunned for religious reasons. It is also a sector which in the wider

5.46-7 A Qāsem Khēl carrying bird cages. Keeping birds is a very popular hobby among the Qāsem Khēl, and raising fighting quails as well as cage-making furnishes additional income for some families (Kote Sangi, June 1975).

5,48 Two Qāsem Khēl men with fighting roosters (Kote Sangi, June 1975).

5,49 In Kandahar, the sievemaker families earn additional income by making decorations for the two-wheeled horse-drawn carriages (Nov. 1976).

geographic region has frequently been associated with itinerant and socially stigmatized groups whether they are called *J̌at* or something else.

Entertainment plays an important role in the daily life of the sievemaker men – particularly among the Qāsem Khēl. In most cases entertainment has the status of hobby, whether it is music, raising singing or fighting birds (the latter for gambling), or traditional story-telling among the elderly; the young boys and men are keenly interested in movies. It is thus true what a Mehrāb Khēl expressed:

> "You may find us rather poor and miserable, but you also see that we have so many hobbies – for example cock-fighting. We are not frugal when it comes to entertainment."

Among the Qāsem Khēl, young men seem to spend considerable time and also relatively much money on their hobbies, at least until they marry. Some of these hobbies may pay off economically; Ghulam, for example, spent six years as a tambour player in a famous band. Upon marrying, however, he resumed sievemaking as he would not leave his wife behind when going on musical tours. Another Qāsem Khēl man was a well-known singer; he lived in Charikar but travelled as far as Pul-i Khumri, Kandahar and Jalalabad to sing at weddings and other festive occasions. He used to rent a house for the families of his brothers and sisters in Charikar so that they would not have to live in tents. Later on, they began to go with him to Jalalabad for the winter, as he was singing there.

Probably the most important hobby among the (male) sievemakers is raising fighting cocks (*murgh ǰangi*) or quails (*būdanas*); for some persons this hobby may also be classified as a genuine profitable activity.[51] This is the case with Khan Agha, a Qāsem Khēl who in 1975 had 8 birds. He catches them himself by putting a caged singing bird near a grain field. The singing bird attracts other birds who are caught either in a net spread over the field or in a nearby trap with grain.[52] Khan Agha will keep "interesting" birds, the rest will be killed and either sold (3 Afs per piece) or eaten.

When a bird has shed its first layer of feathers, it is old enough to be used for bird fighting. For this it is trained some 10 days. The "training" consists of Khan Agha shouting in the bird's ear which makes it dizzy "like a drunk person". Afterwards the bird is given water. Bird fighting is a popular entertainment and the object of much gambling in Afghanistan. A bird bought for 1,500 Afs may be traded at almost double the price after it has won a fight. The bets on birds range from 100 up to 20,000 Afs, if a bird has won some 6-7 times. The annual turn-over of birds for a person like Khan Agha may be 600 birds.

On Fridays, for example, Khan Agha goes with his cocks and quails to challenge other bird-owners for a game, agreeing upon how high stakes they will put on each bird. Some advance money is paid in order to ensure that both will turn up at the game. Both the bird-owners gather partners for their bet; i.e. somebody who trusts the bird and is willing to share the bet. Most of the time Khan Agha makes his livelihood this way, but if he is on the losing side, his father must feed his family.

Cock-fighting (*murgh ǰangi*) is so important among the sievemakers that it has its own legend of origin, tying it both to the Iranian legendary hero of Rustam and to the Ghorbats as the original practitioners of cock-fighting. One informant recounts the legend as follows:

> "Rustam was on his way to another city which he wanted to conquer. On his way, in the jungle, he saw two roosters fighting so fiercely that they were both covered with blood. He watched the two roosters fighting for a while and then continued on his journey to war. He reached the city and after some fighting he was defeated. He made his escape from the city and returned back to the jungle, and on the same spot he saw these two roosters still fighting each other, having torn each other to pieces, both suffering from injuries with one of their eyes pulled out and having cut each other's flesh with their claws. Then he said to himself 'Oh God, my creator. Look at these roosters – these *animals*. Imagine that after having so many injuries they do not give up but still fight one another, that they should have so much perseverance, that they should be so brave. Why should I be less [than they are]? I shall go back and fight until I conquer the city, or else I die'. Rustam resumed his fighting and this time was victorious. He withstood much hardship but refused to yield. He returned (to his own place) and on his way he again saw the two roosters still fighting each other. He took them with him to his

home. He healed their wounds and took good care of them. Then he tried to find a hen in the jungle. He succeeded, ... and then of course came eggs. They placed the eggs under the hen for some days and then chicks emerged. The chicks grew and they multiplied, until today we rear and train the fighting breed of roosters which we call *Kolangi.* So through Rustam we have been the first to have these roosters, and we have given them to other races of people."

Economic Stratification

The average annual income of a sievemaker household is hard to establish because of considerable regional differences, seasonal variations in production and diverse sources of income. However, some estimates will be attempted, here based on the Qāsem Khēl, where individual differences in income appear to be less than among the other *khēls*:

In sievemaking, the main source of income is from the coarse, skin-woven sieves used for grain-cleaning. Depending upon the size, these are sold wholesale for approximately 50 Afs a piece, of which the sievemaker makes a profit of approximately 20 Afs. In retail, the sievemakers make some 5-10 Afs higher profit per sieve, but then he also has to undertake the selling himself.

When the wooden frames and skins have been prepared, a sievemaker can produce around 10 sieves in a day, with minor variations depending on the type of mesh. The preparations of wood and skin, including the purchase of raw materials, cutting and rounding the wood take 2-3 days' work. Finally, the producers spend time selling the product either wholesale or retail. A smaller income comes from repairing old sieves.

In the case of wire-net sieves, a sievemaker can produce some 60 pieces a day when the frames are ready, but the net income is as low as 2 Afs a piece. The profit on these sieves has decreased considerably during recent years, as the price of the wire mesh has increased from 500 to 1,600 Afs per roll, apparently without a comparable increase in selling price of the sieves.

With optimal production, a sievemaker would theoretically be able to maintain a daily income of 50-80 Afs, which compares favourably with the daily wages paid to unskilled labourers. However, such conditions are present only in summer, during which the sievemakers must accumulate reserves to take them through the 3-4 months of winter – where they also undertake some poorly paid activities. To these forms of income, however, should be added the above-mentioned women's earnings as hawkers in most Qāsem Khēl families which may be comparable to the men's earnings, but also subject to the seasonal variations.

A total picture of the Qāsem Khēl's income level cannot be established, but judging from their clothing, tents, houses if any, household possessions and alternative sources of income, it appears that the Qāsem Khēl are generally the poorest of the four *khēls*. The poorest sievemakers are found among the Qāsem Khēl, although the economic differentiation within the Nasir Khēl, Mostafa Khēl, and Mehrāb Khēl is far greater. There are very few Qāsem Khēl families who own a house, while several Nasir Khēls are so well-to-do that they have houses in Ghazni and in Jalalabad; their houses in Ghazni are not mere mud huts but proper, well-built houses.[53]

Part of the explanation for this economic differentiation among *khēls* may be different market situations in their respective regions; i.e. variations in income from selling sieves. Production costs also vary between the areas, since the price of wood and skin is not uniform. Due to the many pastoral nomads of the Ghazni area, skin for example is far cheaper here than in Kabul, while the price of cutting up the wood is much higher in Ghazni. However, the actual production costs may in fact only set a minimal price on the sieves, as the selling price is determined primarily by supply and demand. The formation of prices is not only affected by the number of producers in relation to potential customers. The level of infrastructure in the given area also has a great influence on the commodity exchange process and consequently, on the price level. This is clear from the differing market situation which the Nasir Khēl and Qāsem Khēl face in their summer areas.

During the summer months, the Nasir Khēl apparently make almost double profits on their production as compared to the Qāsem Khēl, because the Nasir Khēl sell their sieves in areas as distant and potentially dangerous as Katawaz, Shindand and Hazarajat. The arrangement may be, for example, that 10 sievemakers rent a truck which they fill up with sieves, 80-100 sieves per person, and even after deducting transport costs they each make a profit of 6,000-7,000 Afs. A Nasir Khēl described the regional price differences in the following words:

> "[The Qāsem Khēl] sell a pair of sieves [*maydabîz* and *chighil*] in Jalalabad and Charikar for 60 Afs. We can sell a tambourine for 100 Afs in Gardez while the same would cost 30 Afs in Jalalabad. In Kabul and *Shamāli* [the area between Kabul and Charikar], a pair of sieves costs 50-60 Afs while in Gardez and Ghazni they sell for 120 Afs."

Hence, according to the Nasir Khēl, the economic differentiation between *khēls* is brought about by the fact that the "Qāsem Khēl go all year round to places where they can never sell a sieve for more than 40 Afs a piece". According to another Nasir Khēl, the Qāsem Khēl men are to be blamed for their comparative poverty:

> "The Qāsem Khēl are so poor because they lose all their money in gambling and only their women go and earn something. But we never let ourselves be idle."

While others also refer to the Qāsem Khēl's "bad habits", regional differences in market situation as argued above, are the main cause for the variation between the *khēls*. Moreover, the concentration of sievemakers in Kabul, the Maidan and Parwan provinces – areas of migration for the Qāsem Khēl – may be higher than in the Ghazni and Gardez areas, with a resulting higher supply of sieves and thus lower prices. One may wonder why these differences are not evened out by migration of the Qāsem Khēl to more profitable areas. It seems that the high integration among the *khēls* inhibits such adaptive responses to the market. The size and composition of migration units are only adjusted to the market within the traditional area of a given *khēl* and not beyond it, a process which may be reinforced by the *khēl*-endogamous marriage practices. The migrations to Turkestan during the last couple of generations should no doubt be seen as such a response, since Turkestan reputedly offers a better market for sieves than eastern Afghanistan.

The Nasir Khēl who are relatively better-off, also explain the differentiation between *khēls* with references to additional economic activities. An elderly informant, for example, states

5,50 The comparative wealth of Nasir Khēl can be seen from this newly built house in the outskirts of Ghazni (Nov. 1976).

"The reason that the Qāsem Khēls are lagging behind economically is because they all year round limit their activities to sievemaking. It pays during spring time but not the rest of the year, so they are never able to save money. We Nasir Khēls – the *Pāchā Khēl* ['King Khēl'] have a lot of other trades, shops in Jalalabad, selling petty things from shops, or engaging in export of vegetables to Pakistan, such as cauliflower."

The Nasir Khēl's assessment seems correct. According to available information, the more well-to-do families (house owners, etc.) are at the same time those who either have changed to another occupation or those for whom sievemaking no longer forms the major source of income. They include families established as small shopkeepers in Jalalabad (who may produce sieves) throughout the year, or only during winter, and others who have been trained within modern crafts. Compared to other *khēls*, there are far fewer Qāsem Khēl families who under-

5,51 A well-to-do man (to the right) visiting his poor Mehrāb Khēl relatives in their tent camp in the outskirts of Ghazni (Nov. 1976).

take such comprehensive alternative economic activities.

It is also possible that sievemaking in the past was so remunerative that the sievemakers could afford to buy houses, something hardly possible in the mid-1970s. This would imply that the occupation has been subject to a gradual impoverishment. However, an attempt to compare the price of sieves in the past and the present did not yield any conclusive results. On the other hand, the sievemakers' economy may also have been composite in the past, in the sense that comparatively well-to-do (house owning) families, have always been those who successfully exploited supplementary economic activities. This question must also remain unanswered, since it has not been possible to establish with any certainty when houses were bought nor the extent of additional occupations.

For the present generation, however, there seems to be a clear connection between standard of living and alternative income sources. This tendency is likely to become even more pronounced, since sievemaking as a traditional craft and occupation is threatened on two fronts: by competition from ready-made products and by the gradual disappearance of the market for sieves.

Industrial products have already led to the disappearance of many traditional crafts. For sievemaking, such a competition has already started with regard to one type of sieves, the *ghalbel* flour sieves.[54] In Jalalabad, ready-made metal sieves imported from Pakistan were sold in the shops along with metal sieves produced by local smiths, resulting in a price reduction of 30-40% on these.[55]

However, until the middle of the 1970, this process had been limited in East Afghanistan and had yet to affect the traditional agricultural crafts. Disappearance of the market for sieves will be unavoidable in the long run, as technological modernization and mechanization change agricultural production all over Afghanistan. The basis for all traditional crafts which produce implements for manual processes within agricultural production will gradually dwindle.

Household and Marriage Patterns

The vast majority of sievemaker households consist of nuclear families. New households are generally formed when the young men marry and separate from their parents after having completed their apprenticeship. Since a man at that time already possesses the necessary work implements, the main expenses in setting up a household are the wedding costs and the purchase of a tent. The latter is a necessity for all but the completely settled Ghorbats.

In case of *badal* marriages, i.e. where two girls are "exchanged" and thus no bride-price paid, marriage may take place at a younger age and actually precede the completion of apprenticeship. In such cases, the boy may join his wife in her parents' household as a *khāna dāmād* for a few years, until the couple is considered mature and able to form its own nuclear family household, frequently after the first child is born.[56] An elderly sievemaker woman with a resident son-in-law explains:

> "My son-in-law separated last year after they had their first child and he was old enough. Sultan [her own son] will separate from his [in-law's] family after having two children, as he is still too young."

The practice of *khāna dāmād* may reflect the comparatively strong position of women among the sievemakers. While this arrangement is also found among other groups in Afghanistan, it is primarily seen where the young man is an orphan or of a considerably inferior background than his wife. Among the sievemakers, however, *khāna dāmād* is not only practiced in such situations, but may be comparable to the initial patrilocal residence of young couples in other social groups, where the newlyweds may initially be living in the parental household of the husband. I have not recorded any extended households comprising a married son living in his parental household. The institution of *khāna dāmād* may also be seen as a strategy to avoid the bride-price, since the son-in-law during the first years of marriage is working off his debt to his in-laws by living and working within their household. A Farāhi married to a Qāsem Khēl explained: "These people don't care so much for money in marriage, but prefer a *khāna dāmād* instead. Especially earlier that was true, but now they take money". However, I have no information regarding the internal economics of extended households, which might confirm that *khāna damād* may substitute for bride-price. The economic part of the arrangement may be of minor importance. A young, unmarried, man explained that "it is our custom to love son-in-laws more than sons", and the girl's mother may well help a young couple with money and gifts during the early years.

Other variations from the nuclear pattern may result from death or divorce. A widow will be included in one of her children's households in case they are all married. She may remarry or form a household of her own with the children, particularly if one of these is a son. If the son is too young to be economically active, the household may be supported solely by the mother's peddling. A widower may also remarry or maintain his own household.

Among the Qāsem Khēl, no instances of polygyny were recorded. In a case where a Qāsem Khēl was forced to marry a settled girl with whom he had an affair (see p. 268), his Qāsem Khēl wife took their children and left him. The economic independence of most Qāsem Khēl women no doubt discourages polygyny, since they are better able than other groups to fend for themselves and their children in case of divorce.

The four Siāwun *khēls* constitute patrilinear descent groups, and from *Fig. 5.52* which covers most but not all Qāsem Khēls it can be seen that the present-day Qāsem Khēl consists mainly of the descendants of four brothers. These have also given name to the emerging sub-groups of Qāsem Khēl, referred to as Hemat Ali *khēl*, Mahib Ali *khēl*, etc. The classification of these subgroups is not absolute, however, and depending on the circumstances reference to even smaller descent-segments is also common by attaching the suffix *khēl* to the name of the prominent (male) figure of a sub-group.

In this registration of Qāsem Khēl, 65 marriages were recorded and among these, further details were collected in 46 cases. Out of these 46 cases, only 7 marriages were contracted with non-Ghorbats (3 with non-Ghorbat men, 4 with non-Ghorbat women). Hence, *qawm*-endogamy (85%) and even *khēl*-endogamy (72%) predominate. Only 6 out of the 39 *qawm*-endogamous marriages were with people outside Qāsem Khēl (4 Mostafa Khēls and 2 Farāhis). Marriage with close relatives is also rather frequent; more than one-third of the *qawm*-endogamous marriages take place within the same sub-group of the *khēl* (12 cases). In fact, cousin-marriages are prevalent, with 16 marriages being contracted with either first or second cousin (8 cases of

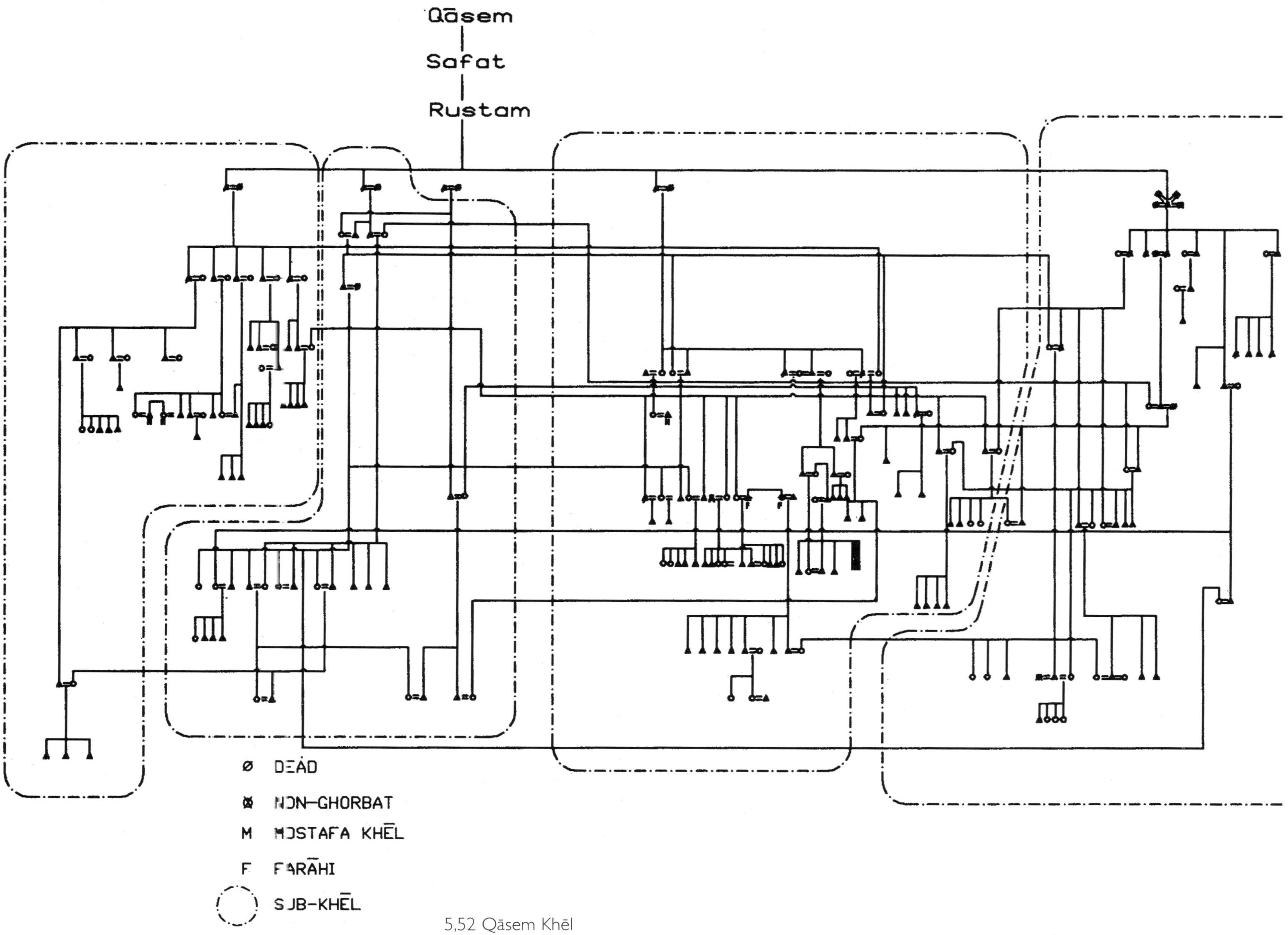

Qāsem
Safat
Rustam

Ø DEAD
⊗ NON-GHORBAT
M MOSTAFA KHĒL
F FARĀHI
( ) SUB-KHĒL

5,52 Qāsem Khēl

each). In 12 cases these were with paternal cousins in the form of FaBrDa, FaBrSoDa, FaFaBrDa, FaBrDaDa or FaSiDa marriages.

In case of inter-*khēl* marriage, the couple will normally remain with the husband's *khēl*, but one case was recorded where the couple lived with the wife's *khēl*, which in this case was Qāsem Khēl. However, the explanation appeared to be that the husband had more or less been banished from his own *khēl*. It was stated that his father had disowned him because he had stolen his sister's savings and jewellery, amounting to some Afs 15,000.

Patrilineal tendencies thus predominate among the sievemakers – both at *khēl* and sub-*khēl* levels. In daily life, however, women play an influential role in the families, both economically as breadwinners and in decision-making. The preference for *khāna dāmād* marriages and the high degree of both intra-*khēl* and intra-sub-*khēl* marriages reflect the importance of maternal relations. FaBrDa-marriage, so prevalent in the Middle East, is generally explained as a strategy for keeping property within the patrilineage or as a means of forming political alliances. This hardly applies in case of the sievemakers, where the Qāsem Khēl particularly have few material possessions, and internal politics seems of minor significance. Marriage arrangements serve rather to maintain connections between a young couple and their parental households, respectively. Paternal cousin marriage fulfills two important functions, in that both husband and wife remain part of their parental sub-group from where the migration units are recruited, and the wife will be able to hawk petty things together with her mother or other close female relatives.

Among the Qāsem Khēl, *badal*-marriages, in which two girls are "exchanged", are rather common, and were identified in at least 10-12 of the marriages. They may take place between close relatives but is generally attractive for poor people, since no bride-price is paid. *Badal*-marriages may be combined with the practice of *khāna dāmād*.

Two cases of levirate were recorded, one of which caused considerable conflict between the two involved sub-*khēls* of Qāsem Khēl:

> Zaher was a famous singer, much loved and cared for by relatives who even adapted their migrations to his tournés. He died in a car accident at a young age, leaving a widow and a small son. Zaher's family wanted her to marry Zaher's younger brother Zaker, but her father was against it. The widow returned to her father's home, while the in-laws kept the child. They went to court demanding that the widow return and stay with them, but as she refused they lost the case. However, one day, during the celebration of the religious holiday *'Eid*, she came (presumably to see the child), and her in-laws kept her. Ultimately she yielded and married Zaker.

The seven marriages with non-Ghorbat spouses are with poor settled people such as shoemenders, potterymakers, barbers or other landless people. The Qāsem Khēl have been wife-givers as well as wife-receivers in this context. At least three of the seven interethnic marriages have resulted from elopement, extra-marital relations, or adoption of a non-Ghorbat.

> Some five years ago, a shoemender's daughter from Badakhshan supposedly "called on" Khan Agha. One of his younger relatives said that Khan Agha had gone to Badakhshan to sing, and had taken the shoemender's daughter as his girlfriend there. When he returned from Badakhshan, she came with him. When

> her father arrived to take her back to Badakhshan, she refused to go, saying that Khan Agha was her husband. His relative claims that Khan Agha did not like the Badakhshi girl, but that he had no other choice but to accept her as wife, whereupon his first Qāsem Khēl wife took their children and left him. She set up a household of her own, which she and her eldest son support without any help from Khan Agha.[57]

In all the cases of exogamous marriages recorded, the non-Ghorbat person has been included into the Ghorbat community. Although the number of cases is low, it appears that the Ghorbats, like the Shaykh Mohammadis, have the ability to absorb outsiders. Among the former it carries prestige to be able to refer to a non-Ghorbat ancestor, while this is not the case among the Shaykh Mohammadis. A case in point are the Mehrāb Khēl, who never miss a chance to stress that although they are sievemakers today, their great grandfather was not. Hence, there circulate two versions regarding the origin of Mehrāb Khēl, one told by the other three *khēls* and one told by the Mehrāb Khēls themselves. The following version is told by a Mostafa Khēl:

> "Zainal was from Baraki Barak ... He was first accepted as a servant into the [Nasir Khēl] community. He grew up in their community. [When he grew up] they told him that now he could take care of himself and could go where he wanted. But he told them, 'If I die, you are going to bury me and I shall not part even from your dogs. I have acquired your habits. So long as I live, I will stay with you.' As he lay down his neck [a sign of total submission], the community accepted him.
>
> "So Qader married off his sister's granddaughter to Zainal. Qader was from Nasir Khēl, so [the married couple] accompanied the Nasir Khēl on their travels to Jalalabad, to Ghazni and anywhere they would go, and Zainal considered himself as Nasir Khēl.
>
> "Zainal had a son and called him Mehrab after his father. So he learned how to make sieves and his children, too, learned how to make sieves. He had four sons and five daughters. All of them married and had children. ... Although Zainal himself was a barber [of barber origin] before he became a servant, his children and grandchildren did not consider themselves inferior to the rest of the community, and they considered themselves Nasir Khēl. And they would just shout insulting words to the barbers: 'We do so-and-so on the graves of the barbers.'[58]
>
> ... So in this way a dispute emerged between these people and the rest of the community. So they separated from the others and called themselves 'Mehrāb Khēl'."

The Mehrab Khēl version confirms that their forefather (Mehrab rather than Zainal) joined the sievemakers, but it certainly places him in a different light:

> "Our forefather [in this version Mehrāb] kidnapped a girl from Kohistan, but they blocked his way and there was a fight. ... He managed to escape and came across our maternal grandfather, Nasir, who was having lunch. Our grandfather [Mehrab] had a big moustache, he smoked his chillum after having tied his horse, and Nasir went to give some water to his horse and told him: '*Khān Ṣāḥib*, would you like to have something to eat?.' Our grandfather's [Mehrab's] cartridge belt was full of bullets. He answered: 'Yes, I would like something to eat.'

After he had his lunch he said to the other persons: 'Wouldn't you like to keep me with you?' They said: 'Are you kidding! We are sure you have 10 servants like us with you.' But he told them: 'By God, I want to stay with you.' ... So he stayed with them. ... One day, during a cousin fight, Mehrab killed a man by slapping him. They wanted to imprison him but could not. As compensation for the blood, Nasir killed his own daughter to get even, so blood was paid for in blood. They had a sister and gave her to *Bābā* Mehrab. Her name was Qamar Gul. God gave him 10 sons. ..."[59]

The bone of contention here may be whether an outsider has joined the sievemakers by marriage or elopement, or has been adopted by them; i.e. come under their protection due to weakness and powerlessness, for example as a child. While marriage implies equality, adoption implies inferiority, as can be seen from the two versions above. There are several such cases where a childless woman has picked up an abandoned child and raised it as her own. The following is from the Qāsem Khēl:

At the time of *Baccha-i Saqqao* (i.e. during the civil war in 1929), a sievemaker woman picked up a 3-year old child, who had been left at a mosque in Koh-i Daman, presumably an orphan or an abandoned child. The story goes that this took place during the Mangal attack on Koh-i Daman (which was supporting the rebel *Baccha-i Saqqao*), and that the child was about to get killed, but was rescued by the sievemaker woman. The woman, who was barren, kept the child and raised him as her own son. When he grew up, he married within the Qāsem Khēl, and he and his descendants are all counted as full members of Qāsem Khēl.

Another case comes from the Mostafa Khēl. As with the case of Zainal, it reveals that adoption implies inferiority, at least temporarily:

"Once Wali Mahmad was a child of 7 or 9 years of age.[60] His people, who were from Matak, had thrown him out so he was wandering aimlessly around when he came across our people in Saray Khwaja. He asked for food and shelter and said: 'If you have got any food for me, I beg you in the name of God to give it to me, as I am homeless.' They gave him food and shelter, and when in the morning they asked him where he would be going, he said, 'I have no place to go'. Tegh Ali asked him if he would accept to be his servant. Wali Mahmad agreed and he started working for Tegh Ali, running errands and helping him in other things. He was happy, and as time passed he made friends with the other children. Then he became like a family-born [*khāna-zād*], and he acquired our habits. Wali Mahmad stayed with Tegh Ali for about 15-20 years and became like a son to him.

"After some years, Tegh Ali's sister, who had no children, adopted him as her son on the recommendation of Tegh Ali, who told her: 'You keep him as your son; he will serve you.' She kept him and Wali Mahmad called her *khāla* [mother's sister]. After some time, Tegh Ali urged his [other] sister's daughter, Bepoi, to marry Wali Mahmad. While her mother agreed, Bepoi refused, as she was very beautiful and ambitious. She became very upset and exclaimed: 'How could I marry that *qarsarlīs-i qawm*! ['plate-licker' of the *qawm*, i.e. one living by the mercy of the community]. I shall not marry him!.' They exerted much pressure on her, and they told her that she had no other choice. The girl wanted to buy some *sanktia* [a kind of poison] and threatened to take her own life if they insisted upon that marriage: 'I shall not accept it, and I swear by God that I will take my own life.' Finally one day, she stood on the floor of a 3-storey building in Kabul and wanted to commit suicide. She said that 'people are going to give me *ta'na* [spite], and they will say that I have married the *qarsarlīs* of the community.'

"Anyway, by fate and destiny, she was finally made to marry Wali Mahmad. ... Now 6 daughters and 4 sons [were born to them] so in that way Wali Mahmad was initiated into the community [through the many children]."

The many descendants of Wali Mahmad, like Mehrab's, may perhaps one day form their own *khēl* or sub-*khēl*, boasting of having a non-Ghorbat ancestor, even if he initially was the '*qarsarlīs*' of the community. In spite of their ability to absorb outsiders, adoption was not found among the Shaykh Mohammadis, and unlike among the Ghorbats, people of 'outsider' descent do not attempt to maintain a separate identity. On the contrary, outsiders had historically joined in order to become Shaykh Mohammadis. Part of the reason is certainly because being a Shaykh Mohammadi, both in the conception of themselves and of the settled community, is infinitely more respectable than being a Ghorbat.

Political Structures

In the past, the four Siāwun *khēls* had an independent political organization of their own. They differ from most other ethnically specialized artisan groups by not being integrated into the political structures of any settled local community. By the mid-1970 their traditional political organization was beginning to break down. In the past, however, it was structured along the following lines: Within the individual *khēl* a *kalāntar* (elder) or *pīrwarta* was elected to settle internal conflicts, assist in marriage negotiations, etc. The position of *pīrwarta* is not hereditary, nor is it associated with particular families. A person is elected simply by force of his personal qualities (respectability, honesty). The functions of the *kalāntar* among the Qāsem Khēls are described as follows:

"When there is a quarrel, the *kalāntar* will come and ask both parts about what has happened. If one is found guilty, he will be punished or fined some 10 *sers* of thin rice and a sheep. He will have to cook it and invite all the *qawm* [*qawm* here presumably means the *khēl* only]. If a person found guilty refuses to pay the fine, the *kalāntar* will tell him: 'OK, go to the government.' In the government, it will then be settled. But the *kalāntar* manages most of the cases."

"As for a person who does not obey any elder's word we will expel him from *sīyāli* [excommunicate him]. We don't go to his 'dead and living' [i.e. do not share his sorrows and joys; no sociality]– and he doesn't go to ours. If he [the *kalāntar*] says that so and so is a bad man, all the *qawm* will condemn him."

A practical example of the *kalāntar*'s functions and power was seen among the Mostafa Khēl, where a family was excommunicated because of a conflict over their daughter's wedding and her subsequent elopement with a non-Ghorbat. A Mostafa Khēl relative tells:

"The wives of Wali Mohammad and Fath Ali were pregnant and they agreed that in case they had children of opposite sex, they were to marry each other. Ultimately, Wali Mohammad got a daughter and Fath Ali got a son. When the children grew up, Fath Ali went to Wali Mohammad and asked for Wali's daughter for his son. But the wife of Wali Mohammad did not agree: 'Did you bring us any *'eidi*, any *baratī*, *naw-rūzi*, *nāmzādī*[61]. You didn't – and I am not going to give you my daughter.' She also cursed him saying: 'Do you agree to marry your wife to my son!'. Fath Ali cried when hearing this and got his son married to his sister's grand-daughter instead.[62]

"It so happened that a Laghmani was living in Wali Mohammad's house. He was a *payzar-dūz* [maker of traditional, pointed leather shoes *payzar*], and Wali Mohammad's daughter fell in love with him and they finally eloped. The community was indignant at this and put Wali Mohammad under pressure. His maternal uncle, Tegh Ali [*kalāntar* of the Mostafa Khēl] drew him out of the house and told him, that he was banished from *sīyāli* [excommunicated].

"After four years, Wali Mohammad returned. He came back, set up his tent in Deh Kepak, away from the rest of the community. In the evening, he came to Tegh Ali's house to ask for forgiveness. The girl with her husband also came from Laghman, and her husband, like her father were re-admitted to the community after paying compensation [*bad*]. Wali Mohammad paid the following *bad*: 2 sheep, 40 *sers* of rice, 10 *sers* of flour, 1 *kharwār* of wood. Tegh Ali invited everybody from the community and after having had dinner, he told the community that 'We will readmit this man into our community. But it should be remembered that nobody should marry his daughter to anybody without the consent of the community.'

"The daughter and her husband were invited from Laghman, and when they came, the community refused to let them return to Laghman. So the Laghmani man was forced to pay *bad*, too, [1,400 Afs, 10 *sērs* of flour, 1 *kharwār* of timber, 2 tins of *rughan*, butter oil], and to live with the sievemakers for the rest of his life."

The more serious cases, which might threaten the relationship between the Ghorbats and the Afghan authorities, were referred to a *wakīl* who covered all the *khēls*, including the Farāhis. Until recently, the *qawm wakīl* was the *kalāntar* of Mostafa Khēl, but the four *khēls* elected a younger man in 1974. However, the selection of the *kalāntar* has led to some confusion, as some Ghorbats claim that there has not been a common *qawm wakīl*, while others disagree as to who is presently recognized as *qawm wakīl*. While the *qawm wakīl* is supposedly elected in a meeting of all four *khēls*, there presently seems to be disagreement about whether or not the old, respected Tegh Ali actually lost the position to Qader, a young, settled man. The conflict is partly a generational conflict, partly a conflict between the "traditional" and the "modern", since Qader can read and write, is settled and earns his living as a shopkeeper in Kabul. Moreover, the election of Qader would also indicate a closer integration with the settled society, as Qader is already elected as *wakīl-i gozar* (street-*wakīl*) in his neighbourhood of Kabul. Apart from the present conflict, the contradictory information may also reflect the break-up of the traditional organization since a *qawm-wakīl* does not enjoy any official recognition.

The Ghorbats' internal organization was based principally on segmentary, patrilinear

5,53 Wakīl Tegh Ali from Mostafa Khēl (to the left) (Kabul, Dec. 1976).

descent. However, the general identity of profession and *qawm* among the Siāwun, the election of *kalāntar* and *wakīl* as well as their functions, are also akin to the organization of the urban guilds, whose elected leaders are also called *wakīl* or *kalāntar* (Centlivres 1972).

The history of the Ghorbats revolves around consecutive periods of settlement and dispersion. Their settlement has invariably been in urban centers such as Kabul, Ghazni, Charikar, Kandahar, and Herat, but whether they have been recognized as one of the guilds here is not known. Through their urban settled life, however, they may have adapted their organization to the predominant urban guild-structure, even though its basis for 'recruitment' is descent rather than occupation.[63]

Irrespective of its specific origin, the Siāwun have constituted a politically independent community both internally and externally. This was in accordance with the general political structure of Afghanistan until the reign of King Amanullah, 1919-29, where the State related to

5,54 Three Qāsem Khēl men (Oct. 1975).

its subjects not as individual citizens but collectively, as members of specific communities, be it tribes, religious communities as Hindus or Qizilbash, or as local, non-tribal communities. In this respect, the status of Siāwun differed from other itinerant, specialized groups like the Musallis and Shaykh Mohammadis: Where the *individual* Musalli families were economic and political dependants of the local landowners, the Shaykh Mohammadis as a *community* were political clients of the locally dominant *khān*. A small illustration of the Siāwun's status as independent community is given by an elderly Nasir Khēl, Salam, who relates that he was previously the *kalāntar* of his *khēl* and had been contacted by the authorities in the following matter:

> "Many years ago, they [i.e. the authorities] asked me to master support from the Ghorbats for pillaging the Pakistani consulate [in Jalalabad].[64] I got out on the street with all the Ghorbats and the mayor was impressed [by our numbers]."[65]

But Siāwun's status as an independent political community was in reality, however, more a sign of their social marginality and ephemeral relations to the settled society than of any higher, more powerful position as compared to the Musallis and Shaykh Mohammadis. This is reflected in a case related by a Mostafa Khēl:

> "Once upon a time, Yaqub had a very nice and fat sheep, admired by everybody in the camp. But during the summer migration, while camping in Qala-i Murad Beg, it was stolen in the middle of the night. A great commotion followed, and ultimately the theft came to the knowledge of the local *ḥākim*. He gathered the elders of the village and told them: 'I want either the thief or the price of the sheep from you, because nobody else would have taken it but you.'[66] The elders collected some 1,000 Afs from the local people and gave it to Yaqub as compensation for the lost sheep. While Yaqub's wife wanted to accept the money, Yaqub said that, 'if somebody steals, it is one person, but this money has been collected from everybody.' So he told the elders of the village: 'Brothers, I will trust in God! While the night is one, the thiefs are thousands. Whoever has stolen the sheep is going to be my defendant in the Other World and is going to answer then. I shall not accept this money.' Then the elders requested Yaqub to go and tell the *ḥākim* that he had dropped the case, and so he did."

5,55 Mostafa Khēl man with his infant son (Saray Khwaja, Sept. 1976).

The above may either be interpreted as an expression of Yaqub's highly developed sense of justice – or as an indication that the sievemakers are willing to renounce their rights in order to maintain good relations with the settled community. The contrast to the Shaykh Mohammadis' zealous defense of their real or imagined rights is striking. Both communities are dependent upon the settled people as their customers, so the difference must lie with their demographic and political strength: living in small, scattered groups, the sievemakers need to be accommodating and inconspicuous to survive. The Shaykh Mohammadis, on the other hand, live in such large groups that they can back their claims with physical power, and if not sufficient they have influential settled patrons to support their case.

The cause of the present disagreement among the Ghorbats regarding the *wakīl* position may be that the modern local administrative structure has undermined it. Hence, the law requires that all men have an identity card with his address. Since most sievemakers lack a permanent residence, they provide the name of a guarantor, normally a close relative with permanent residence. A Qāsem Khēl registered in Charikar explains:

> "We get our identity cards from Charikar, using Sidq Ali [*kalāntar* of Qāsem Khēl] who has property as a guarantee needed for the identity card. Since we are nomadic, nobody can trust us."

The identity cards of the sievemakers are thus not issued at one place, but at various places such as Charikar, Ghazni, and in several districts of Kabul. According to the Afghan authorities, itinerant peoples belong administratively under a district *wakīl* elected in the area where their identity cards are issued. As the authorities do not recognize a special *qawm wakīl* as representative of the Ghorbats, but only the various non-Ghorbat district *wakīls*, the basis for maintaining a common *wakīl* for all four *khēls* has disappeared. Within the individual *khēl*, the identity cards are by and large issued from the same area; hence, the *khēl kalāntar* can still function as middleman between sievemakers and the local administration. However, his position will possibly also disappear, as some of the sievemakers remark that "if something happens among our people, we no longer take it the *kalāntar* but go straight to the government."

Hence, in the modern administrative structure, the Ghorbats are being assimilated into the settled communities. This is part of a more general policy. With the introduction of the Republic in 1973, official recognition of tribal affiliation was disregarded and use of tribal names discouraged. This was an element in the general nation-building efforts, started back in the 1920s, where tribal identities and special privileges were seen as particularistic tendencies counteracting the formation of a general Afghan nationality embracing all the country's ethnic, religious, and linguistic groups.

Group Identity and Cohesion

The sievemakers' internal political structure is gradually dissolving, but group cohesion is still very high among the Siāwun. People who take up other occupations frequently continue seasonal migrations with their kinsmen, and those who have become permanently settled and have taken up more lucrative professions offer housing and economic assistance to relatives and ensure that the young people of the group receive training within other, i.e. "modern", crafts. This is very different from the Shaykh Mohammadis, where "everybody is King of his own hat" and group solidarity is activated in conflict situations but not in economic matters.

Several factors contribute to the maintenance of group cohesion and identity among the Ghorbats: their common occupation, migratory lifestyle, and their status as a linguistic and religious minority. In addition to their custom of endogamy and absorption of non-Ghorbat affines, these factors are essential to the maintenance of ethnic boundaries and social segregation vis-a-vis non-Ghorbats, all further cemented by the particularly low social status of the community.

In the view of the surrounding society, the Ghorbats' low social status primarily involves (1) their itinerant lifestyle and the women's peddling activities, (2) sievemaking as an "unclean" profession, (3) the Ghorbats' supposedly inferior descent, and (4) their adherence to the Shi'a sect of Islam in a society where Shi'as have been a persecuted and despised minority. At a community level, the Ghorbats themselves apply different strategies to tackle this low status, both in their own conception and vis-a-vis the surrounding society: (1) they claim a respectable, royal, descent as *Kayānis*, (2) they recognize that sievemaking is considered "unclean", and hence, attempt to disassociate themselves from the occupation both at the mythical and professional level. (3) Individual families or local subgroups strive to settle permanently, which may be accompanied by giving up women's peddling activities, as was seen among the sievemakers in Kandahar and Herat.

Regarding Ghorbat adherence to Shi'ism, this does not appear, at least among the Siāwun *khēls* to be considered a major obstacle vis-à-vis the majority community. There may be several reasons for this; on the one hand, particularly among itinerant groups, the surrounding society may not easily recognize their religious faith. And on the other hand, among the marginalizing features of Ghorbats, their faith may be less of a problem than their other degrading characteristics.[67]

The Siāwun groups thus do not deny being Shi'as, but they certainly do not stress their Shi'a identity either and tend to undercommunicate any sectarian differences with the settled society as in the following statement:[68]

> "We are Shi'as, our ancestors admitted that we are believers [*mu'minīn*] and Shi'as, so we have remained like that. *Imām* Jafar as-Sadeq was an *imām*, but a special one (a *sayyid*). *Imām* Musa Kazem was his son. About them it is not good to talk so much. There are many details that could cause trouble. Our people believe in the holy five [Mohammad, Ali, Fatima, Hassan, and Hussain]."[69]

The separate religious identity of the Ghorbats is also reflected in death. In Kabul, Charikar, and Jalalabad they have their own graveyards.[70] When the Ghorbats are not in one of the above places and too far away to afford to transport the corpse to one of their own graveyards, they bury their dead at the local (Sunni) cemetery with reference to "*khāk-i Khodā, mulk-i Khodā*" (lit. everywhere is God's place) and "Everybody answers himself on Doomsday, therefore it does not matter where you are buried". They will try to find a Shi'a mullah to perform the burial, or an elder from the group who can read the Qor'an will perform the ceremony.[71]

Cohesion and identity within the larger community of Ghorbats seem to be disrupted in cases where geographical distance inhibits regular contact with the main body of kinsmen. During my short visit to settled sievemakers in Herat in 1976, I got the impression that they had tried to accommodate to the surrounding society by ridding themselves of their "degrading" features. Apart from being settled in comparatively good houses and having given up female peddling and itinerancy, they also eagerly denied being of Ghorbat origin or to be related to other sievemakers in the Kabul, Parwan, Ghazni, and Jalalabad areas (i.e. to the Siāwun), although stating that they had *qawmi*s in Kandahar and Mazar-i Sharif.[72] Only reluctantly did they admit to knowing some words of *Qāzulāgi* but they otherwise denied any knowledge of the language as such.[73] They explained that "they just happened to have this occupation", and that they came from Kandahar and were "Afghan" or Tajik. It should be noted here that in the Herat context, "Afghan" does not imply "Pashtun" as it does in East Afghanistan, but "Sunni Muslim" as opposed to *Fārsī*, which here refers to "Shi'a Muslim". Hence, the Herat sievemakers not only denied being Ghorbat but also their adherence to Shi'a Islam (which, however, is permissible according to Shi'a Islam in case of persecution).

In spite of all the Ghorbats' efforts, social acceptability is hard to come by, and the local people consistently referred to the Herat sievemakers as *Jat* and the *wakīl-i gozar* of their area said with reference to them, that "these *Jat*s are even worse than the *Fārsī*s (i.e. Shi'as)!"

It could be argued that Ghorbats' occupation, lifestyle, descent, and faith all condemn them to social marginality. Their endogamy, social cohesion, and solidarity may on the one hand be seen as positive strategies for survival in a hostile environment. On the other hand, it is also forced upon them by a rejecting society. Hence, tity are internally and externally shaped and even Ghorbats' attempts to change the content of this identity has met with very limited success.

Summary

The four Siāwun *khēl*s display the full continuum, from completely nomadic to completely settled lifestyle, and in this manner shed light on minority versus itinerant characteristics as well as on the process and strategies involved in being assimilated into the mainstream settled society.

The Siāwun's primary occupation of sievemaking is closely associated with their itinerant lifestyle in the sense that their spatial mobility is adapted to the marketing possibilities for sieves, which are largely determined by the agricultural cycle. However, it is questionable whether sievemaking constitutes the primary occupation for all the four Siāwun *khēl*s in terms of economic significance, since women's peddling activities are economically vital for many families. Like sievemaking, the peddling is adapted to the agricultural cycle of their customers. It was shown that during the economically slack winter period, the choice of location was determined less by the market situation for commodities than by the ability of the family to obtain adequate shelter (tent or house) to cope with climatic conditions of a given area.

Unlike the Musallis and Shaykh Mohammadis, the Ghorbats hold a virtual monopoly on the occupation of traditional sievemaking. Yet the sievemakers have evolved a considerable economic adaptability by exploiting various income sources, comparable with that of the Shaykh Mohammadis. For many households, sievemaking is reduced to a temporary activity or a safety net, in case other sources fail or become exhausted. The Ghorbats' and the Shaykh Mohammadis' economic adaptability may well be conditioned by the fact that they, in Rao's terminology (1987), are contiguous to their customers, while the Musallis' adaptability is restrained by the fact that they live attached to their customers and are socially integrated into the settled communities.

Compared to the other two groups, the Ghorbats must no doubt be characterized as more marginal and of a lower social status. Like the Musallis, they are of non-Afghan origin, but unlike these they live socially segregated and have thus been able to maintain their original language. This, in addition to their adherence to the minority Shi'a sect of Islam, and their undertaking of an unclean occupation, consolidates their socially low, marginal and minority status vis-a-vis the settled society.

Under these circumstances, it is hardly surprising that endogamous marriage practices are considerably more pronounced among the Ghorbats than among the other two communities. In fact, from these three cases it appears that the lower the status, the higher the frequency of group endogamy. Rao is thus correct when she points to endogamy as a sign of social marginality (1987). However, as with the Shaykh Mohammadis, integration of outsiders into the community has taken place, although it, besides normal intermarriage, seems to be moulded on completely different patterns in the case of adoption of outlaws and orphans, of which several cases were found among Ghorbats.

Unlike the two other communities, the Ghorbats had and to some extent still have an independent political structure, which by force of their monopoly on sievemaking bears a resemblance to the guild structure. But the close association of occupation and *qawm* which exists within the living memory of informants renders this very distinction obsolete. To obtain social acceptability and respectability, the Ghorbats have to relinquish both *qawm* and occupation. This is somewhat ironic, as occupation and *qawm* in the mythological realm are more clearly disassociated among the Ghorbats than among the Musallis and Shaykh Mohammadis. Although the profession of sievemaking, like many other crafts, is sacralized by an alleged religious origin, the Ghorbats vehemently deny having originally been sievemakers. Rather, they present themselves as being of royal descent of the most prominent kind.

In the preceding chapters, the political impotency of the dependent and separate Musallis was contrasted with the situation of the Shaykh Mohammadis, whose group cohesion and sheer numbers gave them a relative strength in conflicts, irrespective of their low social status. The Ghorbat case adds a new dimension to the picture of conflicts and power between itinerants and the settled society. In spite of their group cohesion and independent economic and political organization, the Ghorbats are not assertive in their relations with the settled society, but appear rather appeasing, minimizing potential issues of conflict. Their migratory pattern no doubt favours such an approach as they live scattered in small camp units throughout the summer. Yet even during winter, where a large number of Ghorbats live in one locality, Jalalabad, they opt for small, inconspicuous camp units. It appears that in this sense their independent political organization leaves them comparatively weaker than the Shaykh Mohammadis, who as political clients of the local *khāns*, also have been able to fall back upon and manipulate the *khān*'s support if need be. For the Ghorbats, their political independence implies marginality, which instead of creating submission, as in the case of the Musallis, leads to avoidance of external conflicts to the largest possible extent. In this respect, the Ghorbats no doubt represent the socially lowest and most marginal of the itinerant communities in Afghanistan.

NOTES:

[1] Apart from my own research, Aparna Rao has conducted a comprehensive study of the Ghorbats, also during 1975-77, in connection with a wider survey of *Jat* groups in Afghanistan. Rao has published a monograph and several articles on the Ghorbats (1982, 1982a). Obviously, some of our material is virtually identical, and we even collaborated during the initial months of our respective fieldworks. However, Rao chose to center on the Ghorbats on a nationwide level, while the main part of my information on Ghorbats is from the Siāwun subgroup, as I was doing the parallel studies on Shaykh Mohammadis and Musallis. Where Rao's data differ from mine, where she contributes additional information, or where she offers a different interpretation, will clearly be indicated in the text.

[2] Ferdowsi's *Shāh Nāmā*, completed in AD 1010, is a poem of nearly 60,000 couplets, based mainly on an earlier prose version of the same name also compiled by the poet. The *Shāh Nāmā* contains the history of the kings of Persia from mythical times down to the reign of Khosrow II (AD 590-628), as well as additional material continuing the story to the overthrow of the Sassanians by the Muslim Arabs in the middle of the 7th century (Encyclopedia Britannica, IV, 1985: 735-6). For an English version of the work, see Alexander Roger's translation from 1907.

[3] For a slightly different version of the mythical ancestry of the Ghorbats, see Rao (1982: 41-2). One can hardly speak of any "correct" version of these tales, as there appear to exist as many versions as there are people telling them – and the same person may not tell an identical story every time.

[4] This was told in 1975. After the Soviet invasion in Afghanistan, Afghans took pride in stating that they would defeat the Soviet forces just as they had defeated British colonial designs through the three Anglo-Afghan Wars (1842, 1879, 1919).

[5] A story of some resemblance is related by Halliday (1922: 177) as an example of the Turkish and Bulgarian tradition regarding the presumed irreligiousness of Gypsies: "When their religions were being distributed to the different nations, the recipients wrote their creeds in books or upon wood, stone or metal, all except the thriftless Gypsies, who inscribed their canons on cabbage leaves which a passing donkey espied upon and ate."

[6] See for example Ivanow (1914) regarding such tales among Persian Gypsies, Clébert (1963: 67), who refers to the presumed curse on Gypsies in Walachia (present-day Romania), that the Gypsies massacred the children of Bethlehem, forged the nails of the Cross, and were cursed by Christ. In Clébert it is unclear whether the Gypsies themselves tell these tales or whether the settled population tell them about the Gypsies. Halliday (1922: 177) presents

them as being told by the settled population in Greece.

[7] Many of the stories and legends told by the Ghorbats can also be found in Rao (1982). In fact, some of them were collected jointly by Aparna Rao and myself during the initial months of our field research in Spring 1975.

[8] Epic hero from the *Shāh Nāmā* and, according to the above tale, also the first sievemaker.

[9] Dawud is the Arabic name for David, king of Israel and a Prophet, to whom God revealed the *Zabūr*, or Book of Psalms (*Zabūr*). He has no special title or *kalimah*, as all Muslims agree that he was not a law-giver or the founder of a dispensation (Hughes 1982(1885): 71). In religious folklore, Dawud is counted as the *pīr* of all metal workers.

[10] Shish is identical to the biblical Seth, the third son of Adam, of whom it is said that God revealed fifty small portions of scripture (Hughes, 1982(1885): 569). Being prophets, the names of Dawud and Shish are followed by the invocation of the blessing *alai-hi 's-salām*, lit. Peace be upon Him.

[11] Adam is reckoned by Muslim writers as the first prophet, to whom ten portions of scripture (*sahīfah*) are said to have been revealed. He is distinguished by the title of *Safīyu'llah*, lit.(chosen one of God) (Hughes 1982(1885): 9)

[12] Halliday, using Evliya Effendi's 17th century account of the guilds of Constantinople, notes that, "Each guild has usually two patrons: (1) the pre-Mahometan traditional inventor of the profession; (2) one of the contemporaries of the Prophet, who was girded by him, or in accordance with his instructions, to be the patron saint of the occupation. Girding of course confers divine grace ..."(1922: 182, note 7).

[13] In 1983 I encountered a group of sievemakers in Eastern Turkey, who were migrating in white tents similar to those of Afghanistan. The technology and terminology for various implements and sieves was identical with those found among Afghan sievemakers. The Turkish sievemakers claimed to be of Kurdish origin and to belong to the Alavi sect.

[14] This is amply illustrated by the materials presented over the years in the *Journal of the Gypsy Lore Society*. Gobineau, writing in 1857 expresses surprise that the Iranian Gypsies by no means appear to originate in India, but from the area between Khorassan and Peshawar. Hence, the explanation that the term *Kauli* should indicate the people who originate from the area around Kabul: "unser Heimathland ist die Gegend von Kabul, man hat uns von dort vertrieben, wir können nicht dahin zurückkehren ..."(1857: 691).

[15] In support of the Iranian origin theory we might also mention the Ghorbats' adherence to the Shi'a faith. My interpreter at the time also pointed out that the Ghorbats' style of singing was in accordance with Iranian musical tradition. The fact that the sievemakers of Eastern Turkey claimed to be of Kurdish origin and adherents to the Alavi faith may also point in the direction of Iranian origin. Barth, too, mentions that the Ghorbati in Iran speaks a certain dialect, but without giving further details.

[16] According to Rao, the background for the escape from Herat was a major war "at the time of the King Timūr-e Kōragān" (Rao 1982: 42).

[17] Rao refers to Kayāni as a lineage on a par with Siāwn and Farāhi, and she states that all Ghorbats in Kandahar are "Kayānis" (1982). I have only heard the expression *Kayāni* as referring to the Ghorbats in general, i.e. Farāhi and Siāwun, as descendants of Kayhan *Pāchā*, i.e. of royal ancestry. For example, a Nasir Khēl of Siāwun states: "Only Nasir Khēls are real *Kayāni*." On a single brief visit to the Ghorbats of Kandahar, I was told a number of *khēl*-names which partly coincide with those Rao has collected among the Kayāni Ghorbat. In Ghazni, however, the Ghorbats stated that the sievemakers in Kandahar are Farāhi, and that those from Herat originate from Kandahar, which tallies with Rao's information. I was also told that two of the *khēls* in Kandahar intermarry with *khēls* of the Siāwun (i.e. Khaleqi Khēl of Kandahar intermarry with Qāsem Khēl of Siāwun and Akhund Khēl intermarry with Mostafa Khēl of Siāwun).

[18] According to an old Nasir Khēl sievemaker, there were 80 sievemaker families in Nasir Khēl (in 1976) 40 in Mostafā Khēl, 60 in Mehrāb Khēl, and 50 in Qāsem Khēl. These figures are far too low in the case of the Qāsem Khēl, which more correctly would be 90-95 families. Presumably, the figures are also too low for the Mostafā Khēl with whom the informant was only in sporadic contact. Rao provides the following figures for the number of families of the different Siāwun *khēls*: Mehrāb Khēl: 79 families, Mostafa Khēl: 95 families, Nasir Khēl: 55 families and Qāsem Khēl: 92 families (1982: 78). The discrepancy between Rao's figures and the old Nasir Khēl's may be caused by disagreement regarding the classification of Mehrāb Khēls and Nasir Khēls. Mehrāb Khēl has relatively recently segmented from Nasir Khēl, and the total figures for the two subgroups are reasonably close (140 versus 134 families).

[19] There is no indication, that the Ghorbat community today as a whole are the followers of a particular *pīr*. Among the Siāwun, however, there are individuals who have "seen the light" and become followers of a *pīr* (Qaderiyya order). Retrospectively, there appear to be many names/titles in Siāwun genealogy indicating some religious association in the past. Apart from "mullah ancestors", there are also living people referred to as *"Sufi"*, *"Faqīr"*, *"Malang"*, *"Ghāzī"*, and *"Ḥajjī*.

[20] See annex in Rao (1982) for further variations.

[21] To stress this point, it should be mentioned that according to Rao (1982: 44-5), the Farāhi houses in Khiaban of Kabul were to be razed to make way for planned road constructions. A similar situation apparently also faced the Ghorbat house owners in Khanabad.

[22] I am grateful to M. Q. J. Bander for the information that Karmisheva mentions that the Mazang migratory Gypsy group in Kazakhstan are sievemakers and knife-smiths. They call the instrument used to make the frames of the sieves *khalaji* (Karmisheva 1963: 597-607). According to a photo, this instrument is identical with the *lurg* of the Afghan Ghorbat, who call the two wooden poles supporting the *lurg alājis*.

[23] According to Rye and Evans' (1976) study of traditional pottery techniques in Pakistan the sieves used to sift the sand are nowhere of the woven type manufactured by the Ghorbats in Afghanistan and used by all potters there. The Pakistani potters used either a simple type of sieve with pierced leather suspended and tied on a wooden frame with leather thong, or they used sieves made of punched sheet metal nailed to a wooden frame. In some areas, it is noted, the potter makes his own sieves.

[24] See also Bahīn (1975(AH(Sh) 1353: 118-23), Rao 1982, and

his own sieves.

[24] See also Bahīn (1975(AH(Sh) 1353: 118-23), Rao 1982, and Wulff's description of the nomadic Koulīs' sieve-manufacture in Iran (1966: 234-6).

[25] For a description of the same process from Iran, see Wulff (1966: 234-6).

[26] Floursieves are in written language called *ghalbīz*, but I have never heard it referred to as anything but *"ghalbel"*.

[27] See also Rao's list of terms and usages (1982: 67-8).

[28] The name describes the way the drum is held: under (*zir*) the armpit (*baghal*) (Sakata 1980: 31).

[29] Wulff informs from Iran that *women* in the nomadic Koulī tribe are sievemakers while the men are tinkers and smiths (1966: 234-6). Similarly, Austin-Lane refers to female sievemakers mentioned by Shirazi in the Fārs-Nāmeh-i Nāsīrī (quoted from Rao 1982: 39).

[30] *Ḥalvā* is a kind of pudding made from rice flour and butter-oil. It is frequently made as a *khayrat*, i.e. offering, charity.

[31] Such business trips are called *ādūr*, the same term as among the Shaykh Mohammadis.

[32] A sievemakers explains: "Suppose we are 12 members of the family, then we estimate how much grain we need for the winter. It will be 1-1.5 *kharwār*. If we have more than that we sell the excess."

[33] This way of expressing past unity by recounting how everybody ate the same dish jointly was also seen in the Musallis' description of a more harmonious and solidary past.

[34] This may be compared with Rao's data (1982: 78), where she provides the number of families in each locality, distinguishing between those who are sedentary, semi-sedentary, semi-nomadic, and nomadic. There are minor differences regarding our information on the *khēl*-affiliation in certain localities.

[35] Before leaving an area, and after having collected their payments, the Ghorbats may visit important shrines. In Istalif, for example, they would visit the shrine of Aishan *Ṣāḥib* (annually, 2-3 feasts take place there), or the shrine of *Bābā* Sanabdal *Walī* in Qala-i Murad Beg. Several families would choose a day to go on pilgrimage together, cook some *ḥalvā*, and spend the day at the shrine, dining there. In the north, particularly the shrine of Sakhi *Ṣāḥib* (*Ḥazrat-i* Ali) in Mazar-i Sharif is important. In Charikar it is the shrine of Fiane *Sharīf*.

[36] See Rao (1982: 83-4) for more details regarding the summer migrations of the Mehrāb and Nasir Khēl in the Ghazni area, of the Kayānis in the north, and a graphic illustration of the annual re-groupings of 11 Mehrāb Khēl families.

[37] Rao (1982: 108) gives an illustrative example of how two sievemaker groups ended up camping in the same locality during their summer migration (in Balkh). They peacefully discussed whether there would be sufficient demand for both groups to stay, and ultimately, the latecomers moved on to another area. However, she also points out that the sievemakers indicated that had the groups belonged to different *khēls*, the solution would not have been reached so cordially.

[38] The special tent construction, which Barth mentions as characteristic of the Iranian Ghorbati is not found among the migrating Afghan Ghorbat (Barth 1964: 91). However, Rao mentions that the Ghorbats in the Faryab province use black tents sewn by the women (1982: 99).

[39] For further details on the structure of Ghorbat camps, see Rao (1982: 111-12)

[40] This description of Jalalabad characterized the pre-1978 situation. In 1992, the city could reportedly offer no shade, as the trees had been cut in connection with the many battles here during the war between the PDPA government and the *mujāhidīn* forces.

[41] The conjurers had just been forbidden to practice their profession by the governor, as one of them had caused traffic problems with his performance on the street. Later on, they also explained that the authorities' negative attitude toward their profession is caused by the fact that when the crowds gather to watch the conjurer's performance, pick-pockets see a chance to practice *their* profession: "So although it is not our fault, the authorities have been forbidding our profession". They were now consulting with each other about what to do and seemed inclined to buy a two-wheeled cart (*karachī*) to work as porters during the winter.

[42] All the Ghorbats who presently live in Kandahar have been settled here apparently for generations. From Kandahar, some families subsequently migrated to Herat (and some to Mazar-i Sharif) after their houses were expropriated and demolished by the government to give space for road constructions. In Herat they bought new houses, but soon afterwards endured the same experience of having them expropriated and demolished. Today, however, the sievemakers in Herat live in houses again, being completely sedentary or semi-sedentary (Rao 1982).

[43] "1 *sarāy's* distance" is, according to my interpreter Mohammad Azim Safi, equal to one day's camel walk.

[44] For further details on the Ghorbat women's medical activities, see Rao (1982: 61-3).

[45] In an article in *Nangarhar Magazine*, Z. Safi writes that traditional soapmaking, according to *Amīr* Abdur Rahman, was introduced into Afghanistan during his reign (1880-1901). It was widespread in the Laghman province until the beginning of the 1960s. The soapmakers of Laghman made soap from poppy oil (*khāsh-khāsh*), mixed with some chemicals. This mixture was boiled and subsequently put in moulds of various sizes and dried. In 1975 in Laghman, soap was made in the traditional way only in the village of Banda-i Nazir close to the *Vilayat* (Safi 1975, *Saratan* AH(Sh) 1354)). The market was otherwise taken over by factory-made products.

[46] In an Afghan context, "Hindu" may well refer to Sikhs, who often trade in textile in Afghanistan, especially in Kabul and Jalalabad.

[47] In this context, it was added that in the decades of Nadir *Shāh* and Zaher *Shāh* (i.e. 1930-73), the Ghorbats used to buy cloth from Jewish cloth traders, and "they were better than the Hindus, they drank tea from the Ghorbats' cups". The Ghorbats were of the opinion that the Jews had been expelled from Afghanistan (rather than having migrated voluntarily).

[48] Rao writes that women do not go peddling at the time of their menstruation and a couple of months after delivery (1982: 61).

[49] See Rao (1982: 70-1) for a description of the cage making.

[50] Loquat, i.e. Eriobotrya japonica.

[51] As far back as 1862 Bellew mentioned quail-fighting as a very popular amusement among the Afghans. He described it as

respective favourites. In the early summer quail visit the cornfields and vineyards in vast numbers; they are usually caught in a large net thrown over the standing corn at one end of the field, and they are driven towards this by the noise produced by a rope being drawn over the corn from the other end, a man on each side of the field holding an end of it. Sometimes they are caught in horsehair nooses fastened to lumps of clay; and these are scattered about the borders of the field where the birds are accustomed to run from one to the other. When a quail has been beaten in fight, and runs from his rival, his owner at once catches him up and screams in his ears; this is supposed to frighten the remembrance of his defeat out of his memory" (1978(1920): 293-4).

[52] A line of nooses made of thin goat hair in front of which is sprinkled some grain.

[53] Some time in the past, all the Siāwun *khēls* owned houses in Kabul. In Nasir Khēl it is said that their ancestor Nasir bought land in Chaman-i Hazori, in the Shahshahid area of Kabul, but it was confiscated by the State during the reign of Nadir *Shāh* (1929-33). As a result of this, the Nasir Khēl became homeless and itinerant, and moved to Ghazni in the summertime. Subsequently, most Nasir Khēls have managed also to buy houses in Ghazni, and some even in their winter area of Jalalabad as well. As far as the Qāsim Khēl is concerned, it is related that they also lost their houses in Kabul, and that one of their ancestors, Bab Ali, had a house in Qarabagh, "but when he died, his son sold it." Bab Ali lived four generations back, and of all his sons and grandchildren, as far as it is known, are sievemakers without any ownership of houses.

[54] The main market, for coarse sieves used to sift grain, has so far not been reduced by any competition. A Sikh shopkeeper in Jalalabad states: "Metal sieves are sold more than skin sieves … . The skin sieves are not totally out as people still buy them for sifting rice and wheat, but now metal sieves with bigger meshes for sifting wheat and rice are being imported from Pakistan and are gradually replacing skin sieves."

[55] Jalalabad, being located close to the border, is apparently ahead of the rest of the country in this respect. Local smith-made metal sieves can hardly be found anywhere else, and the number of metal sieves imported from Pakistan is also rather limited in other localities.

[56] In these instances, where two married couples are sharing one tent, the tent may at night be divided into two parts by placing a barrier or stack of clothes in the middle.

[57] Khan Agha, however, may be a bit of a "womanizer", as he is also reputed to have had an affair with a *Shādibāz* girl. His relatives tease him about this affair by telling the following story of what is claimed to be *Shādibāz*'s marriage customs: "Once there was a king who had asked the *Shādibāz*: 'Why don't you do military service?.' They had told the king: 'Men go to military service – not women.' The king said: 'But you are men – you have moustaches!.' They answered: 'No, we are women. Our men have gone out earning." Then the king thought, 'These so-called men are fed first by God and then by their women. Let them be exempted from military service!' So when these people get married, the bridegroom climbs a tree. Then they call to the bride: 'Oh daughter of *sīyāl*! Can you feed this man of *sīyāl*?.' If she answers 'Yes', everything is all right. If she says 'No', then the man will jump down from the tree ." Khan Agha is teased by his relatives for having climbed a tree only to be rejected by a *Shādibāz* girl.

[58] Even though sievemaking ranks among the lowest of occupations, the sievemakers still consider themselves superior to barbers.

[59] Mehrab presumably had been supporting Nasir in an internal fight ("with the cousins"). This would explain why Nasir not only had to pay the compensation by killing his daughter but also that Mehrab was rewarded with a woman in marriage.

[60] For further details of the background of Wali Mohammad, see Rao (1982).

[61] Gifts, for example of sweets, which the boy's family is supposed to bring his fiancee's family on the occasion of *'Eid*, *Nowruz* (New Year, i.e. 21 March), etc.

[62] Presumably, Wali Mohammad is the previously mentioned boy adopted by Tegh Ali's sister, but this fact was not noted in connection with the story and presumably was irrelevant for the reactions of the community. Instead, my impression is, that Wali Mohammad's wife, who objected so strongly to her own marriage, is the main "troublemaker", by her reluctance to yield to community obligations and pressures in marriage arrangements.

[63] Ivanow mentions that in Nishapur and Sabzawar (Iran) at that time, settled Gypsies had their own quarter in the central part of the bazaar, and were recognized as one of the bazaar's trade-corporations. They had no shops and worked in their houses or simply in the streets. Usually, they had a headman, sometimes a hereditary one (1922: 282-3).

[64] Presumably during 1953-63, in connection with the conflicts and border closures between Afghanistan and Pakistan linked to the Pashtunistan issue.

[65] Salam was *kalāntar* of Nasir Khēl, but at that time presumably only Nasir Khēl (and the associated Mehrāb Khēl) were wintering in Jalalabad.

[66] Such communal punishment has a long tradition in Afghanistan, established during the time where the central power related to its subjects indirectly, on a community basis, rather than as individual citizens.

[67] The three sievemaker households in Bamiyan have, if anything, a more negative experience of living among their co-religionists, the large Shi'a minority of Hazaras, than do sievemakers in Sunni-dominated areas: "Hazaras are not friendly – they always want us to pay in cash. They will not even let us build a house here, but force us to ask permission from the government. ... They refused to allow our children to school as they said we travel so much. The *malik* or *qaryadār* opposed supplying us grain during the drought . We fought him and complained to the *wālīswāl* who decided we should have grain 'as we belong to the same country'."

[68] The Shi'a background of the Ghorbats is reflected in the choice of names predominant in the group: The usage of popular Shi'a names like Ali, Hussein, and Hassan is widespread and certainly far more frequent than in the Afghan population at large. As a supposed strategy for integration in the Sunni majority, Rao (1982: 170-1) mentions that some Shi'ite Ghorbats transform their names from a "Shi'a version" like Ayub Ali to a "Sunni version" like Mohammad Ayub. I have no material to support this claim, but it was surprising to find the name of Mohammad Omar among a Shi'a community, as the names of the first three caliphs generally are shunned, and there even exists a tradition among Shi'as to use these as curses.

and there even exists a tradition among Shi'as to use these as curses.

[69] The supreme position given to the Prophet and his family in Shi'a Islam is indicated in the use of the expression the "Holy Five". The expression is connected to the legend of how they all gathered under the cloak (*abbā*) of the Prophet one day, when they were visited by the archangel Jibrail (Gabriel) who told them that God had chosen them and wanted to remove all their sins so that they might become a cleansed family. Hence, the special importance given in Shi'a Islam to the descendants of the Prophet as infallible and therefore the rightful leaders of the community of believers (Donaldson 1938: 55-6). Jafri (1976: 297) gives the same account within the Shi'a scholarly tradition, stressing the most important part being when the archangel Jibrail came down to announce the "Verse of the Purification" for the "Five of the Mantle".

[70] Generally, Shi'as and Sunnis have separate cemeteries and normally the different ethnic groups and communities use distinct places.

[71] Among the Qāsem Khēl, only three men are able to read the Qor'an, and they will thus act as mullahs in connection with life cycle ceremonies. Two have also turned towards Sufism: "Mulla", Saber *Khāk Ṣāḥib* ("like dust") turned to Sufism after a severe illness four years earlier. He had become *murīd* of *Sayyid Effendi Āghā*, one of the descendants of Ghaus al-Azam *Sāhib-i Baghdadi* (the traditional title of *Shaykh* Abdul Qader Jilani (1077/78-1166), founder of the Qadiriyya Order). The *Āghā* refers to Saber as *malang*. Faqir Mohammad, referred to as *shaykh*, has also turned to Sufism. A woman among the Qāsem Khēl can read the Qor'an, part of which she learned through a revelation (see Appendix).

[72] The Herat sievemakers stated that a group of some 20 sievemaker families lived in Obeh (Herat province), and that they were staying in tents. Apart from that, however, they denied any knowledge of them: "God knows where they have come from."

[73] They did, however, know a number of *Qāzulāgi* words and some local people had heard them speak in a different language among themselves.

CHAPTER VI

CONCLUSIONS

The point of departure for this study of the Musalli threshers, Shaykh Mohammadi pedlars, and Ghorbat sievemakers was ethnic occupational specialization in East Afghanistan, and more particularly its migratory variant. The objective was to determine the position of such groups in relation to the dominant agricultural production system, how this specialization was maintained socio-economically and culturally, and how their position changed with the overall changes in Afghan society. The three communities were selected on the assumption that their different occupations and relations to the settled society could generate conclusions regarding the social integration of itinerant occupational specialists generally. My initial analysis of the field material was cast mainly in economic terms (Olesen 1977, 1982, 1985). Within the framework of the Carlsberg Foundation's Nomad Research Project, however, I came to re-evaluate my material in light of more recent interests and insights. The results of this re-evaluation will be summarized in this chapter related to the general debate on itinerants.

Within the anthropological literature, itinerant groups have been studied under a variety of concepts, such as "wanderers", "non-food-producing nomads", "service nomads", "commercial nomads", and "non-ecological nomads". In contrast to these categories, Rao, following Berland and his predecessors in this field such as Srinavas and Rosander, suggests the term "peripatetics" as a useful analytical category for the study of such basically non-pastoral nomads (Rao 1987). The term "peripateticism" denotes a strategy or mode of subsistence which combines spatial mobility, non-subsistent commerce, and group endogamy (ibid. 1-3). Hence, where "the basic elements of pastoralism are labour, livestock and pastures, those of peripateticism are labour, customers and skills/goods". From this also follows, that "peripatetics per definition are part of a wider economic system" (Gmelch and Gmelch 1987: 134-5).

The Musalli threshers, Shaykh Mohammadi pedlars, and Ghorbat sievemakers conform to this definition of "peripatetics", as they display various forms of adaptation and resource exploitation vis-à-vis the settled, rural society. They are not primary producers but rely entirely on offering their goods and services to a clientele. Their migration pattern is thus primarily adapted to the marketing conditions for their goods and services, which are in turn determined by the agricultural cycle of their basically rural customers. While this market adaptation is supposed to be a general feature of peripateticism, it was also demonstrated that during the slack winter season the localization of the most marginal of the groups, the Ghorbat, was largely determined by the climatic and economic requirements for physical shelter.

The economic strategies of peripatetics have been classified as either generalized or specialized, depending on the degree of utilization of a wide range of strategies vs. a single strategy (Salo 1987). In the present case, it was shown that while the Musallis were basically specialized in grain-cleaning only, the Ghorbat followed a generalized strategy, possessing skills and experiences in different fields. The Shaykh Mohammadis, on the other hand, are specialized in the sense of being pedlars, but their commercial activities reflect a great adaptability to incorporate whatever commodity may generate profit. From these three cases, it appears that the choice of a specialized vs. generalized strategy, with the latter presumably containing the greatest flexibility and adaptability, may depend upon whether the peripatetic group, to use Rao's terms, is attached or contiguous to their customers. The situation of attachment, where the peripatetics live with a given group of customers and work primarily if not exclusively for them, can be observed in the case of the Musalli threshers. In contrast, the Ghorbats and Shaykh Mohammadis are contiguous to their customers, living independently and visiting them at more or less regular intervals. The dependency inherent in the attachment situation of the Musallis severely hampered their flexibility and their adaptability to changing economic conditions as compared to the contiguous situation of the Ghorbats and Shaykh Mohammadis.

The peripatetics' dependent, i.e. non-subsistence, economy generally creates economic and political subordination to the settled society, although considerable variations exist. Attachment results in direct economic dependency, and may become the basis of inferiority in other fields as well, like the Musallis' functioning as village servants. However, we need not conclude that attachment invariably leads to more social inferiority than does a relationship of contiguity. The sievemakers form a case in point, as they unquestionably are the socially lowest-ranking of the three groups investigated. Several other factors may thus influence the social position of peripatetics.

Apart from its economic implications, the question of contiguity vs. attachment apparently has a bearing upon the overall political relations to the settled population. The preceding chapters showed how the Musallis, by force of their scattered settlement and economic attachment to the local landowners, are in a state of complete political dependency on these, having no voice of their own, either individually or as a community. Their dependency renders them politically impotent, since they have to maintain the goodwill of their patrons and are thus largely precluded from engaging in disputes. Similar situations are described by Hayden (1987) and Berland (1977) in relation to peripatetic communities. Where poverty for most Musalli families forces them to live as tenants, *hamsāyas*, the women may even experience sexual exploitation by the landlord without the husbands being able to react in a culturally honourable way. The husband is left with only two choices, either to "lump it" or to leave. A similar situation is described by Berland in his study of the Qalandars of Pakistan, where Qalandar women must often provide sexual favors to village leaders in exchange for fodder and grazing privileges (ibid. 269-70).

It has been argued that in their relations to the settled society peripatetics are by definition dependent, marginal, and in a position of social inferiority, the result of which is rejection and stigmatization (Barth 1987). Still, within this setting, considerable variations are found among different societies, as well as variations from one peripatetic group to another. The situation of the Musalli, Shaykh Mohammadi, and Ghorbat underlines this, as they represent three different forms of political relations to the settled majority society: (1) the individual Musallis' total subjugation, (2) the community-level political clientship of the Shaykh Mohammadis', and (3) the Ghorbats' autonomous, marginalized political organization, which, however, was undergoing gradual dissolution. Other variations may exist among itinerant peoples in the Afghan society. For the individual peripatetic household, community-based political relations work as a buffer against the most extreme forms of persecution and abuse from the majority population. However, it is notable that independent political organization per se, as in the case of Ghorbat, does not automatically entail greater bargaining power vis-à-vis the settled society. On the contrary, the Shaykh Mohammadi community was seen to enjoy a position of comparative strength, partly because they had a stake in the existing local power structure by being political clients of the *khān*, and partly because of their demographic strength, which derived from their concentrated settlement pattern. Another aspect of this situation is, that the social stigmatization in their case is comparatively less than for the two other groups.

Occupational specialization along ethnic lines was an important theme in my original research. However, my re-evaluation of these groups and the case studies presented in Rao (1987), lead me to conclude that peripatetic peoples may be characterized by their ethnic identity rather than by their monopolization or maintenance of certain occupations. In fact, the peripatetics exhibit a high occupational adaptability to changing external circumstances. While occupation may play a role in the mythological ethnic charter, it is ethnicity which is the stabilizing factor in everyday life.

It has also been argued that peripatetics are normally ethnic minorities. In his provisional hypothesis, Barth (1987: ix) labels the peripatetics as "strangers" in relation to the settled majority population. Rao adds, that "each peripatetic community is in its cultural environment a minority ethnic group, and very often it is of different origin from its customers" (Rao 1987: 8). However, my own data on Musallis, Shaykh Mohammadis, and the Ghorbats illustrate that as far as the question of their actual ethnic identity is concerned, Tapper's objections to viewing ethnic groups as constituting objective divisions of a population are fully justified (Tapper 1988). While the distinct (minority) ethnic origin in some cases may be easily defined (Ghorbat and Musalli), it may also be very complex and uncertain (Shaykh Mohammadi). Profession and ethnic affiliation, *qawm*, may in the Afghan context frequently coincide, and in common language be used synonymously, and not only with reference to itinerants. This is further confirmed in the host of legends which all three groups corroborate as explaining both their ethnic origins and their occupational specialities.

The three communities exemplify several of the complex processes at work in the social construction of ethnic identities. The most prominent case is that of the Shaykh Mohammadis, whose membership in a religious fraternity constituted the original recruitment criteria. Over generations, however, the spiritual fraternity developed into a more regular *qawm* based on both patri- and matrilineal descent. The Musallis represent another dimension, as this name is used by others as a generic term for people of a certain profession, irrespective of what they call themselves. As demonstrated, the traditional threshers use the ethnonym Shāhi Khēl. However, to complicate matters further, one section claims to be original Musallis by profession *and* descent, while there is general disagreement about who are "real" Shāhi Khēl. The Ghorbat case appears less "complicated" in the sense that the ethnic boundaries are more well-defined than in the above two cases. The reasons for this is perhaps that the Ghorbat's social and political integration into the settled community is weaker and the number of stigmatizing features associated with the group higher.

The Musallis settled in Helmand also offered an illustration of how the ethnonym Shāhi Khēl can under changed circumstances be turned into a recognized ethnic category with a different content, obtained by successful disassociation of the *qawm* from the profession. The settled sievemakers of Herat, on the other hand follow a different strategy of status mobility. In their case, they have disassociated themselves from the ethnonym Ghorbat and the language of *Qāzulāgi* and changed their itinerant lifestyle, including its socially unacceptable pattern of unsecluded, economically active women. What has remained, however, is the occupation of sievemaking, which in any case is socially degrading in itself. While these sievemakers may succeed in passing as a Tajik community, their degrading occupation may still maintain them in a position as social inferiors.

Casimir (1987) has pointed to the recurrent legendary theme of "guilt and punishment" among peripatetics, suggesting it as a psychological consolation measure and as an adaptive strategy vis-à-vis the settled population. Among the Musalli, Shaykh Mohammadi, and Ghorbat, this theme was certainly present, containing the claim of a respectable, royal or holy origin for the community as well as an explanation of the downfall to their present inferior position. Here, the consolation aspects seemed much more dominant than any possible adaptive function. While the "guilt-and-punishment" theme as such may be part of peripatetics' legends, the structure and content of these legends formed an integral part of the overall legendary heritage of the traditional urban guild system in Muslim West Asia, albeit in a rudimentary and perhaps exclusively oral form. Whether we term the legends as being consoling or "sacralizing" may be a semantic quibble. As Centlivres (1972) observed with reference to urban crafts, it is noteworthy that the socially most inferior occupations claim the most prominent *pīrs*; i.e. the religio-mythical stratification virtually reverses the established social order.

The low social status of groups like the Musalli, Shaykh Mohammadi, and Ghorbat is generally explained by the settled population with reference to their inferior descent, occupation, or lifestyle – or to a combination of these factors. It was previously argued that Shaykh Mohammadi descent, to the extent it is known by outsiders, is not considered inferior; nor are their commercial activities in general. It is the humble economic level on which the Shaykh Mohammadis perform these activities which renders them inferior. What really stigmatizes the Shaykh Mohammadis is their lifestyle, i.e. the fact that they are itinerant, that the women are unveiled and in many cases economically active pedlars, and that the Shaykh Mohammadis are considered noisy and quarrelsome. It could be argued that the latter qualities may also be viewed positively, as the Shaykh Mohammadis are self-assertive and ready to defend their rights and honour, which are otherwise cherished values in the Afghan society.

When it comes to the Musalli, being of Indian origin would for the general Afghan be considered as inferior descent. Threshing work cannot be considered as degrading in itself, as peasants all over the country do it as a matter of course. However, when threshing becomes an *occupation* it turns into inferior work, partly because it is hard and dirty and partly because it is a service which in Laghman has been associated not only with a client position but even with a generalized "servant" function vis-à-vis the settled community. Finally, the lifestyle of the Musallis, despite their seasonal migrations, hardly differs from other poor landless people in Laghman. What is degrading is the poverty, which forces them to live as *hamsāyas* who allow their women to work for the landlord's household, a condition not linked to a peripatetic lifestyle per se.

The Ghorbats, who like the Musallis are of non-Afghan origin, are also considered to be of inferior descent, a view further reinforced by their adherence to the minority Shi'a sect of Islam. Their occupation, on which they hold a virtual monopoly, is clearly looked down upon; work in skin and hides is considered unclean, as were their former medical activities such as cupping, etc. Finally, like in the case of Shaykh Mohammadis their peripatetic lifestyle, including the women's independent economic activities and unveiled appearance, is seen as socially degrading.

A number of itinerant communities are in the Afghan context labelled as *J̌at*. This term does not refer to a distinct ethnic group but is, rather, a derogatory label applied at random to various itinerant, non-pastoral peoples. In fact, the very word *J̌at* is a marker of the social contempt in which the itinerants are held. Rao has argued that the actual unveiled appearance and economic activities of the peripatetic women is central for their popular classification as *J̌at*, while the unveiled women of pastoral nomads do not give rise to a comparable condemnation (Rao 1988). As shown above, however, the term *J̌at* is also used about the Laghman Musallis, although their women observe the same level of purdah and seclusion as settled people in similar economic circumstances. As far as the danger of sexual abuse of the Musalli women mentioned above, other poor, settled people in the same situation of dependency may also have to "eat shame" (Neale 1981, Olesen 1982: 121-2). While Rao is correct that the term *J̌at* has distinct connotations of doubtful female morality, it should also be noted that such insinuations are inextricably linked to general expressions of social contempt rather than being specific ethnic markers of peripateticism. In favour of this argument is the fact that literally any local level conflict in an Afghan settled community invariably involves verbal attacks on the virtue of the opponent's female dependents (e.g. Olesen 1982). Hence, irrespective of actual circumstances, casting doubt on female virtue and hence, male honour, is in the Afghan cultural environment a frequent means of expressing social distance and contempt.

Apart from ethnicity, endogamy was singled out as another important criterion of the definition of peripatetics (Rao 1987). In Barth's formulations, ethnicity and endogamy provide the prerequisites for intergenerational succession, i.e. the continuity of membership that allows comprehensive acculturation into a persisting and adapting culture designed specifically for a peripatetic life (Barth 1987). Rao stresses another aspect, seeing endogamy as an expression of the social marginality of peripatetic groups (1987:

9). This is no doubt the case considering the general attitude of the settled population towards intermarriage with Musalli, Shaykh Mohammadi or the Ghorbat. But their mainly endogamous marriage practices also resemble the general marriage patterns in Afghan society at large. Closer scrutiny of the actual marriage patterns of these groups, however, showed significant deviations from the overall endogamous pattern. An analysis of intermarriage with other communities, the subsequent choice of locality, and the occupation of married couples revealed that these and a number of other mechanisms are at work in the social maintenance of the community and its inferior social position.

Regarding the actual genesis of the three groups studied here, we are left in doubt for several reasons. All of them relate various legends of origin, tying their ancestry and occupation up with mythological heroes or saintly figures. When we seek more precise and recent historical evidence or verifiable genealogical links, the information grows very vague and poor. This is not because these communities withhold the information, but simply because it is irrelevant or counterproductive for them to keep account of elaborate genealogical connections or exact historical events. Most historical accounts are dated as having taken place in the narrator's "father's" or "grandfather's" time, and beyond 1-2 generations events from different centuries are unproblematically mixed. Spatial mobility has no doubt contributed to this situation, as well as the comparable lack of economic assets to be passed on from generation to generation, which would have furthered a precise knowledge of genealogical relations. Being socially marginal and politically unimportant, these groups have hardly ever been mentioned in the comparatively sparse historical records on Afghanistan. Reconstructing the history of these and other itinerant communities is not even comparable to the making of a jigsaw puzzle; most of the pieces are simply missing. This situation, however, is hardly unique to the Afghan scene but seems to be typical of itinerant groups all over the world.

Itinerant communities in general share a number of characteristics in terms of lifestyle, modes of subsistence, social and political relations to the settled society, etc. Attempts have been made to classify and analyze these common traits with Rao and others using a definition of such groups as constituting a category of "peripatetics" (Rao 1987). While these efforts have certainly been fruitful, we still lack the broader analysis encompassing the multitude of features and conditions which the three itinerant/peripatetic communities of my study share with poor, dispossessed sections of the settled population. In the Afghan context at least, an awareness of these aspects seems necessary, as we are dealing with a society where various forms of pastoral nomadism, transhumance, and other forms of mobile forms of subsistence are still widely practiced. In this setting, itinerant groups do not stand out as a particularly alien, deviant, or exotic phenomenon. "Ethnic" occupational specialization is also found among settled communities, and as demonstrated, upon closer scrutiny neither the "ethnic" nor the occupational specialization turn out to be consistent over time. Endogamous marriage practices are also found among stable or pastoral communities and among the poor as well as the rich.

Hence, in order to achieve a full understanding of peripateticism and its implications as a mode of subsistence, as well as to clarify whether it constitutes a fruitful analytical category, it is essential to assess which features are intrinsically linked with this particular lifestyle, and which derive from more general conditions of poverty, dependency, inferiority, cultural hierarchies of social status, etc.; in other words, which features the peripatetics share with other segments of society. The present study has attempted to lay a groundwork for this discussion.

Today, the fate and whereabouts of the Musallis, Shaykh Mohammadis, and Ghorbats remain unknown. Perhaps they joined the ranks of the approximately 5 million Afghan refugees in Pakistan and Iran. Their young men may have been recruited as *mujāhidīn*, to fight for the liberation of Afghanistan and are now participating in the ongoing internecine warfare among the competing *mujāhidīn* factions. Whatever their fate, like millions of other Afghans, the livelihood of the Musallis, Shaykh Mohammadis, and Ghorbats has been irrevocably transformed, if not destroyed. Their itinerant lifestyle, economic adaptability, and group cohesion will undoubtedly prove to be important assets in ensuring their continued survival.

APPENDIX

THE *KESB NĀMA*

The booklet entitled *Kesb Nāma* was recommended to me by the Musalli informant Ainullah living in Qala-i Sardar who said it would enlighten me regarding the actual origin of various occupations. He also told me from which bookstall in Mehtarlam bazaar (the provincial centre of Laghman) we could buy it. The *Kesb Nāma* was written in Pashto and published in Peshawar, Pakistan, but without a printing year or author's name given. My interpreter, Mohammad Azim Safi kindly made an abridged translation into English. The first part he attempted to translate into verse, as in the original, but for the remainder, a prose version is given. Unfortunately, the booklet is no longer in my possession, so a literal translation cannot be presented here, but only the initial abridged version.

However, in their study of potters in Pakistan, Rye and Evans came across a potter in Dir who possessed a copy and meticulously followed all the instructions regarding pottery contained in the booklet, considering it as a holy book. A literal translation of the chapter on potterymaking is included in Rye and Evans (1976). Here the abridged translation of the whole work by M. A. Safi is presented, but to give a proper impression of the structure and content of the *Kesb Nāma*, the first chapter on potterymaking is reproduced from Rye and Evans' literal translation (1976, Appendix 5: 191-3).

In its structure and content, the *Kesb Nāma* is comparable to the *risālat* as presented, for example, by Kassim, Massignon, and Ivanov (1927) from Moghul India or by Gavrilov (1928) from Central Asia, and as mentioned by Centlivres from his 1972-study of the Tashqurghan bazaar. The original religious initiator of a given occupation is introduced along with the *isnād*, the succession of *pīr*s performing it, followed by the ritual aspects of the craft in the form of questions and answers presumably for use in examining an apprentice. As for the *pīr*s mentioned under the pottery section, Rye and Evans have identified most of these as belonging to the Nakhshbandiyya order, having lived and died near Bokhara.

The instructions and general content of the *Kesb Nāma* directly integrate the different crafts into the religious sphere, thus creating a respectability and esprit de corps for the professions. By following the precepts outlined in the *Kesb Nāma*, the occupation becomes religiously worthy, *ḥalāl*, no matter how lowly it may be ranked in the living world. Hence, both Schleifer's observation about the Sufi orders' inherent sacralization of professional life and Centlivres' comments on the *risālat*s constituting a professional code, rendering the craft as *ḥalāl*, can be derived from the *Kesb Nāma* (Schleifer 1983, Centlivres, 1972).

With the courtesy of Smithsonian Institution Press, the translation of the first chapter of Kesb Nāma is presented. (Rye and Evans, 1976, Appendix 5: 191-3)

The craft is beloved of Allah.
PROFESSIONAL BOOK OF POTTERS, CARPENTERS, AND BLACKSMITHS, WASHERMEN AND BARBERS.[1]

COLLECTION OF PROFESSIONAL BOOKS

Ḥāji Faẓl Ahad and Ḥāji Abdur Rahīm and Sons,
Book Sellers
Qissakhwānī Bāzār, Peshawar

Description of the Potters' Profession

I always and every time recite prayers of Allah Who is kind and merciful and understands every work.
He is immortal and will remain forever; everybody except him will die.
He wants for no advice, and conducts his kingdom without assistants.
Even kings with crowns are dependent on him.
Mohammed is his prophet, and he is accepted in His court.
On the day of resurrection he ™Mohammed® will ask forgiveness for his followers.
O believer, have a firm faith in the religion of Mohammed.

Principles of Pottery

O potter, it is necessary for you to know these facts.
From this craft you can earn your livelihood.
O young man, learn the book of your craft quickly.
If you have not the ability to remember or learn, or have not the opportunity to learn, O my dear friend, keep this book in your house.
Look through this book every morning.
O potter, I am telling you that your livelihood will be an honorable one.
If you do not act according to these instructions, then your whole work will be spiritually bad.
Your livelihood will be dishonest. I am telling you these facts.
Question: If somebody asks you the question: From where does the art of pottery come? Then answer him so:
Answer: It has come from Salḥ Abū'l-Hasan,[2] who was the son of Mir Umar,[3] who was a man of fortune in the world. This has been said by Ja'far,[4] who recounts that the experts and teachers in this profession were three hundred and thirteen in number. It has been said in the books that all of them were prophets. After them were seven hundred good-willed teacher-artisans. They were all saints and had adopted this profession.
Question: O potter, if someone asks you the question: who originally laid the foundations of the profession?
Answer: Tell him immediately that in the time of Adam the angel Gabriel brought all the tools, by the order of Allah, to Adam.
Question: If someone asks you this question, and wants the answer without hesitation: Who continued the work after Adam?
Answer: Tell him at once that Noah did this work successfully. After him Abraham did this work intelligently. After him Isaac did this work with great fondness. Then by the order of Allah, this work was done by Moses, the man who talked with Allah. After that this

work came to the prophet Muhammad. After him Ali, [5] the saint of Allah, did this work as a past time. After him Abū'l-Hasan [6] learnt this art and disclosed it to the world. Then this art became well known to all the people in the world.
Question: If someone asks you a question in such a manner: Who was the spiritual leader [of the pottery profession] and who did the research on it?
Answer: Tell him that the first perfect spiritual leader was the angel Gabriel and that the last perfect man in the art was Mir Kulāl, [7] the leader of potters.
Question: If someone asks you how many spiritual leaders and teachers there have been in this profession, then answer like this at once:
Answer: In the answer you should tell them at once, O my wise friend, that the leader of this profession was Abū'l-Hasan, [8] a man of courage who was kind to the poor and generous with his learning.
Question: If someone asks you of this profession, who had the first workshop [9];
Answer: Tell him this fact and make his heart happy. From heaven Adam had brought it first; the stone [10] was brought by him from heaven.

Digging the Clay

When, O potter, you start digging the clay, I tell you O my friend, then you should recite the following verses: "In the name of Allah, the merciful and kind: 'Help from Allah and victory nigh'." [11]

Beating Clay in the House [12]

If you make a heap of clay and prepare it for kneading, then recite aloud the following verse, O my beloved brother: "In the name of Allah who is kind and merciful: 'Labor, O House of David, in thankfulness; for few indeed are those that are thankful among my servants'." [13]

Kneading of Clay

O young man, when you prepare the clay, whether it is sandy or fine, then you should repeat the following verse and your work will benefit: "Blessed is he who has sent down the Salvation [14] upon his servant." [15]

Sitting at the Wheel [16]

When you sit at the wheel then sweep the place with your own hand. Say these words O my good friend: "This is a clay which has been prepared by the leave of Allah."

Placing Your Foot on the Wheel

When you place your foot on the potter's wheel, then you should recite the following verse and you will never get tired; the verse is as follows: "Take counsel with them in the affair; and when thou art resolved put thy trust in Allah." [17]

Placing Clay on the Wheel

When you place the wheelhead on the wheel and place clay in the mold and want to make a pot from it, then recite this verse loudly: "Surely Allah loves those who put trust [in Him]." [18]

Making a Ewer *(Kūzā)*

Listen, O potter friend, so I may let you know the facts. When you want to make a ewer, then you should recite the following words: "There is no strength but in Allah." [19]

Making a Water Storage Jar

When you prefer to make a water storage jar, and place the clay on the wheel, you should recite this verse with love, and your sorrow will disappear: "Truly, Allah is powerful over everything." [20]

Making a Lid

When you want to make a lid from above and below,[21] you should quikly repeat the following verse: "Truly, it is from Solomon; in the name of Allah who is merciful and kind."

Painting the Pottery

O dear potter, when you make the pots ready, and you want to paint them, then you should recite this verse: "We take our color from Allah. Who has a better color than Allah's?" [22]

Smoothing of Pottery with a Stone

When you take a stone in your hand intending to smooth the pottery then ask for help from Allah and recite this verse: "Allah prevails in his purpose but most men know not." [23]

Setting Pots in the Kiln

When you put them in the kiln and heap the fuel on them you should recite these prayers and leave the rest to Allah: "O Allah save them from all calamities and damage and from the rain." [24]

Opening of the Kiln

O potter, before opening the kiln you should perform ablutions, O good mannered one, and after that recite this verse, and the kiln will be blessed: "Come, sweet patience. Allah's succor is there in your misfortune." [25]

Listen, O dedicated ones, it is necessary for potters that each must abide by these conditions. When the kiln has been fired and is ready, you should hear these words; give alms in the name of your spiritual guides. All the former master potters are your guides. Mir Sayyed [26] is their leader, and Mir Ḥusaynī was his son. His second son was Mirzā Shāh, who was beyond value in mystic power. All these three persons were saints and were masters of this profession. Listen to these instructions: When potters give alms, they should name all three in a loud voice. Then the potter who gives these offerings will never be poor and his work will thrive. He will be respected by the people and will be an influence to them. He who does not so practice will be Allah's thief. You should raise your hands and pray for Ni'matullāh.[27]

NOTES

[1] The Potter's Book is a title adopted here for convenience, to distinguish the translated section of the book from the complete work. The pottery section is written in Pashto script; verses from or references to the Qur'an are written in Arabic script.

[2] Probably intended to refer to "Hasan of Basra," a prominent figure in the first century of the Hidjra. Al-Ḥasan al-Basri (A.D. 642-728; 21-110 AH). He exercised a lasting influence on the development of Sūfism by his ascetic piety, and numerous pious sayings are ascribed to him.

[3] Second of the caliphs (khalīfas) after Muhammad.

[4] Ja'far Sādiq, saint in the Nakshbandī succession, the seventh Shi'a Imām.

Chapter 2. The Book of Blacksmiths (abridged translation by M. A. Safi)

In the name of Allah, the Merciful, the Compassionate. Praised be the Lord of the Worlds, and success be to the pious, and peace be upon His Messenger, Mohammad and upon all of his family, and companions .

If someone asked you "Where did the steel and iron come from?" answer him that they appeared from the eyes of Adam – praise and peace be upon him. When he was expelled from Paradise, he was crying a lot. From the tears of his right eye, steel was created and from the tears of his left eye, iron was created.

And if you are asked "Who taught blacksmithery to Adam?". Say it was Jibrail [Gabriel] – peace be upon him. After Adam, Daoud [David] took up the profession. After him, Zikria [Zacharias] took up the profession and from him 40,000 apprentices learned the profession. These apprentices were all Arabs by *kesb*.

If you are asked "Whence comes the bellows of blacksmiths?". Say that it was first made from the skin of sheep which God sent to be slaughtered instead of Ismail – peace be upon him. Now everybody has learned to make bellows from sheepskin.

And then if you are asked "Who made nails, pliers, files, anvils?", tell him that they were all made by Mohammad – the Messenger of Allah. The handle of the hammer was made by Ismail Romi.

And if you are asked: "Who made the sword?", say: "Ruknuddin has made it".

And if somebody asked you "Which verse are you supposed to recite as you enter your shop?", say "Allah is a guardian of the good, and He is the most merciful of the most merciful."

And if you are asked which verse you should recite when you make fire, answer: "And He made fire from green trees so we can make use of it." And when you take the iron out of the shop, and when you put the iron on the anvil, say "[verse from Qor'an]", when holding the pliers, say " [verse from

[5] Khalīfa after the Prophet Muhammad, regarded widely in Sufism as primary heir to Muhammad.
[6] See note 3.
[7] Saint in the Nakshbandi succession. According to Subhan (1960: 190) he died in 1371. Full title *Khwāja Amīr Sayyid Kulāl Sokharī*. Sokhar, near Bukhārā was the place where he was born and buried. He worked as a potter and was for a time the teacher of Muhammad Bahā'al al-Bukhāri, known as Muhammad Nakshband, to whom the origin of the Sūfi order, Nakshbandī, is attributed.
[8] Cf. note 3.
[9] The word *"dukān"* from the Persian means "place of work" and is used to refer to the potter's workshop in general, but it is used also to refer to the potter's wheel. See note 11.
[10] The "stone" referred to is either part or whole of the potter's wheel; cf. note 10.
[11] Qur'an, Surah 61, 13.
[12] In Pakistan clay is brought in from the deposit, dried, and then broken into small lumps by beating the pile with a stick. This method is also used in other parts of the eastern Islamic countries.
[13] Qur'an, Surah 34, 12.
[14] "The Salvation" is the Qur'an.
[15] Qur'an, Surah 25, 1.
[16] Literally "workshop" *(dukān)*. See Plate 14.
[17] Qur'an, Surah 3, 153.
[18] Translated as Qur'an, Surah 153, 3.
[19] Not from Qur'an.
[20] Occurs frequently in Qur'an, as Surah 2, 19.
[21] Apt description; see page 22.
[22] Qur'an, Surah 2, 132. Arberry (1995, I:45) translates as: "the baptism of God: and who is there that baptises fairer than God."
[23] Qur'an, Surah 12, 21.
[24] Not from Qur'an.
[25] Based on Qur'an, Surah 12, 18.
[26] Sayyed Muhammad Gesū Darāz, saint of the Niẓāmī section of the Chishtī order of Sūfis; his full name, with all titles, translates as "Muhammaed Husaiynī of long tresses and kind to his servants." Born in Delhi, later lived in the Deccan. His two sons were Sayyed Husaynī, known as Sayyed Muhammad Akbar Husaynī, and Sayyed Yūsuf, know as Sayyed Muhammad Asghar.
[27] Dr. D. N. MacKenzie (pres. comm.) has suggested that the author was Mullā Niematullāh, of Nowshera, a popular poet of the 1880s period, who versified many romances based on Persian originals.

Qor'an] " when you start hammering, say "[verse from Qor'an]", when tempering the steel, say "[verse from Qor'an]", when you make firearms, say "[verse from Qor'an]", making knives, say "[verse from Qor'an]".

Keep in mind that these blacksmiths who have not learned their *kesb nama*, whatever they earn from their profession shall be *ḥarām* , the clothes they wear shall be unclean, and on Resurrection Day, when 1800 *qawms* will be standing, they shall feel shame and disgrace. But all those blacksmiths, who have learned this *kesb nāma*, who always say their prayers, and who while working say the above verses punctiliously, shall make huge profits from their profession, whatever they eat or wear shall be *ḥalāl*, shall be safe from the Satan of evil and corruption. But if a blacksmith does not have the opportunity to learn his *kesb nāma*, he must still keep it in the house so that the mere presence of the verses in his house will be of help to him, and he shall make huge profits, too. Furthermore, he shall under no circumstances cast any shadow of doubt as to the truth of whatever has been mentioned in the *kesb nāma*, because all of it in every detail has been compiled with great toil from many books of indubitable credibility. The blacksmiths should take advantage of it.

Chapter 3: The Book of Carpenters

First of all, I praise Allah, then His messenger who is the greatest of all prophets. After praising, listen carefully to what I will tell you:

From the time of Adam until the time of our own prophet Mohammad, there have been 1,070 carpenters. Some of them were lamp-owning saints, others were prophets in their own right. One of the saints was Abdul Jalil Mashriqi. The second was Abdul Rahim, the third was Abdul Karim, the fourth was Abdul Aziz Amin. The fifth was Najbuddin, sixth was Nuruddin of Samarqand, seventh Abdul Nabi Fazel, eighth Habib Tarmozi, ninth Niamat Kandahari, tenth Habibullah Kashefi, eleventh Shaykh Latifullah, twelfth Abdullah, thirteenth Hyder Mohammad Sikandar, fourteenth Abu Jafar from Turkestan, fifteenth Shamsuddin, sixteenth Shamsuddin Yousufi, seventeenth Wahid Baghdadi, eighteenth Ali Khorasani.

The masters of the profession are alltogether 3,003. The first was Adam, second was Nuh [Noah]. And if you are asked "Who made the different tools used by carpenters?", you shall say that God ordered Jibrail [Gabriel] to bring them down from Heaven. As the latter was also carrying verses along, it is therefore necessary to recite verses during all the stages of the work process. And if you do not want to learn the verses which a carpenter should recite while working, then do not practice the profession either, because otherwise on Resurrection Day your face shall be black and you shall feel shame; the angels might say: "Oh God, who is this black-faced man? Tell us!" And God will say: "He was a carpenter who practised his profession without learning the verses assigned for carpentry."

Not only on Resurrection Day shall he be punished, but even on earth he will be crippled. So when you take the saw, recite the following verse: "In the name of Allah, the Merciful, the Compassionate. Indeed He has knowledge of whatever is hidden and whatever is publicly known." [in Arabic] And when you take the chip-axe, say "[verse from Qor'an]", and when you take the plane, say "[verse from Qor'an]", and when you take the drill, say "[verse from Qor'an]", and the drill says "[verse from Qor'an]", and the plane says "[verse from Qor'an]", and the chip-axe says "[verse from Qor'an]".

Chapter 4: The Book of Barbers

[After praising God and his Messenger]. When God expelled Adam from Paradise, he had hidden purposes in this. Adam was brought down to the land of Sarandab [the island of present-day Sri Lanka]. He and Bibi Hawa [Eve] were wandering aimlessly and crying for having been brought down from Paradise. Finally God accepted their repentence and entreaty and ordered angels to bring them both to Mecca – which they did. As Adam saw the Lord, he went unconscious. After he awoke, Jibrail got them properly married.

Then Allah ordered Jibrail to shave the head of Adam. God told him how to do it: "Go to Paradise and bring a rock which is called *miqnātīs* [magnet] and melt it into steel and from that steel make a blade and make it as sharp as the leaves of Tuba [a tree in Paradise] – and from the wood of Tuba make a handle for it and then bring some water from Kausar [a river in Paradise] – and then shave his [Adam's] head."

Then God ordered Jibrail to provide Adam with scissors, a cupping-glass [a blood-drawing glass] and also a stone on which to sharpen the blade.

From Adam, Shish Ali Salam got the barber's instruments. And from Shish, they came down to Nuh. And from Nuh, the instruments came down to Ismail, and from him to Youssuf [Joseph] , and from him to Zikria, and from him to Daoud, and then to Suleiman [Solomon] , and from him to Musa [Moses], and from him to Issa [Jesus] , and then to Mohammad and from him to Ali, and then to Suleiman Farsi.

Suleiman Farsi says that the barber should recite verses during the various stages in his practice. The various stages and the particular verses to be cited are as follows: When sharpening the blade on a stone, say "[verse from Qor'an]". When putting water on the hair of the client, say "[verse from Qor'an]". When you are shaving the right side of the head of the client, say "[verse from Qor'an]", for the left side, say "[verse from Qor'an]". For the middle section, say "[verse from Qor'an]", and when the head is shaved, say "[verse from Qor'an]", and when you hold the scissors in your hand, say "[verse from Qor'an]", and when you are trimming the moustaches of your client, say "[verse from Qor'an]", and when you are holding the comb, say "[verse from Qor'an]", the finger-nail clippers, say "[verse from Qor'an]", and when you are holding the mirror for your customer, say "[verse from Qor'an]".

Jibrail was told by God that the Prophet wants to shave His head, and that he should go and oblige Him. God told him, "Go and shave His head and then give Him a special hat made from the leaves of Tuba." So, on the 21st of the month of *Ramaḍan*, which was a Thursday, and while the four senior apostles were present, Jibrail shaved the head of the Prophet, and the *ḥūri*s [fairies] of Paradise carried away the hair of the Blessed One. Then the Prophet asked Jibrail, the angel closest to God in His court, exactly how many hairs he had. The latter answered: "They were exactly 1,200,000 and 13,000 and 30." Then God told the *ḥūri*s of Paradise that "if anyone was to put any one of the Prophet's hair in a *ta'wīḍ* [amulet] , he shall be His friend."

So if you consider yourself one of the faithful and are practising the barber's profession, make sure to recite the above verses and learn the *kesb nāma*. That way your death and agony will pass easier. And you should not consider it disgraceful to practice phlebotomy – that is what the Prophet has said. Jibrail has practised it and also many prophets.

Chapter 5: The Book of Laundrymen and Dyers.

Praised be the Lord and His Messenger. It is mentioned in the *ḥadīth* [traditions of the Prophet] that there was a prophet whose name was Issa [Jesus] who was born without a father, and is now up in the fourth heaven, worshipping God. He was a dyer. And, as one day he was unhappy, tired, and fed up with his profession, when Jibrail came upon him and taught him how to practice his profession correctly, so he felt happy.

He told him: "When you start to prepare the dye in a container, say "[verse from Qor'an]". On Friday night, recite the following verses twenty times "[verse from Qor'an]" [and when you do so and so, recite such and such verses etc.,etc.,]. So when you are washing or dyeing, first make your ablution and then say two *rakāts* [units of prayer consisting of three postures] and then send greetings to Issa, and the first and the last masters and pray for their souls and then for the King of Islam and recite the following verses " [verses from Qor'an]". And those laundrymen and dyers who have not learned the above verses, whatever he eats shall be *ḥarām* and things will be perverse for him, and his future will be doubtful, and Issa will not be pleased with him. It is therefore necessary for all dyers and laundrymen to learn or at least keep this *kesb nāma*. God will save him from all danger.

MUSALLI MYTH
told by the old woman Nurani, Qawal Khel, 9.1.1975

"Our *pīr* is Shams-i Hussaini – there is another called Shams-i Tabrizi, who is the son, but this one is Shams-i Hussaini: He was a *pīr*, and there was a king whose son was dead. He had asked all the mullahs to come and revive his son. He had threatened to massacre everyone in town unless the son was revived. Of course the mullahs could not succeed.

"But [at the same time] Shams-i Hussaini was sitting somewhere praying when a peasant was trying to force an ass to move. But the ass would not move as her foal was dead. Shams said to himself: 'Oh God, offspring is so sweet.' He went and did something, and when the peasant returned he saw the foal move its tail and get up and follow its mother. The peasant was astonished, and all he could see around was a man, that *faqīr* [religious mendicant, i.e. Shams-i Hussaini]. The peasant went to the mullahs [and told them] and they came to fetch [*the faqīr*] as everybody in the area was anxious because the king had threatened to kill everybody if his son was not revived.

"They begged Shams to go to the king's palace. He went there and put some spit on the lips of the dead prince and shouted: 'Raise in the name of God', but nothing happened. He said that two times more, but still nothing happened. But the fourth time, he said: 'Rise up in the name of Shams-i Hussaini.' So by the mercy of God, the prince stretched out and rose. People rejoiced as the prince came back to life, and their own lives were saved.

"But the mullahs got angry as he said: 'Rise up in my name' and not in the name of God. They wanted to punish him. Shams asked them what they wanted to do with him. They said that they would skin him as he had committed blasphemy. Shams said: 'All right – here it is.' He held his hair and with one pull removed all his skin from his body.

"Then he went to the desert. His flesh started to rot, as he had no skin to protect it, and worms grew on it. He got hungry and came down to the city of Hindustan. He went to a butcher for some meat, and then went to a kebab-cooker to make him cook his meat. The *kibābi* told him: 'Go away, you stink and while you are standing here nobody will come and eat here.' Shams said: 'Oh God, I am hungry and nobody will cook meat for me.' He looked at the sun and said: 'Oh sun, come down and cook my meat with your heat.' So the sun came down in spear-distance, and they say that in summertime in India the sun gets closer, about 1 spear-distance [from the earth]. So in this way Shams got his meat cooked, but the rest of the population were all seriously bothered by the heat. You see, all people in Hindustan are dark like me. So people went to *Pīrān-i Pīr Sāhib* [*pīr of the pīrs*] . He said instantly, 'it must be Shams who has done this'. He went to Shams and asked: 'Why have you done this to all the people?' Shams told him: 'Why are you demanding that anybody who mentions your name without having taken his ablution first, shall be put to death?' The latter told him: 'All right, I will not demand that anymore – but in return you tell the sun to go back where it was, for people are dying of heat.' So they agreed. The sun went back, but each year at that time it comes down and then later goes back.

"Shams didn't finish all the meat, but gave it to a passing king on a hunting expedition. He accepted the meat as a present from a poor man, but did not eat it. Later he lost it from his handkerchief, into which he had put it. At home a slave-girl washed his clothes and also the handkerchief. The grease would not come off. She was surprised and tasted some of the fat. Thereby she became a holy woman. The next day, when the king asked for his hot bathwater, she told him to take it easy, as the cocks of heaven have not yet crowed . The king became surprised over her behaviour [i.e., it was very early] – but they found out that she had become holy. The king regretted his earlier behaviour towards her and married her as his queen."

On his visit to Multan, Pakistan, Masson encountered the same myth related to Shams-i Tabrizi, whose shrine is found there. He relates it in the following version (1974(1842), I: 396):

"North of the town [of Multan] is the magnificient and well-preserved shrine of Shams Tábrézí, of whose memory the inhabitants are now proud, though, if tradition be correct, their ancestors flayed him when he was living. To this martyr's malediction is imputed the excessive heat of Múltān, the sun, in consequence thereof, being supposed to be nearer the city than to any other spot in the world. Shams, in his agony, is said to have called upon the bright luminary to avenge him, claiming a relationship, permitted by his name, which in Arabic signifies sun. The powerful orb obligingly descended from his sphere, and approached the ill-fated city."

Ikbal Ali Shah also relates a similar story about the famous Sufi Baba Fareed (Shah 1982: 138):

"There is a *mażar*, or grave, it is said, of Shaikh Fareed or Baba Fareed in the district of Safaid Koh. He was a renowned Sufi. During his younger days as a poor man he roamed about the streets of Kandahar begging bread. None gave him any, and people were all busy with their games and sports. Fareed wanted no alms, for he could at any time produce great quantities of foodstuffs if he desired, but he had heard that people round about were not very charitable and he came to ascertain the truth for himself. As no one took any notice of the poor Faqeer Fareed jumped into the river and caught a fish and held it up to the sun. The sun descended from his height and roasted his fish. The people were all scorched to death. The water boiled in their vessels and the earth became red hot. Fareed left town and henceforth the heat of the sun is great over those parts during summer. That explains the heat-waves of Kandahar."

SHAYKH MOHAMMADI MYTH

Story about *Shaykh Ruhānī Bābā*, told by Abdullah Jan (a Shaykh Mohammadi), Saray Khwaja, 24.09.1975:

"There was a king who was childless for a long time, but finally a son was born to him. When the son became 7 years of age, the king thought of getting him married. The king consulted his wife and they decided to marry him off: 'We might die and it is better to see his marriage now.' The king went and told the son. He answered: 'No. I am not going to get married.'

"On another day, while he was playing with his pigeons on top of the roof, he saw the daughter of a mat-seller. So he lost his heart. She was very pretty, and he fell in love. Three or four more years passed, and his parents did not know about it. They were all the time telling him to marry, but he refused: 'I don't need a wife.' As time passed, he was getting more and more yellow [i.e. pale], like an orange, but he didn't say that he wanted to marry. Every night until morning he was thinking of that girl. Finally, his parents insisted that he should get married, and to whomever he would like, regardless of the country.

"Then he told his father: 'If you insist, I would like to marry the daughter of that mat-seller. I will not marry anyone else.' Then his father said: 'Well, we could get a princess married to you, and they are not few, but you want to marry a mat-seller's daughter.' The son said that he would not marry anyone else. The parents agreed to it: 'It is difficult. It is in our own kingdom, and even if we have to use force or get their consent, we will bring you that girl.' The *wazīr* [Minister], the *wakīl* [representative of the groom] together with the mullah and the *Ṣāḥib Sardār* [leader of the aristocracy] all went to the mat-seller's house and the king told them to offer him everything he asked for, if he would agree to give his daughter to the prince.

"They told the mat-seller that the king wanted his daughter for the prince and asked whether he would consent? The mat-seller said that he did not have a daughter. They said, 'Yes, you do,' but he denied. So they returned to the king and told him that the mat-seller denied having a daughter. The king told them to say to the mat-seller that 'whether he had a daughter or not, the king wanted a girl from him for his son!'. The mat-seller said: 'Give me three days and after that, if I have a girl, I will tell you, and if not, I will tell you.' After that the mat-seller went to his daughter and told her, that the king wanted her married to his son, or otherwise they had threatened to fry him in a pan. Then the daughter said: 'If your life is in danger, I will get married, but on one condition: they shall take either my nights or my days.'

"After three days, while he was working on his mats, the *wazīr* and the *wakīl* came and asked what had happened. The mat-seller told them what his daughter had said. They went back to the king and told him so. The prince agreed to have the mat-seller's daughter during the daytime, as he would be sleepy by night anyway. So he married.

"From morning to evening she would be with the prince, but in the night they would sleep separately. After a month, the prince suddenly changed from bad to worse; unlike other people who become fresh after marriage, he became pale. Then the king asked his son: 'What is going on?' The son complained: 'She is with me only in the daytime.' The father and the son were discussing it when a *malang* shouted from behind the door and asked for charity. This *malang* [religious mendicant] was *Shaykh Ruhānī Ṣāḥib*. The king ordered his servants to give the *malang* everything they had in the kitchen, rice, etc. As they took the different kinds of food to the *malang*, he said: 'I don't want it.' The king said: 'All right. Give him grain in any quantity he wants.' The *malang* said: 'I don't want that either.' The prince then said: 'Give him some gold then – about five *ghūrī* [plates] of gold.' But the *malang* said: 'No, I will not take that either.' The prince then said: 'What do you want? Do you want my kingdom? Then take it!' The *malang* said: 'No. I don't want your kingdom either.' The prince asked: 'What do you want, then?' The *malang* answered: 'I want the secret of your heart. Just tell me what is in your heart. I am a *malang* and I will leave.' Then the prince told him: 'I was married a month ago, but my wife and I are sleeping separately. In daytime she is beside me, but at night away from me.' The *malang* told him: 'All right, that is your problem. You can have my hat. If you put it on, you will see her, but she will not see you.'

"The prince didn't believe the *malang*, so just to test whether what he had been told was true, he put on the hat in the evening, and went to the dining room where his wife was having dinner. She was having rice, and he joined her while wearing the hat. The rice was finished in a very short time, and then his wife asked for more rice, and as he was also eating with her, it was finished sooner than she expected. She was still not full and asked for a new portion. Then she found it strange and was embarrassed to ask for more after four plates of rice. She called a slave girl and asked, 'What is wrong with the rice tonight, not to be full after so much?' So she told her not to bring any more, and the prince believed in the power of the hat."

During the night, the prince discovers that a *Ḥabashī* (lit. Ethiopian, used synonymously for wild, barbarian) appears and carries away his wife on a litter. The prince wears his hat, so that nobody can see him, and he joins his wife:

"The Ethiopian took another girl from another place and they all became four girls with him. All four of them went into the jungle. The four sat down on a litter and the prince was with them with his hat on. When they got down from the litter in the jungle, first the wife of the prince started dancing. After she got tired, the Ethiopian asked her what her wish was. She said that God had given her everything, and that she wanted nothing. So the Ethiopian threw her narcisses, and after her, one of the other girls danced and he gave her some grapes. She ate just one grape, not all. The prince had snatched away the flowers and the grapes and threw them into his bag. And the third girl danced and the Ethiopian asked what she wanted. 'God has given me everything. I don't want anything', she answered. The Ethiopian threw her an apple, which the prince put into his bag. At the end, the Ethiopian rebuked the girls for having come late and threatened to turn them into stone if they ever came late again. The girls all promised not to be late. The Ethiopian finally got them all seated on the litter and carried them to their homes. Just as the flying litter reached the territory of the prince, he jumped off and went home to bed. As his wife followed him, she found him in bed and thought that he must have been there for hours. After his wife fell asleep, he got up and told the slave girl to wake him up earlier than usual the next morning, at which he would get angry and would tell her that his sweet dreams were interrupted because of her stupidity. 'You shouldn't get annoyed,' he told her.

"The next day the slave girl woke him up earlier than usual. He started shouting at her and told his parents how badly she had interrupted his fantastic dreams. His parents tried to calm him down, telling him that it was only a dream, and dreams are never true. The prince, however, insisted that it was not an ordinary dream. After telling his parents about the dream, he showed the narcissus, the grapes, and the apple, while his wife was standing in the other room. As he went there, his wife asked him to tell the truth about how he managed to know about her last night's experiences. He told her about the hat and everything else. His wife told him that she was under the spell of that Ethiopian magician. She also asked him to go with her again, so he could ask the magician to set her free.

"So the next night he accompanied his wife to that garden with the magician. As his wife finished dancing, the Ethiopian asked her what she would wish for. 'A husband', she told him. Upon hearing this, the Ethiopian got angry and turned her instantly into a statue. As the other girls had the same wish, they were also turned into statues. This was all too much for the prince. He got up, threw his hat away and started fighting the magician. For seven days and seven nights, they fought without anyone of them seeming to get the better of the other. On the seventh day, the prince got scared and shouted, 'Oh Allah! Oh saint! *Shaykh Ruhānī Bābā*!' Upon shouting those words, the *Shaykh* appeared, his stick in hand, wearing green clothes and with his *kachkūl* hanging from his shoulder. The *Shaykh* grabbed the hands of the magician, freeing the prince from his grips, and then turning the magician around, his head like a fan and crashing him against the ground. He put his knife against the magician's throat and demanded he turn the girls back into flesh and bones. After the magician had done that, the *Shaykh* killed him with his knife.

"After the slaying of the magician, the whole garden turned into bare mountains. The prince with his wife no longer had the flying litter at their disposal, and they wondered in how many years they would reach their kingdom, travelling by foot. But there was the *Shaykh* again. He asked them to put their feet on his stick and asked each of the girls where they intended to go. All of them said, that they wanted to go to the kingdom of the prince and that the prince be their husband. The *Shaykh* got the three girls married to the prince, asked them to shut their eyes and carried them to the town of the prince.

"As the father found out that his son arrived with four wives instead of one, he ordered a magnificient celebration: giving ripe to the Muslim, raw to the Hindu, the burned to the Hazara, *qurūt* to the *Shaykh Mohammadis*, who love rice with *qurūt*, for seven days and seven nights. May God forgive them there and us here."

GHORBAT MYTHS AND LEGENDS

Of the three communities, the Ghorbats are most eager to relate stories, fairytales, and religious myths, which are elaborations of the West Asian religious folktale tradition. Here follow some examples.

Fairytale told by Neko, a Farahī intermarried with a Qāsem Khēl, Jalalabad, 29.11.1975:

"A king wanted to marry the daughter of a trader. She was rather learned and told him, that she would marry him on one condition: that he learned a *kesb* [profession]. The king agreed, and he learned to make mats. One day he went disguised around in the town to check how things were going. That day he went around as a porter and should bring some mutton to a butcher. This butcher, it appeared, used to supply his mutton by slaughtering a man in order to save money. The butcher therefore caught the king and locked him up, as he wanted to slaughter him. The king asked him how much the butcher would earn by slaughtering him. When he was told, he said 'You can earn much more if you let me make a mat for you to sell for a lot of money to the *wazīr* [minister].' The butcher agreed and said, 'Let us try. If I can get more money that way, I will let you make mats for me.'

"The king made the mat but with the weaving he wrote a message in the mat for the *wazīr*, about how his situation was and that he [*the wazīr*] should come and arrest the butcher and release him. The *wazīr* bought the mat but did not read the message. When the king realized this, he had to try once again. He again made a mat on which he wove a message, but this time he told the butcher to go and sell it to the queen. The butcher did so and as the queen was a learned person, she read the message and immediately had the king released. The butcher and the *wazīr* – because of his negligence – were executed. So it is good to have a *kesb* because otherwise the king would have been slaughtered. "

The following legend concerns the origin of all knowledge. It was told by Gul Hassan, a Mehrāb Khēl from Jalalabad, Nov. 1975. The story combines the advent of modern technology, the old folk belief of the Earth resting on the horns of a cow, and with the Islamic notion of all wisdom and knowledge gathered in one comprehensive scripture in Heaven (from which parts have been revealed to humanity at successive times. Hence, *ahl-i kitāb* (People of the Book), comprising people of the revealed religions – Jews, Christians, and Muslims, the latter having received the last and most comprehensive revelation in the form of the Qor'an).

"In the time of Kayhān *Pācha* [presumably of the pre-Islamic, Sassanian dynasty of Iran] the rivers were all moving to a place in Hindustan and were finally facing a very high mountain, which made the water form a dam ten times bigger than the Sorobi [hydroelectric dam in East Afghanistan]. The king wanted to find out where all the water of the world was going. He offered a prize to anyone who would fathom the depths of the dam and discover its secret. There was someone either from Germany or somewhere else who offered to undertake that daring venture. He built a motor [boat] whose doors were made of diamonds and of very hard metal. So the king was pleased to hear that and told him: 'If you succeed, you will get the prize', which was the king's daughter in marriage. The young man embarked upon his venture, got on board the motor [boat] and reached the dam after some months. Then he went further until the middle of the dam where he discovered a whirlpool, and there he saw that all the water which was pouring into the dam was here moving into the underworld, as it was a deep wide hole, into which water was running. He brought the motor [boat] into the middle of the hole. With the downward flow of the water and also with the motor [boat] he reached the bottom of the world after two years. There he saw a big cow as big as the world, which was holding the Earth. And he saw a sheet of paper as big as the world lying down there. He folded that paper and brought as much of it as he could in his motor back to the surface of the Earth and went to the king and showed him the paper. The king was pleased and told him: 'This was what I was looking for.' From that sheet of paper all knowledge originated. Earlier roads were as narrow as these two lines on that kelim, so that donkeys could walk on them. Now look at the airplanes, radios, and so forth! How did it all come about? It was because of that paper."

The explicitly religious legends, however, occupy the most prominent position in the Ghorbat tales. Mohammad Ayub from the Mostafa Khēl relates how the later caliph Omar was converted to Islam (Kabul, June 1976):

"*Ḥazrat-i* Omar was initially an infidel and was ruler of Medina. In Medina nobody could call the prayer sermons because they were afraid of Omar and thought that if he heard the voice of the muezzin, he would be strong enough to destroy all Medina. Later on, Omar himself was converted to Islam:

"Omar had a sister who had a dream in which she saw *Ḥazrat-i* Fatima [daughter of the Prophet. While sleeping, she became a Muslim and she recited the *kalima* [Islamic confession of faith]. When she woke up, she could read the Qor'an. When Omar returned from hunting, he heard some voice coming from his house, and he tried to find out what was going on. He coughed, and his sister knew of his arrival. She thought that if he saw the Qor'an in her hand, he would kill her. She was sitting near the bread oven [*tandūr*] and threw the Qor'an into it.

"When Omar questioned her, she denied everything, but he suspected and insisted that if she did not tell him he would kill her. Finally she confessed saying: 'I saw the Prophet and his daughter in the dream. He taught me the reading of the Qor'an. So with His miracle I was able to read the Qor'an, so I am thereby a Muslim and I have also read the *kalima*. In your absence I was reading the Qor'an and when I heard you coughing I threw the Qor'an into the [hot] oven.' Omar said: 'All right, we are going to see if Islam is the true religion. If the Qor'an is burned I shall tear you to pieces, but if not, then Islam is the true religion, and I will become a Muslim myself.' His sister removed the cover from the oven, terrified that the Qor'an would be burned and that Omar would destroy all Medina. But Omar saw that there was no fire in the oven but instead, flowers around the Qor'an, and not a single page was damaged.

"Then Omar realized that it was the will of God that he should become a Muslim. So he took his wife and went to the mosque in Medina, where Mohammad was staying. People in the mosque were terrified as he approached and they informed Mohammad that 'Omar is coming towards us but without any fighting or quarrel.' So Mohammad, who was *'ilm-i kul* [omniscient] understood that God had willed Omar to become a Muslim. He invited him inside the mosque. When Omar got inside the mosque he just crawled to the feet of the Prophet. Mohammad raised Omar's head and he kissed him on the forehead, and then Omar told him the whole story and Mohammad said:'It is true – I did appear in your sister's dream'."

Story about the Prophet told by a young Mehrab Khēl (smoking hashish), Jalalabad, 17.11.1975:

"One day the Prophet was going somewhere and on his way in the desert he came across ten people who started running away as soon as they saw Him. The Prophet said: 'Oh God, what kind of people are they? They are human beings and still they run away from me. How am I going to catch them?'

"He continued walking until he met a snake. The snake told the Prophet: 'As soon as I open my eyes to look at You, one of my eyeballs is going to drop to the ground. Dig it in the ground and put some water on it. It will become a bush, and when it bears fruit, make a chillum, put the fruit on fire and then leave it there.'

"The Prophet did that and went away. The ten men were close by. They came closer to the chillum and saw smoke coming out of it. One of them started to inhale it and laughed, and told the others to do it, too. All ten smoked the chillum. So all of them became intoxicated with *chars* [hashish] and lay down somewhere.

"When the Prophet came back, he saw them all lying down. He tied them up and brought them along to Medina. For each man, he built a house and got him married. These ten people were the descendants of Adam, and all *qawms* which exist today are therefore the descendants of these ten men."

Mohammad Ayub, a Mostafa Khēl, relates the following about the expulsion of Adam and Hawa [Eve] from Paradise, Kabul, June 1975:

"Adam was allowed to taste everything in Heaven except wheat. Each grain was as big as a melon [*kharbuza*]. The Devil tried to convince Adam and Eve that wheat was the best thing in Heaven, and for this reason they were forbidden to eat it. Eve, who was created from the left arm of Adam and for that reason with an impaired mind [*nāqis-ul-'aql*], decided to taste the wheat and gave some to Adam, and they were thrown out of Paradise. Until they tasted it, their skin was made of nails [i.e.the clothes of Heaven, *libās-i bihist*]". When they tasted the fruit, this stuff disappeared and what remained was just the finger nails. This is why people throw cut fingernails in water or in a corner or in a hole in the ground so nobody will step on them. It is the clothes of Heaven, and it would be a sin to step on them. They are created by God and are a sign of God and Heaven. The person who throws fingernails anywhere will have to be responsible on Doomsday. From a whole fingernail a person can make magic."

Donaldson (1938), in his study of "Mohammadan Magic and Folklore in Iran", relates a common belief that Adam before his fall possessed a body which was covered with a shell that was made of a nail-like material. After his disobedience this shell was transformed into soft flesh, all except at the ends of his fingers and toes. And it is commonly believed that the nail parings do not decay, and that in a distant future they will again be put to use. Hence, great care is taken to bury or hide them so that no enemy or sorcerer can get them (Donaldson 1938: Ch. XXIII).

*J̌in*s and other supernatural beings are part of people's lives and personal experiences, not only among the Ghorbats or other itinerant peoples but also in settled rural communities in Afghanistan. The following explanations are given by Mohammad Ayub, a Mostafa Khēl, May-June 1975:

"*J̌in*s are that *ṭāyifa* [tribe, Arabic] or those beings who are very dwarf-like. They have long beards, big heads. Some are very dark, some are light golden brown [wheatish, *gandumi*] , and they can disappear totally. When they appear, you touch them, beat them, kill them. They will not harm you, unless you harm them. The only exception is the newborn child, because the baby is as small as them, they would sit on it and [thereby] kill it. They love babies so much. Their young one would be as small as a newborn, the oldest as big as a 7-year old.

"The *J̌in*s have feast and fairs. They live in jungles, especially where there is water, in beautiful places. I have seen a lot near the town of Istalif. They don't want to live close to human beings. During their feasts they are invisible, and when somebody walks, he may inadvertently step on one of their children who are the size of a pack of cigarettes. Then they will harm human beings [in revenge] .

"They disappear by uttering some words and then disappearing. When they seek revenge, they would come upon the person, sit on his shoulders, strangling, biting, throwing him into the river. The person would lose consciousness, and a mullah would be called. The mullah knows the incantations [*qāṣida*], those words used for exorcising the *J̌in*s and *āǰina*. It is a special summon of the *J̌ins* [*qāṣida khasirad*] When the *J̌in*s are summoned, the mullah asks why they are bothering this man. The *J̌in* would tell the mullah, for example, that this man has killed the relative of the *J̌in*. The mullah, after having mastered the *qāṣida*, has control over the *J̌in*s. Then, like a judge, he would prosecute this *J̌in*. The mullah would tell the *J̌in*: 'I have control over you and I can burn you any time [then the *J̌in* would die] .' While the mullah can burn the *J̌in*, there would appear another one, bothering the man before the mullah would be able to help. The *J̌in* cannot harm the mullah. The mullah would tell them that they are to be blamed: 'You are not supposed to be close to human beings and besides, this man has not intentionally stepped on your child, as he could not see it. My verdict is that you shall leave this man, or else I will kill you.' Then the *J̌in* would cry and say: 'Please, don't burn me. Have mercy. This man has injured us.' Finally, the mullah will force them to leave. The language of *J̌in*s is like the language of birds.

"Some people who go insane do it because of the *ǰins*. If the *ǰins* are really hostile to someone, then they might leave him for years before they kill him. Because if the man has killed a *ǰin* they want to torture him. When the mullah force the *ǰin* to leave that man, the *ǰin* says: 'I swear by the Qor'an and God that I will leave this man.' The mullah replies that as they [*ǰins*] don't believe in the Qor'an, he cannot trust them. 'You should swear by the green ring of King Suleiman [Solomon].' Then the *ǰin* would do so and the mullah would trust him. The *ǰins* have to keep the oath. The *ǰins* would always obey this oath because they are subject to the gem of the ring of King Suleiman. The ring was given to Suleiman by God:

"*Ḥaẓrat-i* Daoud was the father of Suleiman. When Daoud had no children, he prayed to God to give him a son, 'who will be close to Your *darbār* [court] and to whom *ins wa ǰin* [all creatures] will bow.' As Daoud was a prophet himself, God fulfilled his wish and Suleiman was born.

"Daoud saw that the child Suleiman was wearing a ring, a gold ring with a green gem, right from his birth. It was written there that man and beast shall be his subjects. Daoud did not understand the significance until 6 days later. He saw that all the *ǰins, dīws, parīs* [supernatural beings] had surrounded the house. He asked what they were doing. They told Daoud that 'A baby is born in your house who is wearing a ring to which we are slaves.' Daoud went to remove the ring from Suleiman's finger but could not. Instead he went and showed them Suleiman wearing the ring, and the *ǰins* and *dīws* and everyone said that it was the ring. There are 99 groups of these sorts of beings, and the ring ruled over them all.

Shāh Suleiman ibn Daoud, nigarī!
[King Suleiman son of Daoud, see!]
Bar sari insi ǰinsi wa dāw wa parī
[Upon humans, beasts, and giant, and fairy]
chār sad khāna sākht az shīsha
[Four hundred houses made from glass]
hama dar band o zi sīm wa zarī "
[All bound by his silver and gold]"

Another version of the same story told by M. Ayub (Mostafa Khēl):

"Once upon a time, Daoud prayed to God for a son who would become master of humans and beasts. God gave him such a son. When Suleiman was born, they saw a ring on his finger. It looked as if the ring was joined together with the finger so it could not be removed. Daoud did not know the significance of the ring, and on the 6th night after delivery, he saw around his house all the *dīws*, *parīs*, *ǰins*, and the like. Daoud asked what they were doing. They told him that God had given him a child wearing a ring and 'Your son is our King. We are subjects of your son'. Daoud was happy and returned to his house. When Daoud asked them whether they were slaves of the son or anybody wearing the ring, they answered that they were slaves of the ring: 'If the ring is with anybody else we would be free. If it is on your son's finger, we are all his slaves.'

"So when Suleiman was 7 years old, he got out of his house and saw all his subjects. Nobody except Suleiman could see them (not even Daoud – he did not know who Suleiman was talking to). When he was 7 years old these beings told Daoud that they wanted to take their king, Suleiman, to their country. He could visit Daoud but had to live with them. So they brought a throne of boiling water [*āb-i jush*] . They bid farewell to Daoud, so they carried Suleiman to the sky and went to the 7th layer of Koh-i Qaf. So they built him a palace and a city and Suleiman realized that they were his subjects. He sat on his throne there and presided over the court. Then the *parīs* urged him to marry a *parī*. He did so when he was about 40 or 50 years old. He lived among these beings.

"Later on, when he realized that all living creatures were his subjects, he wondered if anybody was higher than he was. And he said 'No'. So he became proud. So proud that one day he decided to go back to Earth. When he did that, he sat on the bank of a river and wanted to take a bath in the river. He removed his clothes and covered himself with the feathers of a swan. He went to the water to bathe. All the *parī*, *shīshak*, and other beings were standing around watching. While in the water, the ring fell off his hand and was swallowed by a fish. Suleiman looked around and realized that all his subjects had disappeared and that his throne, on which he had come down from the sky, was also gone. All magical powers had disappeared, too. He dressed and as he was hungry, he went towards town. As he was walking towards town, he saw a fisherman named Nezrah who asked what he was doing and whether he wanted to become his apprentice and servant. Suleiman agreed, and went to his house to work with him. One day the fisherman asked his wife, 'Why don't we adopt him as our son.' Suleiman caught fish with him and went to the bazaar to sell with him every day until the fisherman one day fell sick, and Suleiman went fishing alone.

"The fisherman had a daughter called Uzrah. She married Suleiman. One day he had a son. Seven years later he had 4 children. One day near the river he remembered his past glory, and he cried out: 'Oh God! Where was I and where am I and what became of me from king of man and beast to fisherman?' And he repented and God accepted his repentance [*toba*] . And so Suleiman went to a pond where he had never caught fish before because it was in a jungle. He was lucky, it was a big catch. One fish was very beautiful, shining like lightning. Suleiman decided to sell the entire catch except this one fish which he brought home to cook.

"So he brought it home, gave it to his wife and asked her to clean it and cook it. When she cut it up, she saw something shining in its intestines. It was the Ring. She washed it and kept it and cooked the fish for her husband. While eating the fish, Suleiman told his wife his own life story. While he was telling about the Ring she remembered it. She asked him to describe the former Ring and found the description fit with what she had found. So she showed him the ring. He recognized it and put it on his finger and saw that his kingdom was restored and all the creatures waiting outside. He did not tell his wife but went out to his creatures, and they looked exactly as they did when he had last seen them, when he had gone bathing. Standing waiting for him, he told them his story, explained everything, and so forth. The creatures wanted to take their king back with them. He accepted and went to the house and brought his wife, children and parents-in-law and said that he wanted to bring them along. His creatures suggested that he better leave these mortals on earth. He was persuaded to bring to Koh-i Qaf only his youngest son Mir Bacha."

According to Hughes (1982(1885): 478) Qaf is "the circle of mountains which Easterns fancy encompass the world. The Muhammadan belief being that they are inhabited by demons and jinn, and that the mountain range is of emerald which gives an azure hue to the sky. ... The name is also used for Mount Caucasus." Both the belief in supernatural beings like *jin* and King Suleiman's special power over these, including his understanding of the "language of birds" are supported by the Qor'an (XXI: 81, XXVII: 16-17). Moreover, the commentaries of the Qor'an present the story of Suleiman losing (and finding again) the ring, in which the control over demons and spirits were invested, i.e. God was trying him by letting him lose his kingdom (based on XXXVIII: 34-9).

Donaldson, in his study Muhammadan Magic and Folklore in Iran (1938), also informs that beings like *dīw*, *parī*, *jin* are frequently associated with the mountains of 'Kāf'. But while the *dīws* are under the rule of Satan, *parīs*, for example, have their own ruler in'Kāf' (1938, Ch. III). Donaldson provides no information relating these supernatural beings to the Ring of Suleiman, but states the Qor'an and *ḥadīth* contain references to Solomon's (Suleiman's) control over *jin*, *parī*, and other beings. However, there seems to be agreement upon that while *dīws* are evil, *parīs* generally are good spirits, and *jins* may be good or bad. Donaldson's description of how the wrath of a *jin* mother may be incurred by hurting her baby parallels the Ghorbat version.

Mohammad Ayub, a Qasem Khēl, continues his account of supernatural beings, Kabul, May-June 1975:

"These creatures [*shīshaks* and *mādar-i āl*] are made from the women of Shamali [area just north of Kabul] because these women hardly eat meat, and they wash themselves only once a year. When they start stinking, they leave home. They leave their houses in the night and return in the morning. [During night] they turn into *mādar-i āl* [in this story, modar -i āl and shīshak are used interchangeably]. These *mādar-i āls* are very strong. They can throw a man some metres without difficulty.

"A *shīshak* originates from Pashtun nomads. These people live in tents all the time, in the mountains, and there is hardly a place for women to wash themselves, so they remain dirty and filthy for years. Ultimately, they stink so much that they go crazy. They get out of their tents by midnight, walking in the mountains. Some nights they come across the *mādar-i āl*. The hair of that woman is so long that it reaches the ground. She is called *mādar* because she is old. She eats the liver of human beings. When she sees the crazy (nomad) woman, she does not eat her liver, because the woman are too abnormal. Instead, she carries her away and they become friends and continue to have midnight rendezvous. During daytime *mādar-i āl* would lie under a stone. The nomad woman would go to her tent during the day and at night go to *mādar-i āl*, until she has learned her magic. *Mādar-i āl* 's magic consists of her being able to turn invisible. She can eat grass until she can come across a human being to attack and eat. When the nomad woman has turned into a *shīshak*, she would make *kibāb* of human flesh, giving the liver to *mādar-i āl*.

"*Ajina* are taller than *jin*, but don't wear turbans. They wear hats, both men and women. If you harm them they will do evil. They can kill a man, surround him. With clubs, knives, and stones they will kill him.

"*Parī* [fairies], are female. They don't harm human beings but could fall in love with them. They look like human beings, but their men, *dīw* are ugly. *Parīs* have wings, but *dīw* have no wings. They are very strong, have big heads, and could swallow two people. They are bad and do bad even if you don't harm them. After Suleiman they don't harm any more. Both *parīs* and *dīws* live in Koh-i Qaf, not in Afghanistan."

However, something good can apparently also come out of the association with supernatural beings. Khan Agha from the Qāsem Khēl thus relates a story about his great grandfather, Mahib Ali:

"Mahib Ali had affairs with *shīshaks* and *mādar-i āl*. He went out with them to all the old mills and slept with them and finally he forced them to take an oath in the name of the Ring of Suleiman, that they should not harm the descendants of Mahib Ali.

Now, if fifty of them come, they don't bother us. Several times they have come across us, but they have disappeared..."

Regarding mādar-i āl, Hackin and Kohzad refer to a tradition in the Kabul area of a being called *matar ani* who posseses the power to kill children who catch measles (*surkhakān*) or scarlet fever (*chechak*). This *matar ani* is also known in the Jalalabad area under the name of *Mādar-i alao* (mother of fire) (Hackin and Kohzad) 1953: 163-4. While the above *matar ani* is specifically related to children's diseases, this does not appear to be the case with the Ghorbat versions of *mādar-i āl*, and neither was it the case with similar tales which I heard during 1977-79 in the Khulm area. Here *mādar-i āl* may attack med who in the middle of the night would leave the village to care for their irrigation canals.

Donaldson reports from Iran about the witch *āl* that snatches away tiny babies and steals their mother's liver. "*Āl*'s business is to take babies' lives or to torment the mothers till they die. She attacks only those who are weak" (Donaldson 1938: 28-31). In Donaldson's version *āl* is a witch who is only dangerous to women and children. The Iranian anthropologist Amanolahi, with reference to Luristan, West Iran, also mentions *āl* or *yāl* as supernatural beings attacking women's liver particularly during pregnancy (personal communication). Some resemblance may also be found to the *mari māta* (Mother of Death), mentioned by Crooke (1977(1906): 234) as an example of popular religion and beliefs in Northern India. *Mari Māta* presides over cholera, and Crooke sees her as a malignant form of the Mother goddess in popular Hinduism (ibid.). He also mentions *dīw* among the malignant spirits of North India. The *dīw* is here known as a cannibal and is recognized by his long lips, one of which sticks up in the air, while the other hangs pendent. He often causes tempests, and "were he not stupid by nature, could work infinite mischief" (ibid.: 238).

BIBLIOGRAPHY

Anon. s.a. *Kesh Nama*. Peshawar .

Anon. 1892 For. and Pol. Dept. Sec. F, Pros. Febr. nos. 265-80 .

Anon. 1978 *Afghan Agriculture in Figures*. Central Statistics Office. Kabul.

Adamec, L. W. 1985 *Kabul and southeastern Afghanistan*. Historical and Political Gazetteer of Afghanistan, 6. (Akademische Druck u. Verlagsanstalt) Graz.

Ahmad, S. 1974 A village in Pakistani Punjab: Jalpānā. *South Asia: seven community Profiles*. C. Maloney (ed.). New York.

1977 *Class and Power in a Punjabi Village*. (Monthly Review Press) New York.

Aitchison, J. E. T. 1891 Notes to assist in a further Knowledge of the Products of Western Afghanistan and of North-Eastern Persia. *Transactions of the Botanical Society of Edinburgh*, 18: 1-228.

Allan, N. J. R. 1976 Kuh Daman Periodic Markets: Cynosures for Rural Circulation and Potential Economic Development. *Aktuelle Probleme der Regionalentwicklung und Stadtgeographie Afghanistans*. E. Grötzbach (ed.). (Verlag Anton Hain) Meisenheim am Glan.

1978 *Men and Crops in the Central Hindu Kush*. Ph.D. thesis, University of Syracuse (UMI Dissertation Services).

Amanolahi, S. 1992 The Gypsies of Iran: A Brief Introduction. Unpublished manuscript.

Anderson, J. W. 1984 How Afghans Define Themselves in Relation to Islam. *Revolutions and Rebellions in Afghanistan*. M. N. Shahrani and R. L. Canfield (eds.): 266-89. (Institute of International Studies, University of California) Berkeley.

Arnold, H. 1967 Some Observations on Turkish and Persian Gypsies. *Journal of the Gypsy Lore Society*, XLVI, 3-4: 105-22.

Bahìn, N. A. 1975/AH(Sh) 1353 The Most Ancient Handicrafts of Our Country [in Pashto]. *The Folklore Magazine*, 2-3: 118-23.

Balland, D. 1991 Tents, Yurts, Huts and Caves: On the Cultural Geography of Temporay Dwellings in Afghanistan. *FOLK*, 33: 107-17.

Barin Zuri, A. 1981 *Surplus Labour in Afghanistans Wirtschaft: Methoden und Strategiefragen zur Mobilisierung überschüssiger ländlicher Arbeitskräfte*. (Erdmann Verlag) Tübingen.

Barnabas, A. P. 1970 *Farmer Characteristics in the Koh-i Daman Pilot Area.* Technical Report No. 4. PACCA.

Barth, F. 1959 *Political Leadership among the Swat Pathans.* London School of Economics. Monographs on Social Anthropology, No. 19. (The Athlone Press) London.

1962 The System of Social Stratification in Swat, North Pakistan. *Aspects of Caste in South India, Ceylon and Northwest Pakistan.* E. Leach (ed.): 113-48. Cambridge University Papers in Social Anthropology, 2.

1964 *Nomads of South Persia: The Basseri Tribe of the Khamseh Confederacy.* (Universitetsforlaget) Oslo.

1969 *Ethnic Groups and Boundaries: The Social Organization of Culture Difference.* (Allen and Unwin) London.

1987 Preface. *The other Nomads.* A. Rao (ed.): vii-xiii. (Böhlau Verlag) Cologne.

Bellew, H. W. 1978 (1920) *Afghanistan: A Political Mission in 1857.* (Oriental Publishers) Lahore.

Berland, J. C. 1977 *Cultural Amplifiers and Psychological Differentiation among Khānābadōsh in Pakistan.* Ph.D. thesis, University of Hawaii. Honolulu.

1982 *No Five Fingers are Alike: Cognitive Amplifiers in Social Context.* (Harvard University Press) Cambridge, Mass.

Casimir, M. J. 1987 In search of guilt: legends on the origin of the peripatetic niche. *The Other Nomads.* A. Rao (ed.): 373-91. (Böhlau Verlag) Cologne.

Centlivres, P. 1972 *Un bazar d'Asie Centrale: Forme et organisation du bazar de Tashqurghan.* (Reichert Verlag) Wiesbaden.

Centlivres, P., and Centlivres-Demont, M. 1988 Practiques quotidiennes et usages politiques des termes éthniques dans l'Afghanistan du nord-est. *Le fait éthnique en Iran et en Afghanistan.* J.-P. Digard (ed.): 233-47. (Éditions du CNRS) Paris.

Charpentier, C.-J. 1972 *Bazaar-e Tashqurghan – ethnographical studies in an Afghan traditional bazaar.* Studia Ethnographica Upsaliensia, XXXVI.

Christensen, A. 1980 The Pashtuns of Kunar: Tribe, Class and Community Organization. *Afghanistan Journal,* Jg. 7, Heft 3.

1982 Agnates, Affines, and Allies: Patterns of Marriage among Pakhtun in Kunar, North Afghanistan. *FOLK,* 24: 29-65.

Clébert, J. P. 1963 *The Gypsies.* (E.P. Dutton and Co) New York.

Crooke, W. 1977 (1906) *The native races of the Northern India.* (Sh. Mubarak Ali, Oriental Publishers & Booksellsers) Lahore.

Digard, J.-P. 1988 *Le fait éthnique en Iran et en Afghanistan.* (Éditions du CNRS) Paris.

Donaldson, B. A. 1973 (1938) *The Wild Rue: A Study of Muhammadan Magic and Folklore in Iran.* Reprint. (Arno Press) London and New York.

Dupree, L. 1973 *Afghanistan.* (Princeton University Press) Princeton, N. J.

Einzmann, M. 1977 *Religiöses Volksbrauchtum in Afghanistan.* (Franz Steiner Verlag) Wiesbaden.

Elphinstone, M. 1972 (1839) *An Account of the Kingdom of Caubul*, I-II. (Oxford University Press) London.

EI 1983 *The Encyclopaedia of Islam, II.* (E. J. Brill) Leiden.

EB 1985 *Encyclopaedia Britannica.* Chicago.

Ferdinand, K. 1959 Ris: Træk af dens dyrkning og behandling i Østafghanistan. *KUML*: 195-232. Aarhus .

1962 Nomadic Expansion and Commerce in Central Afghanistan: A Sketch of some Modern Trends. *FOLK*, 4: 123-59. Copenhagen.

1968 Ost-Afghanischer Nomadismus – ein Beitrag zur Anpassungsfähigkeit der Nomaden. *Nomadismus als Entwicklungsproblem.* W. Kraus et al. (eds.). Bochumer Symposium 14.-15. Juli 1967. Bielefeld.

Frommer, G. 1981 *Das Moderne Bildungswesen als Instrument nationaler Entwicklung.* Heidelberger Dritte Welt Studien, I. (Esprint Verlag) Heidelberg.

Fry, M. 1974 *The Afghan Economy: Money, finance and the critical constraints to economic development.* (Brill) Leiden.

Fröhlich, D. 1970 *Nationalismus und Nationalstaat in Entwicklungsländern.* (Verlag Anton Hain) Meisenheim am Glan.

Gavrilov, M. 1928 Les Corps de Métiers en Asie Centrale et leurs Statuts (Rissala). *Revue des Études Islamiques*, 2: 209-30.

Gmelch, G., and Gmelch, S. B. 1987 Commercial nomadism: occupation and mobility among travellers in England and Wales. *The Other Nomads.* A. Rao (ed.): 133-59. (Böhlau Verlag) Cologne.

Gobineau, G. von 1857 Persische Studien: Die Wanderstämme Persiens. *Zeitschrift der Deutschen morgenländischen Gesellschaft*, 11: 689-99. Leipzig.

Grevemeyer, J.-H. 1987 *Afghanistan: Sozialer Wandel und Staat im 20. Jahrhundert.* (Express Edition) Berlin.

Grötzbach, E. 1972 *Kulturgeographischer Wandel in Nordost Afghanistan seit dem 19. Jahrhundert.* (Verlag Anton Hain) Meisenheim am Glan.

Hackin, R., and Kohzad, A. A. 1953 *Légendes et Coutumes Afghanes.* (Publications du Musée Guimet, PUF) Paris.

Hahn, H. 1964-65 *Die Stadt Kabul (Afghanistan) und ihr Umland*, I-II. Bonner Geogr. Abhandl. 34-35.

Halliday, W. R. 1922 Some Notes upon the Gypsies of Turkey. *Journal of the Gypsy Lore Society*, 3rd. ser., vol. 1, No. 4: 163-89.

Hayden, R. M. 1987 Conflicts and relations of power between peripatetics and villagers in South Asia. *The Other Nomads.* A. Rao (ed.): 267-91. (Böhlau Verlag) Cologne.

Hughes, T. P. 1982 (1885) *Dictionary of Islam.* (Cosmo Publications) New Delhi.

Ibbetson, D. 1974 (1916) *Punjab Castes.* (Sh. Mubarak Ali Publishers & Booksellers) Lahore.

Ivanow, W. 1914 On the Language of the Gypsies of Qainat (in eastern Persia). *Journal and Proceedings of the Asiatic Society of Bengal*, New Series, X: 439-55.

1920 Further Notes on Gypsies in Persia. *Journal and Proceedings of the Asiatic Society of Bengal*, New Series, XVI: 281-92.

1922 An Old Gypsy-Darwish Jargon. *Journal and Proceedings of the Asiatic Society of Bengal*, New Series, XVIII: 375-85.

Jafri, S. H. M. 1976 *The Origins and Early Development of Shi'a Islam.* (The Group of Muslims) Qum.

Jones, S. 1974 *Men of Influence in Nuristan.* (Seminar Press) London.

Kakar, H. 1971 *Afghanistan: A Study in Internal Political Development, 1880-1901.* (Punjab University Press) Lahore.

1979 *Government and Society in Afghanistan: The Reign of Amir 'Abd al-Rahman Khan.* (University of Texas Press) Austin.

Kanne, J. 1974 *Interne Investitionsfinanzierung in Afghanistan.* Inaugural-Dissertation, Ruhr Universität. Bochum.

Karmisheva, B. Kh. 1963 Sredni Asiatskie Sigane. *Narodi Sredni Asi i Kasakhistan*, II: 597-607. Moscow.

Kassim, A. M., Massignon, L., and Ivanow, V. 1927 Études sur les Corporations Musulmanes Indo-Persanes. *Revue des Études Islamiques*, 1: 249-72.

Khan, S. M. (ed.) 1980 (1900) The Life of Abdur Rahman Amir of Afghanistan, I-II. (Oxford University Press) Oxford, New York, Delhi.

Lancaster, W., and Lancaster, F. 1987 The function of peripatetics in Rwala Bedouin society. *The Other Nomads.* A. Rao (ed.): 311-23. (Böhlau Verlag) Cologne.

Leach, E. (ed.) 1962 *Aspects of Caste in South India, Ceylon and North-West Pakistan.* Cambridge University Papers in Soc. Anthropology, 2.

Leitner, G. W. 1880 *A Sketch of the Changars and Their Dialect.* Lahore.

Masson, C. 1974 (1842) *Narrative of various Journeys in Balochistan, Afghanistan and the Panjab*, I-III. (Oxford University Press) Oxford.

Neale, J. 1981 The Afghan Tragedy. *International Socialism*, 12, Spring: 1-32.

Norvell, D. G. 1973 *Markets and Men in Afghanistan.* Agricultural Division, USAID. Kabul.

Olesen, A. *Fra kaste til pjalteproletariat?* Field report, Aarhus University. Aarhus .

1982a The Musallis – the Graincleaners of East Afghanistan. *Afghanistan Journal*, Jg. 9, Heft 1. Wiesbaden.

1982b Marriage Norms and Practices in a Rural Community in North Afghanistan. *FOLK*, 24: 111-43. Copenhagen.

1983 The Saur Revolution and the local responses to it. *Forschungen in und über Afghanistan.* S.-W. Breckle and C. M. Nauman (eds.): 131-47. Mitteilungen des Deutschen Orient-Instituts, 22. Hamburg.

1985 The Sheikh Mohammadi – A Marginal Trading Community in East Afghanistan. *FOLK*, 27: 115-47. Copenhagen.

1994 *Islam and Politics in Afghanistan* NIAS. Curzon Press. London

Orywal, E. (ed.) 1986 *Die ethnischen Gruppen Afghanistans: Fallstudien zu Gruppenidentität und Intergruppenbeziehung.* (L. Reichert Verlag) Wiesbaden.

Poullada, L. B. 1973 *Reform and Rebellion in Afghanistan, 1919-1929.* (Cornell University Press) Ithaca.

Rao, A. 1981 Qui sont les Jat d'Afghanistan? *Afghanistan Journal*, Jg. 8, Heft 2: 55-66 . Wiesbaden.

Rao, A. 1982 *Les Gorbat d'Afghanistan: Aspects économiques d'un groupe itinérant "Jat"*. Institut Français d'Iranologie de Téhéran. Bibliothèque Iranienne, 27. (Editions Recherche sur les civilisations) Paris.

1982a The Ghorbat of Afghanistan: Non-Food Producing Nomads and the Problem of Their Classification. *The Eastern Anthropologist*, 35, No. 2: 115-34.

1983 Zigeunerähnliche Gruppen in West-, Zentral und Südasien. *Zigeuner. Roma, Sinti, Gitanos, Gypsies: Zwischen Verfolgung und Romantisierung*. R. Vossen (ed.): 163-86. (Ullstein Verlag) Berlin.

1986 Peripatetic Minorities in Afghanistan – Image and Identity. *Die ethnischen Gruppen Afghanistans: Fallstudien zu Gruppenidentität und Intergruppenbeziehung*. E. Orywal (ed.): 254-83. (L. Reichert Verlag) Wiesbaden.

1987 (ed.) *The Other Nomads*. (Böhlau Verlag) Cologne.

1988 Folk models and inter-ethnic relations in Afghanistan: A case study of some peripatetic communities. *Le fait éthnique en Iran et en Afghanistan*. J.-P. Digard (ed.): 109-21. Paris.

Robertson, G. S. 1974 (1896) *The Kafirs of the Hindu-Kush*. (Oxford University Press) London and Karachi.

Rogers, A. 1978 (1907) *The Shah-Namah of Fardusi*. (Heritage Publishers) New Delhi.

Roy, O. 1985 L'Afghanistan. *Islam et modernité politique*. (Collection Esprit/Seuil) Paris.

Rye, O. S., and Evans, C. 1976 *Traditional Pottery Techniques of Pakistan*. Field and Laboratory Studies. Smithsonian Contributions to Anthropology, 21. Washington.

Safi, Z. 1974-75/AH(Sh) 1353-54 The Artisans of Laghman. *Nangarhar Magazine*, 193-7. [Unpub. translation into English by M.A. Safi]

Sakata, L. 1980 Afghan Musical Instruments – Drums. *Afghanistan Journal*, Jg. 7, Heft 1: 30-3.

Salo, M. T. 1987 The Gypsy Niche in North America: some ecological perspectives on the exploitation of social environments. *The Other Nomads*. A. Rao (ed.): 89-111. (Böhlau Verlag) Cologne.

Sana, S. 1988 Le vocabulaire du fait éthnique en Afghanistan. *Le fait éthnique en Iran et en Afghanistan*. J.-P. Digard (ed.): 277-89. (Éditions du CNRS) Paris.

Schleifer, S. A. 1983 Jihad and traditional Islamic Consciousness. *The Islamic Quarterly. A Review of Islamic Culture*, XXVII, 4. London.

Shah, I. 1982 *Afghanistan of the Afghans*. (The Octagon Press) London.

Steingass, F. 1973 *Persian-English Dictionary*. (Oriental Books Reprint) New Delhi.

Tapper, R. L. 1988 Ethnicity, order and meaning in the anthropology of Iran and Afghanistan. *Le fait éthnique en Iran et en Afghanistan*. J.-P. Digard (ed.): 21-35. (Éditions du CNRS) Paris.

Toepfer, H. 1972 — *Wirtschafts- und sozialgeographische Fallstudien in ländlichen Gebieten Afghanistans.* Bonner Geo. Abhandlungen, 46.

Trimingham, J. S. 1971 — *The Sufi Orders in Islam.* (Oxford University Press) Oxford.

Westphal-Hellbusch, S. 1980 — Randgruppen im Nahen und Mittleren Orient. *Baessler Archiv,* Neue Folge, XXVIII, 1: 1-59.

Westphal-Hellbusch, S., and Westphal, H. 1964 — *The Jat of Pakistan.* Forsch. z. Ethn. und Sozialpsych., 5. (H. Thurnwald) Berlin.

Wiser, W. H. 1936 — *The Hindu Jajmani System.* (Lucknow Publishing House) Lucknow.

Wright, P. 1982 — The Naddaf. *Afghanistan Journal,* Jg. 9, Heft 1: 21-4.

Wulff, H. E. 1966 — *The Traditional Crafts of Persia.* (MIT Press) Cambridge, Mass.

Yule, H., and Burnell, A. C. 1986 (1886) — *Hobson-Jobson: A Glossary of colloquial Anglo-Indian words and phrases, and of kindred terms, etymological, historical, geographical and discursive.* (Rupa and Co.) Delhi.

GLOSSARY

Where nothing is indicated, the word is Persian. Pashto words are referred to by "Psh.," and *Qāzulāgi* words by "Ql." All local terms are explained when first used. Names and words known in a standard anglicized version are retained. Below are listed terms frequently occuring in the text.

ādūr a peddling trip
Ādūrgari the language of the Shaykh Mohammadis
Afghāni local currency. In 1976 1 US $ = 54,55 Afs
alai-hi's-salam "Peace be upon him", phrase added after the name of any prophet
amîr title of Afghan rulers before 1919; lit. commander, chief, or Lord
bābā used as "father", but also a title of respect and endearment when addressing or referring to the head of a religious order
bad compensation
badal "change", "substitution", "return"
banǰaragī selling of petty trinkets
chaǰ winnowing fan made of reeds
chār-dīwālī four-walled enclosure (derived from *chār-dīwārī*: a courtyard)
chighil sieve used for grain-cleaning
chuta'ī, *from chut andāz*, lit. to throw at random; *chuta'ī* is the Musallis' traditional share of grain after cleaning the stack
dulî a litter or simple palanquin
dīhqān sharecropping peasant
iǰāra lease, *iǰāradār*: leaseholder
faqîr itinerant dervish, poor person
Fārsîwān Persian-speaker
futuwwa urban fraternities; various movements and organizations in the Orient
gawdī a light, small two-wheeled horse-drawn vehicle with two cushioned seats placed back-to-back, and covered by a bonnet. Known in the Indian Subcontinent as a *tonga*
gāw-rānī transport work with oxen (*gāw*: cow, ox)
ghalbel, derived from *ghalbīz*: flour-sieve
gharībī 'poor man's work', i.e. work for a meagre living
ḥadīth, traditions of what the Prophet said, did, or approved of
ḥaǰǰ pilgrimage to Mecca
ḥaǰǰī man who has performed *hajj*
ḥākim local, elected leader
ḥalāl religiously commendable, legitimate
hampīr 'of the same *pîr*', used by members of the same guild to refer to each other
hamsāya lit. common shadow; neighbour, also used to refer to tenants who live for free in return for services provided to the host household
ḥaẓrat honorific religious title
imām the originator of an acknowledged norm or *sunna*; a source or precedent for the establishment of religious law; in Shi'a Islam the rightful successor to the Prophet
ǰang fight, skirmish
ǰarīb local measure of land equal to 0.195 ha

jat	derogatory term used about peripatetic groups
kāfir	heathen, infidel
kalāntar	lit. elder. Refers to elected leader of guild. Musalis use the term for the leader of the work groups in the Kabul area
kārīz	subterranean water channel
katabīz	sieve used for grain-cleaning
kachkūl	beggar's bowl
kesb	trade, profession, handicraft
khairat	offering, charity
khāk	dust, earth
khalīfā	successor, vicegerent, caliph
khān	originally this was a title used among Mongol and Turk nomads to refer to the equivalent of a lord or prince. It is now used generally to refer to chiefs and nobles, and has become a sort of respectful title of address
khāna-dāmād	man living with his in-laws
kharwār	lit. donkey-load; a local measure of weight equal to 80 *ser*, which is 565.28 kg
khēl	descent-group, sub-lineage
khwāja	patrilineal descendant of Abu Bakr, the 1. *khalīfā*
lurg	(Ql.) instrument for turning the wooden frames for sieves and drums
maydabīz	finer type of grain-sieve
malang	dervish
malik	(in Afghanistan) representative of a tribe or local community appointed by the government
manda'ī/mandawī	wholesale market
murīd	disciple of a *pīr*
muṣallā	a place of prayer, a mat for saying prayers upon
muṣallā wardar	"prayer rug carrier"
muṣallī-tūb	occupation of the Musalis, i.e. graincleaning
nadāf	cotton codder
namus	reputation, chastity
pāykūb	rice mill
pāykūbt	rice mill worker
pāykūbtī	rice milling work, i.e. de-husking of paddy
patragar	riveter of chinaware
pilaw	rice dish, national dish of Afghanistan
pīr	lit. elder; spiritual leader, notably of a Sufi order, *ṭarīqat*
paw	local measure of weight equal to 0.422 kg
qal'a	castle, fort, fortified house
qawm	people, nation, tribe, family, kindred
qawāl	loquacious, eloquent or fluent speaker. With connotations of noisy, brash behavior
Qāzulāgi (Ql.)	language of the Ghorbat
risālat	treatise
ruhānī	spiritual, holy
sāhib	in Afghanistan and the Subcontinent a title of courtesy equivalent to Mister and Sir
sarāy	a building for the accommodation of travellers with their pack animals, consisting of enclosed yard with chambers round it
sawdā	merchandise of "petty things" like needles, hairpins, etc.
sawdāgar	merchant, pedlar
sawdāgarī	peddling of petty trinkets
sayyid	descendant from the Prophet in the line of Ali
ṣinf	trade and artisan guild (*aṣnāf/ṣunuf*, pl.)
sēr	local measure of weight equal to 7.66 kg
shaykh	superior of the dervishes
sīyāl	respectable equal; religiously worthy person
ta'na	spite; reminding somebody of his failures
ṭarīqāt	road, way, path; the whole system of rites for spiritual training within various Muslim religious Sufi orders (*ṭuruq*, pl.)
vilāyat	provincial centre
wakīl	representative
walī	a saint, a holy man
wālīswāl	sub-governor of a province
watan	fatherland
wazīr	minister
zīyārat	"visit" in a religious sense (pilgrimage). In Afghanistan used to refer directly to the shrine or tomb visited

INDEX

A

Abraham 292
Adam 208, 211, 292, 293, 295, 296, 297, 304, 305
ādūr 143, 148, 158, 161, 180, 203, 249, 281
ādūrgar 143
Ādūrgari 142, 143, 203
Afshar 100
Aghabad 129
Ahmad *Shāh Durrani* 219
Aibak 203
ājina 308, 305
Akhi, Akhi Bābās 54, 56
Akhund Khēl 280
Akram *Khān* 200
alāji 221
Alavi 280
Ali Khel 126, 129
Alingar 57, 58, 61, 112, 114, 121, 123, 128, 145, 150, 151
Alishang 41, 45, 57, 58, 61, 102, 112, 123, 128, 131, 145, 148, 182, 194, 199, 200, 201, 205
'allāf 228, 280
'allāfi 102, 228
Amanullah 221
Amār Abdur Rahman Khān 220
Amīr Abdur Rahman 142, 145, 146, 199, 201, 203, 281
Amīr Abdur Rahman's 128
Amīr Habibullah 145
Anglo-Afghan Wars 279
animal performance 19, 44
Ariaw 150, 151
artisan guilds 211, 212
Asheqan-wa-Arefan 68, 129
āsīyā 78
āsīyāī 78
aṣnāf/ṣunuf 51
awār kūn 223

B

Babaji 114
Babar Khēl 139, 142
Baccha-i Saqqao 199, 205, 269
Badakhshan 40, 148, 267
badal 121, 130, 186, 264, 267
Badiabad 118
bādiyan 153
Badmār 137
Badpusht/Badpakht 72, 145, 148
Bagh-i Alam 154, 192
Bagh-i Mirza 129
Baghlan 75, 112, 238
Bajawur 69
Balatumani 139
Balkans 213
Balkh 206, 220, 281
Baluch 49, 217
Baluchistan 208
Bamiyan 237, 282
Banda-i Sappo Khel 129
bangle-sellers 31, 33, 242, 245
bangle-selling 19

banǰaragī 143
Baraki 100
Baraki Barak 268
barber 18, 51, 54, 57, 65, 71, 90, 205, 207, 268, 282, 292, 296, 297
batta'ī 81
Bayan 154, 192, 193
Bayar 248
baylākhar 233
baylākhars 248
baypār 233
Behar 70
Behsud 129, 140
Bibi Mahru 101
Bini Hissar 100, 121
birinǰ 228
blacksmith 41, 47, 49, 51, 65, 129, 205, 292, 295, 296
Bokhara 291
Bolan 129
bride-price 125, 188, 264, 265
British India 58, 145
Butkhāk 145
Buzak 139

C

cage making 257, 281
caliph Omar 303
carpenter 44, 51, 65, 129, 205, 254, 292, 296
Central Anatolia 56
Chaghasaray 148
Chah-i Mullah Omar 235
Chahārtagān 137
Chahrdehi 75
chaǰ 68, 76, 78, 81, 154, 156
chaǰ-maker 158
chaǰ-making 204
Chaman 248
Chaman-i Hazori 282
Changar 67, 74, 127
Chapriar 248
Charbagh 21, 44, 112, 139, 237
Chardehi 129, 130
chār-dīwālī 239, 242, 243
Charikar 21, 37, 56, 150, 206, 221, 235, 237, 239, 247, 249, 259, 261, 272, 275, 277, 281
Charkhi 145
chārshākh 76
Chashdar 101
Chekkian 74
chighil 223, 226, 228, 261
Chilmati 112, 203
chinaware riveters 44, 242
Chishtī order of Sūfis 295
Chuhras 127
Chūhras 73, 74
chukak 76, 95
Chunduk 129
Chungar 67, 70, 72, 73, 74, 123
chungarī 75
chuta'ī 88, 98, 99
clientship 64, 201, 203, 286, 288
cock-fighting 258, 259
conjurer 242, 245, 281
cotton codder (*nadāf*) 44, 131, 139, 144
cotton codding 143, 197
cumin 146, 148, 149, 150, 151, 152, 153
cupping 44, 206, 248, 252, 288

D

Dahan-i Ghori 33
dāira 230, 232
Danageh 145
Dand 112, 114, 118, 121, 124, 129
Daoud *Khān* 112, 295, 297, 306
Dar al-Aman 76, 80, 100
Darunta 61
Darweshan 118
Dawlatshah 106, 148
Deh Afghanan 100
Deh Bala 101
Deh Kepak 100, 271
Deh Sharana 129
Deh Ziyarat 129
dehusking paddy 82, 87
Delhi 295
Desht-i Rawat 150, 151, 152
dīw 151, 204, 306, 308, 309

Diwa 45, 49, 51, 87, 129, 187
du-kat 87

E

endogamous marriage practices 18, 19, 126, 184, 186, 188, 202, 207, 261, 276, 277, 278, 284, 288, 289
entertainment 256
exogamous marriage practices 184, 188, 192 202, 268

F

faqīr/malang 70, 136, 138, 142, 143, 144, 210, 280, 298, 299
Farah 214, 220
Farāhi 206, 220, 235, 265, 271, 280
Farajghan 101, 142, 145, 148, 149
Faryab 281
Filwan Kocha 246
flail (*gundi-chobe*) 76, 81, 98, 130
fortune telling 44, 203, 206, 248
Frontier 73, 74
futuwwa 51, 52, 56

G

Gabriel 292, 293
Gandab 148
Gardez 134, 261
gāw-rānī 101
Gazak 145
ghalbel 226, 228, 231, 264, 281
gharībī 41, 71, 97, 153, 201
Ghāzī 280
Ghazni 21, 203, 206, 220, 237, 241, 247, 251, 252, 260, 261, 262, 263, 268, 272, 275, 277, 280, 281, 282
Ghilzai Pashtuns 61
Ghorband 37, 148, 238
Ghorbati 213, 215
ghubal 76
Ghulam Ali/Mahigir 54, 135, 145, 159, 163, 168, 170, 176, 179, 183, 184, 190, 192, 204
Ghurbed 213
gilkārī 41
Girishk 248
goldsmith 41, 129, 205, 217, 219
Gonkur 129
guilds 51, 272, 278, 280, 282, 287
Gulbahar 239
Gulkari 129
gulun-i lurg 221
Gumain 112, 129
gundi 228
gundī-takānī 76
gundī/shughak 76
gundīmal 76
gurr 107, 130
Gypsy 208, 213, 214, 216, 279, 280, 282

H

hadith 210, 308
haft-nafarī 198
Haiderkhani 24, 44, 70, 129
ḥākim 135, 136, 275
hamsāya 107, 108, 114, 181, 285, 288
Hazar Meshi 65, 79, 101
Hazara 235, 282, 302
Hazarajat 232, 261
Ḥazrat-i Ali 209, 293
Ḥaẓrat-i Daoud 211, 280, 293, 306
Ḥaẓrat-i Fatima 303
Ḥaẓrat-i Omar 303
Helmand 55, 67, 73, 75, 112, 115, 118, 287
Helmand Valley Project 31, 55, 58, 114, 130
Hemat Ali khēl 265
Herat 21, 206, 208, 217, 218, 219, 220, 252, 253, 255, 272, 276, 277, 280, 281, 283
ḥukmrān 200
ḥūr 208
Hussain Khêl 65, 79, 101

I

Ibrahim Khêl 65
ijāra 104, 106, 130

ilak-i sīmī 228
India 67, 70, 129, 148, 154, 203, 280, 291, 298, 309
Indian jajmani system 100
Indian Subcontinent 57, 64, 73, 127, 129, 205, 207, 221
Indus 73
Inku 245
Iran 23, 37, 208, 209, 213, 214, 216, 282, 290, 305, 309
Iranian Ghorbati 281
Isaac 292
Ismail 295, 297
Ismaili 45
Issa/Jesus 54, 56, 297, 298
Istalif 239, 241, 281, 305

J

Jabar Khēl 142
Jajis 139
jajmani-system 57, 129
jalābs 178
Jalalabad 21, 121, 131, 132, 145, 146, 153, 154, 179, 180, 181, 194, 200, 203, 213, 231, 235, 237, 239, 241, 242, 243, 244, 245, 246, 247, 249, 254, 259, 260, 261, 262, 264, 268, 273, 277, 279, 282, 302, 303
Jalāli 49
jālawāns 194
Jalrez 241
Jat 32, 44, 48, 49, 56, 67, 215, 233, 245, 253, 258, 277, 279, 288, 187, 191, 203
jewellers/goldsmiths 217, 219
jewellery 208, 220
Jibrail [Gabriel] 69, 208, 210, 211, 283, 295, 297
jihād 51, 204
jin 305, 306, 307, 308
jūlahā 68

K

Kabul 17, 18, 19, 20, 21, 24, 25, 26, 28, 31, 36, 37, 41, 44, 57, 58, 61, 68, 70, 72, 75, 76, 78, 80, 87,93, 95, 97, 98, 100, 102, 111,119, 121, 127, 131, 132, 142, 145, 146, 148, 149, 152, 153, 154, 175, 180, 187, 197, 203, 206, 214, 220, 228, 233, 235, 237, 238, 239, 241, 242, 249, 254, 261, 270, 271, 275, 277, 282, 304, 308
Kach [Laghman] 112, 142
Kach-i Aziz Khan 112, 114, 129
kachkūl 136, 138, 302
kāfirs 61, 128, 146, 152, 182, 199, 204
Kafiristan 132, 145, 147, 204
Kahmard 237
Kaja 248
kājek 226
kājek-e tanistāi 223
kalāch 222
kalāntar 95, 97, 111, 270, 271, 275, 276, 282
kalāntari 95
Kalakot 70
kalpī 78, 125, 130
Kama 102, 129
Kamalpur 129
kamān 138, 139
kamāncha 222
Kandahar 21, 115, 133, 137, 139, 142, 199, 203, 206, 208, 210, 214, 218, 220, 248, 251, 252, 255, 259,272, 276, 277, 280, 281, 299
Kandahari Pashtuns 205
Karang 139
Karawoo 70, 129
kard-i pusht-kalāchī 222
Karenj 37, 61, 205
kārīz 133, 134, 163, 193
katabīz 76, 223, 226, 228, 230, 231, 240
Katal 69
Katawaz 261
Kauli 280
Kay Kanus 208, 209, 211, 220
Kay Kayhān 217, 208, 210
Kay Khusrow 208
Kayān Pāchā 210, 219, 280, 303
Kayāni 208, 276, 220, 280
Kazakhstan 280
kesb 46, 127, 295, 302, 303
Kesb Nāma 51, 56, 291, 296, 298
khalaji 280
Khaleqi Khēl 280
khalīfā 70, 295
Khanabad 203, 237, 238, 280

khāna dāmad 120, 121, 130, 264, 265, 267
khāna dāmad marriages 253
kharkār 41, 194
Kharotis 117
khēl-affiliation 281
khēl-endogamy 265
khēl kalāntar 276
khrimum 223
Khuzistan 214
Khwāja Safa Walī 73, 68
Khwāja Tār-i Walī 143, 144
King Amanullah 46, 143, 272
King Suleiman 306
knife-grinders 170
knife-smiths 24, 33, 41, 44, 280
Koh - i Daman 21, 26, 37, 44, 131, 132, 145, 152, 153, 154, 158, 163, 167, 168, 170, 175, 179, 197, 203, 269
Kohistan 102, 132, 139, 142, 145, 148, 158, 187, 188, 268
Kohistan-Panjshir 36
Kolola Pushta 100
Kote Ashro 239
Kote Sangi 17, 19, 26, 132, 139, 191, 203, 221, 222, 239
Kote Sangi, Kabul 212
Koulī 214, 216, 281
Kukur Khel 248
Kulala 95
Kunar 65, 101, 128, 129, 146, 148, 196
Kunduz 40, 203, 206, 237, 238

L

Laghman 18, 20, 21, 24, 37, 41, 44, 45, 48, 53, 54, 55, 57, 61, 64, 69, 71, 72, 74, 75, 78, 80, 82, 87, 91, 93, 95, 98, 102, 108, 112, 118, 124, 125, 127, 131, 132, 139, 145, 148, 149, 152, 153, 158, 167, 179, 181, 182, 183, 187, 188, 198, 201, 203, 234, 237, 247, 271, 281, 288, 291
Laghman-i-Afghania 61, 75, 214
Laghman-i-Tajikia 61, 75, 214
Lahore 73, 74
Lashkargah 248
Laskargah 115
Lataband 95
Lataband road 95
Laundrymen 51, 297
lease land (*ijāra*) 244, 247, 254
leather-work (tanning, shoemaking, and repairing) 44, 129, 207, 221
Logar 203, 220
Logarlam 129
lurg 221, 224, 231, 280

M

Madad Khan 129
mādar-i āl 308
Mahib Ali *khēl* 265
Mahmad Bābā 69
Mahtāb Qala 100
Maidan 145, 154, 234, 238, 241, 261
Maimana 248
malang 203, 300, 301
malang/faqīr 131, 132, 138, 203, 280, 300, 301
malik 17, 109, 150, 194, 201, 205, 282
malikī 109, 112, 126
Mama Khel 248
Mandrawar 95, 118, 129, 139
Mangal 142
Manjuma 118, 129
maraboutic Sufism 144
Marja 116, 118, 130
Maskurah 41, 44, 129, 131, 132, 134, 139, 142, 143, 145, 148, 150, 153, 167, 181, 184, 187, 191, 193, 194, 196, 198, 200, 201, 203, 204
maydabīz 223, 226, 228, 230, 231, 240, 261
Mazar-i Sharif 220, 237, 277, 281
Mehnati Mussali 73
Mehrāb Khēl 206, 220, 237, 241, 245, 247, 251, 258, 260, 263, 268, 280, 303, 304
Mehtarlam 54, 64, 128, 131, 167, 291
metal workers 280
Mir Ali Shah of Laghar 134, 139, 142, 143, 203
Mohammad Khel 59, 100, 129
Mohammadpur 129
Mohammadzai 191, 200
Mohmand 248
monkey-trainers 26, 33

Morghan Kocha 248
Mostafa Khēls 206, 219, 220, 230, 237, 250, 254, 255, 260, 265, 268, 269, 270, 271, 272, 275, 280, 303, 304, 305
mujāwir 132, 203
mukhliṣ 144, 204
Multan 70, 74, 129, 299
Munjan 146, 148
Murghab 248
murīds 69, 70, 127, 144, 204, 283
Musa Khêls 72
muṣallā wardar 71
muṣallī-tūb 57, 68, 69, 70, 72, 73, 87, 99, 100, 103, 106, 123, 129

N

Nadāf Khēl 139, 203
Nad-i Ali 114, 116, 118, 130
Nadir *Khān* 199
Nadir *Shāh* 282
naghāra 230, 232
Naghlu 145, 148
Najibullah 254
Nakhshbandiyya 291, 294, 295
Nangarhar 18, 37, 41, 44, 55, 112, 129, 181, 196, 203, 255
Narenj Bagh 129
Nasir Khēl 206, 218, 219, 220, 237, 241, 245, 248, 252, 254, 255, 260, 261, 262, 268, 273, 280, 281, 282
nawkar 47
Niazi 121
Nijrab 37
Nilan 150
Nilan pass 151
Nimnani 128
Nimnani/Niazi 129
Nirkh 145
Nizāmī 295
nomad women 163
nomads 20, 145, 151, 196, 208, 218, 232, 253, 278, 281, 284, 308
North-west Pakistan 128
Now-i Naqil 115, 124
Nuh, Noah 292, 296, 297
Nukur Khel 248
Nuristan 37, 45, 58, 101, 128, 145, 146, 148, 149, 150, 152, 153, 199, 204

O

Obeh 248, 283
Omar 303
Omarzai 129

P

Pāchā Khēl 210, 262
Paghman 24, 37, 44, 239, 241
Pakistan 23, 37, 56, 69, 74, 98, 154, 170, 175, 180, 183, 203, 241, 245, 262, 264, 280, 282, 285, 290, 291, 295, 299
Panjshir 101, 145, 146, 148, 151, 237
Panjwaii 248
par-boiling 79, 82, 86, 103
parī 306, 307, 308
Parman Khel 129
Parwan 40, 234, 240, 241, 261, 277
Pashai 129
Pashto 20, 245
Pashtun 19, 20, 26, 28, 47, 61, 67, 71, 72, 75, 92, 93, 121, 123, 131, 150, 186, 191, 197, 199, 209, 253, 277
pastoral 147
pastoral nomadism 20, 284, 289
pastoral nomads 18, 19, 25, 28, 76, 147, 116, 241, 242, 261, 288
patragar 140, 203
patragari 203
patron-client relations 65, 100
pāykūb 79
pāykūbt 65
pāykūbtī 79
Persia 211, 279
Peshawar 74, 203, 220, 280, 292
Pikrāj 49
pīr 51, 54, 55, 56, 70, 127, 131, 132, 136, 142, 143, 144, 280, 287, 291, 298

Pīrān-e Pīr Sāhib 299
pīr Shams Tabrizi 69, 73
pīr Shams Tabrizi of Multan 127
pīrwarta 270
Pishin 133
porters 281
potter 18, 21, 23, 33, 41, 44, 51, 53, 56, 129, 194, 229, 230, 267, 291, 292, 293, 294
President Daoud 118
Prime Minister Daoud 115
prostitution 19, 44, 245
Pul-i J̌ogi 129
Pul-i Khumri 29, 206, 237, 255, 259
Punjab 58, 69, 73, 128

Q

Qadiriyya Order 280, 283
Qala-i Akhund 129
Qala-i Fathullah 100
Qala-i Hamisha Bahar 129
Qala-i Khan 129
Qala-i Mansur Khan 129
Qala-i Murad Beg 44, 239, 281
Qala-i Naw 248
Qala-i Pahlawān 129
Qala-i Qafila Bashi 100, 121
Qala-i Qazi 129
Qala-i Sahib 129
Qala-i Sardar 125, 129
Qala-i Sarwar Khan 129
Qala-i Sufi 129
Qala Murad Beg 275
Qarabagh 153, 159, 168, 170, 282
qaryadār 282
Qasaba 118, 129
Qāsem Khēl 206, 212, 213, 220, 233, 234, 237, 238, 240, 241, 243, 244, 245, 246, 247, 249, 250, 253, 254, 257, 258, 261, 265, 267, 269, 270, 275, 280, 282, 283, 302, 308
Qasem Khēl 231, 308
Qataghan 237
qawāls 143, 187, 188, 191, 245
Qawal Khel 75, 298
qawm 45, 46, 47, 48, 49, 57, 58, 65, 68, 70, 73, 110, 112, 119, 126, 127, 128, 135, 144, 188, 192, 205, 269, 270, 278, 286
qawm-affiliation 184
qawm endogamy 119, 121, 123, 127, 265
qawm wakīl 271, 276
Qāzulāgi 206, 216, 220, 277, 283, 287
Qizilbāsh 273
Qorghal 115
Quetta 203

R

rāshbīl 76
Reg-i Shahmard Khan 242
rice mill work 103
rice mill worker 65, 81, 87, 97, 99, 124, 125
risālat 51, 56, 291
riveter of china ware (*patragar*) 31, 131, 141, 144, 170, 197, 203
Rokha 146
ropemakers 47, 55
Russia 145
Rustam 208, 220, 259

S

Sahingar 129
Sahiwal 73
Salmān-i Fārsi 54, 56
sang-chaj 78
Sangar Saray 101
sangchil 88, 89, 98
Sangdar 129
Sanglakh 239
Sangtuda 129
Saray Khwaja 26, 31, 32, 145, 152, 158, 159, 160, 163, 165, 176, 177, 178, 179, 180, 181, 182, 183, 184, 186, 188, 191, 192, 193, 204, 241, 269, 275
Sarboli 145
Sargodha 74
Saur Revolution 21, 55, 118, 130
sawāra 76

sawdā 145, 154
sawdāgari 143
Sayghan 237
Shādibāz 26, 28, 31, 49, 242, 282
Shāh Nāma 208, 216, 279, 280
Shāhi Khēl 208, 287
Shahshahid 242, 282
Shams *Sāhib* of Tabriz, *pīr* 70, 71, 75, 129, 298, 299
Shamsapur 139, 142, 203
Shamsapur pīrs 144
Shaykh Ruhānī Bābā 131, 132, 133, 134, 135, 136, 138, 139, 142, 143, 144, 191, 192, 202, 299, 300, 302
Shegi Qala 93
Shi'a 56, 206, 207, 214, 276, 278, 280, 282, 283, 288
Shi'a Imām 295
Shi'as 34, 45, 277
Shibar 37
Shindand 261
Shinwari 248
Shish 129, 208, 211, 280, 297
shīshak 307, 308
shoe-mending 247, 254, 255
Siakhak 239
Siálkot 74
Siāwn 218, 219, 220, 280
Siāwun 206, 207, 218, 220, 241, 254, 256, 272, 276, 277, 279
Siāwun khēls 265, 270, 276, 278, 282
sievemakers 20, 31, 33, 34, 44, 47, 48, 51, 203
sievemakers, Ghorbat 203
sievemaking, 18
sīkh-i dast 226
sīkh-i gula 223
sīkh-i paigula 223
sīkh-i tala 226
silver-smithery 47
Siyāhpāyak 139, 203
Siyahsang 131, 132, 139, 142, 143, 170, 191, 203, 242
Skandu 150
snake-charmers 33, 242
soapmaking 129, 281
Sorobi 145, 198, 303
Soviet Union 210
Spinboldak 248
spiritual community 131, 192, 202
spiritual fraternity 132, 144, 198, 202
stamp-mill 82, 87
Sufi 51, 52, 191, 204, 280, 299
Sufi order (*ṭarīqat*) 55, 70, 291
Sufi *pīr* 144
Sufism 25, 34, 283, 294
Suleiman Farsi 297
Suleiman, Solomon 294, 297, 307, 308
Sunni 45, 186, 207, 277, 282, 283
supir 76
Surkhrod 129, 203
Swat 74, 128, 221
sweepers 75

T

Tagab 37, 148, 235
tailors 170
Tajik 46, 47, 61, 75, 93, 131, 199, 205, 253, 277, 287
Tajik-dominated 67
Taluqan 203, 237
tānistā 230
tanners 47, 54, 56
ṭarīqāt 51, 70, 144, 204
Tarra Khêl 101, 123, 124, 130
Tashkari 129
Tashqurghan 47, 51, 54, 56, 291
ṭasma'ī 228
tasma kash 223
tawafi 138
Tehran 214
Tela Khēl 139
tin-smiths 228
tinkers 33, 213
tinkers and smiths 281
Tirgarhi 58, 61, 70, 112, 146, 182
transport work 101, 103, 104, 105, 106, 148
Turkestan 55, 56, 237, 239, 261, 296
Turkey 214, 221, 280
Turkmenistan 248

U

Uzbek 47
Uzbeks 237

V

Vangāwālā 31, 49

W

wakīl 112, 114, 116, 118, 130, 271, 272, 275, 300
wakīl-i gozar 271, 277
walī 68, 69, 71, 129
wālīswāl 282
Wardak 142, 238
Washermen 292
water-mills 87, 79
wazīr 300, 302
Wazirabad 100
weavers 44, 52, 68
West Punjab 73

Y

Yakatut 17, 31, 154, 239

Z

Zabūr 280
Zaher *Shāh* 281
Zaku Khēl 139
Zalingar 118
zargar goldsmith 217
Zikria 295, 297
zīrbaghalī 230
Zurmat 133

zîra 101
zīrbaghalī 230
zīyārat 128, 129
ztrbaghat 229
zughak 230
Zurmat 133

Æ

ḥākim 135, 136, 275
ḥadīth 51
ḥalāl 51
ḥalvā 231, 250, 281
ḥukmrān 201
ḥūr 208